A Thinking Man's Guide to Pro Football

A Thinking Man's Guide to Pro Football

PAUL ZIMMERMAN

New York   1970
E. P. DUTTON & CO., INC.

TO FROGGY

Contents

III. CHARACTERS AND CONTEMPLATIONS

I
The Men Who Play the Game

1
A Violent Game

Let us not hear of generals who conquer without bloodshed. If a bloody slaughter is a horrible sight, then that is a ground for paying more respect to war but not for making the sword we wear blunter and blunter by degrees, from feelings of humanity, until someone steps in with one that is sharp and lops the arm from our body.

□ Karl Von Clausewitz, *On War*

It was the night after I saw Sam DeLuca's career wiped out when a Houston player fell across his knees, the night after they bent Mike Taliaferro's arm behind him and fell on it and separated his shoulder for him. I was at a party in Manhattan and I didn't much feel like talking, especially to the little group that was discussing the "mystique" and the sociological implications and the philosophical import of pro football . . . and the one fat guy who kept detaching himself and telling me that he had a shot at the pros but turned it down.

I was thinking about how the sportswriters grumble over the long waits in the chilly corridors after a game, before the dressing room door opens; about the personal insults we feel when a losing quarterback says, "Get the hell away from me; I'm not talking to anybody." But we still feel a protective, almost sacred obligation to rush to football's defense when it gets worked over by the intellectuals, or when a fraud tries to equate himself with it.

I was listening to the party talk but my mind was on Taliaferro in that airport in Charlotte, North Carolina, the night before. The plane was delayed, and he stood at the deserted ticket counter and used it as a prop for his sling. Someone asked him if his shoulder

11

hurt and he said, "Not much," but his feet gave him away. He couldn't keep them still. He'd shuffle them back and forth, keeping pace with the tempo of his pain; faster when the pain got bad, slower when it let up a little.

So you listen to the deep thinkers discussing pro football with a dry, detached objectivity, turning it over and examining it like a fossil, and everything inside you says, "No, no, it's not like that at all."

There seems to be something universal in football. Why does it always seem to produce a personal reaction? ("Well, I went out for it in high school but I was too small," etc.) And why are there always characters who drop that stock line: "Violent athletics are a sublimation of the sex urge." Maybe that theory gives the guy a chance to get even with the football players who took his dates away from him when he was cracking the textbooks back in college.

The fan is being lifted to new levels of awareness. He can see it surrealistically, in the art galleries, or artistically in the beautifully packaged Sabol Productions' "NFL Football" TV shows every week. Television, with its instant replay and stop action, has tried to unlock some of football's inner mysteries. And the fan who once played the game is astute enough to realize that the precise, destructive operation he now watches bears little resemblance to the sport he knew back at Old Nassau.

Analogies have been made to religion and life itself and the family and war. It is war, in fact, that gave the sport some of its vocabulary, i.e., "the bomb," "the blitz," "attack," "offense and defense," "flanker," "two platoons," even "rookie," which is short for recruit.

The players themselves aren't quite sure of the nature of the beast, but some of their quotes about football are more eloquent than the dust-dry observations of anthropologists and sociologists and other fancy people who try to reckon with this new force.

"On Sunday it's like the bullfights," the Minnesota Vikings' quarterback, Joe Kapp, says. "It's an honest thing happening out there. It's the lions and the Christians."

But its brutality sometimes shocks its more sensitive practitioners.

"I don't really realize how brutal the game is until the off-season, when I go out to banquets and watch movies of our games," Jerry Kramer wrote in *Instant Replay*. "Then I see guys turned upside down and backwards, and hit from all angles, and I flinch. I'm amazed by how violent the game is, and I wonder about playing it myself."

I once heard a South African rugby international talking about the sociological differences between the scrum, or linemen, and the backs who play rugby. The scrum, he said, is generally made up of farmers and laborers. The backs are the students and aristocrats. These breakdowns dissolve in American football, though, and some of the most interesting observations come from men like 270-pound Merlin Olsen of the Los Angeles Rams, men whose arena is the very center of the carnage.

"They don't call the middle of the line The Pit for nothing," Olsen says. "We really do get like animals, trying to claw one another apart in there. It is very hard in The Pit. No matter how it seems, no matter what the score shows, it's always hard.

"We get so bruised and battered and tired we sometimes wind up playing in a sort of coma. By the end of the first half your instincts have taken over. By the end of the game you're an animal."

After the New York Jets won the AFL championship in 1968, the league's president, Milt Woodard, mentioned that champagne in the dressing room was against the rules. Joe Namath, of course, had a few words about this, and he paused between swigs of the bubbly to take a look at the game of football.

"Mr. Woodard tried to tell me that it was bad for the image of football," Namath said, "that it was bad for the kids to see it. But you know what the real image of football is? It's brutality. Why don't they tell the kids like it is? Tell the kids that this guy is trying to hurt that guy and knock him out of the game. Or show them some of the letters I get from people who hope some guy cripples me because of my moustache?"

Not all of them like what they do. "Football comes very close to being something I wouldn't want to do," says George Sauer, the Jets' artistic pass catcher. "I'm only happy I play a position where I don't have to be the aggressor. You know, I often get very disturbed by the violence in the game. I have questions about a sport that advocates and administers punishment. I have questions about the name of the game being kill the quarterback. Sometimes I dislike everything about the game except what I do."

"George is a marvelous football player," says DeLuca, his ex-teammate. "He loves the game, but he hasn't brought himself to accept that yet. He's like a college kid intellectualizing it. I think everybody goes through that stage at some time or another, and George is coming to it late. I know I was gung ho about football until I was a junior in college, and then I wondered about football. I came to see that it is a primitive game and accepted it for what it is. George couldn't be so good at football, and work so hard, if he didn't love it."

The San Diego Chargers' former offensive tackle Ron Mix, who made more All-AFL teams than any other man at the position, accepted the game as a job. He neither liked it nor disliked it.

"My attitude about football upset many people who think an athlete should love what he is doing," Mix said. "But I don't think an athlete should love his job any more than anybody else. The only important thing for an athlete to realize is that he has an obligation to do well. I've always realized that. If I could have loved the game besides, that would have been a little frosting on the cake. But that wasn't the case."

Except once—when he faced the Rams' great defensive end Deacon Jones in a 1968 exhibition game, after Jones had outplayed him the year before.

"Until then I had always discounted emotional involvement," Mix said. "I found I could do the job mechanically. But that second time against Deacon I found out that it can be good to have the adrenalin flowing. I played mad the whole game."

They question what they do, and sometimes the answers come out as incriminations of the whole mystique of football, from player to spectator, right down to the culture of American society.

"If you don't believe that people in America have a need for pro football," said the St. Louis Cardinals' linebacker, Dave Meggyesy, "you writers should sit in the stands more and hear what goes on. Football is just short of war for some of those people. It brings them right up to the edge. The fans can really get their hostilities off. There's mayhem but no killing. It's a titillation.

"Football is an archaic ethos. The black athletes know more

than anyone who's kidding whom. Face it, football's passé. It's a game for the Yahoos. It's like the old Roman sports. Throwing the bomb—blitzing—now what the hell does that mean? If this society changes like I hope it will, football will be a dead issue. The people will be able to get their hostilities off in a healthier way.

"The top football players are psychos. They are very unhealthy people, but society views them as some of our healthiest people. When you have men perpetuating violence in sports, in television or anything of that nature, you can't call that sane. You can't call the people who do it sane. You can't call me sane.

"So why do I play? People tell me I'm biting the hand that feeds me when I speak out. Well, I'm not. I can live on $5,000 as well as what I make now. I have no worries on that score. My wife is great. I have no allegiance to football. I can knock it if I want. I have nothing to hide. If change is going to come, the revolution has to occur in people's heads."

But the question remains unanswered. Why *does* he play football? Why do any of them?

"Easy," one vintage Chicago Bear once said. "If you do it on the street you get put in jail for assault. Here you get to do it for free."

It's not that simple, or they'd be recruiting pro football players out of jails. It's not really like the bullfights either, because no one gets led in, blinking and pawing, to be systematically butchered. They come in on their own. But often the most brutal of players challenge you when you remind them of that brutality.

I once did a dressing-room interview in Oakland. I had dropped the line in my advance story, "The Raiders' brute of a defensive end, Ike Lassiter," and after the game the 270-pound defensive end turned a baleful stare at me and pointed his finger— "You," he said, "you're the one who called me a brute."

"Christ, Ike," said tackle Tom Keating from the next locker. "I wish someone would call me a brute. I'm always 'clever,' or 'quick,' or 'tricky.' "

The image of the Dumb Football Player haunts so many of them.

"I'm not trying to suggest that pro football players, as a group, are the intellectual equals of, say, the staff of the *Paris Review,*"

Kramer wrote. "But I've sat with lawyers and politicians and with writers, and frankly, when I want an interesting conversation, I'd just as soon chat with a bunch of pro football players. At least the players are willing to discuss something beside football."

"Listen," Deacon Jones says, "I'm not an animal. I don't go around scaring women and children. They don't have to lock me up after a game. What I do is as athletic as rushing the net in tennis, stealing a base in baseball, faking a guy out of the pivot in basketball. Sometimes it's even like a poker game. I gamble a lot out there. You have to have style out there or you get eaten alive."

But before style can take over, they have to have the ability to hit—to punish. This, all the good ones have, even if they don't always talk about it.

"In the pros," says the Rams' former linebacker and defensive captain, Don Paul, "you know how to get that extra leverage to be able to hit hard. You know how to hit and then be able to keep your feet to hit again. On top of everything else, you're 40 to 60 pounds heavier than the players in college. And 500 percent meaner."

A few years ago a physicist figured out the collision force involved in football. Assuming that a 240-pound lineman who runs the 100 in 11 seconds collides with a 200-pound back who runs it in 10 seconds, the kinetic energy equals 66,000 inch-pounds— "enough to move 66,000 pounds, or 33 tons, one inch," he said.

Running rampant on the field, this force often produces tremendous collisions—and injuries. These, too, must be accepted as part of the business.

"You play so many years in this league, it gets to be matter-of-fact," says the Detroit Lions' defensive tackle, Alex Karras. "Like, for instance, when John Gordy, who had been my roommate for 10 years, hurt his knee and ended his career.

"I saw him get hurt. And as much as I love him as a person and a friend, it didn't come as a big shock. As he was lying there, hurt, it was as if it wasn't him. It could have been me or someone else. It was just a cold fact. It's the way it is in our business. You just have to accept it."

There are other things they have to accept, like the cheap shotters and late hitters, the sadists that exist in every walk of life.

"I'll get him," the old New York Titan tackle, Sid Youngelman, once said of the Houston Oilers' Al Jamison, who had been nicknamed Dirty Al for obvious reasons. "I don't know where or when or how, but I'll get him."

"How can you?" someone asked. "With the face bars and equipment and everything now. How can you get a guy?"

"Lots of ways," Sid said. "The easiest is in a pileup. You pick your spot, and then you get his helmet off . . . and kick his damn head in."

"There are a million ways to get a guy legally," says the Green Bay Packers' Dave Robinson, "but you have to wait for the chance. I have the patience to wait."

Winston Hill, the Jets' offensive tackle, once analyzed the difference between a rough football player and a dirty one.

"Larry Eisenhauer from the Patriots is a rough player," Hill said. "He comes at you clawing, and he yells and screams and slobbers at the mouth. He even bit me once, right here on the arm. But he's not dirty. When a guy hits you after the whistle blows or when your back is turned, or when he tries to kick you in the groin, that's a dirty football player."

"When you come right down to it," Merlin Olsen says, "your life is at stake out there. I'm not a weak man, and I've had quarterbacks bent under me in such a way that I'd only have to twist them a little to end their careers. I don't do it because I don't want to and I don't want it done to me.

"Few do, or there would be far more serious injuries than there are. Sometimes I'm twisted in such a way that an opponent could break my neck as easy as snapping his fingers. If he did, he might kill me. I'm still alive, if only barely."

They have their own styles and peculiarities. Ralph Kohl, a syndicate scout, tells about watching a scrimmage at the Vikings' Mankato, Minnesota, camp. He heard someone screaming— routinely—as he played, and the screamer was identified as ex-Notre Dame tackle Alan Page.

"So that's where that guy is," the scout said. "I've been back to Notre Dame for two years and haven't heard that sound. I never knew who made it until now."

And there are touches of humor even in the brawls on the field. "I pulled at the shoulder pads of a guy in a blue jersey," the

Kansas City Chiefs' center Jon Gilliam said after a Houston-Kansas City battle royal in a 1967 exhibition game. "Then I looked up and saw it was Ernie Ladd [6-9, 300-pound defensive tackle]. So I said, 'What do you say we go break this up, Ernie?' "

Intruders into this world often get firsthand lessons in its violence. Charlton Heston, the actor, tells about the time he broke a rib while he was filming a blitz scene for the movie, *Number One*.

"It was kind of my admission ticket, my dues," he said. "I can remember Jerry Sturm standing over me, slapping me alongside the head and saying, 'Welcome to the NFL.' "

2
Offensive Line
(Anonymous)

An offensive lineman is like a blacksmith. At one time it might have been a good job.

□ Anonymous

Someday the former offensive linemen of the world might sit down and pool their pension money and decide to erect a monument to Vince Lombardi, because if any man could be called the Great Emancipator of the offensive line, it would have to be him.

He gave them a better way of life, a more sensible way of earning a day's pay. He freed the great masses of congestion in the middle of the line, and, indirectly, he helped bring them what small measure of publicity has come their way.

He came to the New York Giants as Jim Lee Howell's assistant in 1954, his head full of Jock Sutherland's sweeps and Earl Blaik's finesse. And when he got there he found a world in which the blocking linemen performed their work like gladiators, digging away at the tightly packed defenses, occasionally straightening up to take their punishment on the pass blocks.

Lombardi put in his old St. Cecilia's High School end run stampedes, and the same blocking principles carried down to his Green Bay Packer and Washington Redskin days. He lifted a Giant running game that had been last in the league in 1953, averaging less than 90 yards a game, into respectability in that first year, and a year later, when Alex Webster and Mel Triplett joined

Frank Gifford in the backfield, Lombardi knew he had something unique.

He had three big backs who could run with power and speed. Best of all, they could block. All of them. Lombardi pulled his guards on the sweeps, and used the blocking ability of his backs, and the whole thing put unbelievable firepower on the defensive flank men.

He employed the exceptional talents of Roosevelt Brown as a pulling tackle. And he took the heat off the center by moving the guards out wider, creating splits in the middle of the line and rendering obsolete the huge defensive middle guards, such as Detroit's 350-pound Les Bingaman, or Washington's 275-pound Jim Ricca, or Green Bay's 290-pound Ed Neal, whose 19-inch forearms had left a trail of unconscious centers around the league.

But Lombardi's biggest contribution in those Giant years (1954–58) was his option system of blocking. Now the linemen had the option of moving the defensive man in either direction, riding him the way he was going, using his own momentum against him. It was a tremendous break for the blockers, who had grown old before their time trying to move out 260- and 270-pounders planted squarely in the hole like sequoias.

Lombardi gave his offensive linemen some respite from the horrible tedium and the terrible abuse of pass blocking, a highly specialized form of masochism, where a man's ability is graded by the ways he absorbs punishment—and the duration of time that he can stand it.

The outside world first became aware that Lombardi was stirring things up in Green Bay on December 26, 1960, when the Packers lost the NFL championship to the Eagles, 17-13, in Philadelphia's Franklin Field. The stories that came out of that game were all Philadelphia: quarterback Norm Van Brocklin and coach Buck Shaw, ending their careers in a wondrous blaze; and, of course, Chuck Bednarik, a 60-minute center and linebacker after 12 years in the game. Still, Lombardi had shown people a slight peek into the future.

My paper, the *New York World-Telegram & Sun,* had sent me down to Philly to get losing dressing-room quotes for Joe King, our regular pro football man. I was assigned to the Packers, who had gone down following Lombardi's reversion to what the columnists considered Stone Age football in an era of the high flyers. One man, I remember, began his Monday column: "They should have parked a Stutz'-Bearcat outside of Franklin Field yesterday . . ."

But the Packers had gained 223 yards on the ground against the Eagles that day, and even from my seat in the skyscraping Franklin Field press box, where you lived in mortal fear that a strong wind would blow the whole thing over and drop it, plop, right on the 50-yard line, I could see that right guard Jerry Kramer and left guard Fuzzy Thurston and center Jim Ringo were doing terrible things to the middle of the Eagles' defensive line. The Eagle tackles had been nullified, and even the great Bednarik was having trouble getting out of the way of Ringo's precise cutoff blocks.

My interest was somewhat personal, too, because that was a year in which I had been spending my Saturday nights playing offensive guard for the Paterson, New Jersey, Pioneers of the semipro Eastern Football Conference. And when I hit that Green Bay dressing room, I wanted to hear from Kramer himself—and Thurston and Ringo—how they called their audibles and what the Philly tackles were doing on their pass rush.

Yes, a lot of pass-block pressure was relieved by the runs, Kramer patiently explained, and any one of the three of them had the option of making calls, and why was I bothering to talk to an offensive lineman anyway?

Pretty soon Ringo and Thurston came out of the shower, pleasant, friendly men who were amused at the idea that a reporter seemed interested in their world—even if it was only one reporter.

The four of us had a nice little chat, and I came away from that dressing room thinking, gee, covering the pro football beat must be a real breeze. And, of course, then the awful realization came that I was totally blank on Starr and Hornung and Lombardi quotes, and Joe King nearly heaved me out of the press-room window, with a few carefully delivered words to help get my mind off option blocking and audibles and the whole subject of offensive linemen.

Next day I was back covering the high schools, where I couldn't get into trouble, and it was a full two years until I set foot inside a pro football dressing room again.

You just didn't read stories about offensive linemen in those days, a condition that lasted right up to that famous block that Kramer delivered on the Dallas Cowboys' defensive tackle, Jethro Pugh (a double-team block) in the 1967 NFL championship game, a block that led to Kramer's book, *Instant Replay,* and its successor, *Farewell to Football.* But things have calmed down again in the offensive lineman's world, and backs and receivers are again the newspaperman's staples.

I remember one interview with Bob Talamini, the New York Jets' offensive left guard, a few days before the Jets-Baltimore Super Bowl. A couple of us asked Talamini about the Baltimore defense, and he broke it down for us, carefully detailing its personnel and its means of operation. A few other writers drifted by, and pretty soon it turned into a real press conference.

"Hey," said a writer from Houston, where Talamini made All-AFL for six years before he came to the Jets, "you were never this good a talker when you were with us."

"How the hell would you know?" Talamini said. "No one ever talked to me."

"One of the Cleveland Browns once told me," Kramer wrote in *Instant Replay,* "that if he ever had to go on the lam from the law, he'd become an offensive lineman."

A lineman will insist: "My job is to protect the passer, and if I do my job I'm happy," which is of course a lie because no man is happy getting slugged in the teeth—for considerably less pay than the people he's protecting. So you write that old chestnut about the thankless job of the offensive lineman. Sometimes writers will try and goad a player into making a crack or two about the man he'll be facing, and only a player who is extremely naïve or very confident will risk psyching up an enemy before he faces him. But a writer can drum up a feud story this way, and it'll carry him along for a day or two.

There's no way you can lean on statistics for help, because offensive linemen aren't covered by any. Passers, runners, receivers, interceptors, kickers, punters, returners—they all work their way into the stat sheet. Even defensive linemen have come into some statistical recognition, and most pro clubs hand out sheets marked, "tackles and assists," with "pass deflections" thrown in as a special concession to defensive backs.

Fans who crave numbers can locate statistics for every man playing a professional sport in the United States—at every position. Hockey, basketball, baseball; everyone winds up with either saves or assists of put-outs or shots taken—something statistical. Only football's offensive linemen remain uncovered. So the fan thinks of them in nebulous terms, a magazine piece he once read, the All-Pro teams at the end of the season, a sensational downfield block he once saw and remembered, a TV commentator's hypnotic repetition: "So-and-so's playing a whale of a game."

"We don't leave any statistics to be remembered by," said the Packers' great offensive tackle, Forrest Gregg, in 1970, "so I don't want anyone to overlook the fact that I haven't missed a game since I came into the league in 1956."

The meat-and-potatoes blocks on running plays—tackle on end, guard on tackle, center on tackle or middle linebacker—are so difficult to isolate and analyze that the statisticians never have considered devoting any effort to them. The head coach can't help much, because his horizontal view of the game doesn't give him any kind of perspective on the work in The Pit. He can tell if a man is getting beaten on his pass protection, and if it gets too brutal he'll yank him and talk things over. And if he doesn't like the way the conversation is going, there will be a different guard or tackle on the next series of plays. The hard-core analysis is handled by the movie camera, and the coaches reach their verdicts on the offensive linemen in a dark room, running the plays over and over and over.

That's when the linemen finally get their shot at the statistical tables, but it's a very private affair. The coaches grade the blockers on every play. The grades are sometimes on a percentile basis (pass blocking is expected to draw a lower score than blocking for the run), sometimes on an aggregate score system. And they're a secret between coach and player, but the book always makes a reappearance during next year's contract talks.

"I've always felt," Kramer said, "that the real value of grades is providing a helluva good lever for them during next year's contract talk."

If you focus your attention on the offensive line, you might miss some of the game's other elements, such as the first few fakes a receiver puts on a cornerback who's covering him. And, of course, you'll miss the sight of the quarterback taking the snap from center and either handing the ball off or moving back to set up for a pass, a sight which, for some mysterious reason, seems to hold the attention of 95 percent of the fans.

"It's crazy, I know," Gregg says, "but when I'm just watching a game on the tube, I start off looking at the offensive linemen. But then if it's an exciting game, I'll react just like any other fan and look at the quarterback. Or sometimes I just get lazy and start off by watching him right away."

Actually, the televiewer has a better chance to zero in on the linemen. The receivers move out of the camera's range after the first few steps, but nowadays you don't mind anyway. Your security is the instant replay which will probably pick up anything dramatic that happens in the area. So you're left with the choice —disciplined watching of the line or a casual look at the backfield action. Sometimes a little mental discipline can pay heavy dividends.

The battle between a great offensive lineman and a fine defender can prove fascinating. If you watched the battle between the Minnesota Vikings' six-time All-NFL center, Mick Tingelhoff, and the Kansas City tackle that played him head on in the 1970 Super Bowl, you might have been an eyewitness to a historical event—the end of the "greyhound" center, that small, agile lineman who had become fashionable in the NFL.

The Chiefs lined up in an "odd" formation, placing a lineman directly over the offensive center, a variation that the AFL has favored over the NFL's traditional 4-3 defense, with each defensive tackle squared up on the offensive guard, and the middle linebacker set between them. But Kansas City gave Tingelhoff either 6-7, 275-pound Buck Buchanan to cope with, or 6-1, 260-pound Curly Culp, and the battle turned into an overmatch, with Tingelhoff the loser (see Fig. 1).

Tingelhoff, whose 235 pounds had been adequate for cutting off the middle linebacker, or chopping at the legs of the defensive tackles, was physically overpowered and outmaneuvered by the Kansas City tackles. The eyes of the coaching world were on this drama, needless to say, and coaches, being natural copiers, might just decide to try out the odd alignment next year. It could mark the end of the undersized center.

The 4-3, Or Traditional NFL Defense

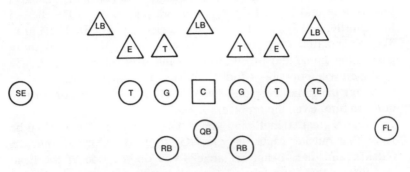

The 4-3, Or Traditional NFL Defense

The Kansas City Version Of The AFL Odd-Front Defense

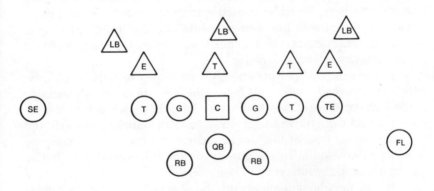

Fig. 1

If you watched the 1967 Green Bay-Los Angeles game for the NFL's Western Division championship, you might have enjoyed the war between Forrest Gregg and the Rams' perennial All-Pro defensive end, Deacon Jones. Gregg won. He kept Jones, who had a five-year age advantage (29 to 34), a 15-pound weight edge (260 to 245), and infinitely more speed, away from Starr all afternoon by using leverage, superb body control, and a complete knowledge of Jones's attacking techniques. He used the man's own speed and strength against him.

"We were all waiting for that battle," Kramer said. "Deacon kind of tore into Forrest the first time we played them. He chewed him a little, and Forrest had gotten bawled out by Mr. Lombardi. The second time they met, Forrest was ready. He'd taken those game films home and run them over and over, all by himself. He could tell you more about Jones's moves than Jones could.

"After the game, everyone knew what kind of a job Forrest had done on him. Even the reporters knew."

"Jones's great strength and speed make him very tough when he takes that outside route on you," Gregg said. "Outside, outside, outside, and then, bang, he smacks you on the side of the head and throws that little fake of his and he's gone inside and beaten you cold.

"I just kept riding him wider and wider, until he took himself out of the play. When he started getting frustrated and cutting inside, I pivoted with him and rode him into the traffic. Of course, beating those smacks to the head was another matter, and that would take too long to explain."

Every coach or player who ever sat down to write a *How to Watch Football* book, will drop the line in there somewhere: "Watch the guards. They'll tell you where the play is going."

I would dearly love to get away from this ancient proverb, but except in the case of the "sucker play," a bit of legerdemain that will be discussed later, the guards are the tea leaves—they'll give you a look at the future.

If they fire out, straight ahead, the play will usually be a run inside. If they fire out low, it could be a run or a "quickie" pass over the middle. If they set themselves in a pass-blocking stance, the play will be a regular pass or a draw, a delayed hand-off to a back coming through any area of daylight between the tackles. And if they do a pivot and pull out, running parallel to the line of scrimmage, the play will be an end sweep and you're an eyewitness to one of football's classic dramas.

Many things can happen to a guard on his journey from his set position on the line to the final destination—the corner linebacker or defensive back. You can get a whole chronicle of success or failure. If one guard is half a count late getting out, his man might get a piece of him, upsetting his rhythm and causing the other pulling guard to run him down. Stripped of his two interference men, the runner finds himself rounding the corner into a mob, since the middle linebacker, watching all movement along the line for tip-offs, has raced over to meet the sweep, and he's brought his gang with him.

Or maybe both guards have pulled out in textbook fashion and are well on their way, say around right end. But the offensive right tackle, or perhaps the tight end, whose duty it is to block straight ahead and contain, has been pushed back, into the path of the guards, those dutiful guards who always worry about losing the speed necessary to beat their runner to the corner.

So there's a stack-up along the scrimmage line, and the runner puts his head down and prays for deliverance. Ninety percent of the fans watching the game ask, "What the hell's the matter with that runner?" And the other 10 percent, the ones who have picked up the picture from the beginning, smile and recite their expertise —"Well, you see, the defensive end beat the tackle and got penetration, and this knocked off the pulling guards, so the ball carrier's interference was stripped right away. . . ."

A fan really earns his hot dog, though, if he tries to follow the actions of the offensive center, the toughest of all offensive linemen to pick out and the hardest to follow once you have managed to locate him. But if he's a Tingelhoff or a Jim Otto, the Oakland Raiders' 10-year All-Leaguer, you just might want to see how he earned his credentials.

If the opposing middle linebacker is having a particularly big day, for instance, you might want to watch your center and see where he's going wrong. You also might see some surprising things going on down there in the middle of The Pit. You'll see a lot of holding and grabbing, even tackling, by the offensive linemen, particularly the centers, who are provided the best concealment by the flow of traffic. You might wonder why the officials don't call it, why they don't see it when it's so clear to you. Sometimes I wonder about that myself.

I've got my own theory, not perfectly developed yet, but a kind of a hunch. I think that the officials possibly are taking just the slightest bit of pity on the offensive linemen and the unbelievably difficult job they have to do—both emotionally and physically—every time they're called on to pass-block.

"Sure, I'll grab a guy if I see he's going to get in there and take a clear shot at Namath," the Jets' Dave Herman says. "I don't care if it's 15 yards or 15 miles. What's worse, 15 yards or a crippled quarterback?"

"If I were an offensive lineman I'd probably hold, too, because my responsibility would be to keep the guy off the quarterback," says Dallas' All-NFL defensive tackle Bob Lilly, who probably gets held more than any defensive lineman in football.

"I wouldn't make it obvious, though, like some people do. But what the hell, it's not called that much anyway."

"I've got a pretty good catalog of the way different tackles attack your head," says Dallas' right guard, John Wilbur.

"There's Alex Karras of Detroit. His specialty is the karate chop. It can numb you for a second if you don't learn how to get out of the way of it.

"Merlin Olsen of the Rams likes to keep banging his hands over the ear holes of your helmet. Both hands at the same time. It hurts like hell, from the pressure change or something. And the noise scares you. He knocked me flat out twice before I learned how to dodge it.

"When I played against Billy Ray Smith of the Colts I learned a new one, though. He kept sticking his fingers through my face guard. I think he might have been after my eyes."

Alex Kroll, an articulate and witty man who once played offensive tackle for the New York Titans—at a modest 230 pounds—wrote in his *How To Be a TV Quarterback,* about his introduction to pass blocking.

"My particular job on this play was to keep Denver's 270-pound right end, Don Joyce, from rearranging our QB, Lee Grosscup's lean physique. We ran up to the line of scrimmage, Grosscup called the snap number, and I took a step back into a very formful pass-blocking stance.

"Abruptly, a forearm about the size of a fire hydrant collided with my helmet. Crack! And then a thud, as the fire hydrant found something softer. I lost my balance but managed to dive at what looked like Joyce's knees, and the two of us went tumbling down in a swirl of New York grass and dust.

"I got up. But unfortunately, so did he. And sadly, underneath the flesh of my left wrist, several little bones seemed to be moving with unaccustomed freedom. I didn't know if my wrist was broken, but I certainly didn't have time to find out because round two was beginning.

"Again, the fire hydrants attacked, and that went on for still another play, and we punted. On the bench, my first impulse was to think about my job. It was a simple thought. If that wrist was busted, I probably didn't have a job. So I wrapped the wrist in an Ace bandage and returned to the front.

"The two of us spent that sunny afternoon in September making sincere efforts to mutilate each other. And in truth, Don Joyce's efforts were not unrewarded. My consolation came from the fact that the quarterback remained unbowed, and I held my job—at least for that week."

The New York Jets' center, John Schmitt, has special memories about Ray Jacobs, a 6-3, 285-pound defensive tackle from Texas, who drifted around the AFL for a while, finally settling with the Boston Patriots last year as a reserve.

"Everything was going OK, a nice sensible game," Schmitt said after the Jets beat the Patriots in Shea Stadium. "Then they called time out and I saw No. 87 coming onto the field, and I said, 'Boys, fasten your chin straps, here comes the head crusher.' He's got that forearm shot to your left ear down pat, and about the sixth time he hit me, I didn't see the huddle anymore.

"I told the ref, 'Watch him, he's winding up. You're not allowed to wind up on a blow.' It was kind of a desperate move on my part, and I didn't give it much hope, and the ref kind of looked at me like he felt sorry, but what could he do about it?"

"Jacobs," said Dave Herman, "will cause a lot of offensive linemen to celebrate when he retires. Last year he was playing in Miami, and Jeff Richardson was in at center for us. Jeff came back to the huddle, tugging at his helmet. It was twisted all the way around and he was looking out of the ear hole.

" 'I didn't know Jacobs was in the game,' I said to him.

" 'Yeah, he just came in,' he said."

I remember the Jets' offensive guard, Dan Ficca, talking about playing against Ernie Ladd, a 6-9, 300-pounder with little finesse, just a straight-ahead charge and a sadistic desire to cave in helmets with his forearm or fist.

"Well, he broke my nose and then he broke my cheekbone," said Ficca, ticking off the injuries like a guy tallying up a gin rummy scoreboard.

"Then he broke the cheekbone on the other side, but by then my head was numb anyway, so it didn't matter."

"All that my wife looks for," said the Jets' offensive guard, Randy Rasmussen, "is to see whether I get up or not."

And yet, there's a strange kind of respect that the quality players on both sides of the line have for each other, a severely defined sense of right and wrong.

"Someone once told me before we played Minnesota," Gregg said, "that the way to beat their big end, Carl Eller, was to get him around the knees, because he had bad knees and you could tear him up real easy that way.

"I told him I knew it, but I'd hate to do anything like that to him because he's a helluva guy, a good clean competitor."

Each position on the offensive line carries its own headaches and rewards, and they're worth a closer look.

CENTER: "Offensive center is a racket," says San Diego's former All-AFL offensive tackle, Ron Mix. "It's the place to hide a weak brother.

"All he does on pass blocking is help someone else out. On running plays he throws cutoff blocks to one side or the other. Big deal. It just means falling down in front of someone."

"I've heard that theory," says Otto, who made All-League for every one of the 10 years the AFL was in existence. "Let me ask one question. If it's so easy, how come no one ever wants to play there?"

One drawback is the fact that centers don't tape their hands, as the guards and tackles do. The tape would take away their feel of the ball, so the result is usually a set of badly mangled fingers each Sunday.

And there's always the traditional mental picture players have had about centers, poor fools who are busy snapping the ball, or some other foolish job like that, while the sadists across the line wind up and deliver their blows to that most wonderful target of all—the helmet. And in the old days, when "birdcages" were for sissies, and helmets were made of leather, and the center always had a middle guard playing directly over him, it was truly a position for martyrs. It may be again, if the AFL's odd-front defense catches on everywhere.

You used to be able to tell a center by his nose. The longer he played, the less cartilage it had.

"I guess it's something you've got to get used to, like olives," the Giants' old star, Mel Hein, once said, pointing to his own flattened nose.

"I remember one day I was playing against the Bears, and their middle guard George Musso, 270 pounds and mean as they came, kept slugging me on the helmet.

"Finally on one play I brought my fist up and got him under the chin and it dumped him on his back, but you know what, he didn't even get mad. He just said, 'Gee, I didn't think it was bothering you.' "

"When they first put in the 5-4 defense in the forties," recalled the Bears former center, Bulldog Turner, "they put the biggest, toughest guy they had right over the center, and he'd let you have it in the face as soon as you snapped the ball. Green Bay had this 290-pound guy, Ed Neal, with an arm as big as my leg and just as hard as that table.

"You didn't have a face guard then, and so Ed Neal broke my nose seven times. No—he broke my nose five times. I got it broke seven times, but five times he broke it."

In the mid-1950's, though, face bars became mandatory, and the battle between the center and the middle guard became more even. The head became a blocking weapon.

"Every man has a slight fear for his face," Ringo says. "God made you that way. When I first came up to the pros, a face mask was the sign of cowardice, but when it became standard equipment, you could stick your head into a block. Thank God for the face bars. I don't think I could have made it without them."

Ringo played against 4-3 defenses for almost his entire career, which meant that he could survive at 230 pounds.

"You have to ask now," says Gil Brandt, Dallas' director of player personnel, "whether Ringo would survive an odd-front defense, whether he'd even survive the squad cut in camp."

But the odd-front has not taken over yet, and until it does, the center must be agile. Ringo came up in the era of the huge middle guard, but when the 4-3 defense replaced the 5-2, and the middle man gave way to the mobile middle linebacker, the centers also shrank in size. Body control was more important than sheer strength.

On passing situations, against the standard 4-3, the center drops back and gives help where it's needed (Mix's "weak brother" accusation), always giving his first look to the middle linebacker, who might decide to put a rush on the quarterback at the last minute. Before the ball is snapped, the rusher, or "blitzer," or "red-dogger," is doing everything in his power to look the picture of a man who is planning anything except a blitz.

"Take your eye off him," Ringo said, "and he'll be in on your quarterback before he can even get a grip on the ball." There can be a back, or even two, set behind the center for additional help against the blitzers, but the center, unless he's helping a guard with a particularly troublesome defensive tackle, must give the blitzer his first look.

On running plays against the 4-3, the center usually angle-blocks, shooting out at either defensive tackle on an angle, cutting him off. If he goes for the middle linebacker, it will be with a delaying type of block, a scythelike sweep of the man's legs, with the idea of slowing his pursuit, or cutting him down if he can, rather than actually moving him out. On a running play up the middle, he must take on the middle linebacker straight ahead, but to come up too high on a block like this is to invite severe punishment. No middle backer worth his keep will stand there and let a center, in full line of vision, attack his upper body. A taped and padded forearm, jerked upward in a quick, murderous arc, usually ends such foolishness.

A few years ago, when Lombardi's power sweeps were in full flower, the exceptional center was measured by one type of block, the cutoff on the defensive tackle on the side of the sweep. It's still an effective gauge. When the guard pulls out to lead the interference, there is a split second in which his opponent is left uncovered, and it is up to the center to cut across the defensive tackle's body and nullify his charge. If the center is too slow in his execution, the guard can't get out, because the tackle will penetrate and disrupt the whole play.

If the center can make the block consistently, the wide attack, with its whole stream of variations and modifications, can be established. If he can't, the whole concept is handicapped.

"It became so much a part of me that I didn't even think about it anymore," Ringo said. "It was automatic and I took it for granted. Maybe a bigger man would have more trouble with it, but for a little guy like me, the toughest block was always the straight-ahead drive, when one of those 300-pound monsters was playing me head up. I don't envy the centers now, if that odd-front defense becomes popular."

In the last couple of years, though, defensive tackles have been chosen for their mobility, as well as their bulk, their ability to penetrate quickly and foul up the sweep before it develops. And the old Lombardi sweep, at times still effective, is not the killer it once was.

The center has an added responsibility, snapping the ball to the quarterback. A smooth exchange is the result of thousands of exchanges on the practice field, over and over until it becomes automatic and natural for both players. There is no special technique. Every quarterback has his own preference for how he wants to get the ball. It's a matter of sheer repetitive learning, like juggling three oranges.

Much harder is the long snap to the punter or the holder on field goals and extra points. The center is under a double strain here because he must devote his full concentration to making his pass absolutely accurate, and at the same time getting the ball back as swiftly as he can. (Watch a field goal or punting drill in practice and you'll usually see a coach measuring every tenth of a second with a stopwatch.) And in back of the center's mind is the knowledge that for one long moment his head is unguarded, an inviting target for a fist or a forearm, anything that will shake his concentration, along with other things.

"It's a right awful feeling," says Miami Dolphins' Tom Goode. "It's like trying to sink a putt for a $20,000 championship in golf and not even being able to see the hole.

"It's like there are only two people in the world, you and that guy who has to get the ball. You have to put the ball right on the button for him, and you'd better get your head up in time or the linebacker is apt to give you a killin' lick."

Some coaches bring in a different center for these specialized tasks. A man like Otto, though, prefers to do the job himself. He takes pride in his art, and has his own theory about the raps in the head a center had to take.

"It sounds funny, but I firmly believe that your head gets in shape like any other part of your body. Early in training camp I always get headaches after practice. My head isn't in shape yet. But later on in the season it's not so bad. I wonder if you can toughen and condition the material around your brain? Anyway, the headaches always go away after a few beers."

GUARD: He must be strong and tough enough to take on the tackle head on, the gigantic defensive tackle that is his responsibility for the day; he must be fast enough to lead a halfback around end on the sweeps; he must be unemotional enough to hold his pass blocks while his head and upper body are getting savaged.

"On pass blocking, you've got to be patient and you've got to let the man come to you," says ex-Jet Sam DeLuca, who played seven years in the AFL.

"You've got to resign yourself to the fact that you're going to take punishment from those big tackles. If he wants to stand there and slug, it's OK, because he's not rushing the passer while he's doing it. A young player has trouble understanding this, and he'll get impatient and fire out and pop his man. That might work for a while, but when he does get beaten, he gets beaten quickly, and that's the worst thing that can happen to an offensive guard."

DeLuca, calm and introspective, offered an interesting contrast to Herman, an emotional fireball, when they were the Jets' guards. (Joe Namath once said before the 1969 Super Bowl, "I don't envy Bubba Smith, having to play against Dave Herman. Bubba's going to find a machine gun in his chest all afternoon.") Sam always used to say that Herman would be one of the great guards in the game as soon as he learned to control his emotions. Sam would teach him patience, which was like trying to teach a wild stallion the moves of a Tennessee walking horse.

I once saw DeLuca spend a rough afternoon against Ernie Ladd and his knockout punches. DeLuca would take the shock and give ground; absorb, recover, and retreat; absorb, recover, retreat. Ladd got so frustrated on one play that he wheeled on DeLuca and hammered down on his helmet until he had literally beaten him into the ground.

Ladd stood there snorting and staring down at Sam like Hercules surveying the fallen Antaeus, but the whole grim business had taken time, and during that time Namath had completed a touchdown pass. In a physical sense Ladd had won, but in football's pattern of execution he was a loser, because his job was to reach the passer. His private assault had taken him out of the picture.

Ladd's tactics of shattering the AFL's assorted cheekbones and noses often proved effective against guards less disciplined or courageous than a DeLuca. They would fire out on him, hoping to cut off his charge before it could gather momentum; they would whip into a body block, trying to cut his legs.

Both measures could be successful as a change of pace, and many quarterbacks prefer the quick removal of a 6-foot-9 obstruction. But Ladd, who had a certain amount of agility, developed the habit of jumping over a cutting block. And then, once again, the guard was beaten quickly and decisively. On a quick pass over the middle, the linemen are taught to use body blocks to cut down the wheat field in a hurry, so that the quarterback's vision is clear. But on a long pass play, which takes a full three or four seconds, there's no substitute for the plain, old-fashioned absorb, recover, retreat.

The newer trend in offensive guards is the tall, physically powerful man who can match the defensive tackle's height, long arms, and leverage. An example is Oakland's 6-5, 255-pound Gene Upshaw, a physical match for most of the tackles he will meet.

The better offensive guards aren't really bothered by the match-ups with the forearm-swinging 280-pounders, "the fat slobs," as Kramer liked to call them. Their nemeses are the toe dancers, the Alex Karras types. Karras is small for a defensive tackle at 6-2, 250, but his weapons are intelligence, and of course his karate chop, and a weird assortment of moves developed from 12 years of learning.

Ask Herman who the toughest tackle in the AFL is, and he

won't mention Ladd or any of the other helmet breakers. His personal candidate is Boston's 5-11, 255-pound Jim Hunt, a dancer and slider with speed.

On pass blocking, the guards have two advantages over the tackles. There is a center right alongside them to help out when things get tough. And the area gets highly congested, limiting the operating room of the defensive tackles.

The first advantage can turn into a crutch. A guard who is constantly looking to the center for double-team help might lose his job to a man who is eager, even though not fully able, to take on a tackle by himself.

Next time a pass play develops, watch the center and see what side he instinctively looks to. This should tell you one of two things—which is the better defensive tackle, the one deserving of double-team treatment; and which guard is the weaker one, the one who consistently needs help.

The traditional move of the pass-blocking lineman is the forearm pop, catching his man in the center of the body—the numbers. All other moves come off this one delivery, but if it proves effective, the offensive guard or tackle may stay with it all day. His head must be up, which goes against all of civilized man's better instincts, his body coils, uncoils, and then recoils. In practice, the line coach is always yelling, "Square up! Square up!" In other words, take your man head on.

About five or so years ago the system of pass blocking changed a little. The hands became weapons for the offensive lineman. He was taught to guide his man with his hands, pushing off, controlling here and there. In the strictest sense of the word it's illegal, but officials will usually look the other way as long as the blocker doesn't get ridiculous with his hands, as long as he doesn't grab and hold on. So this slight bending of the rules is now taught by offensive line coaches on all but a very few professional clubs.

According to most guards, the toughest block on running plays is the straight-ahead pop, since not much momentum has been generated. But it's personally satisfying.

"Head up, eyes forward, drill him with your forehead right on the numbers," Kramer says. "Of course, these guys don't always cooperate. They'll whop you on the head with their forearms, or sometimes they're just too damn big and strong."

Once the basics have been established, the nuances enter: the crab block, so named because the defensive tackle's legs are tangled up by a low-cutting block, and then pinched by a contraction of the blocker's body; the reverse body block, in which the blocker angles his frame in the opposite manner, using his rear end and legs to seal off his man; and all manner of wall-off blocks, using a swinging arm as a pivot and a screen. They can all be effective, but only if the basic element is there—the successful head-and-shoulder drive block that earns respect for the physical power of the blocker.

The pulling guards are football's matched rhinos, and the sight of 500 pounds bearing down on a single cornerback or linebacker can be memorable. It's like Dublin on a Saturday night; something always happens.

The textbook defines their duties in precise terms. They pull out together, and when they get to the corner they take slightly different routes. The onside guard (right guard when the sweep is to the right) will block out on an outside man. If there is no one to his outside, he'll turn upfield. His running mate, the left, or off guard, will turn sharply when he gets to the corner and look to seal off his inside. This is the textbook version. What usually happens, if both guards are fortunate enough to arrive outside still in good health, still as a tandem and still ahead of the ball carrier, is that they'll take on any object in a different-colored jersey. But if they follow the book and perform their assigned tasks as written, then you're watching a vintage Packer operation, a unique picture in any sport.

"The greatest sight in the world for a pulling guard," says the Jets' Rasmussen, "is a cornerback. I remember in one play in the Cincinnati game, Roger [right tackle Roger Finnie] had knocked the defensive end right on his back, and someone had gotten the linebacker, and when I turned the corner all I saw was that little defensive back. What a great sight!"

The battle to take the corner has provided some unforgettable moments. One that I'll never forget came in a 1948 All-America Conference game when the New York Yankees' 175-pound defensive back, Tom Casey, split a pair of pulling guards and stopped Cleveland's 238-pound Marion Motley head on.

Casey was taken off the field on a stretcher, amid the thunderous cheers of the Yankee Stadium fans. He was ambulanced to Bronx Veterans Hospital, where his heroism was diagnosed as a severe concussion. The announcement a few days later concerned his retirement from the game, but kids on sandlots all over the Bronx spent the rest of the season re-creating Tom Casey with low, hard, albeit nonconcussive, tackles.

"You hope for a linebacker who'll stand there and take you on," Kramer said. "But he has to be either very big or very courageous to give you a standing target like that. Our outside linebackers, Dave Robinson and Lee Roy Caffey, were both 250, so they could get away with it. But how many 250-pound corner linebackers are there in the game?"

The pulling guards won't always throw their body at a defender. Dallas' John Niland has developed a technique called a butt block, which isn't like it sounds. It's a billy-goat technique in which he draws a bead on his man's chest, butts him, and keeps going.

Oakland's Gene Upshaw has drawn some criticism from AFL coaches because of his reluctance to leave his feet on open-field blocks. I once watched an Oakland game on TV with a few assistant coaches, and every time Upshaw pulled out they would chant, "Throw, throw," and when he didn't throw his body they would cackle, "See that, he just won't throw."

But most of the time he cleared the area simply by running over somebody, which reinforces the old theory that it doesn't matter how you get the job done as long as you do it.

Most of the time the linebacker who has come up to meet the challenge will spin or dance around or do just about anything to avoid giving the pulling guard a clean shot. And it is in these moments that a guard proves himself, especially when the runner isn't close enough behind him to set up his block for him. He'll lower his shoulder and drive. Sometimes he'll miss completely, and sometimes he'll knock the defender a few yards downfield, where he'll wind up making the tackle.

But sometimes you'll see a clean kill, one of the great joys of dedicated offensive lineman watching.

TACKLE: Why are pro football's offensive tackles bigger than the offensive guards, since guards play against monsters and tackles play against the sleeker, swifter defensive ends? The answer is height. Offensive tackles are drafted for height, to match the towering defensive ends. In 1969 the defensive ends in the NFL averaged 6-4½, 252. In the AFL they went 6-4¼, 258.

A defensive end will seldom attack his man head on, punishing him as a tackle would. Instead he uses his long arms as levers, pulling and jerking the blocker one way or the other. If the tackle is handicapped by a pronounced height disadvantage, he's in for a rough afternoon.

Since the defensive ends carry the greatest pass-rushing responsibility, the heaviest pass-blocking duties fall to the offensive tackles. Usually, their margin of error is less than that of the guards, since they work in a more open area. The good tackles take great pride in their jobs of pass blocking.

"I like pass blocking because you're not just a machine out there," says the Jets' Winston Hill, an All-AFL tackle.

"You're not just punishing people. You're coming close to doing the work of an athlete, matching the agility of a man 20 to 40 pounds lighter than yourself [Hill weighs 280] with your own. I've had pass blocks that were so pretty I wanted to take them and frame them and hang them on the wall. And I've been whipped so bad that I wanted to cry."

Offensive tackles are generally of two varieties. There are the athletes, the mechanical perfectionists, trim 250-pounders such as Mix and Gregg. They conditioned themselves with weights and sprints in the off-season, and always kept an eye on the waist-line.

At the other end of the scale, if you could find a scale big enough, is the mountain, the massive type of tackle who uses his body as a great wall between defensive end and passer. This breed, epitomized by the Jets' 330-pound Sherman Plunkett, who retired before the 1968 season, now seems to be dying out.

Sherm never lifted weights and seldom watched his own. God had blessed him with an unusually quick pair of feet, and he used them to keep his ample body constantly positioned in front of his man. He was effective enough to make the All-League team one year, and there is a memorable film clip of the 1967 AFL All-Star game, in which the West's coach, Hank Stram, watches Plunkett and sighs to one of his defensive linemen, "Getting past him is like taking a trip around the world."

"In pro football," Mix says, "if you're a tackle who can protect the passer—you can't do anything else but protect the passer—you can make the team. You may even make the All-Star team.

"You can be worthless as far as the rest of the game is concerned. Your downfield blocking can be nonexistent. Your blocking at the point of attack can be below average. But if you can pass-protect, you are considered an excellent football player, not only by your contemporaries, but by the fans."

When the end comes for one of the big fellows, it comes suddenly and without warning. During the 1967 season Plunkett started losing his quickness afoot—and this was coming off an All-Pro year in 1966. The word went out to the defensive ends, via movie projector, that Plunkett could be beaten to the outside.

Moves were laid aside, and every battle became a footrace to the outside between the defensive end and Sherm, a race Sherman wound up losing too often.

"Twisting him was like twisting a building," said Kansas City's left defensive end, Jerry Mays. "But his legs eventually went on him. Legs are so important. Even if you're properly conditioned, you usually can't get anywhere against a blocker for three quarters. Then his legs tire and he can be had."

The wall of pass protection must be formed inside, forcing the rushers to take a circular route outside the blockers, and creating what is called the passer's pocket.

"That pocket's got to be sealed up like a balloon," says Baltimore's offensive line coach, John Sandusky. "Just one hole in it and the whole thing blows up."

A leak in the middle of the pocket, with a defender taking a full shot at the practically immobile Joe Namath, could have ended the damaged quarterback's career at any moment. So Jet coach Weeb Ewbank played Plunkett for years, subordinating all offensive plans to the overall concept of keeping his quarterback healthy.

In Plunkett's prime, there were few tackles better at maintaining that vacuum inside. An inside rush against him was almost useless, since he could lean on a man and cave him into the logjam in the middle of the line. He knew how to practice the subtle arts, too. His hands and arms were always busy, always flirting with a 15-yard holding penalty. A quick push with both hands, a quick grab of the jersey; he knew all the tricks. But his best technique was a short, jolting punch to the midsection, not enough to cause any real injury, but enough to create sufficient distraction to destroy timing. It used to be fun watching someone play against Big Sherm for the first time, the look of shock and amazement when he tasted that first solar plexus blow.

It was as if a great canvas dummy had suddenly struck back, or the faithful, family Labrador retriever had suddenly turned and inflicted upon its master a deep, painful bite.

A team that uses a Plunkett type, though, must sacrifice part of its running game to that side. Screen passes, in which the tackle has to sprint to the outside and turn upfield, will tire him out and affect his pass blocking, since he has to carry around 60 or 70 more pounds than the average offensive tackle. Even the active 270- and 280-pounders, All-Pros such as Hill and Kansas City's Jim Tyrer and Los Angeles' Bob Brown, men whose quickness off the mark allows them to cave in a whole area to their inside, won't be called upon to do much screen-pass or pull-out work. It simply isn't worth tiring them out.

The tackle's normal blocking assignments on running plays are less arduous than those of the guard, who must dig in and drive a man who might outweigh him by 30 or 40 pounds. The tackle's job requires a certain amount of finesse, but often he can get by on mere containment, since the split between tackle and tight end is wider than the guard's spacings. The hole, in a sense, is already partially created. And if he catches his block just right, and drives his man back for yardage, it's a bonus.

A tackle like Mix, whose body control was exceptional, could often permit a coach to put in plays he wouldn't think of using with another man. On an end sweep to his side, Mix could hook-block a defensive end and wall him off from the action, an almost impossible block for a tackle. On a quick pitch to the outside, he could pull out and lead the play, along with Walt Sweeney, the guard next to him. The interference could form quicker this way, quicker than on a standard two-guard pullout, since the distance the linemen have to travel is decreased. All you need to make it work is a sprinter at tackle.

For years the San Diego sweeps have made reputations for backs like Keith Lincoln and Paul Lowe and Dickie Post. But it was Mix who made them go.

TIGHT END: The tight end lines up outside the tackle, close enough to help out on double-team blocking, but far enough away so that he can get clear on pass patterns. He is a combination blocker-pass catcher, and on most defenses he'll have a corner linebacker playing him head up. On the majority of running plays, he'll have to block him with a straight head-and-shoulder charge, which is where the tight end proves his manhood, because the linebacker is waiting for him. Occasionally, though, he'll take a slightly wider split and try to cut the linebacker with a body block. And on even fewer occasions, he'll be called upon to handle a defensive end by himself, which can prove an experience.

"All I could think of," said San Francisco's John David Crow when he was converted from running back to tight end and had to face Los Angeles' Deacon Jones, "was the coach asking me how I'd like to shift to tight end. He never did ask me how I'd like to block on Deacon Jones. I figured after that first experience everything else would be downhill.

"As a running back I thought I'd had everything done to me that could be done. I'd been hit every way you can be hit. But as a tight end I don't know where it's coming from. I guess I've made more mistakes in the six games I've been there than I made in the last two years. There's something new all the time.

"When I played against Jones, I felt like a rookie. It was the strangest feeling after all these years. I didn't know what Jones was going to do, the way he charges with his left hand out and hits you on the head with that big fist of his. The one thing I was thinking at the time was, 'My God, I can't let him hit me on the head with that hammer.' I gave him my best shot and held on and let him carry me back. The second time I got inside the hammer, and he hit me behind the head."

Crow's predecessor on the 49ers, Monty Stickles, wasn't much of a pass catcher, but he said he welcomed the contact.

"I love to be on offense," he said. "I love to beat a man who can use his hands. When I knock a man down who can use every technique against me it is very satisfying. It's a lot of fun, hitting a man."

When the play calls for a tight end to block down on the defensive end, he's usually double-team blocking with the tackle next to him. But occasionally you find a man big enough to get the job done by himself, such as the Colts' John Mackey, the Chiefs' Fred Arbanas, San Diego's Jacque MacKinnon, and the best ever—Green Bay's 6-3, 250-pound Ron Kramer.

"He was big enough and strong enough to wipe out a man by himself," Lombardi said, "and because this freed another blocker, it was almost like owning a permit to put 12 men on the field."

Football psychologists have always wondered why a man would want to become an offensive lineman in the first place. A defensive player can give full vent to any destructive urges. He can play "mad" the whole way, while the offensive player must always stay within the mechanics of his position. And defensive efforts are always rewarded by a "tackle by . . ." on the public-address system.

"I think it's a desire to create, I really do," Ringo once said. "A smooth offense is a creation, a beautiful thing. Defense is destruction. I just don't think I have it in me to play defense. I love to watch a good offense. It's the prettiest part of the game, watching a sweep go or seeing a well-executed trap play pick up 40 yards.

"Watching someone like Forrest Gregg work is like watching a great bullfighter or ballet dancer."

Often, an individual's emotional makeup will determine what side of the line he will play on, assuming he is physically able to perform both jobs.

"You look at a kid coming into camp and there's just something about his attitude that seems to earmark him for offense or defense," Lombardi says.

"It's not a bad thing, it's just something in his makeup. I've assigned backs to wrong positions when they first came here. I almost made the mistake of playing Herb Adderley [All-Pro defensive cornerback] as an offensive receiver. But you don't seem to make those errors with linemen.

"An offensive lineman usually has a technical approach to the game. He can be trained and developed. A defensive player can get by on instinctive reactions and emotion."

Try this test. Watch the linemen after a play is over. The defensive man who has missed a tackle might put on a small horror show, kicking the turf, pounding the ground with his fist, maybe slamming himself on the helmet hard enough to create a low-key headache. The offensive player will seldom show any emotion after he's missed a block, even though he may be dying inside.

"An offensive player is a thinking man; he doesn't get as much mileage out of an emotional state," Mix says. "He might be just as vicious a player as a defensive man, but his viciousness is usually within the rules.

"Why did I become an offensive lineman? For one thing, my size was only ordinary; my skills were mechanical, not instinctive; and emotionally I have the temperment of an offensive lineman.

"I don't have to lock myself in a room before a game and try to get mean or incensed in order to play well. Football is still a game for me."

The thrill of letting one's body go wild in a sudden mad urge of abandon, the wild rush of the blitzing linebacker, the ferocious bull-elephant charge of the defensive tackle; they're all practically unknown to the offensive lineman. Even on his open-field work, when he pulls out and leads a ballcarrier downfield, he must be in control, always in control. But there are moments for revenge.

"This is football, this is what football should really be like," Rasmussen said last season, after the Jets used 43 running plays and only 21 passes, to defeat Boston.

"Four yards and a cloud of dust. Green Bay football. God, I love it. Now I know why the Packers loved to play this game so much."

"When you run a team into the ground, it's your turn to dish it out," Schmitt said. "It's what we call get-even football. You don't just stand back getting popped all the time. You pop a little yourself."

The block that looks best on the TV screen, the open-field block that sends a defensive player cartwheeling and causes the commentators to fall all over themselves in search of new synonyms for "great," is usually the easiest to perform. The reason is that the defensive player is desperate at this point. It's a last-resort type of thing for him. He has totally committed himself; he is going at full speed, practically out of control, and often the merest bump will send him flying.

Many times, the offensive lineman must use guile to even the odds between himself and the fist-swinger across the line. Draw plays, screens, and traps are his weapons, and the basic premise in all of them is the same—make the defense think something is happening, and then hit them with the exact opposite. Acting ability helps.

On a draw play, the lineman drops back, sets himself to pass block, and then rides the defensive lineman along his chosen course while a back takes a delayed hand-off and races through the vacated area. The runner can pick any spot he likes, but a wrong choice of holes will give him minus five yards on the stat sheet and some very unpleasant conversation in the huddle.

The trap is a two-man operation. A tackle or a guard will leave his man alone, allowing him to penetrate, perhaps bumping him first to "set up" the trap. Once the defender is suckered into the enemy backfield, he will be cut down by a pulling guard, charging across from the blind side, low and hard. There are two kinds of traps: the short trap, which is simply a variation on the normal running assignments, and the long trap, which covers a greater amount of lateral distance and is designed as a potential long gainer (see Fig. 2).

The screen pass is a bit of hokum in which three men, usually the center, guard, and tackle, pretend to falter on their pass blocks. They have to give some kind of blocking effort, though, or they'll tip off the play (in which case the defensive man will veer to the outside and holler, "Screen!" in a voice that will carry into every living room with a TV set). Worse yet, they'll allow a speedy defensive lineman to get in so quickly that he'll upset the whole operation.

After a delayed count, usually two seconds, one of the actors in the drama will yell, "Go!" at which time all three men will head for the flank, the open country, where a back and a lazily thrown ball have drifted out, hopefully in that order.

My favorite play in all of football, though, is the "sucker play," which calls for the ultimate in deception and pure raw courage. It's the wildest of gambles, the most naked of bluffs. And like the poker maxim, "You can't work a bluff on a fool or a drunk," you can't work a sucker play on a subpar defensive lineman, only on a superior player, whose own qualities of alertness and pursuit work against him.

An offensive guard or tackle pulls out of the line, away from the direction in which the play is going. The purpose is to "influence" the man over him to go the same way, to pursue it. If the

Short Trap: Right Guard Traps Right Defensive Tackle

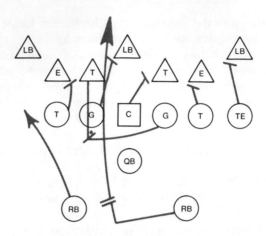

Long Trap: Right Guard On Right Defensive End

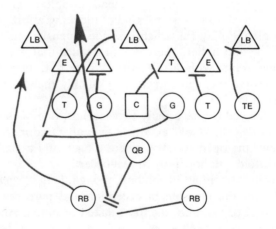

Fig. 2

defender takes the bait, he takes himself out of the play. If he doesn't, he remains squarely in the hole, with no one blocking him.

Ballcarriers aren't happy about running this play, and one Boston College assistant coach named Bill Campbell calls it The Letter to the Bereaved Parents of Your Fullback—"Gee, we're awfully sorry about what happened to your son, Mrs. Comella, but the tackle just didn't take the fake."

In the last few years there have been two famous applications of the sucker play. In the NFL championship game in Green Bay in 1967, Chuck Mercein went from the Dallas 11-yard line, to the three with a minute to go. The man suckered was Bob Lilly, one of the NFL's finest tackles. In the Kansas City-Minnesota Super Bowl, the Chiefs' Mike Garrett scored the game's first touchdown on a perfectly executed sucker play that actually combined the principles of the long trap, just to stay on the safe side.

Kansas City's left tackle, Jim Tyrer, pulled out to his left, trying to influence right defensive end Jim Marshall, an active pursuer. Marshall took the fake, and it was so effective that Alan Page, playing the tackle next to him, started to go for it too, perfectly setting up the long trap by the Chiefs' right guard, Mo Moorman. The rest of the Chiefs' line merely angle-blocked away from the hole, and perhaps the most perfectly executed block was by tight end Fred Arbanas, lined up on the left side, who knocked middle linebacker Lonnie Warwick off his feet.

"We must have called that play seven or eight times this season," Garrett said, "and that's the first time we've ever scored on it. We tried it four or five times against Oakland, and Keating [defensive tackle Tom Keating] nearly took my head off. I guess it only works against NFL teams." (See Fig. 3.)

Holding, on pass blocking, is a calculated risk by the offensive lineman. If the official catches him, it's 15 yards. But he doesn't catch him that often, or doesn't choose to. The defensive lineman can either inform the referee or umpire that he is being held, which doesn't amount to much, since every other-play is punctuated by shouts of "Watch the holding!" or he can deal with the offender his own way. Since this method merely involves a step-up in volume and intensity of what he's been doing all afternoon anyway, the offensive player figures it's worth the price. Very few offensive linemen don't hold.

"I used to get a lot of holding penalties on me," Hill said. "Then I took off the gloves I wore in cold weather. They gave the

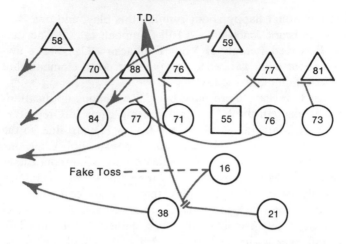

KANSAS CITY
84   Tight end Fred Arbanas
77   Left tackle Jim Tyrer
71   Left guard Ed Budde
55   Center E. J. Holub
76   Right guard Mo Moorman
73   Right tackle Dave Hill
16   Quarterback Len Dawson
38   Fullback Wendell Hayes
21   Halfback Mike Garrett

MINNESOTA
70   Right end Jim Marshall
88   Right tackle Alan Page
76   Middle guard Paul Dickson
77   Left tackle Gary Larsen
81   Left end Carl Eller
58   Right linebacker Wally
      Hilgenberg
59   Middle linebacker Lonnie
      Warwick

Fig. 3

referees something to look at—a target. When I took off the gloves, they forgot about me."

Most experienced offensive linemen have the option of changing their blocking assignments among themselves if the defense switches. Instead of blocking straight ahead, the center and guard, or guard and tackle, might cross-block. This would happen if the enemy is packed tightly inside. They can call "area blocking," in which each blocker takes a zone, or an area, and this is a logical call if the defense has been stunting, or varying its normal moves.

Usually the center will call the switches among the five interior linemen, since his voice can be heard on both sides of the line. In some systems he is required to make a call on every play, some of them dummy calls, so the defense will hear the same type of thing every time. Occasionally a guard and tackle, or a tackle and tight end, will call switches to each other.

The rewards for all this dedication and application are small compared with those of the rest of the offense, the runners and passers and receivers. Newspaper notice is thin, and many times coaches introduce incentive-type awards to keep up spirits.

When he was with the Giants, Lombardi presented a weekly "Blocking Award," $10 a game for the winner. In 1958, a divisional championship year, eight-time All-Pro tackle Rosey Brown won it 11 out of 12 weeks. When he was with the Packers, Lombardi made a big thing about his numerical grades, and often he'd stop the movie projector to zero in on a particularly good—or bad—block.

"You'd wonder about him sometimes," Kramer says. "Here we were, all college men, and he'd use something as basic as that. 'He's psyching me,' you'd say to yourself, but damned if it wasn't effective.

"I remember one particular block I made. It was against Chicago and I pulled out and got Bennie McRae, the cornerback. I got him with my helmet under his chin and knocked him flat on his rear. Then I stepped over and picked off the defensive end cutting across, and then I headed downfield, but by that time the runner had made his cut and was gone.

"When it came on the screen, Lombardi started yelling, 'Hey, that's a helluva block, watch this!' and he ran it over again. I don't believe one single word was written on it in the newspapers, but all the ballplayers saw it. You've got to have that."

3
Quarterbacking for Fun and Profit

I wish there was a Caribbean League in football like they have in base-ball. Then I could play all year.

□ John Unitas, 1964

Then we ran the clock out. I told Unitas just to take the ball and fall down. But even on the sneaks he was looking for a hole to run through. He likes to make yardage even running out the clock.

□ Don Shula, after beating Minnesota, 14-13, in 1964

"Never mind how many passes he throws and what his competition percentage looks like," my old high-school coach, Charley Avedisian used to say. "My quarterback's got to be the guy who can take you in in the last two minutes, when it's getting dark and the fans are booing and the wind is blowing and there's so much ice on the ball he can't grip it."

Charley, who had once played guard for the old Giants, had a sense of the dramatic, and we used to chuckle at him behind his back—"Win it for the Gipper," and all that. But when you look it all over, is there really anything else to being a quarterback?

Well, yes, there is, of course. There's reading defenses and knowing how to decipher the defensive flimflam of the masked zones and "combinations," and, naturally, when a guy reaches the pros he can't have a fish arm. But what it all comes down to is those last few minutes, with the fans booing and the wind blowing, etc.

Joe Namath can do it. In the Jets' Super Bowl year, Namath brought them from behind in the dying minutes of four games, including the AFL championship against Oakland. Y. A. Tittle could do it; it seems that he always could. Even in his diaper days with the Baltimore Colts of the old All-America Football Conference, he could leave you for dead in two minutes.

Bobby Layne had it, and John Unitas, and Otto Graham, and of course the Dutchman, Norm Van Brocklin. In those last two years at Philadelphia, he might have been the best of them all.

"The year we won the championship in Philly, we trailed at half time in five games, sometimes by 24 points," Tommy McDonald says. "But each time, between halves, Van Brocklin went to the blackboard, explained what the defense was doing, and we came back to win in the second half." Which makes you wonder what coach Buck Shaw was doing while Van Brocklin was chalktalking, but that's the way it goes.

I can't comment on Sammy Baugh's style as a quarterback. I saw him through a kid's eyes, and he was merely the guy who scared you to death while he was beating your Giants. I remember him throwing bull's-eyes while he was falling all over the place, but I also remember that he could bring the team down the field in a hurry and beat you. When people tell me about his fine wrist action and the kind of spiral he had on the ball, I tune out, but I'll listen when they say he was a great quarterback.

The quarterbacks get the most money and pull the most people into the stadium. They get quoted the most and analyzed the most, and naturally the fans reserve the greatest volume of their cheers and boos for them.

The Pro Football Hero of the Year is odds-on to be the quarterback—the winning quarterback, which doesn't strain the imagination any. Bart Starr was the headline name in the Packers' glory years, although some writers still reserved their heavy coverage for Joe Namath throughout this period, marking time until he could be a winner, which he finally was in '68. Then everybody zeroed in on him, forgetting Earl Morrall, who had been the pre-Super Bowl glamour boy. It all happened too quickly for Len Dawson to be accepted as a matinee idol, except in that one Super Bowl week in 1970. Everybody was too busy looking at Joe Kapp, and Kapp still emerged as the hero of '69, a bit tarnished after the Super Bowl, maybe, but still the kind of a guy you like to read about—and write about. Earthy. Real. Takes no crap and knocks a linebacker on his can if he gets in your way. He laughed in the face of people who said that a passer must have a quick release and a controlled spiral, and that quarterbacks only run out of sheer terror—Van Brocklin's quotable old chestnut. A "Q" and "A" session with Joe Kapp:

Q: Are you an unorthodox quarterback?

A: When we were losing, they didn't say I was unorthodox, just that I was losing.

Q: Some people have written that you are not a classic quarterback.

A: Classics are for Greeks.

Q: Is it true that you throw the ball without putting your fingers on the laces?

A: What good would it do?

Q: Have you ever tried any other position?

A: I'm not good enough to be anything but a quarterback. They made a cornerback out of me when I was a freshman in college, and I got beat three times for TD's. It was degrading.

Q: What does football mean to you?

A: Football is a kid's game. It's also a game for animals.

Q: So you're crude, then.

A: What does 'crude' mean? Not graceful? Well, they pay a quarterback to win, not on how pretty he looks.

Q: Why don't you run out of bounds when you run with the ball.

A: Running out of bounds is for gringos [his mother is Mexican].

Before Kapp came down from Vancouver in the Canadian Football League to join the Vikings, sportswriter Wells Twombly asked a Vancouver reporter what Kapp was like as a player.

"Well, he's a great quarterback," the man said, "if your idea of greatness is a guy who takes 12 seconds to stagger back and set up."

But after the NFL Championship game, *Sports Illustrated*'s pro football chronicler, Tex Maule, wrote: "What Joe Kapp may have done is to pretty much destroy the mystique of pro football. The arcane mysteries of the flexed line and the overshifted defense and the combination man-to-man and zone defenses mean nothing to him. He attacks defenses basically, with no frills and no excess ratiocination."

It isn't all that simple, and it isn't quite as complicated as some coaches would have us believe. Kapp and all his lack of ratiocination wouldn't have been anywhere in 1969 if the Viking defense hadn't been superb. And don't forget that in 1968 the Jets' defense was No. 1 in the AFL (and held the Colts scoreless until the last Super Bowl quarter). And the whole Starr-Lombardi operation was predicated on a great defense.

A quarterback must be physically tough and durable. The days of the "containing" defense are over, and the passer must now be able to take a beating. The injury rate has been stunning in the last two years, and it is interesting that the man that everyone said would drop first, Namath, with his pasteboard knees, scarcely missed a series during the '68 and '69 seasons. A QB's passing and play calling and faking talents can't help him if he can't lead a team, and the team just won't respond if it detects any sign of physical cowardice in its No. 1 man.

"It took me three months to learn to ride a chariot for *Ben Hur*," said Charlton Heston, who played the part of a quarterback in the movie, *Number One*.

"I learned enough about painting in a couple of weeks to do *The Agony and the Ecstasy*. Parting the Red Sea, with the help of De Mille and God, took no time at all. But I've been trying to learn to play quarterback for eight months, and I find it incredibly difficult, by far the toughest preparation I've ever had for a film."

Heston said the toughest part was learning to step up into the pocket in the face of an all-out pass rush.

"This is going against every instinct in the human animal. Every nerve in your body is saying, 'Keep going, keep going, get rid of it, get rid of it!' "

Everyone who has ever played with or against Unitas speaks of his great courage. At times it almost sounds masochistic.

"You can't intimidate him," says the Rams' defensive tackle, Merlin Olsen. "He waits until the last possible second to release the ball, even if it means he's going to take a good lick. When he sees us coming, he knows it's going to hurt and we know it's going to hurt, but he just stands there and takes it. No other quarterback has such class.

"I swear that, when he sees you coming out of the corner of his eye, he holds that ball a split second longer than he really needs to —just to let you know he isn't afraid of any man. Then he throws it on the button. I weigh 270, myself, and I don't know if I could absorb the punishment he takes. I wonder if I could stand there, week after week, and say: 'Here I am. Take your best shot.' "

And some of the shots are horrendous. Just watch a quarterback after he releases the ball a few times. The officials are supposed to protect him from the late shots, but there's the split second of indecision—could the defensive man stop himself in time or couldn't he? And when a law is overlooked long enough, like the one against spitting in the street, it loses its bite.

Whatever they may say to the contrary, the majority of defensive linemen don't have much love for quarterbacks.

Alex Karras, the Detroit defensive tackle, once had a radio show in which he answered fans' questions. The phone rang one night and an effeminate voice asked: "Don't you think a quarterback should get more protection from the linemen?"

And Karras answered: "Really now, they get more money than we do, sweetheart."

Karras also traces his dislike to remoter grounds. Half of what he says is a put-on, but most good comedians rely on an element of truth, and Karras is one of football's established comics.

"If you took a survey of most quarterbacks," he once said, "you'd find that they go to the Presbyterian Church and the cafeteria afterward, and there they drink ice tea and eat a hot dog with a dab of mustard.

"They're all milk drinkers and they're all alike . . . pretty boys, all in the same image. The only one I know who isn't is Sonny Jurgensen."

Karras is speaking symbolically, of course. He knows that Namath doesn't drink milk. What he means is that there is a fundamental difference in the life-style of a quarterback and a defensive tackle. One is slim and the other is fat. One gets the girl and the other one doesn't. And if the quarterbacks don't like the pounding they have to take, then the hell with them.

Unless a quarterback can stand back there and say, "The hell with you too, Jack," he's in trouble. There are different ways of saying it. He can curse and snarl at the defensive linemen, like Layne used to do (he snarled at his own, too). And he can keep his mouth shut and beat them to death with his passes. No matter what his style, his teammates must believe that he knows he can do it, or they'll give him a funny look when he claps his hands and says, "Let's go, gang!" They'll ask themselves who's kidding whom.

"There's a difference between a quarterback coming away from the center and saying to himself, 'I hope I find my receiver,' and a quarterback coming away saying, 'You better stop this one, pal. I'm putting it right there in his gut,' " Allie Sherman once said.

Sometimes an uncertain feeling comes across as soon as a man steps on the field. Jerry Kramer, in his book, *Farewell to Football,* describes rookie Billy Stevens stepping in to quarterback the Packers in 1968 in a game in which they were beating the 49ers.

"He called a play I'd never heard before. It must have been a play from his college days. He tried to pass a couple of times and the 49ers hit him late and turned him on his head and stomped him into the ground and just about killed him." Worst of all, the 49ers scored 20 points in the last quarter and won, 27-20.

Raw physical courage isn't always enough. Many rookies have it, but the only rookie who ever won an NFL or AFL title was Bob Waterfield, and this was in the wartime football era of 1945. Off the field, a quarterback can be a wild man. On it, though, and in the movie room, he has to be disciplined. He must learn.

Namath's life on the field—careful, conservative, meticulous— is the reverse of his life off it. People have a hard time believing that Namath is one of football's most intelligent and fundamentally sound signal callers.

The Colts certainly didn't believe it before that '69 Super Bowl. They were astounded by his confidence and flippancy (some of Namath's teammates later said that they didn't actually give themselves much of a chance until Namath started throwing around those "I guarantee you" quotes). Billy Ray Smith, the defensive tackle, spoke of Namath's knees—and his teeth—and Unitas said that Namath had never seen a defense like the one the Colts were going to throw at him.

Namath didn't look at the Colts in terms of personalities— Mike (The Animal) Curtis, the linebacker who hates everybody; and Smith, who could jump over blockers to get to a quarterback; and the mountainous Bubba Smith, who responded to those "Kill,

Bubba, kill!" roars like a Ferrari responds to high octane gas. What Namath saw, watching the projector with his backfield coach, Clive Rush, or in his room by himself, was a little set of moving X's and O's, playing a rotating strong side zone defense.

He knew that he could snap the ball into the creases of such a defense. He'd done it before. The Orange Bowl turf was firm and fast. The weather probably would be good. And he had been dumped for losses only 15 times during the season, less than any other starting quarterback in football. He wasn't worried about his offensive line breaking down. He was a student, and if there was any trepidation about that final exam, he kept it to himself.

"This might sound like baloney," Rush said, "but Joe did not misread a coverage all year. Sure, we'll send in a play now and then, but he has a 100-percent prerogative to check off, or change anything we send in. (Tittle once said that a man doesn't really become a mature quarterback until he can tell his coach to go fly a kite.)

"Joe knows as much out there as we do. I remember one time the year before when we called Mike Taliaferro on the phone down by the bench and said, 'Mike, send in play so-and-so. Before Mike could get to coach Ewbank, Weeb had already sent in the same play with Mark Smolinski. And before Smolinski had gotten to the huddle, Joe had already called the play. That's what is known as thinking together."

And Ewbank, who 11 years before had salvaged Unitas from the Pittsburgh sandlots, gave Namath a system that placed a tremendous mental burden on him, but also gave him complete control—unlike the wheezing choo-choo-train of a messenger-guard system that Paul Brown employs to control his quarterbacks.

"We always gave Joe a little more leeway in changing his calls at the line," Weeb said. "Maybe that's why he learned so quickly. The system is basically simple. He calls a color, and if it's a 'live' color, then the real play will follow. Sometimes we change the live color every game, sometimes we change it during a game itself.

"If Joe suspects that the defense is picking up the live color, he can simply call 'Check with me,' in the huddle, and then when he comes up to the line he gives a color—dead or live, it doesn't matter—and the real call follows. He can change that one, too. He can say, 'Double-check with me,' and then he'll call two plays at the line and the second one is the real one.

"He was calling practically all 'Check with me's' in the Super Bowl game, and a few 'Double-check with me's.' "

A pro, according to Gus D'Amato, the fight manager, is a man who does what he knows has to be done. And Namath was a pro that day against the Colts. People who only knew him through the quotes about his hair and his mink coat, his great passing arm and quick release, saw a scientist at work that day. It was a textbook job, a clinical study on how to beat the strong-side rotating zone.

Afterward, Namath said it had been easy. "It was the easiest zone I ever read," he said. "They stayed in it almost the whole day. They hardly made any adjustments."

The strong-side rotation zone is a defense geared to stopping the deep threat of the flankerback. In this case the object of it was Don Maynard, who had scored 10 touchdowns for the Jets and averaged 22.8 yards a catch, the highest average in the league. The flankerback, or wide receiver on the strong side, is the man who lines up on the same side as the tight end. The weak-side wide man, or split end, was George Sauer, who came in with more modest credentials—three touchdowns and an average of 17.3 yards a catch. He lined up on the left side, and the Jets seldom varied this basic alignment by loading up with slot formations (both wide receivers on the same side). They didn't have to.

Namath wanted to work against this strong-side zone because he knew the potential of Sauer. He knew that Maynard had come in with a bad leg. He didn't want the Colts to start ganging up on Sauer, forcing the quarterback to rely on Maynard as his primary receiver. So to get the Colts worried about Maynard—and stay in their strong-side rotation—Namath threw some first-half bombs to him, which is what you're *not* supposed to do against a defense geared to stop exactly that. Maynard didn't catch any of them, but he showed his straight-ahead speed, narrowly missing one touchdown and scaring the daylights out of cornerback Bobby Boyd and strong safety Obert Logan, who had rotated over to cut him off.

So the Colts stayed in their strong-side zone and Namath picked them to pieces, throwing to Sauer 12 times and connecting with him eight times, which gave Sauer a Super Bowl pass-catching record. The Jet line negated the pass rush, the backs picked up the blitzing Colt linebackers, and Namath had time to operate.

Figure 4 shows the strong-side rotation zone defense. The dotted areas are the areas of coverage for each man. The shaded areas represent Ewbank's "places where the zone is vulnerable," or cracks in the zone. Namath hit the cracks 11 times in 15 attempts. He completed five of six checkoff passes to his backs against blitzes; and he threw into coverage areas seven times (four times to set up the threat of Maynard), completing one pass.

Len Dawson ran a cool and efficient Kansas City attack against Minnesota in the 1970 Super Bowl. His thinking was the same as Namath's—conservative—and he relied on a strong defense and ground game to set up his passing. His statistics were moderate, and his completion percentage high, but there was one big difference between his style and Namath's.

Dawson beat the Vikings without completing a single pass he had thrown farther than 10 yards. Even his 47-yard touchdown to Otis Taylor was a little sideline pass that turned into a big gainer when the corner back and strong safety missed their tackles. Dawson is not a good long passer, but he did what he knew best, and he inched the Vikings to death with his short tosses. Twelve of the 17 passes he threw, incidentally, went to his two wide receivers.

Namath and Dawson both played confident, conservative games, which used to be the trademark of Bart Starr in his preinjury days. When they faced a zone defense, they took what was given to them. The cockiness of their command basically came from modesty. They knew how to read defenses, and the team knew it and responded to their leadership, which in turn bolstered the quarterbacks' confidence. The whole thing feeds on itself.

Kapp is an outlander among quarterbacks, a fluke, a freakish type, but his own boiling desire ignited his teammates so that they played at full throttle all the time. The mechanical and intellectual shortcomings Kapp might have had on the field were almost compensated for by the wave of emotional fervor he generated. But Kapp is an original, an Eddie Stanky. Don't forget that he's been a winner wherever he's been. He took California into the Rose

Bowl, Vancouver into the Grey Cup, and Minnesota into the Super Bowl.

Probably the two most unhappy quarterbacks of 1969 were the men who made All-NFL and All-AFL, respectively, Roman Gabriel and Daryle Lamonica. There's a parallel there. Both are fine athletes, both have seemed on the verge of greatness, without ever quite being there, and both have ego problems. With Gabriel, who's personally liked and respected by his Ram teammates, it's not enough ego. With Lamonica, who has split the Oakland Raiders into the pro-Lamonica and anti-Lamonica factions, it's a case of too much. Both men, incidentally, are backed up by fine defensive teams.

"We zoned Lamonica the whole game," said Cincinnati assistant coach J. D. Donaldson, whose Bengals beat Oakland during the regular season. "We took away the long pass, but he still tried to go long. Force, force, force; it was like a personal challenge to him to see if he could drop the bomb on us. I think we intercepted him four times."

Oakland's offense is a big-play thing, with the quarterback looking for the bomb whenever the opportunity presents itself. When the Raiders get you going, Lamonica can pass you right out of the park. He is what Namath used to be three or four years ago, but Lamonica's football intellect hasn't developed along with Namath's. His physical courage is above question, and it might even be that blind courage that cost the Raiders a Super Bowl shot in '70, when Lamonica stayed in the AFL championship game against Kansas City, trying to throw the ball with a banged-up hand that could barely grip it.

Gabriel's problem is self-doubt. "The primary emotion I take into a game is fear," he once said. "I fear that the club we are going to play could beat me. If it beats me, I'm in second place. I fear my opponent. When a play breaks down, I'm not able to handle the emotional letdowns. I come back to the huddle thinking: 'Who broke down? What happened?' I get the feeling it is an impossibility—almost an impossibility to get back the yards we've lost."

It would take a psychiatrist to figure out why a man who's 6-4, 220, who breaks tackles like a tight end and hurts the people who

Fig. 4

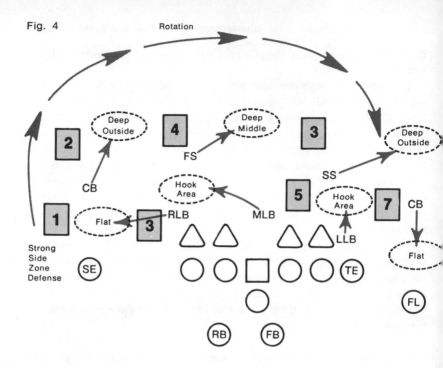

NAMATH'S SUPER BOWL PASSING FREQUENCY

1st HALF

	INTO VULNERABLE (SHADED) AREAS		
1	**2**	**3**	**7**
inc—Sauer (Lyles & Shinnick def.— switched to weak side rotation) +4 Sauer +13 Sauer +11 Sauer	+35 Sauer	+6 Sauer +13 Mathis	inc—low, Turner

2nd HALF

1	**4**	**3**	**5**
inc—Sauer, wide	+40 Sauer	+14 Sauer +10 Sauer	+14 Snell inc—Lammons (Logan plays Lammons man-to-man) +11 Lammons

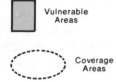

Vulnerable
Areas

Coverage
Areas

	Colts
Jets	RCB: Lyles
SE: Sauer	FS: Volk
RB: Boozer, Mathis	SS: Logan
FB: Snell	LCB: Boyd
TE: Lammons	RLB: Shinnick
FL: Maynard, Turner	MLB: Gaubatz
	LLB: Curtis

CHECK-OFFS VS. BLITZ	INTO COVERAGE (DOTTED) AREAS
+6 Mathis +9 Snell inc—Snell, dropped ball +12 Snell	inc—Sauer, hook left (Shinnick & Lyles def.) inc—Maynard, fly right (got behind Logan) inc—Maynard, fly right (Boyd & Logan def.) +2 Lammons, hook left (tackled by Lyles)
+1 Mathis +5 Snell	inc—Maynard, fly right (Logan def.) inc—Maynard, dropped ball on right sideline inc—Maynard, fly right (beat Logan but caught ball out of end zone)

do tackle him, who has never copped out with an injury, who can throw the ball as well as anyone, shouldn't have the one basic ingredient—confidence. Again, the problem might be a matter of football intellect, the ability to read defenses.

Most veteran quarterbacks will tell you there are certain things that come only from on-the-field experience. Not even the films can give them to you.

"Zones are disguised these days," Namath says. "Usually you'll pick up the key by watching the tight safety. But different clubs disguise them differently with exchanges and their own particular wrinkles. That's where playing experience helps. You look at a team for years and you get an instinctive feeling about them. Take San Diego, for instance. I like to watch Kenny Graham, their tight safety, and see how he moves. You can look at movies forever, and it's not the same as seeing it in the flesh."

The whole area of "reading" a defense is something that came up in the last decade or so, ever since the zone defenses started taking on new looks and faces. When some people drafted quarterbacks, they thought of them as either smart or dumb, depending on things like IQ testing and college grades. It's amazing how many supposedly dumb collegians turned into smart quarterbacks.

Namath, for instance, scored 104 on one IQ test a pro scout gave him before the draft. Unitas flunked his entrance exams at both Pitt and Louisville, finally passing the Louisville test the next time around. And once upon a time a quarterback's brain was measured by his selection of plays.

"During the 1941 season, we were away out in front in one of the games," the Bears' old quarterback, Sid Luckman, says. "I decided to try something. I asked the lineman if they would like to call the plays, to see how far the team would go without the quarterback doing it. The plan was to let each lineman call one play —the one he liked best.

"They all thought it was a great idea and we started in. We started on the 20 and five plays later we scored. That beat one tackle and an end out of their turn to call a play."

"Reading" is the measure of intellect these days, and the whole thing starts as soon as the quarterback gets the snap from center. As he drops back, his eyes are following his primary receiver, although he might look the other way for an instant—to throw the defender off. His brain is working like a computer; inhaling, digesting, and discarding information as it is recognized. This all must be done in the space of 2.7 seconds or so, 3.5 tops. Namath says he'll throw to his primary receiver 75 percent of the time, "Either that or your game plan is no good—or you're not reading well." Then comes a quick look at the secondary receiver, and against some defenses the second man will automatically become the primary target. Then there might be time for a quick peek at the third one, and then the three-second gong goes off and it's time to unload the ball or have your head taken off.

If everyone is covered, the rookie quarterback will stand there and take his loss, like a good little soldier, or try and scramble for some yardage, like Fran Tarkenton. The old pro will throw the ball away, unload it out of bounds or into the ground, where no one can intercept it. This usually sets up a round of booing in the crowd, especially if money has been wagered on the game. And up in the press box, the writers are saying, "Gee, he's really off today."

"One time we had a blitz on," said Houston's linebacker, Ron Pritchard, "and I know I didn't give it away. But Namath picked it up before I even hit the line of scrimmage. Pete Lammons was in behind me and Namath had the ball to him. He reads, man, he reads."

All the reading in the world, though, won't help if a passer doesn't have the knack of hitting his receiver at just the right time, hitting him on the break, if the pattern calls for it. A lot of it comes from pure dog-labor, the after-practice stuff, or "specialty work," as Ewbank likes to call it.

Unitas and Ray Berry got to know each other during Ewbank's hours of specialty work. Namath got firmly acquainted with Sauer and Maynard that way, too. If the passer is in perfect harmony with his receivers' moves, he can snap off his throw in less time, putting less of a burden on the offensive linemen and considerably improving their outlook on the game of football.

When the Giants played the Jets in a 1969 exhibition game in New Haven, Connecticut, I brought a stopwatch with me into the press box and kept stats on how long it took Namath and Tarkenton to unload their passes. I timed them from the time the center fed them the ball until it left their hand. Namath averaged 2.7 seconds per pass, Tarkenton, 3.4. It may have been partly the fault of Tarkenton's receivers, or possibly the fact that the Jets' deep coverage was better, or perhaps Tarkenton didn't mind holding the ball longer, knowing he could probably scramble out of trouble if things got sticky. But the Jets' approach just seemed like the sounder way of doing things.

If a passer develops the knack of hitting his receivers on the break—or if he is born with it—he won't get intercepted as much.

The late Paul Christman once drew a diagram for newsman Murray Olderman in which the old Cards' QB showed a receiver running a diagonal pattern. He drew a circle around the point where the line veered, and another one where it stopped.

"If a receiver is covered," Christman said, "the passer can't hit him here [pointing to the first circle], because he hasn't shaken free yet, or here [the second circle] because by then it might be too late. The defensive back might have caught up to him. He has to hit him here [a point between both circles]. That's where the receiver has made his break and that's when he's open for a fraction of a second.

"A hundred kids today can throw the ball as well as Sammy Baugh did. In practice. They've got the arm and the strength. And they can fire it on a line, overarm, sidearm, any way you name it. But what makes a passer is this—the ability to hit his man on the break. Some of them never develop it."

OK, so assume your receiver is breaking off his pattern 20 yards downfield and you have three seconds to get the ball to him, and in front of you a panorama of shifting zones and switches is unfolding. You have to make sure to look the defenders off so they can't read your eyes and know exactly where the ball is going —so how do you ever pick your man out in all the traffic?

"Suppose you're in a crowded railroad station, and you look across the waiting room at a nondescript man and you want to watch him walk across the room," ex-Cleveland quarterback Frank Ryan says. "If you watch him all the time, it's easy to follow him as he makes his way through the crowd. But if you look away for a second, you won't be able to find him again. It's the same with receivers."

Ah, but what about that moment when you have to look the defense off him? The question is unanswered. It's just something you have to do if you want to win big in pro football, which might give you an idea why Heston said it was easier to split the Red Sea than play quarterback.

As for this business about a quarterback having peripheral vision, how he can look at the left sideline and see out of the wee corners of his eyes what's going on on the right side—Minnesota's backup man, Gary Cuozzo, says it's a myth.

"When I was young, I used to read about quarterbacks with peripheral vision," he says, "and I honestly believed they could see the whole field. But it's impossible. Don't believe it. I've asked several players about that, and I've never found one of them who told me he could see all the way across the field at the same time. You look here and you look there. This peripheral vision thing is one of the misleading things you read. A quarterback has to have good vision, period."

Quarterbacks are drafted for height, as well as strength of arm and brain these days, and often an inch or two can mean a difference of $50,000 or so in bonus money. Six feet is supposedly the absolute minimum for quarterbacks, or the redwood trees on the defensive line would totally obscure their vision.

"Name a quarterback under six feet tall who has ever led a professional team to a championship," an assistant coach once asked. I couldn't name one, but I couldn't name one taller than 6-3, either, who had ever won a title. It might involve the correlation of height and coordination with the speed of impulses between brain and arm, arm and ball, ball and receiver, or something like that. But we'll never be sure until a shrimp or a stork produces a championship.

The art of pure passing has been dissected and put together many times. Tittle says that you can teach a poor thrower to be OK, but you can never make the so-so guy great. What a pro coach can do, though, is take the untamed arm of the college quarterback and teach it the subtleties.

Most college quarterbacks have to have their delivery softened when they get to the pros, since the common misconception is that you have to be able to knock down a building with your ball or it will be intercepted. In fact, on many long passes, a higher trajectory is preferred, because it allows the passer to release the ball earlier and let his man run under it—if his timing is OK. But to throw a 40-yard line drive, the quarterback has to wait longer, until his receiver gets free, and this can wear down the offensive linemen.

The deliberate underthrow is something that Unitas and Namath both perfected. A receiver goes deep, turns and comes back for the ball, at which point the defender gets his feet crossed up and falls down, and the offense is six points richer. In the press box we're saying, "What luck. An underthrown pass and they get a TD out of it."

"The deliberate underthrow, if your timing is down pat, is a good way to beat that bump-and-go style where a cornerback stays with your receiver all the way, right from the line of scrimmage," Namath says. "Once your man goes long, the cornerback has to run like hell to keep up with him, and the deliberate underthrow —the comebacker—will get him all screwed up."

For all the commotion about throwing—pure passing never got a team anywhere. Pro football's all-time top ten for completions is as follows:

November 1, 1964: Houston's George Blanda went 37 for 68 against Buffalo.

December 5, 1948: New York's Charley Conerly went 36 for 53 vs. Pittsburgh.

December 20, 1964: Denver's Mickey Slaughter went 34 for 56 vs. Houston.

December 1, 1940: Philadelphia's Davey O'Brien went 33 for 60 vs. Washington.

September 23, 1962: Philadelphia's Sonny Jurgensen went 33 for 57 vs. New York.

October 25, 1964: Chicago's Billy Wade went 33 for 57 vs. Washington.

November 26, 1967: Washington's Jurgensen went 32 for 50 vs. Cleveland.

November 13, 1960: Houston's Blanda went 31 for 55 vs. Los Angeles.

November 10, 1963: Dallas' Don Meredith went 30 for 48 vs. San Francisco.

November 21, 1948: L.A.'s Jim Hardy went 28 for 53 vs. the
   Chicago Cards.

Those are the 10 passingest performances in pro history, and in
each case the passer's team lost, repeat lost, the game. This
doesn't mean that we're calling for a return of the flying wedge
. . . just that passing doesn't help much unless there are other
means of expression to go with it.

The running quarterback was the style at one time, mainly because all the good NFL signal callers were run-or-pass, single-
wing tailbacks in college—Layne, Conerly, Tittle, Baugh, Luckman, Waterfield, even Frankie Albert in his sophomore year at
Stanford. As the T formation grew up, though, coaches realized
that the most effective place for a quarterback to operate from
was the blocking pocket. And the sight of a freewheeling scrambler like Tarkenton makes purists like Ewbank positively ill.

"Scatter guys," Weeb says. "They keep scattering around out
there until one day they don't get up."

Tarkenton is called upon to defend his actions a few dozen
times a season, and he says that he only runs when his protection
breaks down. But around the league, the players suspect that he
gets a kick out of all the dodging and dancing. The defensive lineman who have to chase him don't dig it at all.

"We think Tarkenton uses audibles when we're chasing him,"
says Roger Brown, the Rams' 300-pound tackle. "Audibles like
'Help!'

"We chase him and we chase him and when we get him, we're
too tired to enjoy it. He makes for a long afternoon. Guys our
size, when we do that much running, we're ready for a stretcher.
He gets enjoyment out of running our tongues out."

But when the QB's do get caught, the results can be disastrous.
It has become open season on quarterbacks, and never before has
the attrition rate been so high for what used to be the safest of all
positions. In 1968, for instance, 18 of football's 26 starting quarterbacks were lost for either all or part of the season. The figure
calmed down a little in '69, but it was still higher than that of any
year except '68.

"The other day," Namath told a Touchdown Club banquet in

Miami before the Super Bowl, "somebody asked Don Meredith who was the most important member of the team, and he said, 'The doctor.' I agree, because the name of the game is Kill the Quarterback, brother."

"Man, I didn't know what Don was giving me when I took over this job," Dallas quarterback Craig Morton said when he replaced the retired Meredith. "I'm 26 years old and I feel like I'm 56. I am a total wreck."

Why all the injuries, since the art of the passing game, with its premium on timing and sophisticated blocking techniques, has become so refined? Blitzing might be one reason, but the era of the all-out blitz is coming to a close. It's too easy to hurt it with a little checkoff pass to a back, and all quarterbacks know how to do that. The answer is probably the nature of the pass rush itself, and the individuals who are rushing.

In the old days, only the ends put the real rush on the quarterback, and that was only if they were "crashing," instead of playing their normal "boxing" game—waiting for the end run. The three interior linemen, two tackles and the middle guard, were containing types, or run-stoppers. These days, though, you've got four defensive linemen who can put on a pass rush, and the era of the 300-pound tackle might also be ending. Speed and agility seem to be the new weapons now, even for defensive tackles, and when one of today's speedy defensive tackles or ends hits the quarterback, he's arriving with more speed than the meatballs of 20 years ago could generate. It's the speed of the collision, not the size of the vehicle, that determines the accident.

Gabriel says that most of the "high" injuries, i.e. shoulder and collarbone, occur because of the flimsy pads that quarterbacks wear. A lineman's bulky shoulder pad, he reasons, would hamper throwing.

"I've been hurt, but nobody knows about it," he says. "That's my secret of staying healthy. All you've got to do is announce where you're hurt and they'll go for it."

They'll go for a quarterback's head, and they'll get their hands up to obscure his vision, which places their arms in the general neighborhood of his head, anyway. But only an out and out sadist (and there are a few) would go for the "hospital zones," such as Namath's knees. They slug the QB's in the head, and the fans gasp and say, "Oh, my, how horrible," but the sound of jingle bells is a lot healthier than the sound a knee ligament makes when it rips.

"The defense," Tittle once said, "can take you out anytime it wants to. As you release the ball, your left foot is solidly planted on the turf and your left knee is rigid. All a defensive lineman would have to do, assuming he has the choice, is wait for the right moment and go for that knee."

The 1969 season introduced a new hazard—arm and shoulder trouble—and all of a sudden people were comparing quarterbacks to sore-armed baseball pitchers.

"It's not too unusual for a baseball pitcher to come up with a sore arm," Gabriel says. "And the pitcher works every fourth day. On an off day he'll throw only 15 or 20 minutes.

"I bet I throw between 150 and 200 passes every day. The football weighs more than the baseball, and you throw with just about the same velocity. You've got to throw it farther, and don't forget there's a pad on your shoulder that restricts your motion a little. When you add all that together—plus the knocks—you get arm injuries."

In 1969 Starr and John Brodie and Unitas and John Hadl and Greg Cook and Bill Nelsen were some of the more publicized arm and shoulder cases. Starr originally hurt his arm in pregame warm-ups, on a 74-degree day. People have tried to analyze quarterbacks' throwing motion to figure if that would supply a clue. But the experts who once described Unitas' delivery as "pure" now say that he ends up with the back of his hand pointed inward, like a pitcher's follow-through after he throws a screwball (which is what Ewbank had been saying all along). There are still the little mysteries of the arm.

"Watch those two guys warming up," Whitey Ford once said while Yankee pitchers Jim Bouton and Al Downing were practicing. "You see the way Bouton throws, with all that unnatural motion and his hat flying off all the time? That's why he's going to have arm trouble. Now watch Downing, a free-and-easy motion, natural, but the ball explodes in there just as hard. Guys like that don't get arm trouble." Next season Downing spent the year nursing a sore arm, which never did come around.

Quarterbacks have been unfairly maligned by everyone, even

their own teammates, ever since the position achieved importance. Unitas hung around Walt Kiesling's 1956 Pittsburgh camp like a lost soul, before he finally got his release.

"I don't think coach Kiesling knew I was in camp—literally—until the AP put out a picture of me showing a Chinese nun how to hold a football," Unitas said.

Even Starr, whose patience and conservatism gave him the remarkable statistic of only three interceptions out of 251 passes in the Packers' championship season of 1966, saw those same traits criticized. Two years later the linemen were grumbling about the Statue of Liberty standing there with the ball so long that they couldn't hold their blocks.

The amalgamation of quarterback and team is the thing that can make an offense seem smooth or erratic. The Colts always had that amalgamation—coach, quarterback, team; it was all the same function. Dave Anderson, in his book *Countdown to Super Bowl,* mentions the irony of Ewbank coaching his quarterback, Namath, to beat his old quarterback, Unitas. When John entered the game in the fourth quarter, Weeb lapsed into forgetfulness on the bench and murmured, "No interceptions now, John."

The Colts have shown that they can win under almost any quarterback. Earl Morrall brought the Unitas-less Colts into the Super Bowl in his first year with the club, and three years earlier a series of injuries had stripped the club of all quarterbacks. So the job fell to halfback Tom Matte, who performed with the plays taped to his wrist. The Colts beat the Rams, with Matte in command, and he led them all the way in that historic sudden-death playoff against the Packers, which might still be going on if a referee hadn't ruled a missed field goal good. And Matte ended his weird fling with two touchdown passes in the 35-3 win over Dallas in the Runner-Up Bowl.

You wonder how a team reacts to the strange anachronistic Cincinnati system in which Paul Brown calls Greg Cook's plays for him. It takes originality away from the quarterback and deprives him of independent thought processes. It slows down the time element, with the delay caused by the messenger guard having to run on the field every play. It gives the quarterback some moments of indecision—right up until the time the breathless messenger arrives into the huddle ("Coach Brown, puff, wants, whew, you to call, oof, 36-trap, uhhh, on two"). But worst of all, it deprives the quarterback of his most up-to-date weapon, the automatic, the change-up at the line of scrimmage.

"Oh, he lets me call automatics," Cook says. "I've called as many as three or four a game. But if I change a play of his, I'd damn well better have a good reason why I did it."

"What it does," says the Jets' linebacker and defensive signal caller, Larry Grantham, "is to give us the last say. It's a guessing game between the quarterback and me all the time anyway. He calls his play in the huddle. I call my defense. He looks us over and calls his automatic. I can call mine. But he can call another one because he knows when the ball is going to be snapped, and I can't take a chance of getting caught in the middle of a switch. So he gets the last call.

"Against Cincinnati, I just call a defense—or a change-up—and that's the last word on the subject. But Brown is so tricky anyway that he's probably anticipated my call before he's even sent the play in."

"Letting the quarterback call his own plays would be the easy way for me," Brown says. "But there are people with our team, assistant coaches and myself, who have devoted a lot more time to this guessing game than the young quarterback has, and I think our judgment might be a little more sound. If a quarterback were around long enough, he might eventually start making his own calls [Otto Graham never did in 10 years under Brown].

"And as for the practice of my calling plays upsetting a young quarterback, mentally . . . I sure wouldn't want to sit around and suffer just to make a guy feel good."

At the other end of the scale was San Diego coach Sid Gillman, who drafted a Columbia quarterback named Marty Domres in the first round in 1969, flew him out to San Diego on June 8, and began an intensive cram course that nearly blew the kid's head apart.

"I checked into the Lafayette Hotel in San Diego on June 8," Domres said, "and they started working with me right away. Six days a week, eight to nine hours a day—sometimes as many as 12 hours. Nothing but watching films and studying them. I'd start at 7 A.M. with coach Gillman, and then other coaches would take over, then Sid would relieve them. They worked in two-hour shifts. I did that right up until the Coaches' All-American game in Atlanta at the end of June. Then when I came back, I did it again—right up until camp started.

"It gets you tired after a while, sort of puts you to sleep. You reach a period when you just can't absorb any more. When camp started, I just felt mentally exhausted. It took me a month to shake it off—until the exhibition games started. That's the thing I never expected from pro ball, all the classroom hours, all the studying."

But 15 years from now Marty's brain might still be quick enough to carry him along in the game, even though his body would be creaking a little. The elderly quarterbacks are some of the sports world's most fascinating people.

"Do you know what I really like here in training camp?" the Jets' 40-year-old Babe Parilli said one July, as he was going through his sixteenth year in pro ball.

"I like it right after lunch, when I come back to the room and take my shoes off and lie down and get my feet up on the bed. I light a good cigar, and turn on the TV set—to the afternoon stock market reports."

"Lord a' mighty," said defensive back Jim Hudson. "There it is. You've just heard it. The all-time description of the 40-year-old quarterback. You ought to make a tape recording of that and sell it."

4
Divers and Survivors: The Runners

Many shall run to and fro, and knowledge shall be increased.

□ Daniel, 12:4

They come into pro football all instinct and nerve, without the surgical scars on the knees or the knowledge of what it's like to get hit by a 240-pound linebacker. They burn brightly, and by the time they're 30 or so they might still be around, but they're different players. They know how to pass-block, and they can run their pass routes without making any mistakes; they can block in front of a ball carrier, and they run just well enough to be considered runners. They dive—and survive.

Running back is a position governed by instinct, and many of the great ballcarriers were never better than they were as freshman pros. It's the most instinctive position in football, the only one in which a rookie can step in with a total lack of knowledge of everything except running the ball, and be a success.

Ask Red Grange to detail the moves he made on that 60-yard touchdown against Michigan and he'll look at you blankly.

"I was never taught to do what I did, and I know I couldn't teach anyone else how to run," says the great halfback. "I don't really know what I did, and I'd have a hard time telling you what I did on any individual run, even if it's one of the runs that everyone always talks about.

"I read about my change of pace, and it was news to me that I ran at different speeds. I know I used to have a crossover step, and I had an instinctive feeling about where the tacklers were. I read that I had peripheral vision. I didn't even know what that meant. I had to look it up."

All right, you say. Grange was running around in the Dark Ages of football, when everyone was 185 pounds and slow, and no lineman pursued downfield, etc. Listen to Donny Anderson, the Green Bay halfback who set a pro record for bonus money:

"I think running ability has to be bred in you. You can't learn, and I did something back at Texas Tech, against Texas A & M in my junior year, that I couldn't do again in a thousand years if I tried to show you.

"I was supposed to go off left tackle, but it was closed up. I must have seen an opening to the right out of the corner of my eye. My left foot was already planted to the left. Then somehow I put my right foot about five or six feet to the right and changed directions.

"Teddy Roberts, our safetyman, and I were looking at the films and he said, 'How'd you do that?' I said, 'I don't know.' We ran it back and forth six times, and I still couldn't tell him."

A lot of nonsense gets written about runners' styles, analyzing their moves—left foot here, right foot there, etc. Usually the writing is terribly dry and not very informative. It reads like an eye chart, and the act of diagraming and capsuling the moves and feints of the great runners is like pinning butterflies under a glass pane. For instance, you read that old limp-leg quote that is attributed to Thorpe—"I just give them a leg and then take it away again." The quote probably originated with Walter Camp, and then was tacked onto any decent runner until it became a cliché. Thorpe probably gave them the leg, and took it away, and gave it to them again—hard—plus the knee and the boot and anything else that would let them know that the old Indian was not to be messed with. He had that way of punishing people.

Some qualities seem universal. The great ones usually run with their feet close to the ground—Sayers, Jimmy Brown, Jimmy Taylor, Joe Perry; they all did it. Even Lenny Moore, who was noted for his high knee action, brought his feet down when he got near the line. The reason is balance. And they were all quick starters, even the seemingly slow men like Taylor and Alex Webster (who ran about a 5-flat 40). They all got off the mark in a hurry.

Pure speed doesn't mean much in itself, although it's nice to have. You see defensive tackles racing downfield to overhaul running backs; you see safetymen, even linebackers, catching them from behind, and it makes you wonder. The reason is that the actual mechanism of carrying the football naturally slows people down.

Marty Glickman, the radio announcer, once did a study of it. He had been an Olympic sprinter who doubled as a halfback for Syracuse.

"I was timed for a 100 in a track suit, and then I was timed for that 100 again, only this time I was carrying a football under my arm," Marty said. "The conditions were the same each time. I was wearing the same clothing, the same spikes. I repeated it a few times, and each time I was one to two seconds slower when I carried the ball.

"The arms play a part in pure running. Coaches always show the sprinters how to use their arms for balance and power while they're running. Anything that impedes that free arm movement —like a football—is going to cut your speed."

Trackmen who pop up in the pro football drafts come in as wide receivers—occasionally defensive backs—but seldom as running backs. Their speed is used for running *without* the football, and, once they've got it, they slow down. You'll even see a sprinter such as Dallas' Bob Hayes caught from behind.

But the good runners all have the quick start and the knack of avoiding objects, and a rookie can use exactly the same skills he had in college. And if he's got the physical qualifications, he will make a good, often a sensational first-year pro. He hasn't learned fear—or self-defense. The repeated hammering hasn't yet taken the zip from his legs. Everything else can be taught, the faking and blocking and pass routes, provided he has the desire to learn and the courage to execute some of these more tedious jobs. But if he's a pure and gifted runner, a club will sacrifice the other traits to keep him in the lineup. He's going to draw people into the stadium, and football is still a moneymaking proposition. People never yet paid to see a great blocker.

Many of the fine running backs made All-Pro their first year—

Gale Sayers, Jimmy Brown, Alan Ameche, Hugh McElhenny, Doak Walker, Steve Van Buren, Bullet Bill Dudley; all had arrived by the time they put on a pro uniform. Calvin Hill made All-NFL as a Dallas rookie in 1969, and Paul Brown built his Cincinnati attack around a rookie, Paul Robinson, in '68, earning Robinson an All-AFL berth (although Brown chose to develop his offense around his quarterback the next year).

Scouts generally have a better percentage when they recommend rookies. Occasionally there are failures. No one can scout the future. But the percentage rate on running backs is high. Five runners were drafted in the first round in 1969, and all five—O. J. Simpson, Ron Johnson, Hill, Larry Smith, and Leroy Keyes— became starters as rookies.

Outside of some of Sayers' more electric moves, I've never seen a better cut executed than one I saw Dick Bass make against Stanford when Dick was a senior at the College of the Pacific. It was a sideline move. He had turned the corner and the tacklers were running him out of bounds, and he give it one of those sharp, full-stride cuts to the inside, knocking one man over and gaining 10 more yards before he was dragged down. It was a move of a man who's much better than the competition—and knows it; a confident, almost disdainful move. And it was one you'd practically never see in pro football, for the simple reason that it violates all the instincts of survival.

It brought him right back into the flow of traffic, and laid him open to blind-side contact. But the Stanford boys weren't the Packers, and in the pros the runners give up those extra few yards to keep in mind the long-range picture, the preservation of a career.

"I watch some ball carriers fighting along, long after the issue is closed," says the Browns' Leroy Kelly, who, like Jim Brown, has never missed much playing time because of injuries. "That's how a back gets hurt. There is a time to give that second effort you read so much about, and there is a time to find yourself a soft spot.

"They always said that Jimmy Taylor was a punishing runner, which was the reason he got *his* by so many punishing tackles. I guess that was just his way."

They tell a rookie back to run with abandon, but they also tell him to protect himself and avoid taking the unneccessary chance, which is like telling a man to bet the favorite and the long shot with the same two dollars. The great rookie back might go through his first few games in a sort of fog.

"Frankly, most of the defensive players are still something of a blur to me," Hill said during his first season. "I'll be told who they are and what to watch for, but then I get into the game and they're a blur. I've had to learn the hard way. For instance, I was warned about Lonnie Sanders of the Cards. I was told Sanders would submarine the blockers and tackle the ball carrier. He has the knack of doing this, and that's just what he did do to me when I got the ball. He wormed right in there and nailed me."

In those first few games with Dallas, when Hill was shocking everyone with his mad gallops, he was asked what he found most difficult in pro football. His quotes weren't about the physical punishment or the savagery of the game (he is studying for the ministry) or the actual pain. He talked about the classroom work, the learning of assignments, memorization of pass routes, the brainwork involved in choosing the right man to block. The physical part of the game was instinctive.

Frank Gifford once listed four basic requirements for a good running back. First, he should have the physical talent—size and speed. Then he had to have knowledge—pass routes and blocking assignments and execution of his fakes. He had to be realistic; able to adjust and improvise, if the situation called for it. And he had to be durable. He had to avoid injury.

If the runner is strong in the physicals, though, he can get by without an overload anywhere else. The pure runners draw the big salaries, and their weaknesses in blocking or faking, or their fogginess on pass patterns, will drive the coaches crazy but it won't cost them a spot in the lineup. The gifted set of legs can hide a multitude of shortcomings. The pedestrian runner who is a solid pass receiver and a good blocker in front of the quarterback might last for years. But his position on the squad is always shaky. So is his salary.

In building a wall around his weak-kneed quarterback, Joe Namath, Jet coach Weeb Ewbank has always managed to have a supply of backs who know how to punish a blitzing linebacker. If they don't know how, they learn quickly or sit on the bench. A quarterback such as Namath always means there will be a place for backs who may not be breathtaking runners, but who aren't afraid to take on the linebackers—or even defensive ends, once they get past their man.

Emerson Boozer showed brilliance as a runner ever since his first rookie weeks with the Jets, but he languished on the bench behind Billy Mathis. Mathis' best runninng days were behind him, but he could block and catch. The press roasted Ewbank, who finally started using Boozer when his blocking began to come around. The young halfback was on his way to a scoring record when a knee operation wiped out the 1967 season for him. He came back slowly, but strangely enough, his blocking kept improving.

Ewbank's 1969 training camp quotes were all about Boozer's exceptional blocking, which was sad, in a way. It was like a man pointing to a thoroughbred and saying, "Boy, he sure does a great job pulling that old milk wagon."

A coach with any sense of realism will always try to keep his solid pass-blocking backs and good fakers and diligent students happy with constant newspaper reference to their excellence. I've always felt that part of this is sincere, and part of it is an attempt to make up for their weaker salary scale. They get praised on the practice field, but I wonder what happens during the contract talks when they say, "I think I've got a $5,000 raise coming. Coach says my pass blocking and faking have been out of this world."

That's usually when the rushing statistics get dusted off, along with the All-League teams, and they might hear, "Yeah, but, uh, you only averaged 2.8 yards per carry and 23 backs finished with more yards than you."

Only certain types of individuals can become good fakers, because the act itself is a giant swindle. A back runs into the line without the ball, but pretends he has it. The better the acting job, the harder he is hit by the linebacker or defensive lineman and the more time the passer has. And the madder the linebacker or lineman gets. So the running back who has carried out his fake gets hit just as hard as he would have been if he were carrying the ball. Except that there's no run-to-daylight to look forward to. He is a poker player who is pulling a bluff after he has folded his hand.

"Artie Donovan, the old Baltimore tackle, used to concentrate on fakers," said Don Paul, the old L.A. linebacker. "He would subject them to so much punishment that they would make it obvious they didn't have the ball to avoid Artie's beating."

And Kansas City halfback Mike Garrett tells of the game in which he was taking such a ferocious pounding on his fakes that each time he ran into the line he would yell, "I don't have it!"

Sometimes there are backs who seem to endure forever. Not blessed by any noticeable talents in any particular direction, they hang on, year after year, playing their usual steady game, competent in all departments, exceptional in none. And then one day you start counting up the yards and you're amazed.

During the off season of 1970, the Pittsburgh Steelers' publicity man, Ed Kiely, put out a release about Dick Hoak. Hoak is a name that no high-school boy west of the Monongahela or east of the Allegheny can identify. There are no Dick Hoak fan clubs in California or New York. But Dick Hoak, by gaining the very normal total of 535 yards rushing in 1969, moved into the No. 25 spot in lifetime NFL ground gaining. Which, again, might not mean much until you consider that he's ahead of such glamor names as Jon Arnett, Charley Trippi, Frank Gifford, Tank Younger, Cliff Battles, Paul Hornung, Dutch Clark, and Bullet Bill Dudley. And in the 1970 season, given his normal rate of increment, he will move ahead of Clark Hinkle, Timmy Brown, and Bronko Nagurski, among others.

Dick Hoak has played with the Steelers for nine years. He has missed three games. He can't run 40 yards any faster than five seconds, which is considered too slow for a linebacker. He has led his club in rushing only three times during those nine years, and he is small—5-11, 190. He dives and survives. He has never been a salary holdout.

"I don't think he knows there's such a thing as a pension fund yet," Kiely says.

"I'm tired of this stuff about not being fast enough," Hoak says. "I'm tired of hearing it and reading it. It's the only thing that's ever bothered me in the papers. We've had a lot of fast running backs here, guys that could really fly. But some of them don't know where they're going.

"There's one thing about some of these kids coming out of college. They're not that smart. It takes a lot of brains to play this game. Plays are changed at the line, and you have to recognize defenses. You have to know who to block and when, how to run patterns. You can't sit back and say, 'What are they doing now?'

"As far as speed—you never run in a straight line. You never run a 40-yard dash, and usually you're following a guard. On most of your wide plays you have a guard pulling out ahead of you, and if you go full speed, it doesn't help you."

Some of them, such as Jimmy Taylor and Tom Woodeshick of the Eagles, survive through sheer ruggedness, the desire to inflict as severe a blow as they receive.

"It's a tough game, and the tougher it is the better I like it," says Woodeshick, like Hoak, an invader of the all-time ground-gaining domain.

"I come from the hard-coal region around Wilkes-Barre. I've always played where it's cold and tough. I enjoy hitting. If I can't evade tacklers, I try to run over them, and there's no greater satisfaction than running over them. I don't mean I like hitting so much that I enjoy being hit—nobody wants to be knocked into the bleachers—but you couldn't survive if you didn't like contact. There's no place to hide out there."

The love of contact takes all forms. For some, the job of pass blocking assumes added meaning when there's a chance to deliver a punishing shot. The Jets' Matt Snell, an All-AFL fullback in 1969, is one of football's better pass blockers. The interesting thing is that there's no love lost between Snell and the man he is blocking for, Namath, but it doesn't interfere with Snell's work on the field. Ewbank enjoys pointing out Snell's talents to the writers who cover the club, and the coach showed up at one of the regular press luncheons with a film clip of one of Matt's particularly vicious shots—a helmet and forearm spearing of the midsection of Buffalo's 280-pound defensive end, Ron McDole. It crumpled the big man as if a bullet had hit him.

If the Jets' staff decides to hold a clinic on pass blocking, they'll probably include film clips of Snell's best shot of the 1969 season. It also came against Buffalo, this time on the Bills' 6-4, 219-pound tight safetyman, John Pitts, who was foolish enough to try a safety blitz.

"I caught him a good shot, right on the chin," Snell said. "I knocked him right on his tail. He fell flat on his back and his head bounced, and when he got up, I just laughed at him. I get hit all the time. It's rare when you get a chance to hit somebody back like that."

Ohio State coach Woody Hayes is probably responsible for the viciousness that made Snell such a devastating pass blocker. God might have had a little something to do with it, too, but it was Woody who gave the Jet fullback a taste of the rigors of the game. He didn't know where to play Snell. So he played him everywhere.

"At Ohio State," Snell says, "I played every offensive position except quarterback, center, and guard. On defense, I played everywhere except tackle and middle guard. But when I began to pass-block in the pros, I realized I had to nullify the size of those big linebackers on a blitz. I moved a couple of steps closer to the linebacker, cutting down his velocity of impact, and none of the coaches complained. Now Weeb teaches the rookies to do it that way."

When the linebackers don't blitz and Snell isn't running a pass pattern, he acts as a mop-up man on defensive ends or tackles who filter through. Minnesota's great defensive end, Carl Eller, didn't touch Namath when the Jets played the Vikings in a 1969 exhibition game. The reason was Snell, who chopped at Eller's legs when the big end showed signs of beating the offensive tackle. Snell was a blocker that night, and for the first time he showed a little peevishness with the role.

"I don't mind getting the blitzing linebackers," he said, "but this is a little too much. If they're going to play me at fullback and offensive tackle at the same time, let 'em pay me two salaries."

The ends don't care for it much, either. When New York played Oakland in 1969, Snell helped out his right tackle with the Raiders' 270-pound defensive end, Ike Lassiter. Finally Lassiter got a little annoyed with his double treatment.

"Hey, the man's doing a good job," he told Snell after one play. "Leave me alone."

Snell is in the $40,000- to $45,000-a-year pay bracket, but the giant salaries for running backs are still pulled down by the flyboys, the game breakers. People pay to see them. And the runners pay the fans back by some memorable pictures. The best in the game now is Sayers, whose instincts seem to be one level higher than those of the rest of the people in this world.

"In my book, the first objective is always getting the TD," Sayers says, summing up the game-breaker's philosophy. "It's nice to get the first and 10, but I'm looking for the TD and the first downs come second. You can't stop to look for it. It's there and you know it's there. I can't explain it.

"I know that a lot of backs are happy at the end of the season to have a 5.0 average, but 5.0 averages don't win ball games for you. Touchdowns win games. This is what I'm looking for—touchdowns. I feel that I can always beat my man one-on-one. And two-on-one, I can beat them 75 percent of the time."

"The thing that makes Gale different," said one of his teammates, "is the way he's able to put a move on somebody and lot lose a step. He gives a guy a fake while he's going full speed. I give a guy a move like that and it takes me 15 yards to get in stride. Watch any runner. They'll all slow down a little when they have to cut a corner or throw a fake—all of them except Gale."

There were many people who criticized the Bears' George Halas for using Sayers on dive plays from tackle to tackle. The critics drew on some unseen "Football for the Fans" axiom that said Fast Backs go Around End, Big Backs go Through the Middle. But the inside route offers the explosive back the best chance to explode. He might get stopped four or five times in a row, but when he hits one right, he's gone.

"It's the best route," Sayers says, "because after you get by the line, you've got maybe one or two halfbacks to beat and a whole field to maneuver in. The sideline will kill you, though. If you step out-of-bounds it's the same as being tackled. I love running through the middle.

"The hard tackles are the open-field tackles, the ones where you get chopped by the ankles, or they hit you from the side. When I get hit after a two- or three-yard gain inside, I'm falling on somebody else, so it's like a cushion. It may look bad because there may be seven players around you. But you might be lying on four. It looks rougher on TV than it is."

Sayers made the statement a few games before the 49ers' Jim Johnson took him out for the season with a low tackle. It tore the ligaments in Sayers' knee. The tear was diagnosed immediately—before fluid had a chance to gather—and it was operated on that day. The quick diagnosis and surgery gave the injury the best possible chance to heal completely. And the fact that Sayers regained full mobility next season was a constant reminder that a super-athlete can recover from knee surgery within a year.

The physical recovery for a great back is only part of it. Knee surgery isn't as dreadful a thing for a plunger, a straight-ahead power back. But for a Sayers' type, whose game is all cuts and fakes (which put added strain on the knee's lateral movement), it can be devastating.

Boozer had a unique billiard-ball style that let him bounce off tacklers and hit a new hole without losing his balance. The recovery from his 1967 operation has taken two years.

"Just watching football games now," he said in training camp the following year, "I see things I never saw before—like pain. The other night, I saw Billy Joe get hit and someone landed across the back of his legs and I saw pain. It's the same with games I watch on TV.

"It startled me. I never looked at football with that in mind. I always heard fans oohing and aahing when someone was really hit, and I couldn't understand it. It had no meaning to me. A solid shot was just a solid shot. It was never painful. But now I look at games the way fans do."

A year later he gained 129 yards against the Bengals and got a game ball, but he still didn't feel he was all the way back.

"I won't feel right until I've broken a long touchdown run," he said. "A couple of the runs I had today should have been 60-yarders, but I got in the secondary and I was run down and tackled. I haven't been in the secondary in so long that it felt strange. I kept saying, 'I wonder what to do now.' I just didn't have that long-run philosophy."

When people talk of running backs, they like to speak in terms of trends—first the little back, the speedster; then the "big backfield" offense, created by Vince Lombardi's power sweeps with the Giants and the Packers; then the smaller back again, not really little, or the blitzing linebackers would run over him, but the smaller, quick-hitting, 190- or 200-pounder.

If there has been any noticeable trend, it's been toward slightly shorter backs. But their weight has remained pretty much constant for the last 10 years. There is, and always was, a place for the good, quick, 195- 205-pounder, big back or no big back offense. If a man has talent, he'll find a spot.

The following table shows a breakdown, by weight, of the 15 leading ground gainers in pro football, combining both leagues when two leagues existed. The table is for the last 20 years, choosing the seasons that occur at five year intervals.

1949 (NFL & AAFC): Average, 5-11½, 195

> Under 180 pounds—2
> 180–190—5
> 191–200—4
> 201–210—2
> 211–220—1
> Over 220—1

1954 (NFL): Average, 6-0½, 206

> Under 180—2
> 180–190—2
> 191–200—2
> 201–210—4
> 211–220—1
> Over 220—4

1959 (NFL): Average, 6-1, 211

> Under 180—0
> 181–190—1
> 191–200—2
> 201–210—4
> 211–220—6
> Over 220—2

1964 (AFL & NFL): Average, 6-1, 212

Under 180—0
181–190—2
191–200—2
201–210—3
211–220—5
Over 220—3

1969 (AFL & NFL): Average, 6-0, 212

Under 180—0
181–190—1
191–200—4
201–210—3
211–220—2
Over 220—5

Lombardi has been credited with restoring the running game to favor. Actually it had never been out of favor. There was one brief period in the early 1950's when the Los Angeles Rams drove everyone crazy with their passes, and analysts were brooding that the defense would never catch up. The team everyone points to was the 1950 Rams—Bob Waterfield and Norm Van Brocklin throwing to a covey of wide receivers—Elroy Hirsch, Tom Fears, Glenn Davis, Vitamin Smith, etc. But the Rams that year threw 453 passes and called 404 running plays. And next year, when they won the NFL title with an aerial attack that was only slightly less productive, the Ram runs outnumbered their passes, 426 to 373.

There has *never* been a team that won an NFL championship by passing more times than it ran. Never. The AFL had a few in its formative years, but the teams that gave the young league its two victories over the NFL—New York and Kansas City—both ran the ball more than they threw it. That's right, the Jets, the Joe Namath Jets, ran more than they passed.

The running back has always been an important figure, even when it seemed that the pass-catch operation would sweep the game into the skies. And the running back has always taken his share of the lumps.

"I've got 189 carries," Snell said after 13 games in 1969, "and I'll bet that 180 were between the tackles. When you carry into the line, you take a helluva beating.

"Most people think that Don Maynard takes a beating as a receiver because sometimes when he gets tackled, it looks like he's being torn apart. And sometimes maybe he is. But when a receiver is hit, it usually involves two forces going in the same direction. A running back is in a head-on car accident.

"I've been in 189 head-on car accidents."

5
Catching the Football

I tell myself that I'm faster than 95 percent of the people in the world. It's just that the other 5 percent happen to be cornerbacks.

□ George Sauer, Jr.

It was in Kezar Stadium in San Francisco, and the Baltimore Colts had a third down, goal to go, on the 49ers' seven-yard line, right below where I was sitting.

It must have been ESP that made me decide to hold my binoculars steady and unwavering on split end Raymond Berry, neglecting everything else on the field. Or maybe it was just the law of averages. But in the next 2.7 seconds or so I saw a tableau that is still vivid in my memory as the perfect coordination of passer and receiver.

Berry cut straight down toward Abe Woodson, the 49ers' right cornerback, launched himself at Abe's knees in a straight head and shoulder block. Abe, figuring some sort of sweep was on the way (there must have been some play action simulating a sweep), fought to get Berry off him. Then, in an instant, Berry turned and hooked to the inside and John Unitas' ball was right there as he hooked. TD. Six points. And the 49ers' fans gave poor Abe a tremendous booing. What the hell was he doing a yard away from Berry anyway?

There is no higher standard of excellence in the art of pass receiving than this intricate knowledge of timing, a knowledge of the workings of someone else's body as well as those of your own.

There have been many great passers and many fine receivers, and quite a few good combinations of both. But the Unitas-Berry combination was the greatest of all.

History awards a special place to the Arnie Herber-to-Don Hutson pass-catch combination that exploded onto the NFL scene when the league was still tuned in to Bronko Nagurski and Tuffy Leemans. It was daring and spectacular—"You go long and I'll throw the hell out of the ball"—and the defense wasn't ready for this stuff yet. But Unitas and Berry arrived when the defense had gone into a careful study of guarding against the pass, after suffering through the wild passing orgies of Los Angeles, and any receiver who got troublesome was quickly awarded double or triple coverage.

This chapter is a study of the pass catchers, but a receiver is negated without a good arm to get him the ball, and vice versa. Unitas and Berry fed off each other, and the greatness of one was a mirror of the greatness of the other. It helped that both were of the same emotional makeup—careful, meticulous, and a word that has become almost a cliché now—dedicated.

Berry in practice was a Colt legend. He would always show up in full pads. He would spend time checking the fields for hidden holes and impediments. He would leave nothing to chance. He had a set of moves that he would painstakingly rehearse every day, mentally checking them off as he did. The many Ray Berry chronicles have pointed out that he had no outstanding speed, but this could have been an aid rather than a hindrance to his development.

You can generally divide receivers into two groups—workers and flyers. Berry was a worker, and perhaps if he had been born with a sprinter's speed, life would have come easier and he never would have developed his scientist's approach to the game. It's a nebulous argument ("If Namath had the good knees, it would have taken him two or three more years to learn to stay in the pocket"), but a man without the flyer's speed cannot stay in the league without moves and a well-disciplined knowledge of patterns, while a flyer can make it with little brainwork but a lot of leg.

"I've never before seen the speed-and-hands combination that he has," San Diego's Sid Gillman said about his gifted flanker, Lance Alworth, in 1969. "Nobody I've seen can touch him. If he were as conscientious about playing football as, for example, Raymond Berry, he wouldn't be believable.

"It's not a question of courage. He doesn't mind traffic, and he catches balls in a mob. There are just some things Lance doesn't like to do, certain types of routes; some he loves, some he doesn't. I suppose it's a natural thing with an artist—a violinist has certain music he likes to play, some he won't."

Nevertheless, the cornerbacks would just as soon do without Alworth, who also catches his share of short passes, because the back is usually playing a little farther off him than usual.

Sometimes you get a combination flyer-worker, such as Cleveland's Gary Collins, a man who has been curiously neglected by the All-Pro pickers from year to year, but another player the cornerbacks always rate as almost impossible on man-to-man coverage. Collins has lost some of his speed since he came into the league, but he still thinks like a game breaker.

"I want those first downs," he said. "And touchdowns. Third and long yardage is my play. I'm not going to try and catch a lot of less important passes just to look good on numbers. I'm not interested in statistics. I like money."

Some of the flyers are pure athletes, like St. Louis' Dave Williams, who once scored more than 7,000 points in a decathlon competition, and who jumped center for his high-school basketball team, even though he stood only 6-0. His forte is the battle for the ball, when he and a defender go up for it.

"I get a kick out of taking the ball away from them," Williams said. "When there are two of you up there, it's a question of who wants it more. I feel it's my ball. It's up to me to take it—like a rebound in basketball."

Every team strives for a "balanced attack," like a good meal, neither too heavy on sweets nor pure protein. But a long passing attack must be part of the picture, and a receiver with pure speed will always get an extra-long look (witness the string of "World's Fastest Humans" who keep coming in year after year).

"Sometimes you'll go along all season and never get your long passing game going," Berry said, when he was an assistant coach at Dallas. "But you have to keep going to it. You have to use it like a club over the defense's head or they'll shut off everything else."

The ordinary cornerback lives in fear of the flyers. The exceptional defender, like Oakland's Willie Brown, who plays the tight bump-and-go style, generally fears the worker. A split end like New York's Sauer, whose game is moves and timing, rather than sheer speed, impresses Brown more than a sprinter.

"When you come out of a game after covering Sauer," Brown says, "you're more tired than you would be covering a bigger guy or a faster guy. Sauer keeps working on every play, whether he's the designated receiver or not. All receivers should do it, but they don't."

Sometimes it's laziness that causes a receiver to loaf on a pattern. Sometimes it's a preconceived plan. Sauer's running mate on the Jets, Don Maynard, is like a soloist in a flute concerto. He's one of the few men who seems to have *gained* rather than lost speed during his 13 years in football. Maynard's style is deception; three patterns half-speed, then six points.

"He lulls you and lulls you," says the Jets' strong safetyman Jim Hudson. "Pretty soon you're asleep, and he gets that inside angle on you and it's all over. I know him like a book. I've covered him enough in practice. But it still happens. He's hypnotic."

Maynard's most devastating pattern is the post, termed by Gillman, "the long and the short of it," in which he heads straight downfield for 10 or 15 yards, then breaks inside, angling toward the goal posts. It's the route most feared by cornerbacks, since their primary responsibility is the outside. When a receiver is running a post pattern, his body is between the defender and the passer. An interception is almost impossible, unless the pass is misthrown.

"One of the few things in football that hasn't changed," Don Hutson says, "is pass patterns. I suppose they never will. What more can anybody do?"

And the Browns' old receiver, Mac Speedie, who was an assistant coach at Houston and Denver, and a head coach of the Broncos until 1966, says that the pass patterns he coached in the AFL were the same ones that he and Dante Lavelli ran 15 to 20 years before that with Cleveland.

"The only difference," he says, "is that now the players are bigger and stronger and faster."

The basic patterns are listed in Fig. 5. Different clubs use dif-

Fig. 5

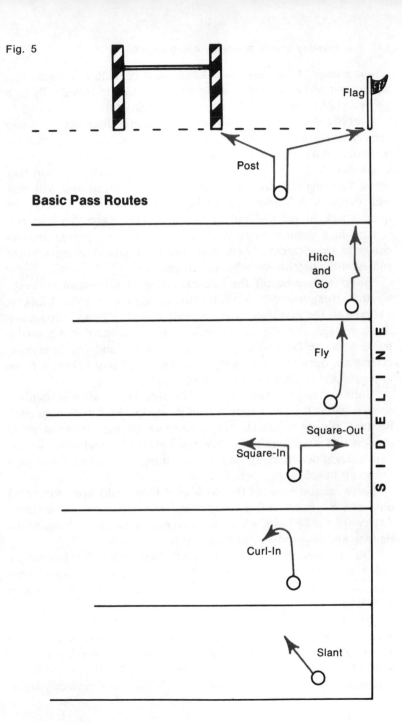

Basic Pass Routes

ferent names. A sideline pass could also be called a hitch or a square-out or just an out; a deep pattern could be called a fly or a go or an up; a turn-in is also a curl or a hook, etc.

Every receiver has his own style of running these routes. Sauer runs his square-outs with geometric precision, everything sharply angled. Maynard rounds off the same pattern, making it more of a circle-out. A flyer might not be as precise in running his short patterns, knowing that the defender respects his speed and will play well off him. A worker has to be more precise. He expects the quarterback to get the ball to him when he makes his first cut.

And in a mature passing attack, in which the passer and receiver know each other well, there are preordained changes in the routes, if the defense switches coverages.

"Suppose I come off the line expecting man-for-man coverage by the strong safety?" says Baltimore tight end John Mackey. "Maybe in the huddle Unitas has called a play I can run against that coverage. But when I get under way, I find them in a zone defense with the linebacker covering me inside and the safetyman taking me outside. So I change the pattern, hook between those two guys and come back for the ball.

"John is on the same page with me. He reads the defense around me at the same time I read it. He knows I'm coming back because, during the week, that's what we decided to do if we're ever in that situation. The difference between us and other teams, which might occasionally do the same thing, is that our entire pass offense is based on this one idea."

There are some passes that look as if they could work forever. I once saw Sauer catch five straight square-out passes on one drive. Afterward I asked him what's to prevent him from catching 20 little five- and six-yarders like that.

"Oh, I probably could," he said. "Assuming the linebacker didn't start dropping back into the area to help out—and even then, we could probably run some stuff at him that would get him back where he belonged.

"But I don't think a wide receiver could stand it physically. When you reach up for that square-out pass, you stretch for the ball and you leave your whole side open. All the cornerback would have to do would be to lay back, wait until you catch the ball, and crack you with his helmet each time. It's perfectly legal;

it's good hard football. Your ribs wouldn't hold up for a whole game, and even if they did, you'd have a terrible time getting yourself on the field the week afterward. You'd certainly never be able to get through a season like that."

The catchers come in all shapes and sizes—and at all speeds: from medium fast to fastest. Scouts prefer someone like New Orleans' No. 1 draft choice for 1970, Kenny Burroughs, who stands 6-5, weighs 212, and can cover 40 yards in 4.6 seconds. But they'll take a 5-10, 180-pounder with the absolute minimum speed allowance (4.7 seconds . . . 4.8 really to stretch a point; anything slower won't get him past the stopwatch session), if he can go up in a crowd and come down with the ball and do it five times a game. Sometimes they're just natural receivers, i.e., Tommy McDonald and Don Hutson. No one can quite explain Hutson. He came up at a time when defense ruled with an iron fist. The leading passer in the league, Ed Danowski of the Giants, averaged less than five completions and 70 yards a game; and the leading runner, Doug Russell of the Chicago Cards, averaged just over 40 yards a game.

All of a sudden it was whoosh and whoosh, Arnie Herber cranking up like a javelin man and letting 'em go to Hutson, while 13,000 fans in the stadium gasped. Ty Cobb once saw Hutson play and he called him, "the second-best judge of a fly ball in athletic history," which makes you wonder who Ty considered No. 1, himself, or Tris Speaker, or maybe Arnie Herber.

"He was so difficult to defend against," says the old Bear halfback, Luke Johnsos, "because half the time he didn't know himself where he was going. He'd signal the passer how he was going to break."

It's interesting that when Hutson and Sammy Baugh teamed up in various All-Star games, they never quite managed to click. Baugh was a spot passer, great at hitting a man on the break, *provided* he showed up where he was supposed to be. But Hutson was a free-lancer who took no orders from a playbook. He was an early-day Don Maynard.

At Green Bay, Cecil Isbell and Hutson did manage to work out one devastating pattern later on. It was the original tag-out, in which Hutson did a hook, or stop move, dropped to his knees, and caught Isbell's low pass. It was impossible to intercept.

One final Hutson note: Edmond P. Rovner, a lawyer from Bethesda, Maryland, says he will take a lie detector test that he once saw Hutson catch a low pass, one-handed, in full stride, with the palm of his hand facing *downward*. Sorry, but this I don't believe.

Hutson would probably be a good man today, busting zones with his instinctive ability to avoid people, but for the ordinary mortal, the Berry training is probably the best. He used to suggest that Dallas' rookie receivers take a football up to their rooms, handle it, fondle it, toss it up and down while they were lying on their beds. When the receivers were playing catch in practice, Berry would advise them always to tuck the ball under their arm before they threw it back, and even as a coach, Berry couldn't catch a ball without instinctively putting it away.

Berry and Sauer are blessed with an identical gift—absolute concentration, the kind Ted Williams had. Sauer said he developed his from his father, Boston's general manager George Sauer, Sr.

"We had about 13 trees in our backyard when I was a kid in Waco, Texas," George, Jr., says. "When my dad would throw the ball to me close to the trees, I'd bounce off 'em after I caught it. I remember my father telling my mother one time, 'With his hands he should be an end.'

"Up here, when I catch a pass, sometimes it's like I was still bouncing off those trees in our big ol' backyard in Waco. Except that now those trees are chasing me."

Catching the ball long or short, a receiver must have confidence in his hands. New Orleans' Danny Abramowicz led the NFL in pass receiving in 1969, but even though he broke all of Xavier University's receiving records, he wasn't drafted until the last round. His physical statistics—size, speed, etc.—didn't measure up, and he probably wouldn't have been drafted at all if New Orleans' coach Tom Fears hadn't been a slow receiver himself, once upon a time. Abramowicz' dual message is concentration—and hands.

"I just concentrate on catching the ball, never dropping it, even in practice. If I get my hands on the ball, I should catch it. Oh yes, I rub my hands on a ball before a game. I watch the ball into my hands, watch it all the way. I don't trap it against my chest, like some receivers do. I've got great confidence in my hands.

"Even back in school, every time I dropped a ball and asked myself why, I always got the same answer. I was thinking about something else. Maybe I was thinking that a guy was going to whack me or maybe I was thinking about where I was going with the football. If you don't keep after it, these things creep into your game."

There are other things that can creep in, too, like cornerbacks who slug you to your knees as you come off the line of scrimmage, or tug at your jersey or trip you. The defensive back is allowed to make contact before the ball is thrown. The reasoning is that, on a running play, the flanker is allowed to block the defensive man, and in order to shed the blocker, the defender must use his hands. So he can always argue that he didn't know whether the play was a run or a pass, and he can dish out his wallop—within reason. The flagrant stuff might not be seen by the officials, but there is a special room in the league office devoted to a film study of naughties that might have gone undetected. And all of a sudden a defensive man might get a letter telling him he's $100 poorer.

"Everyone gets a free lick at the flanker," Alworth says. "They give me a pounding, a forearm, a kick. One team held me 23 times in a game, and I've been clotheslined by the defensive end as I was coming off the line. 'Just thought I'd let you know I'm here,' he said. I can't do anything about it. Some of these linebackers could beat me to a pulp. I haven't yet seen one I could whip."

He got even one night, though, in the opening game of the 1968 season—against Cincinnati. The Bengals' Fletcher Smith, at 6-0, 178, a physical match for Alworth, was giving Lance a terrible time—punches, clothesline swipes, etc. Alworth took it until the game was safely out of reach, and then he jumped Smith, pummeling him to the ground. The ref threw him out of the game, naturally, but Alworth had made his point.

"Look, we have to play these guys again," he said. "I don't want anybody thinking they can get away with stuff like that for a whole game. People look at movies, too, and if they see that, they'll start thinking that I'm softening up and I'll get it every week. Besides, the guy only weighs 178.

And it's interesting that John Sample, a notorious head-banger and talker and out-of-bounds tackler, which proved effective against the Giants' Frank Gifford in Sample's NFL days, finally gave up on Alworth and just played him straightaway.

"What was the use?" Sample said. "He'd just come back and say, 'Way to go, John.' Covering a guy like that, you've got to save all your breath—for breathing."

Veteran L.A. flanker Pat Studstill said that the defensive backs' favorite trick was rapping him on the back of the helmet, just as the ball was coming. It broke his concentration. Sometimes his helmet, too.

"It jogs you enough so you take your eye off the ball and miss the catch," he said. "They'd rather do that, because they usually can get away with it. If the defender puts a hand in the middle of your back, he's going to get flagged by the official. Night Train Lane was the best I ever saw at rapping the receiver at just the right time. He had it down perfect."

Sometimes the receiver can use his own tricks, though. Berry would try to memorize the calls different defensive backs would use among themselves. He would run his pattern at a rookie and yell, "Switch!" for instance, hoping the youngster would mistake the voice for that of the safetyman and veer off him.

"It didn't work too often," Berry said, "but it was worth a try every now and then."

And a wide receiver with a streak of meanness can become a punishing blocker. A good one, such as the Packers' 6-5, 220-pound Boyd Dowler, can be a big asset on a sweep, since his block is usually the crack-back, or blind-side shot that can flatten a linebacker or cornerback, if he catches him right.

"We're usually called on to crack back on the linebacker, or MDM—most dangerous man," says San Diego's Gary Garrison. "That blocking is a must. Our sweeps depend on it. Anyone can block when he puts his mind to it. All you've got to do is really throw your body in there."

The world of the tight end, though, is more elemental. He's got to be a blocker, of course, and he's also got to learn how to get away from the linebacker who plays him head up in most defenses (the AFL's "stack" defense is getting away from that idea, preferring to hide the linebacker behind the defensive end, leaving the tight end alone).

After the tight end escapes from the linebacker, who can use his hands, forearms, or fists to try and keep him in, he faces the tight, or strong, safety. It's generally a physical overmatch—6-3, 230, to 6-2, 200 or so—in favor of the receiver, but if the linebacker has slowed him up first, the odds even up.

"The play of the tight safety is predicated on the linebacker on that side," says Baltimore's John Mackey. "He'll play you looser if the linebacker is big and active like the Packers' Dave Robinson, tighter if the linebacker is weaker or if he doesn't know you. We're expected to clear out the middle, though, to break up the double coverage on the wide receiver. It can be a tremendous help to him.

"The whole key to keeping the linebacker off you is getting off exactly on the snap count, or maybe half a count early if everybody else does it. Miss it by a fraction of a second and he's on you. Most of your pass routes are inside, and if you're trying to go inside the linebacker, you're going to have to shove him out of your way. There's no way to avoid it. On a quick pop pass inside, you hit him a good shot and then release quickly. That little slant-in pass is still very effective."

The physical demands of the tight end are as frightening as those of the linebacker on defense. The tight end has to be a pass receiver-blocker combination, and he can expect contact on every play. Most of his routes are to the inside, the perimeter of The Pit, where violent experiences are the reward for anyone sucked into its sphere.

The attrition rate on tight ends is high, and they usually don't last too long, or if they do, their years of peak performance are limited. Mike Ditka, Ron Kramer, Mackey—the three best ones of recent years—ferocious blockers and punishing runners once they got their hands on the ball—all fell victim to injuries.

"When I was 23 or 24, guys used to warn me that I'd begin to feel the beating I was taking, and I just laughed at them," Ditka said. "I never missed a game in Chicago—84 straight. Now I'm 28 and I defy you to show me another end who's taken the beating I have. Maybe Ron Kramer, and look at him. The Lions just cut him."

An anomaly in this punishing world is the Cardinals' vastly underrated Jackie Smith, who at 6-5, 225, can block well enough to get the job done and can also lope downfield for long passes, an unusual quality for a tight end. In 1966 he gained 1,205 yards on his receptions, an all-time record for tight ends, and he averaged 21.5 yards a catch, a higher average than all but four of the league's wide receivers.

"The secret isn't in pure speed," he says, "but how you make your cut. You've got to learn to make that cut, even if it's a 90-degree-angle cut, without chopping your stride. The defensive back can read you once you start shortening your stride so the cut will be more comfortable to execute. That's where you separate the good receivers from the ordinary ones, making that cut in full stride so the defensive back can't adjust. That's where you beat him. You also have to set him up—lure him away from the cut, so if he bumps you after your fake, it'll send you into the pattern, not out of it."

The receivers must read the style of their passer, as well as the pattern. A hard thrower means one kind of catching technique. A gentler arm may necessitate another. The Redskins' Charley Taylor has made a study of the flight of the ball.

"With a hard thrower like Sonny Jurgensen, you've got to let your hands ride with the ball, because he throws so hard," Taylor says. "You can't do it facing him. Unless you have huge hands, the ball will bounce off.

"With Fran Tarkenton, my teammate in the Pro Bowl one year, if you try and ride the ball into your hands, it'll fall short, because he throws a soft pass. You've got to catch him facing him, like Homer Jones used to. Homer can catch that way with practically anybody, though, because his hands are so large. He sort of clamps the ball."

Some receivers defy classification. Tommy McDonald, of the Philadelphia Eagles, a 5-9, 176-pounder with good, but not breathtaking speed, lasted for 12 years in the NFL, long enough to establish himself as the sixth leading receiver in pro football history. He had little knowledge of patterns when he first came up, but he had the confidence that he could beat any defense, including double coverage. He also had some very individual habits, like rubbing his fingertips on the concrete wall before a game. The idea was to give them sensitivity, in the manner of a safecracker using sandpaper on his fingers.

He would bite the tips of his fingers to get the blood circulating, and he played in shirt sleeves, no matter how cold it was.

"The bare skin of your forearm is sensitive," he said. "But your jersey isn't. It binds you. It can take an inch off your reach. And when the ball hits your bare skin, the immediate reaction is to grasp it."

The passers were cool to McDonald at first. They were alarmed by his size, and his overwhelming confidence puzzled them. But once they started going to him, he developed.

"When a quarterback goes to you early in a game," Gary Garrison says, "even if the pass doesn't connect, it helps your confidence tremendously. It shows that he has faith in you."

The days of the McDonalds might be numbered, if the bump-and-run style becomes effective. A tiny man simply won't be strong enough to handle a cornerback who attacks him at the line of scrimmage, and stays with him all the way. The NFL style is still the 4-3 defense, with the cornerbacks playing a cautious five to seven yards off the line. The answer to the bump-and-run game might be bigger, tougher wide receivers, who can dish out a little punishment themselves, before the play gets under way.

"You have to attack the guy if he's playing you tight all the way," says Kansas City's Otis Taylor, who is 6-3, 215. "Maybe sometimes he thinks I'm being dirty or rough in a way, but I think it's perfectly legal and I try to attack him to keep him off me. I try to make him afraid that I might do more to him."

It lends a slightly brutal tinge to what always has been pro football's most aesthetic phase, the long pass, the arc of the ball, the grace of the receiver.

"I love the physical act of catching a ball properly," Sauer once said. "That's why I enjoy the practicing. The action of having control over your body is tremendously satisfying.

"And when a ball is thrown in my direction, I know it's my ball—not the man who's covering me, not the ground's, but mine. I follow it into my hands with such concentration that I can see the grain. I can even see a letter of the printing.

"It says J5V on it—I think."

6
Defense

Defense is the stronger form with the negative object, and attack the weaker form with the positive object.

□ Karl Von Clausewitz, *On War*

Tackling is more natural than blocking. If a man is running down the street with everything you own, you won't let him get away. That's tackling.

□ Vince Lombardi

The defensive troops are football's counterpunchers. They can score knockouts, but they won't lead. When they've stunned the enemy, when they've got him on the ropes, the offense takes over.

The history of defense reads like a conditioned reflex, a reaction to new offenses, to new trickery, deception, and power. When the offenses started getting more mobile way back in the twenties, the old 7-Diamond defense gave way to the looser 6-2-2-1. When the T formation with man-in-motion came in, the defense loosened up into the 5-3-2-1. When halfbacks started running downfield for passes, Philadelphia coach Greasy Neale brought in his Eagle defense, a 5-2-4, or 5-4-2 alignment, depending on how you wanted to look at it. When the Los Angeles Rams attacked it by sending four and five receivers downfield, short and long, the Giants came up with a 6-1-4, gradually loosening up into the 4-3-2-2 of today. And this has been varied by odd-fronts and stacks and all manner of zone pass coverages, hidden and open. See Fig. 6 for how the history of defense would look.

The 4-3, with variation, seems to have settled on football as the ideal defensive alignment. But it is constantly honed and perfected. And Dallas coach Tom Landry, perhaps the most innova-

Fig. 6

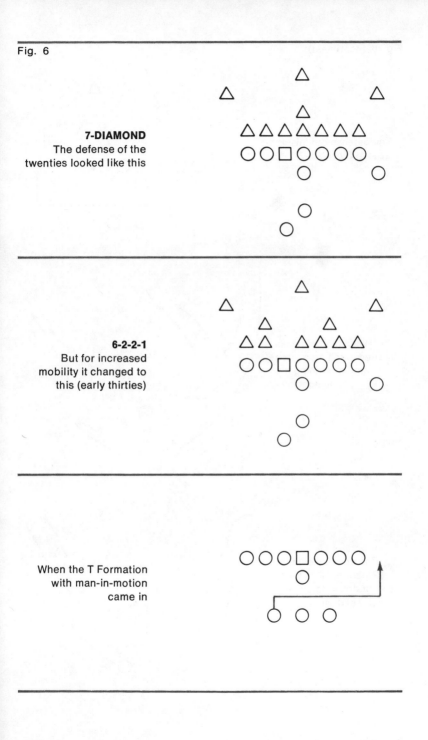

7-DIAMOND
The defense of the
twenties looked like this

6-2-2-1
But for increased
mobility it changed to
this (early thirties)

When the T Formation
with man-in-motion
came in

Fig. 6 (continued)

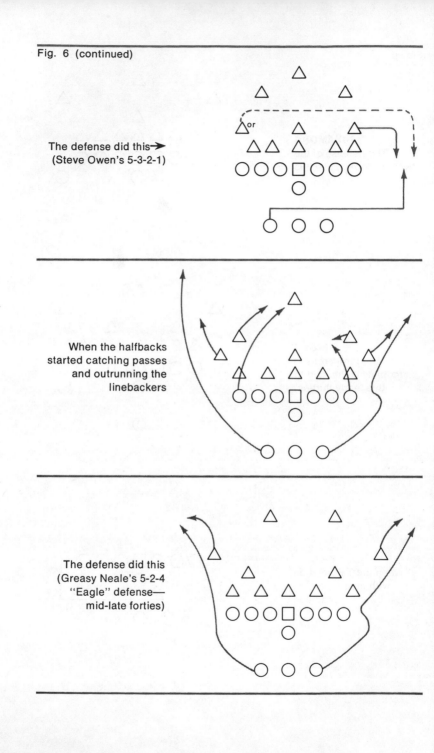

The defense did this→
(Steve Owen's 5-3-2-1)

When the halfbacks
started catching passes
and outrunning the
linebackers

The defense did this
(Greasy Neale's 5-2-4
"Eagle" defense—
mid-late forties)

Fig. 6 (continued)

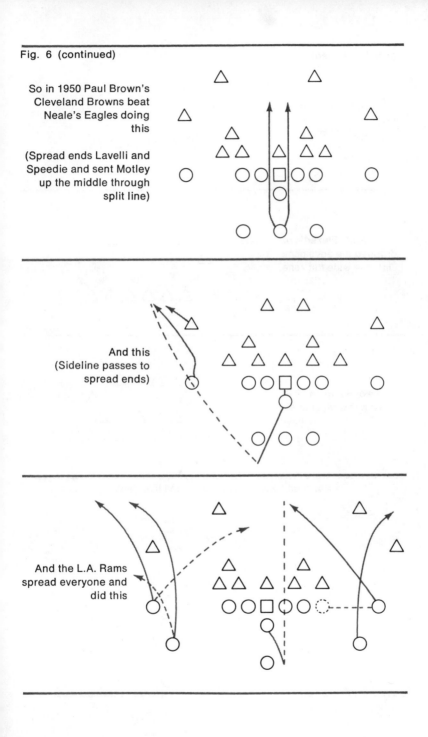

So in 1950 Paul Brown's Cleveland Browns beat Neale's Eagles doing this

(Spread ends Lavelli and Speedie and sent Motley up the middle through split line)

And this
(Sideline passes to spread ends)

And the L.A. Rams spread everyone and did this

Fig. 6 (continued)

So the Giants lined up
in this
(6-1-4 "Umbrella")

And "Flexed", or
dropped the ends back
into the wide flat zone
like this

And wound up, in 1956,
with this Modern 4-3
defense

Which now has "zone" variations like these:

1. (Strong-side rotation)

Fig. 6 (continued)

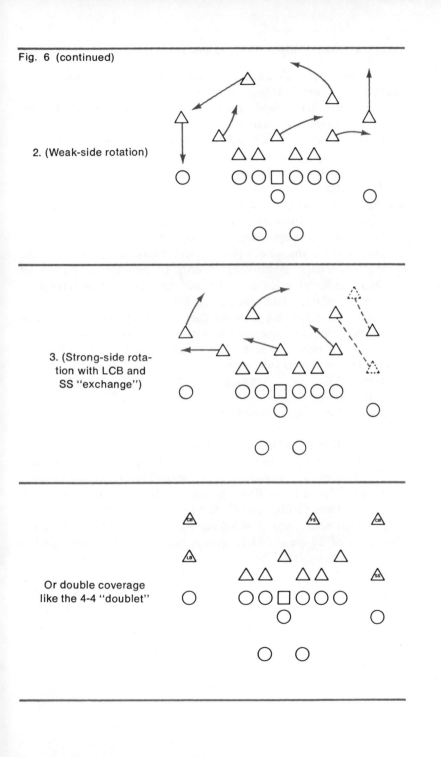

2. (Weak-side rotation)

3. (Strong-side rotation with LCB and SS "exchange")

Or double coverage like the 4-4 "doublet"

tive thinker in the game today, might have reached the ultimate in containment with his Doomsday Defense.

"There are eight gaps along the line of scrimmage," Landry says, "six between offensive linemen and one in each flat or outside area. In each of our defenses, one man is assigned to each gap. If the play comes in a defender's direction, he covers his gap, rather than going directly for the ball."

He can draw little triangles in these gaps and when all the gaps are filled, then his defense has reached total containment, a theoretical departure from the traditional idea of "total annihilation."

It is in this concept—the containing rather than the attacking defense—where the whole thing might break down. Because the history of defense is also the history of emotion: a parade of toothless, colorful assassins who weren't always that strong on playbook stuff but could sure as hell deliver a blow.

Landry modified his defense for the 1969 Eastern Division championship game against Cleveland by installing a couple of switches. His linebackers, Chuck Howley and Dave Edwards, alternated from side to side, depending on the alignment the Browns presented. His free safetyman, Mel Renfro, did the same with Otto Brown, the rookie right cornerback. It would take only perfect execution to defeat this defense, Landry reasoned.

The Browns executed well; if not perfectly then at least close enough to defeat the Doomsday Defense. Bill Nelsen, who is not a great quarterback but who follows the game plan, as written, was given plenty of time to pass, and he picked the Doomsday Defense apart with his precise little passes to Paul Warfield and Milt Morin and Gary Collins and Bo Scott.

The final score was a shocking 38-14, and Nelsen had completed 18 of 27 passes. The quotes that came out of the Dallas locker room expressed bewilderment. Yes, there had been confusion created by the steady flow of shifting personnel. Some of the older veterans even talked about retirement. And Landry began asking himself questions about his overall concept. Might it not be profitable to step back in time and revert to a more basic tee-off defense?

The people who make their living from the game always stressed defense, even though its subtleties mystify most fans. In the one-platoon era, the coaches used to devote as much as 80 percent of their practice schedule to offense, but since then the practices have been just about equally split.

When people looked at the decline of the Baltimore Colts in 1969, they mentioned Unitas' arm and the lack of punch in the attack. But their offense, which had finished fourth in yardage in the NFL in '68, was still fourth in '69. The defense had sunk from second in the league to thirteenth.

The leading defensive teams were always at championship level. But great offense didn't always ensure success. In the three-year period, 1967–69, the three NFL Super Bowl teams finished first, second, and first, respectively, in defense, while the offenses ranked ninth, fourth, and tenth. The AFL teams could get by with a spectacular offense and so-so defense in the league's formative years, but in '69 and '70, when the AFL beat the NFL in the Super Bowl, the AFL's two representatives were its top defensive teams.

In 1954 the San Francisco 49ers had a showpiece offense—Joe Perry and John Henry Johnson, the league's No. 1 and No. 2 runners, plus Hugh McElhenny, who averaged eight yards a carry and finished eighth. There was Y. A. Tittle passing to his fine pair of ends, Gordy Soltau and Bill Wilson. But the team finished third in the six-team Western Division.

"Defense—that's where you have to start rating a team's chances for the championship," Landry said back in 1963. "You can never count a good defensive team out of the race."

"When I came down from Canada in 1967," Minnesota coach Bud Grant says, "I asked myself, 'How can you be successful in the NFL?' I decided the successful teams were the ones with the best defenses. Can you recall a single great professional team that didn't have a great defense?" (Cleveland in 1964, but nobody can figure out how the Browns ever won the title that year.)

"When we were getting started," the Jets' former owner, Sonny Werblin, says, "I remember Weeb Ewbank saying that defense is the name of the game. He said, 'Let's draft athletes, no matter what position they played in college.' That's how we built the defense. Jim Hudson was a quarterback at Texas and he became a safetyman for us. Ralph Baker was an offensive end at Penn State, and he became our corner linebacker. We were even thinking of playing our fullback, Matt Snell, at linebacker, because we had no one else, but Woody Hayes talked us out of it."

In Lombardi's overhaul at Green Bay, he stocked his defense with men who were offensive players in college, i.e., cornerback Herb Adderley (halfback); linebackers Ray Nitschke and Lee Roy Caffey (fullbacks); safetyman Willie Wood (quarterback); linebacker Dave Robinson (end); cornerback Bob Jeter (halfback).

Sometimes you'll find a head coach who is strictly an offensive thinker. Jimmy Brown says that Cleveland coach Paul Brown, for instance, would get so annoyed when the defense beat the offense in scrimmages that he would get in the huddle and devise trick plays on the spot. But you can be sure that Paul Brown always had good assistant coaches to handle the defense for him, and he gave them carte blanche.

"When you get down to it," Giant quarterback Fran Tarkenton said in answer to his critics in 1969, "no team wins without a good defense. Namath is great, but he couldn't do it until the Jets defense developed into what it is. That's the situation now with the Giants. You don't need a great offense to win a championship, but a great defense is a must."

The Kansas City Chiefs didn't ride into the Super Bowl on Len Dawson's right arm or their multiple offense. They did it with the defense that held the Vikings to seven points. They gave up a total of one touchdown in the two playoff games against New York and Oakland. They kept the Jets out of the end zone with a goal-line stand that began on the one-yard line. And they kept the Raiders from scoring three times in the last quarter, when the Chiefs' offense fumbled the ball away inside the 25-yard line each time.

"It was the most inspirational thing I've ever gone through on a football field," said Kansas City's defensive captain and left end, Jerry Mays. "There has never been a group of men closer together than we were then. Emotion? You should have seen what was going on in that defensive huddle. There was Willie Lanier, our middle linebacker, the ol' honey bear, with the tears streaming down his face, yelling, 'Dammit, they're not going to score!' All the offensive guys, even people like Jim Tyrer who never open their mouths, were standing there on the sidelines yelling and shaking their fists. I want to tell you, there was some emotion out there."

There is very little science in a goal-line stand, just emotion and adrenalin and the physical battle of beating the man over you. Miami coach Don Shula calls it an emotional hypodermic.

"There is no single thing in a football game that turns the fortunes of the two teams more suddenly than a goal-line stand," Shula says. "If you have the ball with first and goal on the other team's five and you don't get a point, it disheartens your team, offensively and defensively. It inspires the opposition."

There can be inspiration and emotion in a sustained offensive drive, especially if most of the yardage comes on the ground. But for the most part, offense is technique and defense is emotion—assuming, of course, that the basic knowledge is there.

"Defense is more exciting," says the Rams' tackle, Merlin Olsen. "On offense you're part of a machine. Defense is more individual. But I'd say the techniques of offense are harder to master."

"Get a few fiery guys on defense, and they can inspire your whole squad," says the Jets' defensive coach, Walt Michaels. "A 40-man squad with 15 real studs on it will be a winner. It's like a riot. Get three people yelling and pretty soon you've got 50, all chanting and hitting. Instigators—that's all it takes."

It's understood that pure noise won't do it. People have to know what they're doing. But unless the players are exceptionally mature, a cold, precise, uninspired defense won't produce a winner. Coaches such as Grant and the Rams' George Allen, who are primarily defensive thinkers, installed systems that cater to the destructive urges in their players. Usually the names of these systems —"tee-off," "blow-and-go"—are as colorful as the people who practice them. A defense that attacks might produce mistakes, but it will also leave a lot of lumps.

"Our theory is to explode into the neutral zone and then to move and react with the play," Olsen says. "Other teams may wait instead of exploding and then react later than we do. Ours seems like a more basic approach."

"When the Rams get a lead," Bart Starr says, "their defense is especially dangerous because it will take liberties it wouldn't take if the game were close or if they were behind. The linemen will come at you with contempt, unafraid of what audibles you might call to burn them."

The Vikings have been burned by their tee-off approach to the game. Kansas City took advantage of left end Carl Eller's free-wheeling pursuit by faking him three times on end-around plays. And the first Kansas City touchdown came on a "sucker trap" that took advantage of the quick reactions and pursuing tendencies of Viking linemen Jim Marshall and Alan Page. But the percentages are still with Minnesota, and the result of one game will not make Grant go into a deep strategy session and decide to junk the principles of reckless abandon.

When Phil Bengtson came to Green Bay to take over the defense in Vince Lombardi's first year, he found a collection of talented, but cautious, defensive players.

"They had been coached to play a cautious, waiting game, doubtless the result of being burned so many times in the lean years," Bengtson said. "They were a defense in every sense of the word, the Switzerland of pro football.

"To remedy the situation, I had to explain that in modern football the defense attacks. The defense has plays, formations, and strategies—and it can produce points. Most important, the aggressive defensive team must have a morale of its own: a goal, a leader, a reward. It all comes under the heading of Pride, which is what I tried to instill in my defense that long, hot summer of 1959, when they had none."

But there's another aspect to pride—Maturity. Before the 1963 season, Landry analyzed his young expansion team, the Cowboys, and talked about the defense.

"After a defensive team is set," he said, "it takes about three years of working together before it reaches its peak. The first year is the year of confusion. During the second year, you begin to see some success as the players learn their assignments well enough to carry them out instinctively. During the third year the team gains confidence and pride and the defense starts maturing.

"Right now our defense is all on a level. No heads pop up higher than the level. There aren't any players anyone is afraid of. We haven't established an image of monsters on this club. It's too young. That comes with time. I mean, the longer you play, the

better you get, the easier it is, and not just because you, personally, have improved. Other clubs become afraid of you. When you
get ready to play the Giants, for instance, you play away from a
Jim Patton. He has earned the right to be feared. We can upgrade
the quality. We still lack depth. But what we're trying to do now
is instill confidence and pride."

Grant says that the prime of life for a defensive lineman is 28
to 32, and most coaches agree that the line is the keystone of the
defense. Grant also adds: "There is no instant success. It is impossible to acquire experience without some losing efforts."

"You just have to be older," says the Cowboys' six-time All-
NFL tackle, Bob Lilly. "Check the great defensive teams—Green
Bay, the Giants in the early sixties and late fifties. Old. On offense
you can get by with young backs and receivers, but on defense you
rarely see a man come in as a starter unless he has three or four
years experience. Maybe a few linebackers and cornerbacks, but
maybe they are not given any real responsibility at first, either. As
they get older they get more responsibility, more complex assignments."

Lilly also points to another quality as the mark of a good defense. Pursuit. It can't be coached, but the coaches always mention
it. Lilly says it's a barometer of desire.

"It's the secret to a really good defense," he says. "All the good
defenses have good pursuit. Every player can get beat on a play,
but pursuit keeps the 40-yarder down to 15, holds a TD to a field
goal. If you don't have the desire to pursue, then you don't need
to be out there anyway. And that's something you don't have to
work on. All you do is push yourself."

Coaching defense is a matter of psychology. And Michaels, a
psych major back at Washington and Lee, always reminds everybody of that.

"An offense can't help typing itself," he says. "It works on
what it does best. Everybody does. The great teams—Green Bay
of a few years ago, Kansas City, Minnesota, Oakland—are easy to
type, and easy to design a defense for. Executing that defense is
something else. Don't let Kansas City's multiple formations fool
you. When it comes time to actually running the plays, they fall
into a pattern. It's the sign of a solid team.

"The team that throw 50 different things at you all at once are generally doing it out of weakness, not strength. No one has such great personnel that he can do everything exceptionally well."

"There are some teams that play a guessing game, constantly trying to fool you, to go away from their own basic strengths," says Billy Baird, the Jets' free safetyman for years. "They can carry it to ridiculous extremes.

"We scout ourselves. We know where we're weak. And sometimes you sit back there waiting for a team to hit that weakness, and it never does. You say to yourself, 'God, what are they waiting for? Why don't they do this to us?' And you never find out. Maybe they're too busy trying to fool you.

"We don't jump around much. We sit in our defense and assume it's the right one and wait for them to get on with what they're going to do. Just like the Jet offense is a pretty basic thing. Its strength is execution."

Michaels carries the strategy a little further into the realm of psychology. He likes to read *people* as well as the methods they teach.

"It's like literature," he says. "You read a writer, and many times you can see the other writers who had an effect on him when he was young. You can see something of them reflected in their work. It's the same in coaching.

"I look at Cincinnati, for instance, and I can see their defense as an extension of their defensive coach, Vince Costello, my old linebacking buddy on the Browns. I look at the Cincinnati middle linebacker standing out there and I see Vince—the same mannerisms. When I look at the Rams I see Tom Catlin. The Philly linebackers look like Chuck Bednarik. He coaches them in camp. I can even see something of Abe Gibron in the Chicago defense, even though Abie didn't play much defense. But he was always on the goal-line teams, and it shows.

"I'll tell you another thing that helps when you're coaching a defense. That's some experience playing offense yourself. I was a fullback in college, and I played one year of offense in the pros —with Green Bay my first year. I didn't like to play offense; it wasn't really my bread and butter, but the experience is still with me. Your defensive game plan has no rhyme nor reason if you can't try and project yourself into the other team's offense."

There is still a limit to what a coach can expect a player to grasp. And the ultrastrategists who are brilliant in their conceptions often find that a great gulf exists when they try to get that knowledge into the brain of the player.

"A lot of us merely expect too much of the players," Michaels says. "You have to realize that some positions don't require geniuses, say some of the defensive line positions, so you don't give them as much to do, but you demand good execution of what you do give them. Other positions might require more intelligence, so you draft accordingly. I've never yet seen a dummy off the field that became a great thinker once he had the uniform on. But the reverse is often true—a smart person will be a dumb football player.

"Often it isn't a lack of football intelligence; it's a matter of coordination between mind and body. The mind just isn't relaying the signals fast enough to the body. So the player hesitates, and he's dead. Sometimes coaches forget that a defense is only as strong as its weakest player."

The idea of defensive brainwork didn't always exist. Look at some of the vintage game plans, and their simplicity stuns you.

"The Giants assigned Mel Hein, their center, to cover our man-in-motion," Chicago quarterback Sid Luckman said after the 1942 Giants-Bears game. "Hein was a great player, but he wasn't fast enough to cover men like McAfee or Bobby Swisher. So we just threw to them all afternoon, and that was the ball game."

"I played in the middle of the seven-man defensive line," said Boob Darling, the center on the 1928–31 Green Bay Packers. "I pulled out of the line if I smelled a pass, and stayed in if I suspected a run was coming."

Defenses nowadays, though, with their "masked," or hidden zones, put a quarterback's thinking processes to the ultimate test.

"The way they disguise those zones," Joe Namath says, "I wonder how a young quarterback can come into the league and survive. There's so much reading that goes into it, so much recognition. I wonder how I did it myself, except that they didn't try and hide the zone as much then."

The basic premise of the zone defense is that people cover an area, rather than a prescribed man. So if a pass receiver has beaten his man, he is merely drifting into someone else's zone of coverage. It will generally shut off the deep pass, because a safetyman is always there. The idea is that it's better to let a team inch along against you, while you hope that somewhere along the line it will foul up, than it is to give up the quick six points.

The weakness of a zone defense is that a precision-passing team, such as the Jets or the Cleveland Browns, will exploit the gaps in the defense, the holes. The receiver will find those cracks, and if the passer is skilled at hitting him as he makes his break, he can puncture the zone defense. And the wider the offense spreads itself, the more pronounced those gaps in the defense become.

A team can use a zone defense through strength or weakness. A strong pass-rushing team, such as the Rams or the Vikings or the Chiefs, will play a zone because it figures that the quarterback won't get enough time to "read" the zone, and even if he does there will always be some tall defensive lineman sticking his hands in the air, blocking the passer's line of vision and the ball's line of flight. A quarterback with a bad arm, or a rookie quarterback, can be destroyed by a good zone defense. But a zone defense can also be used to hide a weak cornerback or two, since it eases their intense one-on-one pass-coverage responsibilities.

Before the 1969 Super Bowl, people assumed that the Baltimore zone defense was predicated on the great pass rush of the defensive line. After the Jets beat the Colts and Namath punctured the zone, the same people said that the Colts' zone was merely a means of hiding its weak cornerbacks. The truth probably lay somewhere in between.

Quarterbacks were traditionally told that the way you can spot zone coverage was to give your first look to the defensive strong safetyman. If he moves toward the tight end, his normal responsibility in a straight man-to-man defense, then the defense is in a man-to-man. If he backs up, or veers over to the side, then the defense is playing zone.

But the defense has responded by disguise. A tight safetyman might fake a move toward the tight end, and then drift into a zone. Or he might "exchange" assignments with another defender, who looks as if he's heading for the tight end. Or the defense might use "combination" coverage, part zone, part man-to-man. This confuses everybody, sometimes even the defense.

"I once had a coach who had a theory that man-to-man defense was always the best," Grant says, "because he would always know who to blame if something went wrong.

"We use a zone defense because we feel that we can get to the quarterback or exert enough pressure to make him unload the ball before the zones get too big."

"I've always liked to watch basketball," Michaels says, "and try and relate the coverage there to pass coverage. And I've always had the feeling that the perfect pass defense might be like the NBA's concept of a sliding man-to-man coverage. It's not really a zone and it's not really a pure man-to-man, but something in between. Anyway, I'm working on it."

The basic alignment, the 4-3, has undergone changes since the Giants first went with it in '56. The AFL clubs have always liked the idea of an odd-front defense they call a 5-1 or 5-2. There aren't really five men on the line, but one of the tackles lines up directly over the center, giving the appearance of a 5-man line. This has its variations, including the "stack," which is a means of hiding one or two—even three—linebackers behind a defensive lineman, thereby giving the backers-up tackling room. It keeps the blockers off them, provided a defensive lineman is quick enough to charge into the gap and contain two offensive linemen.

Kansas City achieved the ultimate in "stacking" in the 1970 Super Bowl, when the Chiefs occasionally hid all three linebackers behind their linemen.

"We were in some form of stack over 90 percent of the time," Mays said, "and we never played it that much before. Minnesota's recognition was destroyed. Kapp would roll to the strong side when we were overshifted that way. We got the message the third or fourth time the Vikings got the ball and couldn't get a first down. We felt stronger and the pace quickened."

The stack doesn't have to originate from an odd-front defense. Lombardi employed stacking principles when he assigned his defensive tackles the job of pinching inside, keeping the blockers off his middle linebacker, Nitschke. And the Packers lined up in a pure 4-3. The Jets often stack from a 4-4, which gets its name not from the fact that there are actually four linebackers (although the club does that, too, to provide double coverage on pass receivers on both sides), but because the inside linebackers are aligned di-

Kansas City 3-linebacker "stack"
vs. Minnesota

Fig. 7

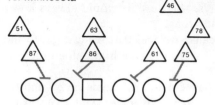

KC "stack" vs. Minnesota (two
LB's stacked and strong safety up)

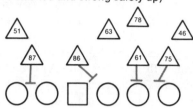

KC normal, or true 5-2 vs.
Oakland, 1969

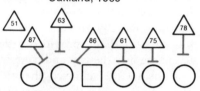

87: Brown, RE   75: Mays, LE   78: Bell, LLB
86: Buchanan, RT   51: Lynch, RLB   46: Kearney, SS
61: Culp, LT   63: Lanier, MLB

Oakland 5-1 "under" vs. KC—allowing the strong-side run, with R.T.
Keating's quickness counted on to penetrate and stop running power

*The normal LT, 85, Oats, is the "Rover" or "Chaser" man, fre-
quently playing as an
end on either side

*Chaser as RE

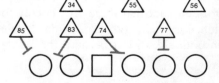

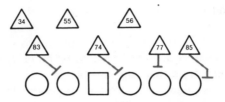

Oakland 5-1 "under" vs. KC
*Chaser as LE

83: Davidson, RE   77: Lassiter, LE   55: Connors, MLB
74: Keating, RT   34: Otto, RLB   56: Oliver, LLB
*85: Oats, LT

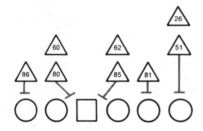

Jets' 4-4 "Stack"

Jets' pure 4-4, with extra LB, 56,
Crane, substituting for SS, 26,
Richards

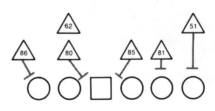

81: Philbin, LE   85: Thompson, LT   80: Elliott, RT
86: Biggs, RE   51: Baker, LLB   62: Atkinson, MLB
60: Grantham, RLB   26: Richards, SS

rectly behind the defensive tackles, giving the defense a squared-up look.

"You have to have the right kind of defensive linemen to use a stack," Michaels says. "They have to be quick types. They have to be able to penetrate that gap and tackle people, not big lardasses who can't close their arms around anybody. Don't forget that a lineman's hands are covered by miles of tape, and sometimes it's tough for him to close them on a ball carrier.

"But I'm not married to the stack. We use it because of the type of personnel we have, quick people. If I had some powerhouse 270-pounders at the defensive tackles, I might go with the 4-3. Who knows?"

The stack, plus some other defensive alignments, are shown in Fig. 7.

7
The Front Four:
Half a Ton of Defense

Doug Atkins wasn't born. The Arctic ice cracked, an explosion followed, and he came out.

□ Ed Staton, *New Orleans Times-Picayune*

You build a defense with a foundation of ends and tackles. You add the linebackers, and you top it off with cornerbacks and safeties. If the foundation cracks, the whole thing comes down, because the line is where it all starts.

A weak pass rush means terrible pressure on the defensive backs, which means that the linebackers have to help them, which means that the running defense is weakened. Weak front four against the run means that the linebackers have to stay in close and play mop-up all the time, which means that the defensive backs can count on no help on pass coverage, which turns them into psychos.

But stick a couple of real studs on that front four, and the whole operation takes on a different look. The quarterback will have to pass from positions he doesn't especially care for. The defensive backs will intercept, and so will the linebackers. The defense can indulge in more trickery and artifice. More interceptions. Better field position for the offense. More points. More wins. More money.

The coaches draft accordingly. Five of the 26 first-round draft choices in 1970 were defensive linemen, the heaviest first-round representation of any position. Seventeen defensive linemen were picked in the first three rounds of drafting, compared to 11 line-backers and 11 defensive backs. A good year for defensive line-men? Well, maybe . . . but in '69, the defensive line led the line-backers and secondary, 10-8-7 in the first three draft rounds. In '68 the score was 14-8-5; in '67 it was 12-11-11; in '66, 15-7-6; in '65, 15-9-3, etc. The linemen won all the time.

More important is the way the salary scales have reflected this concern for the big pass rushers. In the old days you gave 'em a bale of hay and a bucket of water, bedded them down for the night, gave them a few dollars if they played well enough, and sent them on their way. People paid to see Red Grange. People still pay to see the Simpsons and Namaths, but players are also paid to stop them. And defensive ends and tackles, according to the latest study of professional salaries, earn more than offensive linemen, much more than defensive backs and kickers, and about the same as linebackers. Only the glamour boys, the runners and throwers and catchers, are wealthier.

Vince Lombardi says he can usually look at a big lineman and tell whether he will play offense or defense. If his hair is combed and he says "yessir" and "nosir," and "I'd really like to become an outstanding professional football player," he's an offensive man. But if he comes in an old leather jacket and a two-day growth of beard, he spits on the floor and asks you, "How much you paying me?" then he's defense all the way.

The pattern of offense is control, everything within its pre-scribed limits. Left foot here, right foot there; mustn't hold too much, mustn't forget the play. Defense has its mechanics, too, and its plays, but a lineman can just say "the hell with it," and start teeing off and smacking helmets and generally raising the kind of hell he did in the saloon back home, and he will be a success. De-fensive line play is innovation. Offensive work is precision.

The best locker room quotes usually come from defensive line-men. Or if they're not from them, they're about them—the quar-terback talking about the lick that so and so delivered, the offensive tackle talking about the blow that spun his helmet half-way around. When defensive linemen talk about a game, they get right to the point.

"We're like a bunch of animals kicking and clawing and scratching at each other," says the Rams' great defensive end, Deacon Jones. "Going in, going into The Pit, I like to slap the guys' helmets. It shakes them up. When I get to the man with the ball, I hit him as hard as I can. If I can hit a man hard enough so he has to be carried off the field, I'll be glad to help him off."

"What I like to do," says Kansas City's 6-7, 275-pound defensive tackle, Buck Buchanan, "is come down around the quarterback's head with the club—this [his forearm]—the club. You try to ring his bell. You just sort of shake it down around his head all the time. I very seldom tackle a quarterback around the body anywhere. I try to strip 'em through here—the head. You miss a lot of them. They'll duck you. But a lot of times you catch him, especially if he's throwing to the other side and doesn't see you. You really crush him to the ground, and the next time he'll be looking for you."

It affects all of them, even the pensive and analytical Merlin Olsen, who plays left tackle, next to Jones.

"Even if the quarterback is going to get the pass away," Olsen says, "you have to bloody him up a little, to remind him you were there. You have to punish him to discourage him. He begins to listen for your footsteps. He begins to hurry. As he loses his rhythm and timing, you've got him. The good ones never break—you can only bend them, not break them."

These men aren't sadists. It's just that intimidation is part of their game. A man has never yet been thrown out of the league or cut from his team because he cracked too many quarterbacks' helmets.

It was a little different in the old days, when players performed both offensively and defensively. The lineman you freely use your fists on this time will do the same to you on the next series, when the ball changes hands. Every team had its "policeman," its enforcer, and the man who made a reputation by putting players out of commission soon got his. But even that give-and-take world didn't discourage some of the real murderers of history, such as the Bears' Ed Sprinkle.

Ed was a defensive end whose weight was around 205 and whose meanness was legendary. A hard-jawed Texan with dirty blond hair and pale, flat eyes that said, "I'd just as soon kill you as look at you," Ed make his reputation on quarterbacks for 12 years, and no one ever managed to finish him off.

"Sprinkle—The Claw—I'll never forget him," Y. A. Tittle once said. "He had a left forearm like Sonny Liston's. When quarterbacks went against the Bears, they looked with only one eye for the pass receivers. With the other, they looked for Sprinkle." (There were only four officials instead of today's six.)

It was a different game then. Defensive ends were expected to rush the quarterback only after the ends had taken care of their primary duty, protecting against the run or closing for the off-tackle play. Interior linemen were "contain" men, who jammed everything inside. The four-man pass rush was unknown, and some of the pass-blocking assignments were ridiculous, i.e., guards pulling out to pick off the ends, a practice that wouldn't stand a chance today.

The Browns' Len Ford was the best pass rusher of his day, but his style had no subtlety. He'd merely overpower his man. The Colts' Gino Marchetti developed his own pass-rush style. Tremendously powerful through the chest and arms, Marchetti would take an outside route, holding the offensive tackle by the shoulder pads while he got into position. Then he would yank him aside, violently, and charge the quarterback. The Cowboys' Bob Lilly, a tall, rawboned defensive tackle, is one of the leading practitioners of the art today.

"I'm a grabber and thrower," he says. "I use my hands to keep them off my legs. If they get to your legs you can be had. I'm not a forearm-smash type of player because I'm tall, and if you swing your forearm at a guy and miss him, he's got you. Your whole body is open."

Sometimes college players who work against teams with heavy running attacks have to adjust their whole style of play when they come into the pros. More colleges use pro offenses today, but the run is still the staple of collegiate football, and unless a lineman watches the pro game with a clinical eye, he probably won't be a skilled pass rusher when he arrives.

"The pass rush was the hardest thing for me to learn," says 6-8, 270-pound Doug Atkins, who spent 17 years in the NFL. "At Tennessee, you spent your time trying to stop the run, so once I hit the pros I had to school myself not to stop once I got past the fullback. I just had to realize that the big prize is always the quarterback."

There are always those little tableaux of defensive linemen knocking a quarterback on his tail, then helping him to his feet and dusting him off. I get the feeling that half of that stuff is for the crowd, or it's a kind of a sneer. There is a built-in professional hatred that exists between defensive lineman and quarterback. The QB draws the big salary, the big press, the big cheers—and boos, too—and don't forget that booing can be a real spur to a defensive-lineman. A QB can torment the defensive lineman in subtle ways. A quick-release quarterback can snap off his pass at the last second with a flick of the wrist, just as the lineman is zeroing in for the kill, leaving him only with the sound of the referee's "Leave him alone! Don't touch him!"

And a scrambler can run a poor tackle or end until his tongue hangs out, until his body is tired and spent and the injury factor becomes a real hazard. The reward is that clean blow that might come once a game, or every two games. And when people talk about making the game safer for the quarterbacks, the defensive ends and tackles pause from their mauling and hammering in The Pit and give one long, loud laugh.

"Sure I think quarterbacks should be given more protection," says Detroit's tackle, Alex Karras, "if they want to put on a ballerina outfit and slippers. Then we won't hurt them.

"As long as they put on a jock, shoulder pads, and a helmet, they should be just as easy to knock down as it is easy to block us on the defensive line. As long as they're getting paid to do what they do, they don't need any more protection and they shouldn't gripe."

When the Lions' Roger Brown, a 300-pound tackle, was traded to the Rams, he was immediately rushed into action. He had only a vague notion of the Ram defensive signals.

"I didn't have much time to learn the plays," he said, "so I invented my own. It was called No. 12, which happened to be the jersey number of the quarterback we were playing. I just kept calling the No. 12 play all day."

The thing that turns a good pass rusher into a great one, once he has mastered his own special set of moves to beat his man, is consistency. It is physically impossible to go full throttle on each of the 55 to 60 plays a man takes part in. On obvious running situations—third and inches, etc.—the defensive line will not devote its first effort to the pass rush. It will contain and try to fill the gaps.

But the greater the rusher, the more all-out pass rushes he will have in him. Adrenalin, desire, determination, a good supply of benzedrines in the locker room—they're all part of it.

"The main thing is to keep going," said Deacon Jones. "If I get blocked, I claw my way in, even if I have to crawl. I don't give a damn who's coming. The competition gears me up."

Olsen has called Jones and Marchetti the two greatest defensive ends the game has ever seen. He gives Jones the physical edge, Marchetti the edge in concentration.

"Marchetti was my idol," Olsen said late in the 1967 season. "But physically he was no match for Jones. You can't believe Deacon's quickness and speed, even when you're playing next to him. It's really quite frustrating. You'll have a good shot at the ball carrier when all of a sudden, whap, Jones is sitting on him. The other day I said, 'David, will you please let someone else have a chance?' I doubt if there's ever been a quicker big man [Jones is 6-5, 255] in competitive sports.

"Marchetti had marvelous concentration. You could set a bomb off under Gino and he'd still get to the passer. It's hard to concentrate 100 percent on every play, but this is what makes a good athlete great. Even last year there were times when Deacon couldn't stir himself up to go all out on every play. This is where Jones—and all of us—are still improving."

There is no set style. Emotion can find its outlet in the loquatiousness of Atlanta's defensive end, Claude Humphrey, or in the silence of the Jets' end, Gerry Philbin.

"I was talking to No. 72 [offensive tackle Fran O'Brien]" Humphrey said after one game against Pittsburgh. "I just told him I'd like to keep him around to play for L.A. against us a week later, things like that. You keep talking to them and maybe they'll overextend next play—and you get that step on them.

"I'll talk to the quarterbacks, too. They like to watch and think after a play, making mental notes of who might be open or what play might work next time. If you can make them talk to you, he can't concentrate on his play calling. When we played San Francisco I talked to Brodie all day, and finally I got him talking back. He tried not to listen, but I got behind him and yelled his name as loud as I could. And after each play I'd introduce myself— 'Claude Humphrey, No. 87.' "

Most defensive linemen aren't talkers, though . . . except for an occasional, "Watch the damn holding." For one thing, it takes energy and breath. And then it can break concentration.

"What the hell is there to talk about out there?" Philbin says. "You prepare yourself mentally. You get yourself 100 percent psyched up to punish, to destroy. You don't want to waste it on a whole bunch of gab."

I once asked him if he ever talked to an opponent on the field, except to warn him about holding. He thought for a minute.

"Just once that I can remember," he said. "The week after we beat Baltimore in the Super Bowl, I played in the AFL All-Star game in Jacksonville. I was playing against Ron Mix, who always gave me more trouble than any tackle in the game. On one pass play he caught me just right and knocked me right on my back. I mean it was a helluva shot. I got up and I was walking back and he said, 'Gerry, that was a great Super Bowl.' I said, 'Thanks.' I think that's the only time I ever talked to a guy. But you'll notice that Mix did his job first, before he said anything."

Philbin is 6-2, 248, which is undersized for a defensive end. His game calls for a highly developed set of spins and fakes, plus driving, repeated effort. He is mean, too, but it is a small man's meanness, not the overpowering bullying of a Len Ford or a George Andrie of Dallas.

"What would you be like," someone once asked Philbin, "if you were as big as Verlon Biggs?" Biggs is the Jets' 6-4, 270-pound right defensive end.

"If I was as big as him," Philbin said, "people would have to pay me to let them live."

Often a man like Philbin has to fight to keep his weight from dipping too low. In college he lifted weights and saw his own poundage rise from 195 to 225 in the spring of his junior year.

"I couldn't believe it," he said. "I was just as agile, even quicker. And the power . . . the power."

But sometimes the bigger men decide to cut back on their size.

The Kansas City linemen slimmed down for their 1970 Super Bowl. Left defensive end Jerry Mays went from 255 to 242. Buchanan dropped 15 pounds—from 290 to 275. And the Chiefs' 6-6 left offensive tackle, Jim Tyrer, who weighed 320 in his first year, and 295 when the Chiefs played the Packers in the '67 Super Bowl, weighed 265 before the Vikings game. The theory is that once you've got enough size, any more of it won't help hitting power. That's where speed takes over. It's like driving a golf ball or hitting a baseball. A man won't get any more distance because he builds his biceps up from 16 inches to 18.

"Unnatural size is useless," Olsen says. "Some players pack on poundage until their legs cave in. I've never even lifted weights. My size came natural, as a result of the sort of work I always did when I was younger, hefting hod and bucking bales of hay. I also worked as a ranger in Yellowstone Park until visitors began to mistake me for a bear."

Brains are becoming more of a factor in defensive line play; not so much at end, where a man can get by with an effective pass rush, but inside, where the blockers shoot out at different angles.

In 1968 the Jets had a rookie defensive tackle in their camp named Karl Henke. His brother was Ed Henke, a bald and grizzled veteran of 11 years as a defensive end and tackle in pro football. The second day Karl was in camp he opened a letter he got from Ed.

"Look at what this guy writes me," he said. The letter was on yellow, legal-size paper, and it was headed: Tips on Playing Defensive Tackle.

"Choose your route, inside or outside your man, but make sure you coordinate with the middle linebacker," it said. "Fight the pressure to your inside at all times, and when you feel that pressure relax, slide to your inside and play the trap block from the off side, or watch for the screen pass. Use head fakes and quickness to defeat your man on pass rush. Punish him with your hands. Jerk him in the direction he is going. Read as you charge and watch for the draw play. Be careful of the tackle blocking down on you, and watch the pulling guard, and read the sweep accordingly and pursue. Don't get caught on the sucker play, though, and watch for the fake pitchout."

"For Christ sake," the rookie said. "You have to be 10 different guys to be able to do all that."

Perhaps no man has made as exhaustive a study of defensive tackle play as Olsen has. But it took him years of concentration to gain the knowledge that permits his instincts and reflexes and strength to take over.

"There are 22 different types of blocking that can be used to defeat a defensive tackle," he says. "So I agree with our defensive coach when he says that a defensive lineman should be like an IBM computer. If you have to stop and think, you're licked. It's got to be instinct. The feet must move quicker than the mind. Those running backs are only two or three quick strides away from the line of scrimmage, and if they're coming at you, friend, you'll never have time to think about it. You either react perfectly to one of those 22 blocks you're getting, or the runner is gone.

"When you're tired and hurting and in a coma, your instincts will carry you. I think it takes as many years to develop a topflight defensive line as it does a quarterback. Intelligence, determination, concentration, deception, agility, and quickness are all my weapons as much as are my size and toughness. But without size and toughness, none of the rest would be of any use to me.

"You have preconditioned responses to the offense. When I line up before a play begins, my mind acts as a scanner. I look at the formation, I know the situation, and a tremendous load of information comes to me. The play begins and the information is still coming in. Then I make my decision. I respond. Remember, this is all happening in an instant.

"We have a drill here where only half the line is used. I don't like it. It feels uncomfortable. The reason is that my normal input of information is limited. It's unnatural. Similarly, when a back runs a play in practice at half speed, I get annoyed because I'm not getting the right information. There is something wrong.

"Football can be played on many different mental levels. I play it at the highest level I can. I challenge myself to be the best there is."

And, of course, not all the defensive tackles in pro football play at one-half or even one-quarter of the level of Olsen—mental or physical. And that is why Olsen ranks with Lilly as the best in the game today, two of the best ever. And a rookie defensive lineman, all fire and determination but very little brain, gets a rude awakening when the game's dimension of the mind is revealed to him.

"You wonder what they are going to be like," said rookie defensive end Fred Dryer before he faced the Jets in the College All-Star game in August, 1969.

"You wonder if they're going to split your helmet open, crush you, or what, every time they block you. A lot of things like that pass through your mind. But it wasn't like that. That offense doesn't come at you and blow you out of there, one-on-one. They finesse you with their experience. Winston Hill had me doing things I thought I wanted to do. But then I found out I was out of the play."

As defensive linemen get older, they develop more intricate and fancier moves. When they first start they are either brute strength or sheer speed; on rare instances, a combination of both. A defensive end named Ron Nery, an NFL reject but a terror in the AFL in its early years, used to say that he had his moves numbered. And if he was having a particularly big day, he would torment the offensive lineman in front of him by saying, "Here comes move No. 3; here comes old No. 4." The league advanced more rapidly than he did, though, and by 1964 Nery was gone, numbers and all.

The basic move for a defensive tackle is still the punishing, straight-ahead bull-like rush, not as a steady diet, but as an educator, a convincer, just to show his man what he's capable of if he wants to turn it on. "So many moves you can make, so many stunts," Olsen says. "But the best philosophy is to simply keep hitting them with your best lick."

But the best lick, or the strongest rush, also takes the most energy. Some of the great defensive tackles of the past were able to turn on that rush right up until the very end. Except they couldn't do it on every play. They might have one or two really good charges in them for a series. The 49ers' Leo Nomellini, a 270-pounder with tremendous power, started slowing down that way, and toward the end of his career, he would cut loose with a free-wheeler about every fourth play.

Sometimes the tackles who once played like rhinos develop different instincts as they get older. The become "waiters and readers," stay-at-home men. They stay back and watch for the traps and draws and delayed stuff up the middle, or the delayed screen passes outside. And a team that has a bull at one tackle often wants a waiter at the other one, to cover up for his running mate's mistakes.

One of the best readers was the Packers' Hawg Hanner, whom they called the Piano Player, because he was up and down the line like a man at the keyboard, covering the mistakes of the quick-penetrating Henry Jordan. With Hanner covering behind him, like a getaway man at a stickup, Jordan could blow in fast without worrying about the trap.

Often two bull-type tackles in the center of the line can foul up the operation, although two speed men, such as the Jets' John Elliott and Steve Thompson, generally work well together. In Olsen's first year with the Rams, his running mate was 285-pound John Lovetere, a powerful straight-ahead man.

"We fouled each other up," Olsen said. "We'd take the same inside route and bump into each other. The offensive linemen loved it. They'd just pile us up in the middle."

So the Rams and Giants made a tackle-for-tackle trade. The Rams got Rosey Grier, an eight-year veteran who could stay back and read if he had to. The Giants got Lovetere, who teamed with Dick Modzelewski, a reader and waiter. And both defenses improved. After Grier retired, right end Lamar Lundy took over as the reader, or "garbage man."

"On some plays, " he said, "I'll make the tackle because the other guys have made the quarterback commit himself my way. 'You just stand right there, Lamar,' they tell me. 'And we'll chase him to you.' "

And as a defensive line matures, each member of it gets to know the moves of his running mate. Players can instinctively cover for each other. But coaches have a hard time teaching this. It comes with experience, an entire defensive line aging together. Often a coach who's going for a title will bring in an old defensive lineman, even though the same age on an offensive man would disqualify him.

An end and a tackle often work together on what are called stunts, or "games." All they're doing is switching routes. The tackle will charge diagonally outside, and the end will loop around him to the inside; or the end might take the diagonal charge, the tackle the loop. It's designed to foul up the blockers' assignments and create that moment of hesitation or doubt, or even a totally blown assignment that precedes disaster. It's generally used against a young or inexperienced lineman.

Karras works his stunts all by himself. He is probably the most unique defensive tackle in the game, with his little steps and feints and moves, occasionally broken up by a single, powerful straighta-way charge.

"He has to be played tight, very tight," says the Giants' offensive guard, Doug Van Horn. "If you give him just a little bit of room, he'll take advantage of you. He likes to take it out on youngsters. Most defensive tackles have just one move. They bull head on. Not Alex. There is no other tackle like him. He has inside and outside moves, a bull move where he puts his head down and runs over you, or he'll just stutter-step you like a ballet dancer."

Once a tackle gets too good, though, too quick, he graduates into a new dimension—the world of the double-team block. Center and guard are now permanently assigned to him, and he now has to beat two men before he has a shot at the quartetback. Sometimes an exceptional tackle, like Lilly, will even draw triple coverage—a guard, a center, and a fullback who stays in to give him that final shot if he manages to sneak through.

"In a game, you don't realize why you're getting in there," says Dallas defensive end George Andrie, who plays next to Lilly on the right side. "The movies show why. Lilly is taking three men with him. That means I just have to break the one-on-one block and I'm free."

"In one game against the Rams," said San Francisco defensive coach, Paul Wiggin, "they threw 40 passes. On 23 of those pass plays, the guy blocking our tackle, Charlie Krueger, needed help. We developed a new statistic in our grading of performance on game films because of that. If we keep track of how many times a defensive tackle is double-teamed, we get a good idea of what kind of a job he's doing."

It's possible to double-team a defensive end, and the man usually assigned to help the offensive tackle over the rough spots is the fullback. His job is to chop the end's legs if he manages to get through. What it amounts to for the defensive end is a constant high-low, with an ever-present danger of a knee injury because of the continual pounding his knees are taking. The good ones all experience this.

In a 1969 exhibition game, the Jets assigned Matt Snell, their fine blocking fullback, to help the tackle out with the Vikings' Carl Eller. It was a frustrating evening for Eller, a physically exhausting one for the two men blocking him.

"Two men all night. It's a helluva tribute to you," a writer told Eller after the game.

"My friend," he said, "I don't get paid for tributes."

"Anytime two men are being used to block one all day," the Jets' defensive coach Walt Michaels said, "I'll shake his hand and say, 'Buddy, you're doing a helluva job out there.' "

The worst emotional and intellectual experience a defensive lineman goes through is called holding; a frustrating, maddening, illegal (but not called every time) device that tests the sanity of every defensive lineman in the game. Somewhere, sometime, every offensive blocker in football is going to hold at least once. Some are chronic holders—their game plan depends upon it— some do it only as a last resort, to save the quarterback from certain annihilation. But the effect on the defensive man is the same. Instant madness.

Picture yourself coming home one night, and you find that your house has been robbed. You see the guy who has done it, and you're starting to chase him. Except that you feel something tugging at your sleeve. Someone's got hold of it. So you try and shake him off—punch him, kick him, anything you can to get rid of him —all the while keeping your attention on the person you're trying to chase. And still the guy has your sleeve and won't let go, and by now you're frantic. You're screaming at him. You'd like to kill him.

That's what it's like for a defensive lineman who's being held.

Gary Pettigrew, a defensive tackle for the Eagles, said that he was surprised by only one aspect of the professional game—the holding.

"I just never knew what holding was until I began playing in the pros," he said. "I couldn't take it at first. The first time I played against the Browns, I thought I was in against an octopus.

The Browns are the best holding team in the game. Dick Schafrath has more hands than a dirty old man."

Pettigrew rated his top five holders in the NFL, and No. 5 on the list was Giant guard Pete Case. "He tries hard," Pettigrew said, "but I just swat him. He's not heavy enough to hold. One time Chuck Walton of the Lions held me so bad in an exhibition game that I started asking people for advice. They told me to head-butt him."

On the next play Pettigrew grabbed Walton by the shoulders, pulled him sharply to him, and clunked him under the chin with his helmet. Walton calmed down for a while.

The Jets' All-AFL defensive tackle, John Elliott, had another method. It's frowned on by purists, but it's effective. Before the Jets played Oakland in 1969, Elliott gave out midweek interviews about how flagrant a holder the Raiders' Gene Upshaw was. The stuff was widely quoted, and that Sunday Upshaw was flagged twice for holding.

"Yeah, I know, it violates the code or some damn thing to talk about it in the papers," Elliott said. "But if the man is going to keep holding me, I want people to know about it. The refs read the papers, too."

"It gets more and more ridiculous," says Lilly, who probably gets held more than any tackle in football. "They're not only holding they're also tackling now."

"Who's the best tackler in the NFL?" someone asked him. He thought for a while and came up with Junior Coffey, the fullback who was traded from Atlanta to the Giants.

"Every time I'd get close to the quarterback when we played Atlanta," Lilly said, "Coffey would tackle me. Yes, I'd rate him the best tackler I've ever faced."

"The better you are, the more you beat your foes, the more they're driven by desperation to illegal tactics," Olsen says. "I've had men hold me on the opening play of the game, before they even tried to stop me fairly. I hate it, but it's difficult to detect and you just have to learn to live with it."

Then there's shoving, which is more subtle than holding, but it gets the job done.

"It doesn't get called," Lilly says, "because the ref can't be sure he saw it—heat of battle type of thing. But when you're taking an outside rush, it can be just about as effective as holding. They shove you out wide, the quarterback steps into the pocket, and you have to take a 180-degree turn to get him."

Deacon Jones has another gripe—cheap shots—clips—the illegal crack-back blocks he suffers because of his great speed. After the 49er game in 1968 Jones sounded off about tight end John David Crow and his illegal crack-backs, the last of which got called for clipping.

"He snuck up from behind and clipped me as I was rushing the passer," Jones said. "The play was designed to wipe me out. And if Crow knew how to block, he would have put me out of the game, and maybe out of football forever. It only takes one clip, you know. It was a lousy cheap shot. I wouldn't do that to anybody."

The holds and shoves and clips and cheap shots are natural reactions to the legal overmatch the defensive linemen enjoy. There comes a time when even a man with the masochistic job of offensive lineman rebels, when the body just can't take any more head shots and stinging blows and grabs that can leave marks on his flesh for two weeks. The defensive man's hands are destructive, but legal, weapons. Not every blocker agrees.

"It's amazing how much they get away with," says the Giants' offensive tackle, Rich Buzin. "Defensive players are allowed to use their hands, but only in certain limited ways. The end, for instance, can clout you on the head, but only if it's done in one motion of arm and body as he comes up out of his stance.

"They once penalized Tim Rossovich of the Eagles for hitting me on the head. And it's the first time I've heard it called. But he hit me on every play, so how do you figure it? It doesn't really hurt, but the blow knocks your head to the side and it can make you blink. And that gets your eye off the man you're blocking."

Most defensive linemen agree that constant domination of a man is tough—unless he's an abolute dog, and then he won't be around long anyway. But even if they do have a "cousin" on the offensive line, they won't talk about it. It works both ways.

In 1969 the Rams' offensive tackle, Bob Brown, had an outstanding game against the Colts' giant defensive end, Bubba Smith. The rematch was a little better for Bubba, but still a standoff. After the game some reporters tried to work Brown for a quote, something along the "What's wrong with Bubba Smith? " line. Brown would not be drawn into the sucker trap.

"I guess you people of the press," he finally said, wincing as he drew on his clothes over the fresh bruises, "will never know how good Bubba Smith is until you put on a uniform and play him. I voted for him on the players' All-NFL team. He is a load. And you can quote me."

Bubba had an off year in '69, but he did reach a crescendo in one game—a preseason tune-up against Dallas and the Cowboys' All-NFL tackle, Ralph Neely. Smith's emotions had been tampered with, and he responded with a display of ferocity he didn't approach for the rest of the season. But it all stemmed from a bum rap. The week before, someone asked Neely who were the best defensive ends he had ever faced. He named three—Eller, Jones, and Philbin.

Bubba's name didn't figure in the conversation one way or the other, but his teammates decided that it would be a cool idea to bug the big man with the quote, "Bubba who?"

So they kept on him all week . . . "How do you like that Neely, saying a thing like 'Bubba who?' " and even the CBS television men doing the game chuckled about it over the air and hung the quote on poor Neely. And, of course, the innocent Dallas tackle paid for it all, in flesh.

"People sometimes ask me to rate the best offensive lineman I've played against, and the worst," Olsen says. "I'll never tell. Not again. When I first came into the league, I once told an interviewer who I considered the hardest and easiest blockers. I had to meet the hardest man the following week. He felt he had a reputation to uphold, so he gave it everything he had.

"A couple of weeks later I met the easiest man. He was all wound up to show me up. He played beyond himself, and beyond me. I'm not giving anyone any inspiration from now on. They're on their own."

And there are some defensive people, like the giant Atkins, who play good aggressive, football—until aroused. Then they turn into maniacs. Word gets around quickly, and no one bugs these people.

"Atkins aroused," an old teammate once said, "is a once-in-a-lifetime sight. You see those crazy cowboy movies where the hero picks up guys in a barroom brawl and throws 'em through walls? That's Atkins."

And finally there's the rare chance the defensive lineman gets once every decade or so, the opportunity of scoring a touchdown, which I've never heard any TV commentator describe as anything but a Lineman's Dream (has anyone ever asked a defensive lineman what he dreams about?). Olsen came close once. He picked up a fumble against the Cardinals in 1965, ran 59 yards, and fell down.

"Merlin just tripped," said Ram coach Harland Svare, "over the horizon."

8
The Linebackers

Reading your keys gets you into the area, but then it's up to you. It's seek and destroy.

□ Dave Robinson

The man who invented football never figured there would be a position like linebacker.

You just couldn't walk up to Walter Camp and say, "Walter, old boy, someday there's going to be a chap who weighs 240 pounds, and he won't be just a big boy like Fat Tom over there; he's going to have to run downfield with the halfbacks, and then next play he's going to have to charge through the guards and tackles to get to the ball carrier. He's going to have to be vicious, you see, because when the interference forms, he'll have to wade through it and knock it to pieces; but he can't just be a killer. He's going to have to be a genius, too, because we're going to give him a choice of, oh, maybe 50 different plays to call, so we want him to be able to figure out what the other team's going to do before they do it."

And, of course, Camp . . . or Stagg . . . or Rockne . . . or any of football's pioneers would have looked at you and said, "Please, we're busy. We're trying to coach a football team."

The truth is that nobody expects a man to be able really to play the position. If they did, the linebackers would be drawing $100,000 a season, instead of the $19,000 to $20,000 they're paid now, putting them right about in the middle of the wage scale—more than the offensive linemen, less than the offensive backs and receivers.

It's a position of compensations. "We know you're not really fast enough to cover O. J. Simpson, man-for-man, straight down the field," the coaches say, "but we'll write it into the playbook anyway. Don't worry, he'll get bumped around a little coming out of the backfield, and if he does get lose and breaks downfield, just hang in there. Our line will pressure the quarterback so he won't have time to hit O. J. deep. And if he does . . . well, every pass isn't thrown perfectly, and pass coverage isn't so bad, anyway, once you get the hang of it. Yes, we know it's almost impossible to stop a screen pass when a guard and a tackle are out there leading the play, but just for playbook's sake we'll write it in as your responsibility. Just get out there and be tricky . . . or if you can't fake 'em, take 'em on, and who knows, maybe someone will back you up and bail you out.

"What's that you say? You're supposed to drop back for pass coverage when the quarterback is cocking his arm, and you have to come back and fill in for the draw play at the same time? Well, buddy, that's your problem. We're not paying you to look pretty out there."

The schizophrenic world of the linebackers: Come in, back up, go deep, stay tight, be fast, be big, be mean, be smart. Actually, be everything.

So when you read those little *Football for the Fans* primers that start their linebacker chapter with: "The ideal pro linebacker must be tall and he must weigh 225· to 250 pounds," etc., you've got to say, hold on a minute. They come in all shapes and sizes, and they play it any way that it works. The important thing is getting the job done—and surviving.

They could look like Dave Robinson, 6-4, 245 pounds, with the speed of the pass-catching end he was in college and the reactions of a piranha. Or they could look like Larry Grantham, 210 pounds with a little potbelly just starting to show. They could be like Ray Nitschke: bald, toothless, mean as a landlord. Or they could be like Paul Crane, sleek and trim, a carefully combed young man of high religious principle.

You watch the movies of the Jets against the Buffalo Bills. It's a screen pass to Simpson, except that the play is over before anything has happened. Grantham has somehow managed to split both blockers, and he's flipped O. J. like a guy emptying a wastebasket. Second and 18, Buffalo. Little Larry, with his banker's belly and that funny little stiff-legged run. It's amazing that it happens, but it does. Again and again.

"Well, there's something to this being old," says Grantham, who is in his early thirties. "It's not all bad. I couldn't coach anybody to play linebacker like I do. When you've been around for a while, there are just certain things you pick up. When a back leans forward, he's coming out in a pass or he's getting the hand-off. When he leans back, he's setting himself to pass-block. The young ones tip it off most of the time. Sometimes the old ones do, too.

"The screen pass? You just sort of see it opening up. They give you the inside. They invite you in. So I start going wide right away. We've got our keys to play, but if you start figuring them out, you're dead. You've got to look for that first movement, and that's the time you react—not your brain, but your legs. Your brain catches on later. I look at one man, but I'm really seeing about five. And there's absolutely no waiting involved."

OK, so how about splitting the blockers? You're too little to take them on and there's not enough room to run around them.

"Well, it's the kind of move a back might use, a fake or a limp leg, call it what you like. I can't really explain it. It's instinct, I guess."

Whatever it is, it's not taught. There is no stereotyped way of playing linebacker.

"In college you're taught never to run around a block," says the Steelers' Andy Russell. "Fight the pressure, the coaches tell you. But if the blocker is bigger and stronger than you, and most of them are, and you fight the pressure, you wind up making the tackle and giving up six or seven yards to do it. Watch Howley of the Cowboys. He's like a matador out there. He'll dart inside, actually running around the block, and he'll make the tackle for a three-yard loss.

"When I was a rookie I used to watch our guy, John Reger, doing that and I'd think, Well, that's the sloppiest way to do something. But he'd make the tackle, and I'd be playing it honest and getting killed. So I tried to develop some of those moves, and now I can do it. But I'm sure it would drive my college coach crazy. He'd say, 'you've turned into a sloppy ballplayer.' "

When you're a super-athlete like Dave Robinson, the Packers' great left linebacker, the route is generally a little more direct. His game is "keys," the little tips a player might give when he pulls out of the line or starts his block, the little clues to the play that will follow.

"I love hitting, blockers as well as ballcarriers," he says, "but you have to be selective in who you're hitting, because all the fakes are aimed at linebackers. And that's where your keys come in.

"You can take one key and go with it all season, but you're going to be just average, or less. If you have two keys to work from, you'll be better. Three keys, you might be outstanding. If the tight end is on my side, for instance, I have to check the tight end, the near tackle, the near guard, the far guard, the near back, and the far back. But I've got less than a second to do it, so I just do the best I can.

"You've got to be careful of the phony key, too. A man who blows a play might give you a phony key, because he isn't going where he should. That's why it's important to have more than one key. They can throw one wrong key at you, one fake, but it's very hard to coordinate two. How do you get a key? One way is to hit the man when he's not trying to block you. The tight end wants to block me on a running play, so he's resigned to getting hit. But if I bust him when he doesn't have to hit me, he's going to learn not to like it.

"And he might do something about it—set up a little bit off the line, lean, something like that—to avoid being hit. When he does that, I've got a key. I can tell when he's supposed to block me and when he wants to do something else. Backs can give me a key, too, the way they tilt.

"Oh, I might be off one blocking hole, but I've got the general area pinpointed. Once I do, I'm free to play football. That's what the whole idea is, to get me into the area of the play so I can play football."

But a Dave Robinson comes along maybe once or twice in every coach's lifetime, and while that coach is waiting, he'd better learn to adjust, and to accept something less than the Athenian ideal of excellence. The supposed "musts" for a linebacker that every scouting manual carefully points out can be bent a little, too.

"First of all, there's the matter of his height," says the Jets' defensive coach, Walt Michaels, the corner linebacker and captain of two Cleveland Browns championship teams. "The book says he's got to be 6-2 or 6-3, certainly no smaller than 6-1. Well, I'll take him an inch smaller if he's got the brains. I want to know what he's thinking when he sees them breaking out of the huddle and lining up in front of him.

"Then there's his speed. The book says 4.9 for the 40. But the speed comes into it when he's dropping back to cover passes, and what I want to know is how fast is his drop, not how fast he goes straight ahead for 40 yards.

"Next, they say he's got to weigh 225 pounds or more. But I've had 210- or 215-pound people with 235-pound strength. And I've seen some awful weak 240-pounders."

There's another dimension the linebackers step into—signal calling. Usually the job falls to the middle linebacker, since his "automatic" calls, in which he has to change a defense at the last minute, have to be heard on both sides. Occasionally a corner linebacker whose experience is as vast as that of Grantham's will handle the job. And sometimes the coaches will call the defenses from the sidelines, signaling the alignment by a move or gesture. The theory is valid. A linebacker has enough to worry about without the burden of setting his team in the right alignment . . . and the defensive captain has the option to call an automatic, anyway.

Los Angeles' Maxie Baughan said that the audibles are the only way of coping with the multiple offenses, but he admitted that the 125 or 150 Ram defenses will be "audibilized" by only a few basic calls. Many linebackers brag about figuring out the audibles the offense is using, shaking up the quarterback by shouting out the play he's called after he has switched to it.

"Yeah, I read about that, and between you and me it's a lot of crap," Grantham says. "Sure, you might hit it lucky once or twice, but the offense will usually catch on and burn you good. That's the easiest way to foul yourself up, standing back there trying to dope out the audibles or the 'hut-hut-hut' at the line. It's a good way to break your concentration and take your mind off the job. I think player tendencies are a much better tip-off.

"But even if you've got everything figured out before it happens, there's still the matter of physically stopping it."

And that's where the middle linebackers come in, the physical destroyers such as the Packers' Nitschke and the Atlanta Falcons' Tommy Nobis and the Bears' Dick Butkus.

The jury is still out on which is the best of the three. *Sport* magazine once conducted a poll of famous old linebackers to see if they could pick the best middle linebacker in the game. Nothing was decided. Chuck Bednarik said that Nobis is the best because he plays with a worse team so more pressure is on him. Bill Pellington said that it's easier to stand out with a bad club, because a middle linebacker with weak support can free-lance all over the place and turn in more spectacular performances every Sunday. His choice for No. 1 was Nitschke, an opinion shared by Les Richter, who cited Nitschke's leadership qualities. Bill George said that the Chicago defense put more responsibility on its MLB, therefore Butkus had to do more things well, therefore he was the best. And unlike Nobis and Nitschke, Butkus had to call all the defenses himself.

The magazine tried it another way and asked the linebackers to point to the essential quality that makes a great middle linebacker. Upper body strength, stopping the run right at you, said Joe Schmidt. Quickness on end sweeps, general pursuit, said Bednarik. The deep drop on pass coverage, said George. Toughness, added Bednarik. And so on, and so on.

Butkus is the epitome of violence on the football field. "There are guys who make tackles and then there's Dick," says his linebacking teammate, Doug Buffone. "He's a mauler. I hit pretty hard, but no matter how hard I hit, I don't hit *that* hard."

"Every time I play a game," Butkus says, "I want to play it like it was my last one. I could get hurt and that would be it for keeps. I wouldn't want my last game to be a lousy one."

"Butkus—if he doesn't tackle you himself, you can hear him

coming," said Pittsburgh quarterback Terry Hanratty after the Bears beat the Steelers in November, 1969. "You know he's going to be there eventually. You have to be conscious of him. He has an instinct for the ball—pass, runner, anybody. It doesn't matter."

"With the highest respect, I've got to say Dick is an animal," says Butkus' old Bear teammate, Mike Ditka. "He works himself up to such a competitive pitch that on the day of the game he won't answer a direct question. He'll grunt."

And after a Colt-Bear game in Chicago, the Baltimore team bus was going to O'Hare Airport. It had stopped for a light when a trailing car hit the rear bumper. "There's Butkus again," said one of the Colts in the rear.

Actually Butkus established his image before he ever reached the pros. When he was at Illinois, a magazine quoted him as saying that he went to college to be a football player, nothing more, nothing less. It was typically blunt and honest, but it didn't sit well with the administrators at Champaign-Urbana, who were trying to help the NCAA establish their euphemism, the "student-athlete."

"They didn't recruit me to be a scientist or an engineer," Butkus said. "They brought me in to be a football player. If I was smart I'd be a doctor, but I'm not smart, so I'm a football player."

He stepped into the middle of a Chicago Bear defense that George Halas liked to point to with pride and say: "One hundred and sixty-five defenses. Eleven basics, with 15 variations on each one."

"Back at Illinois," Butkus said during his learning process, "you were graded from zero to three on each play. Hell, you could get one point just for lining up right."

In two months he was expected to absorb, in its entirety, Halas' defensive world, with its strange, almost mystical vocabulary. The middle linebacker was Mars, the outside backers, Bump and Streak. There were Stunts with the linemen, Revolves with the deep backs, Storm formations to the strong side, Bullets to the weak side, Blitzes, Blasts, and Blows, plus all manner of red-dogs—Pink, Green, Blue, Purple, Turkey, Tweedy, Pelican, and Mad Dog, which Butkus liked best because it meant everybody in on the quarterback.

He had to make the calls, so he had to know his teammates' nicknames—Weasel, The Head, Benny the Bat, Lightning, Bone, and Cement Head. Passes were X's and Y's. Receivers were Skymen, Skins, and Skows, running to the Post, the Flag, or the Arrow. "It's all I can do to figure out where I'm supposed to be," he said.

Halas saw Butkus at the College All-Star game, 260 pounds of raging meanness, but he saw something else, an overweight middle linebacker who was going to have to cover pass receivers. "You can be a good linebacker at 260," Halas told him, "a very good one at 250, but to be a great one you'll need that extra step, which means you'll have to weigh no more than 245." Butkus reported to camp at 245 and his weight has stayed the same.

He mastered the art of pass coverage, although, at first, he didn't think it was possible. He memorized his Captain Midnight Code Book and figured out all the Bear defenses. He has become a dedicated, intelligent, albeit highly destructive football player, and it bugs him when people toss off their lines about the Cro-Magnons who play the game, much in the same manner that Nitschke took deep offense when Tommy Brookshier introduced him to the TV cameras as "Green Bay's madman," after the '68 Super Bowl.

"Some people think I have to get down on all fours to eat my couple of pounds of raw meat every day," Butkus said in an off-season interview in 1969. "Others think that George Halas taught me to walk upright and I have an agent to do my reading and writing for me.

"But people who really know me know that I can read a little. I move my lips sometimes, but I can read things on a second-grade level—like newspapers. I don't need a rubber stamp to give an autograph."

The outside, or corner linebacker has the responsibility of stopping or at least forcing the end sweep, turning it inside, into the flow of traffic. He must read the wide screen pass and somehow get in front of it and generally foul it up. If the offensive back on his side of the line swings out wide to catch a pass, he must go with him. If the back continues on deep, down the field, the linebacker must keep up with him, or at least try to. If the tight end is lined up on his side he must "jam" him, or pop him at the line, to break up his possible pass route, although some defenses are getting away from that theory.

And in some varieties of zone pass defense, the corner linebacker might wind up covering a flanker back.

Agility is his game, and the coaches are willing to sacrifice a little size to achieve it. A little . . . but not much.

The middle linebackers patrol the tackle-to-tackle area, tackling anything that tries to get through. If the defensive linemen are skillful enough to attack the gaps between offensive linemen, thereby tying them up and freeing the middle linebacker, the job is so much easier. On normal pass coverage, the middle linebacker may be called on to read screen passes, and then he swings wide to help his outside linebacker—or to take it on himself, if the cornerman is doing something special, like blitzing. If two backs swing out of the same side of the backfield, and the play is a pass, the middle linebacker generally sticks with the back closest to the line, the one who is going deep. This is the play that ages the middlemen, that gives them nightmares, particularly if the back is a 9.3 sprinter like Simpson.

"I was kind of scared at first, the idea of covering a fast back one-on-one," Butkus said. "I was scared because of the way everyone talks, you know, the stuff you hear on television about how that's what the offense wanted to do all day, isolate a back on a linebacker, and 'Let them get one step on you and they're gone.' That kind of stuff. And for a while when I first started, I thought this must be true, because I was getting beat.

"But I was just inexperienced. I wasn't reacting well. As the games went by, I was picking up my coverages right away. I'd play closer, too—bump him, crowd him, and pretty soon I was picking off a pass here and there."

"Sometimes, all a linebacker has to do is keep near his man," Michaels says. "He may not even be called on to defend against a pass. What you want him to do is discourage a throw. Remember the quarterback only has a split second to look downfield and read the coverage, and if he sees a big linebacker near the back, that might be the only look he's going to have time for. He won't throw.

"I'm always happy when our defensive line is doing a good enough job so that the linebackers can drop back into the passing lanes every now and then, sort of pop up where they're not supposed to be. They'll do things that don't show up on the stat sheet. They might not actually intercept the ball, but who knows how many interceptions they create for somebody else?"

Pass coverages for the linebackers are like the vegetables Mama tells every good little boy to eat. But the blitzes are the ice cream and pie. Blitzes: also called red dogs, or shoots, or stunts. They amount to the same thing. The blitz is the all-out rush on the quarterback, the chance for a linebacker to repay him for all those little screen passes and swing passes and draw plays.

The birthday of the blitz is officially listed as December 1, 1957, when the San Francisco 49ers (defensive coach, Phil Bengtson) beat the New York Giants (offensive coach, Vince Lombardi) 27-17, by sending their linebacking trio of Matt Hazeltine, Marv Matuszak, and Karl Rubke pouring in on Charley Conerly. Charley fumbled five times that day, losing four of them, and the brand-new weapon called the blitz supposedly turned the trick. It might have been done before (I have an image of Sam Huff swooping in on quarterbacks from his middle linebacker position in 1956), but the 1957 Giant-49er game is its acknowledged birth date. And two years later, when Lombardi became head coach of the Packers, the first assistant he hired was Bengtson.

The early Lombardi-Bengtson Packers blitzed heavily, and they were masters at unhinging quarterbacks by this mass of unblocked linebacking fury pouring in. But just when the rest of the world had picked up the blitz and wielded it like a giant cudgel (the Bears occasionally used, and still use, a blitz that sends in all three linebackers, plus a defensive back), the Packers started to taper off. The theory was that it left too many holes in the vacated areas, and a quarterback who kept his cool and didn't get rattled could pick it to pieces. The great Packer defenses of the mid-sixties blitzed very little, but when they did, they came like the hammers of hell.

"A blitz," Lombardi once said, "is used to cover a weakness."

And so it follows that your blitzing teams today are generally your teams that are fundamentally unsound, weaker.

"We'll blitz because we're not strong enough to lay back and hold them," says Nobis, who is one of football's more destructive blitzers. "We've got to force something.

"But you can't just shoot in there like a maniac. You've got to be reading while you're coming, or you'll just run by everything. I've seen it happen too often."

A blitz may be effective, though, against a team that has a fast set of backs who like to run downfield under passes, but aren't really big enough to block a linebacker. The set backs are the traditional guardians of the quarterback when the blitzers threaten. And the quarterback's traditional way to sting a blitz is to dump off a little pass to one of those backs swinging behind the blitzer, into the zone he has vacated.

"We don't blitz much," Michaels says, "for the simple reason that it's too easy to read. But then again, we don't do a lot of things other people do. Our outside linebackers don't hold up the tight ends, because most of the time the concept is unreal. Who are you kidding? Tight ends like Mackey and Jackie Smith are going to get loose. Why tie down your linebackers with a job they won't be able to perform?

"When you blitz a lot you're also kidding yourself, because the first thing a quarterback learns nowadays is how to read blitz coverage—and how to beat it. But hell, if we found a quarterback who couldn't read it, we'd blitz the hell out of him. You do what works for you."

The blitzing linebackers, though, and the spectacular gamblers such as Huff in his early Giant years, are still the people who make All-Pro. A successful blitz is something the fans and the press and the people who pick the All-All teams notice. You forget a good pass coverage. Most of the time it isn't even seen. But the sight of a quarterback knocked flying lingers.

In a way it's unfair to such middle linebackers as Kansas City's Willie Lanier and the Jets' Al Atkinson, fine fundamental players and good pass defenders, but nonblitzers and nongamblers. ("If I gamble, I might make nine great plays in a row," Atkinson says, "but the tenth is a touchdown.") The All-Pro pickers have yet to give them much recognition.

"I like linebackers who aren't afraid to hit you, but at the same time always operate from an area of high intelligence," Michaels says. "They don't go berserk on the field.

"You can find people to play the defensive line—strong, dedicated, crazy people. But you have to have players to cover up for them. That's why linebackers were invented."

9
Last Line of Defense: The Secondary

Defensive backs. Nothing but reactions. You train 'em like seals.

□ Sam Baker

The Jets had been beaten, 27-14, by the Oakland Raiders toward the end of the 1969 season. It was three days later—press luncheon day—and the newspapermen headed down to the locker room to ask for the umpteenth time: "What's wrong with the Jets?"

Only this time they knew the answer. It was right cornerback, Cornell Gordon, who had given up two touchdowns to the Raiders' Warren Wells and had allowed Wells three more catches—all for good yardage. A cornerback's lapses cannot be hidden. They are right out there in the open, out of the traffic. Just you and me —and 60,000 fans.

So Gordon sat up on a rubbing table while half a dozen writers asked him what was wrong in half a dozen ways.

"It was pretty brutal," John Dockery, the left cornerback, said later. "Sort of like the Grand Inquisition. Confess and conform and ye shall be absolved. I sure felt sorry for Cornell, but you know what I was thinking while all that was going on? I was thinking, Thank God it's not me up there on that table.

"Do you know how tough this position is—how unbelievably tough? You're standing there all by yourself, and you're looking at a guy like Wells who can fly, I mean really fly. One missed step, one stumble and that's it. Curtains. I wish everyone who sat there in the stands and booed Cornell Sunday would get a chance to see what it's like—just once."

The position demand's a sprinter's speed, no nerves, and no memory. Brood about a mistake and you'll repeat it, the coaches say. In fact some scouts say they draft for intelligence at every position except cornerback, where too much introspection can hurt. They figure that once a man starts thinking deeply about how impossible the job is he comes apart.

Which doesn't mean that cornerbacks are dummies. Dockery was a Greek and Latin major at Harvard and he does fine. What cornerbacks are, though, is underpaid. Next to kickers, cornerbacks are the lowest-paid players on a football team. It doesn't reflect the low regard in which management holds the position, only the fact that cornerbacks are often youngsters who come from obscure colleges, and their bargaining acumen is way behind that of the glamour players from the big name schools. John Sample says he got canned in Washington because of a contract squabble with Otto Graham.

"I wanted to get paid the same as the men I was covering," he said. "It was logical to me. The job I have to do is just as tough as the job they do. Why shouldn't we get paid the same?"

The answer is that cornerbacks don't draw fans and receivers do, and that's the traditional salary index, fair or unfair.

The week after his disastrous day against Oakland, Gordon had a magnificent afternoon in the Houston Astrodome, shutting out all the wide receivers the Oilers sent his way.

"What did it was getting out of New York," he said. "We played seven straight games there, and that's just too much. I was getting so that if I'd have had to face those fans one more week I would have cracked up. There's more pressure in New York. They get 62,000 people out there every Sunday, rain or shine. That means you can be sure of 124,000 eyes on you—every week."

The one standard quote you get from cornerbacks concerns the basic toughness of the position—physical, mental, emotional. It's all part of the game. Oakland's Willie Brown, the best cornerman in the AFL, wants to hold a clinic every June for cornerbacks. He says he will run it, and it makes no difference whether or not the men are from competing teams.

Cornerbacks of the world belong to a common fraternity, he reasons. A fraternity of misery.

"Nobody has it any tougher than us," he says. "The game is usually won or lost depending on how well a cornerback stops his man. But we still aren't paid what ends get. The clinic I have in mind would be on how to play the different receivers in football. And to discuss money."

"Defense is an all-day effort," said the Steelers' Clendon Thomas. "Offense is, too, but the pressure isn't on every instant as it is on a defensive man. Playing back there, you've always got this thing in the back of your mind—I may be the one who lets the touchdown score. I may be the one who loses the game."

"I think almost every defensive back in the NFL could play offense," says the Rams' free safetyman, Eddie Meador. "But not many offensive backs could play defense." Or put up with the pay.

Pure speed isn't enough. Henry Carr, the Olympic 200-meter man, found that out in his few years as a defensive back with the Giants and Lions.

"Running backwards was the hardest thing I had to learn. My speed was actually a detriment at the start. I depended too much on my legs."

And not only cornerbacks feel that terrible one-on-one pressure. Bruce Maher, the Giants' strong safetyman, says it can be just as bad for a safetyman who has to play a tight end, one-on-one.

"The worst thing is what happens after a guy catches one on you and goes for the score," he once told writer George Plimpton. "The first thing you see as you run toward the bench is all the big linemen going down to kick the extra point. Your own guys are looking at you like a worm, and the other team's linemen sort of have a half grin on their faces, conspiratorial like, like you conspired to fall down and let their guy score. You run toward the bench and you know you're going to get hell there. You can see the coaches, with their clipboards, watching you come."

And the defensive back has a nice long stretch on the bench to think about that touchdown and brood about it. The coaches say that the good ones wipe it out of their minds and bounce right back. I'm sure the psychiatrists would have an opinion about that.

"The thing to remember is that you're going to get beat," says Herb Adderley. "If you don't, you should be coaching, not playing. The question is, when you get beat, can you recover? You never give up on it. So someone scored a TD on you? You should never think about the play that's past, except briefly, and then only how you're going to keep your man from doing that again."

In 1967 the Cowboys cut Warren Livingston, who had been a regular cornerback for six years. He never caught on anywhere else. The end, for him, was sudden and final.

"What happened to Livingston," said Cowboy coach Tom Landry, "was that he lost his confidence. That's fatal for a cornerback. It destroyed his concentration. The only thing you can compare it to is the pro golf tour—four and a half hours of pure concentration in a round. A defensive back has to sustain three hours of concentration. Getting beat on a pass is like three-putting a green. Before the next play, before you get to the next green, you've got to shake it off, like it never happened."

Jack Christiansen, Detroit's former All-NFL safetyman and one of the game's finest defensive coaches, says that it's rare for a rookie to make it big as a defensive back. Physically it's not impossible. The mental conditioning takes longer.

"I didn't do very well my first year with Detroit," he says. "In fact the only defensive backs I can remember who made it big their first year were Night Train Lane and Lem Barney."

Players sometime find that the maneuvers that seem so simple when they were diagramed on the blackboard turn into nightmares on the field.

"The toughest thing for me," says the Jets' free safetyman, Billy Baird, "is to pick up a loose receiver. My job is all angles. On a blackboard, you always make the angles intersect, but out there the chalk doesn't always get there on time."

The Jets' technique of man-to-man pass coverage, taught by Walt Michaels, is the "slide" principle, as opposed to the backup technique.

"I want my backs to slide their feet," Michaels says. "I don't want them backpedaling. When you backpedal, your whole body straightens out. And if the receiver makes a move then, you're dead.

"The essence of man-to-man coverage is concentration on your man, though, but I could show you instances of guys taking their eyes off the man they're covering. And when you do that, it's very difficult to know where the man is when you try to get back to him.

"It's like being a good defensive basketball player. Look at the Knicks' Walt Frazier. His eyes never leave the man he's on."

Jet cornerbacks are expected to line up three to five yards from the receiver they're covering. The alignment is more conservative than that of the Oakland bump-and-go cornerbacks, who crowd their men all the way, but more radical than the traditional Green Bay idea of coverage—five to seven yards. Green Bay cornerbacks, slightly farther from their men from the start, are taught the backpedal technique.

"They backpedal furiously, at the same rate as the offensive man who is coming at them," the Packers' Phil Bengtson says. "They're ready to shoot to one side or the other when the receiver makes his cut. When they're running backward or sideways, they must run 'out of gear' like a flywheel that can suddenly catch hold and take off in any direction.

"That's why you see the defensive backs working their legs madly in place and pumping their arms out in front of them. The maneuver helps them to maintain their balance, and if they should opt to run forward into the line, the perpetual gyrations become part of their pummeling, punishing, shoving fierceness."

When a defensive back gets his playbook in camp, pass defense is generally broken into five basic coverages. They look like this:

1) Basic man-to-man. There are two types of man-to-man coverage, and the difference is the free safety. The Jets, for instance, play what they call "team defense." This means that the free safety, whom they prefer to call "weak-side safety," is not really free at all. He has a definite assignment, for instance the weak-side halfback flaring, or veering, out of the backfield, close to the line might be the weak-side safety's responsibility. (If he veers wide he becomes the linebacker's concern.) The theory of team defense is that nobody gets hung up alone. There's always help available, although it seldom really works out that way. A team with a gifted ball hawk at the safety—for example, Oakland's Dave Grayson,

St. Louis' Larry Wilson, or the Packers' Willie Wood, might play a true man-to-man, with the free safety genuinely free. He is given his head and he pursues the ball. The Packers under Lombardi were just about a pure man-to-man defensive team.

2) Man-to-man with double coverages. It could mean that the strong safety doubles on a wide receiver and leaves his regular man, the tight end, to a linebacker. It could mean that the free safetyman leaves his normal area of responsibility and devotes full-time help to a cornerback on a particularly dangerous receiver.

3) Zone defense, involving all the variations of the two basics —strong-side and weak-side rotation.

4) Blitz coverage. This describes the pass coverage adjustments the secondary must make to compensate for one, two, or all three linebackers shooting in at the quarterback. The key adjustment concerns coverage on the running back, who is the textbook receiver to beat a blitz, swinging into the area the blitzer has left. A safetyman usually will be responsible for crowding the back and preventing him from getting open, but it's not as easy as it sounds. There is traffic to wade through, and if the safetyman cheats up too close to the line, he will alert the offense that a blitz is coming.

5) Keys and mixers. Key defense is a very specialized type of coverage in which a mature group "reads" the offense and acts according to a prearranged set of keys, or tip-offs. A mixer is a variation from normal, such as a 4-4 defense, with an extra linebacker replacing a safetyman, or a five-back prevent, in which an extra back or two comes in for a lineman or a linebacker—or both—leaving an alignment that might look like a 3-5-2-1. This is a long-yardage defense, and the object is to shut off the deep pass.

Some coaches brag about the variety of defenses they can use —200, 300, even more. What this usually amounts to is different combinations of maneuvers out of different alignments, a geometric progression sort of thing.

"I'd say our basic game plan from week to week calls for only 24 defenses," says Larry Grantham, the Jets' right linebacker and defensive signal caller.

"We use three fronts, or formations, and we can call eight different defenses off each one. When a team says it has 300 defenses, it's just a matter of terms. What they call a defense, we might simply call an adjustment."

Every defensive player has his assignment, but the experienced veteran sometimes picks up a key on his own and plays his hunch. Coaches allow it, unless a man gets burned too often. Then there's a heart-to-heart talk.

"It's like bridge," Baird says. "Sometimes you get a one-bid from your partner and you jump to four hearts, a closeout bid. The only rule involved is be certain you can make it. It's the same in football, when you decide to guess on something. You've picked off some giveaway that tells you what's coming. You might guess wrong. It might even happen two or three times a game, but this doesn't mean that you'll get beat. It might only mean that you won't get where you're supposed to be. Anyway, it took me three or four years to get to the point where I would dare to guess."

Sometimes, though, the defensive backs who march to their own music can drive a coach crazy, particularly if he's trying to get across the concept of a coordinated defensive effort.

"John Sample was like that with us," Michaels said. "You tell the four backs how to play, and three of them listen to you and one doesn't. Then he gets an interception, and what do you tell the other three guys? What do you say? It's like playing poker and a guy pulls to an inside straight and hits it. You try and tell him how dumb it was, but there he is, sitting there with all the money in front of him."

Most of the veteran defensive backs have picked up their own clues on how to play the different receivers. Larry Wilson keeps a book on receivers. So did Sample, whose mysterious "Little Black Book," had a numerical rating on all the receivers he faced in his 11-year career. He graded them from one to five points (five is the best) in each of five different categories—speed, ability to run patterns, toughness going for the ball, blocking, and ability to avoid being intimidated—by John Sample.

Lance Alworth of the Chargers was a 25-point perfecto, in Sample's book. Sample's old teammate on the Colts, Ray Berry, lost a point on speed, but everything else was fives. Sample was generous to his old enemy, Frank Gifford, but gave Frank only two points in the intimidation category. They'd had their jams.

Often John upgraded the book, as he did when he played against the Colts' Willie Richardson in the 1969 Super Bowl. He added a point here and there, took away one or two, and his four-year-old memories were revised and ready for the printer.

"Some people laughed at John's Little Black Book," Jet coach Weeb Ewbank said. "But I wish some of my guys now would start keeping one."

The Cowboys' Cornell Green keeps his own set of do's and don't's.

"There are certain rules for certain passes," he says. "Take a turn-in toward the middle, for instance. If the ball is accurately thrown, you can't intercept it unless you run through the man, which is interference. The only thing you can do is wait until the ball gets there, time it right, and really crack him to knock the ball loose.

"Usually, on a sideline pattern you can read a man and tell whether he's really going to turn out for the ball, or whether he's just throwing a fake and then he'll head upfield. If he's going to get the ball after that five-yard turnout, he's going to look back, right then, for the ball. You close on him when he looks back. If he doesn't look back, he's going to cut upfield—a hitch and go. They'll tip it every time."

Sometimes a cornerback will deliberately flatten his man and take the penalty, figuring the long-range advantages—making him hear the footsteps—will outweigh the short-term discomfort of the 15 yards. Buffalo's Butch Byrd got beaten for a touchdown by Boston's Charley Frazier in a game in 1969. The next time Frazier ran a pattern he was flattened.

"The play was illegal and I realize that," Byrd said. "But the only thing I was worried about was whether the 15 yards would hurt us or not. A cornerback is asked to cover a man who's just as fast as he is, possibly faster, and who knows where he is going, and when. All the cornerback has is reaction, nerves, and whatever it takes to keep the receiver from catching the ball.

"Whatever it takes."

There are some cornerbacks so outstanding, though, so feared, that coaches devote a special scouting report to their capabilities (see Fig. 8, report on Herb Adderley, which was prepared during the 1968 season). Such is their disruptive potential on enemy of-

Fig. 8

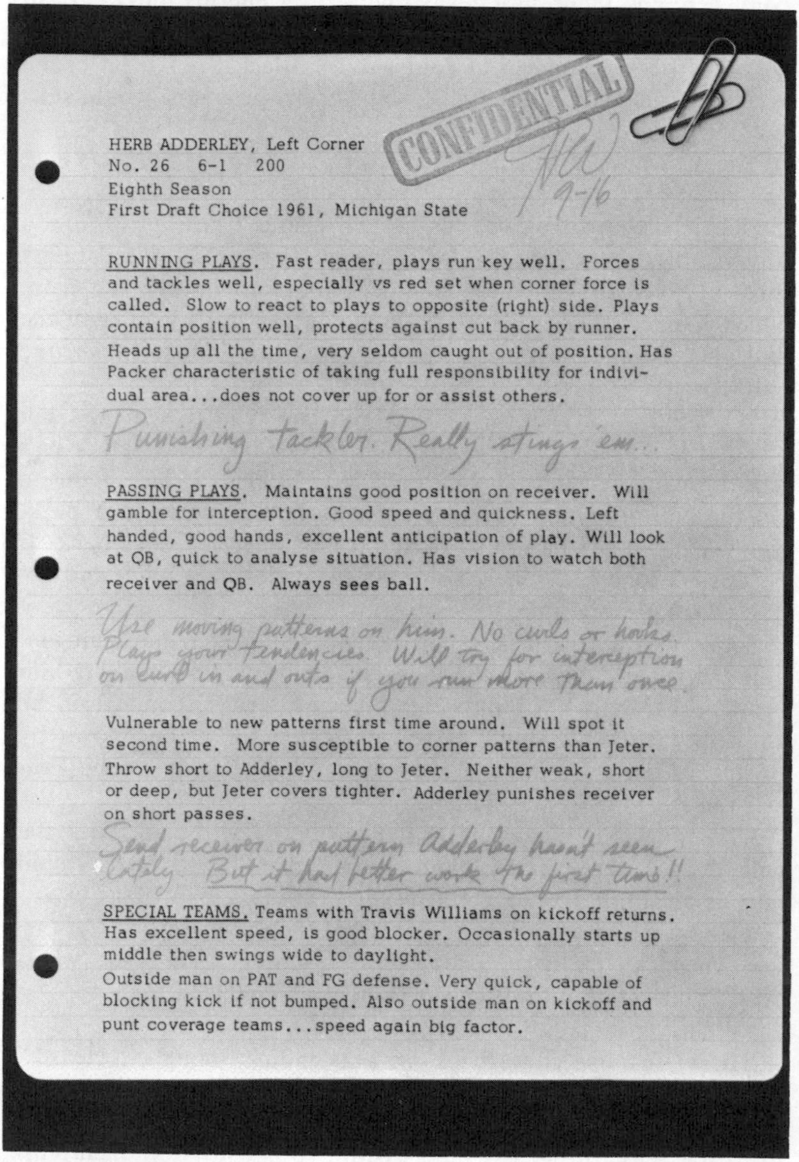

HERB ADDERLEY, Left Corner
No. 26   6-1   200
Eighth Season
First Draft Choice 1961, Michigan State

RUNNING PLAYS. Fast reader, plays run key well. Forces
and tackles well, especially vs red set when corner force is
called. Slow to react to plays to opposite (right) side. Plays
contain position well, protects against cut back by runner.
Heads up all the time, very seldom caught out of position. Has
Packer characteristic of taking full responsibility for individual area...does not cover up for or assist others.

Punishing tackler. Really stings 'em...

PASSING PLAYS. Maintains good position on receiver. Will
gamble for interception. Good speed and quickness. Left
handed, good hands, excellent anticipation of play. Will look
at QB, quick to analyse situation. Has vision to watch both
receiver and QB. Always sees ball.

*Use moving patterns on him. No curls or hooks.
Plays your tendencies. Will try for interception
on curl in and outs if you run more than once.*

Vulnerable to new patterns first time around. Will spot it
second time. More susceptible to corner patterns than Jeter.
Throw short to Adderley, long to Jeter. Neither weak, short
or deep, but Jeter covers tighter. Adderley punishes receiver
on short passes.

*Send receiver on patterns Adderley hasn't seen
lately. But it had better work the first time!!*

SPECIAL TEAMS. Teams with Travis Williams on kickoff returns.
Has excellent speed, is good blocker. Occasionally starts up
middle then swings wide to daylight.
Outside man on PAT and FG defense. Very quick, capable of
blocking kick if not bumped. Also outside man on kickoff and
punt coverage teams...speed again big factor.

fenses. For many years, Herb Adderley's trademark was the long interception, the quick karate chop that could turn a game around in a few seconds. Adderley keeps his own book on playing the receivers, and some of his observations are worth noting:

ON CHICAGO'S JOHNNY MORRIS IN 1964, THE YEAR HE SET AN NFL RECORD WITH 92 CATCHES: "I play him loose for maybe the first six or seven steps. He's going to throw a few fakes at me, but he's got to make the final move sometime. When he commits himself and I've played him correctly, I'll have a good shot at breaking up the pass. Timing is the key." (Adderley held him to two catches in the final game in '64.)

ON GARY COLLINS: "I've had more trouble with Collins than any other receiver, and when Frank Ryan was throwing to him, this was the best combination I saw. They had great timing and you couldn't crowd Collins. The young receivers will tip you off by looking in the direction they're going to run. But Collins keeps his head down and keeps you guessing. Collins will also disguise his charge, so you don't know whether he's going deep or short."

ON JOHN UNITAS: "Unitas is more of a gambler and I'm a gambler, too. Maybe that accounts for my success against the Colts" (In a crucial game in 1965, Unitas beat Adderley with a 57-yard TD pass to Jimmy Orr, but Adderley came back with two interceptions, the second for a 44-yard TD. The Packers won, 20-17.)

ON THE POST PATTERN: (A deep pattern in which the receiver starts straight downfield and then breaks inside, diagonally, toward the goal posts.) "It's the most feared pattern in football. You're outside conscious most of the time, so if the receiver cuts for the middle and catches the ball going away from me, it can usually be six points. A quarterback like Ryan did a great job throwing the ball on this play. He threw a high pass that was either caught or overthrown. It's almost impossible to break up without getting called for interference."

ON AGING: "I've changed my style of play a little. I used to back straight up and wait for the receiver to make his move. Now I turn to the side and get ready to run. Kids coming out of school these days are so doggoned fast that if you back up they're on you and gone. I want to play as long as I feel good and as long as I feel I can do the job. How I feel mentally is very important, too. When the time comes that I think I can't cover this guy or that guy, it's time to get out of the game, because if you think that way, it's going to happen."

Adderley's greatness comes from his speed (he was a hurdles champion at Michigan State), his great instincts and moves, his knowledge of offense (he was an offensive halfback in college), and his size. But there's another factor. He played on the left side, behind Dave Robinson, an All-NFL corner linebacker, and Robinson, in turn, played behind Willie Davis, an All-NFL defensive end. The great pressure that Davis exerted allowed Robinson occasionally to loosen up and drift back into the short, wide-pass lanes, where his 6-4, 245-pound frame presented a definite obstacle to the quarterback's line of vision. This allowed Adderley greater freedom than most cornerbacks enjoy.

"Pass defense is a coordination between the rush and the coverage," Ewbank says. "The linemen must pressure the passer, so the cornerbacks' job isn't so tough, but you can't have the rush unless the coverage is there, too. If the backs are playing too loose, the quarterback can throw quick passes for yardage and he isn't affected by the rush that much."

"The boys today are smart," the Lions' great cornerback, Night Train Lane, once said. "They throw head fakes at you, body fakes. They make a study of the game, too. I can follow two fakes. But when they throw three of them at you . . . well, it means somebody isn't getting to the quarterback."

One machine that the cornerbacks can't really lean on too heavily is the movie projector. When you see a team on film, you can't measure emotional intensity. Nor speed.

"It's hard to judge a man on film," said Bobby Boyd, an NFL cornerback for nine years. "You don't get the small things, the intangibles. Like how your man comes off the ball, whether he looks at the quarterback, his gestures, movements and expressions that you catch only when you've worked on him head to head.

"You can't pick up speed off the films, but speed alone wasn't that much of a problem to me. The thing I don't want to see in an opponent is quickness. It's the guy who can barrel down at you, then break it off quickly, who means trouble."

Before the 1969 Super Bowl against the Jets, Boyd and the rest of the Colt defensive backs took great pride in the team's ability to shut off the long touchdown pass, the bomb. It was the mark of the good zone defense team.

"Not one bomb has been dropped on us all season," Boyd said. "They all kept plugging, but none connected. Dallas—heck, they threw four bombs at us and we came up with four interceptions."

This is the epitome of the zone defense theory. Slightly less permissive is the traditional NFL-Green Bay method of man-to-man coverage, the seven-yard-deep principle that Bengtson calls the Fisherman Theory.

"The idea is to give the enemy the short ones and wait for his mistake. Be patient and shut off the score, not every gain.

"It's terribly frustrating for our defensive backs to do what is right when their human nature, their buddies on the sidelines yelling, 'C'mon, you guys, grab that thing,' and their fans all tell them differently. Like patient fishermen, they have to wait until just the right minute to make their catch. If they wait, the quarterback is eventually going to misthrow a pass and they can pick it off without getting out of position or committing themselves to the ball instead of the man."

The AFL was a young, impatient league, though, and its theory of pass defense, the bump-and-go principle, reflected that impatience. The idea behind it is total annihilation, turning off all the lights.

The cornerback lines up a yard or so off the line of scrimmage and bumps the receiver as he makes his first move, tries to knock him out of his regular route. Then he has to stay with him the rest of the way downfield. All you need in order to be a good bump-and-go cornerback is roughness, the size to apply it effectively, the speed to recover and chase, and the emotional makeup that permits you to take the field knowing that if you miss the bump, your man can be long gone.

It's a frightening concept, but certain AFL teams have had success with it. Oakland is perhaps the best bump-and-go team. Kent McCloughan started the practice a few years ago, and Willie Brown is the best in the business at it right now. San Diego's Speedy Duncan is a little guy, but he has been a bump-and-go man for years. His overwhelming speed bails him out. John Dockery is only a baby in the league, but he is a bump-and-go cornerback. Kansas City's Jimmy Marsalis played bump-and-go even as a rookie in 1969, but his style was more of the "influence" technique, steering his man into places he didn't care to be.

"An Arthur Murray dancing instructor," was the way the Jets' Don Maynard described Marsalis. "He dances you all over the field."

Everyone is united in praise when Brown's name is mentioned.

"He doesn't give you a thing," Joe Namath says. "He tries to take away the short pattern, so the receiver can usually get half a step on him on the deep one. But Willie's reaction is so good that if the pass isn't perfectly thrown, you can't complete it. He's the best."

The emotional advantage of the bump-and-go style, or of man-to-man coverages in general, is that a player who responds to challenge will enjoy the idea of direct confrontation with the enemy, rather than the more nebulous zone theory. Bob Cousy once described the idea in basketball, when someone asked him why he taught man-to-man rather than zone defense at Boston College. The same applies to pass defense.

"When you give a young, competitive athlete a straightforward assignment, like a man to guard, and say, 'Here he is. He's yours. Go get him,' " Cousy said, "the guy will generally respond better than when you assign him a zone to cover. He gets up for the man. He says to himself, 'Dammit, I'm going to shut that guy out.' He'll be diligent when you give him a zone, and he'll want to help the team and all that, but the adrenalin just won't be flowing the same way."

The zone defense in football provides an important psychological advantage, though. It gives the defense the "hidden" interception, the unexpected one, when a free safetyman or a linebacker comes swooping out of a blind spot in the passer's vision and picks off the ball. It can destroy the QB's concentration—and his execution—for the next few series, or for the rest of the game.

"The year I led the league with 10 interceptions," says the Cardinals' free safety, Larry Wilson, "I got them all out of a zone defense, a strong-side rotation. The quarterback looked downfield and thought he saw an open man. But he wasn't really open because I was coming just as hard the other way."

Safetymen aren't drafted into the pros. A team drafts a cornerback, and if he doesn't have the speed for head-to-head coverage, or the temperament for it, he turns into a safetyman, a free safety if it's discovered he has a nose and an instinct for the ball, a strong, or tight, safetyman if he's bigger and rougher—and slower. Sometimes free safeties are discovered by an accident—a great move in practice, an instinctive break-off of a coverage into a more profitable route.

"There comes that special moment when it's time to go for the ball and instinct takes over," Christiansen once said. "In that moment, great free safetymen are made."

"I learned early," said the Raiders' Dave Grayson, an All-AFL cornerback who became an All-AFL free safety, "to watch the receiver, the tight end, and the quarterback as the play develops. I learned to tell by the arc of the ball where it was going and what the descent would be like."

"I always knew that a free safetyman is supposed to watch the quarterback and the receiver, too, but it was always difficult for me," said the Steelers' Paul Martha. "Old pro quarterbacks like Unitas and Jurgensen would look me off the guy they were throwing to. Then all of a sudden, midway through the 1967 season, I realized I was following the quarterback all the way—and the receiver, too. It just happened. It was like I had stepped into an entirely new dimension."

Cornerbacks who become free safeties often feel like the coal miner who kisses the ground when he gets a job on the surface.

"Say I'm covering Dave Williams of the Cards," says Atlanta's Jimmy Burson, "and I shut him out on nine of 10 plays, but on the tenth he catches one for a TD. The reception I'd get from the fans wouldn't be too nice. They'd all blame me for it. Now the free safety doesn't have all that responsibility, that one-on-one coverage; consequently he's not as conspicuous when he makes a mistake. Everyone sees a cornerback's mistakes."

It's possible for the offense to isolate free safeties in one-on-one coverage, but it takes some readjusting to do it. In 1969 the Jets flanked halfback Emerson Boozer on one side and tight end Pete Lammons on the other, with George Sauer and Don Maynard, the normal wide men, stationed inside them. This was against the Oakland Raiders, and the Raiders responded by assigning Grayson to Boozer and tight safety George Atkinson to Lammons, leaving the cornerbacks to their normal coverage—Sauer and Maynard. The Jets weren't trying to pick on Grayson. They merely wanted to get him away from Maynard and Sauer, pin him down in a restricted coverage area so he couldn't free-lance and interfere with Namath's passes to his two favorite receivers.

What happens, though, when an offense resorts to such a gimmick, is that it is going away from what it normally does best—passing to its regular wide men from a regular alignment. Maynard and Sauer were working out of unfamiliar "slot" positions, and Boozer and Lammons didn't catch a pass between them from the wide spots. The formation didn't last for the whole game anyway. It was just a "mixer."

Another method of isolating a free safetyman is to "slot" a wide receiver, or line him up on the same side as the other flanker, slightly inside him. Some defenses cover this by swinging the cornerback over to the other side of the field to stay with the man he was originally responsible for, wherever that receiver may pop up on the field. But the Jets' theory is to keep the cornerback in the territory he knows best and let a safetyman, who is more familiar with the terrain around the middle of the field, cover the slotted receiver.

The Chiefs slotted 6-3, 215-pound Otis Taylor against the Jets in two different games in 1969. They got a Taylor vs. Baird overmatch, and pulled two long gainers out of the move, one for a touchdown.

The bigger and slower tight safeties sometimes get this treatment, too, but if a defensive coach has a slow man as his tight safety, he doesn't usually trust him with man-to-man coverage on a slotted wide receiver.

The tight safeties invariably give away pounds and inches to the tight ends they cover, and this can cause a physical overmatch—particularly if the tight end isn't "jammed" or held up at the line or if the quarterback has plenty of time to hit him. A great defensive end, though, can nullify the effectiveness of a tight end as a pass receiver, if the tight end has to stay on the line to help the offensive tackle block the troublesome character.

"Who throws to their tight ends against us?" says the Rams' strong safety, Richie Petitbon. "The ends are all too busy blocking

Deacon Jones. Playing behind the Deacon will add three years to my career."

An exceptional strong safetyman can do wonderful things for a defense, as the Jets found out when they lost Jim Hudson during the 1969 season. In 1968 Hudson was a combination safetyman-linebacker. He was fast enough to stay with any tight end in the league, and big and strong enough—and a vicious enough tackler—to come up close to the line and work as a linebacker. As a matter of fact the Jets often worked Hudson into what amounted to a pure 4-4 defense, four linebackers and four linemen, in '68.

"It's a shame," Michaels said, "that people learned about the true value of Hudson only after we lost him."

Finally there's the safety blitz, the ultimate in devilry, a move that sends the free safetyman charging out of nowhere to put a rush on the quarterback. It is football's most daring gamble, a pure surprise move that relies on the skinniness and speed of the safetyman to squeeze him between the blocking linemen. Larry Wilson was a master at it.

"We don't do it much anymore," Wilson said in 1969. "You really need experienced people back there to cover up the hole you've left, and we have a young secondary. Coach Drulis started it here and I was lucky enough to be the guy to be here to do it. Nobody knew what I was doing at first. I hit a different hole each time. Now the linemen are catching on and they'll slide block and take your head off."

His craggy face lit up as he reminisced about the good old days.

"I sure enjoyed it, though. It was really fun. It was a chance to get back at the quarterback, the guy who stands around all day smiling at you."

10
The Games Kickers Play

Let's face it; this isn't a very good life if your team keeps kicking from the end zone, where you have to run so far from the bench.

□ Sam Baker

In 1966, the New York Jets beat Denver, 16-7, and nine of the points came on Jim Turner's three field goals.

"Nice kicking," Weeb Ewbank said after the game.

"Nice kicking," said backfield coach Clive Rush.

"Nice kicking, Jim," said PR man Frank Ramos.

"Frank," Turner said, "you're the only guy who said anything to me about it."

"What are you talking about?" Ramos said. "Weeb and Clive Rush just told you, 'nice kicking.' "

"Is that right? Were they talking to me? I thought they meant Curley Johnson's punts."

Turner spent four years with the Jets until he really felt that his job was secure. What pushed him over the top was an all-time professional record of 34 field goals in 1968. The next year he kicked 32. Moody and introverted, he lives in his own little area that is measured by wind currents and tufts of grass and bald spots on the field.

People have learned to leave him alone.

"I don't want anyone talking to me during a game, unless it's something about the field that I might have missed," said Turner, who is no stranger than any of the kickers. "I stand in my own area at the end of the bench. People don't get too close to me. Sometimes the rookies will come over and say something at the beginning of the season, but they learn to leave me alone, too.

"In practice I check the wind in all parts of the field. I keep a record of how it blows at different hours. I can tell you what the stadium grass is like in September and late and early October and every other time of the year. Look, this is my business, my bread and butter. One inch can mean a ball game."

Turner probably will never feel completely secure, despite his records. (Only five men in history have kicked more field goals.) He has seen too many strange things happen in his six years with the Jets.

In 1966 he went 18 for 35 on field goals, a slight drop in percentage from 1965. He was having contract troubles, too, so the Jets' 1967 training camp was marked by a progression of soccer-style sidewinder kickers.

"We don't let them try out while the whole squad is watching," said George Sauer, Sr., who had to supervise the weird crew. "It's not good for morale."

So Turner brooded, but he didn't have to worry. The results were more humorous than ominous.

A German kicker brought a little book of clippings with him. He had been the star of the New York German-American Soccer League, and around the Eintracht Oval people were whispering that he couldn't miss. He took the book with him when he left the Jets' camp 20 minutes later. The grass was too high, he said.

A 19-year-old high-school graduate asked Ewbank, "Should I kick 'em left-footed or right-footed? I can do it either way."

"Just kick the damn ball," the coach said. The switch-kicker lasted about five minutes.

An Englishman planned to make it a big-money affair. He brought his agent with him, and they sat in the stands before practice, a sporty-looking young man and a little bald-headed gentleman of 50, with a potbelly. The bald-headed guy was the kicker. He had a unique style—grass skimmers. They never went a foot above the turf.

"Damn 10-percenters," Ewbank said that night. "Those agents ought to know better, pulling a stunt like that."

The widely traveled Booth Lusteg put in an appearance one day while the Jets were practicing in New York's Randalls Island Stadium, so he and Turner had a head-to-head battle, winner take all. Turner won that one, too.

"Well, what am I supposed to do when these guys show up and tell me they can kick 10 out of 10 from the 50?" Ewbank said. "Chase 'em away? Suppose one of them catches on with another pro team and does great. You newspaper guys would blast me from here to kingdom come."

It's probably the weirdest position in professional sports—punter and kicker. You need absolutely no knowledge of the sport to be successful in it. With the old 33-man roster, places on the squad were too valuable to be squandered on a pure specialist, but the 40-man limit provides him with an entrée. If he can do something else, too, if he can play a little, so much the better. Coaches and general managers are always looking for bargains. But an accurate foot will draw a professional football paycheck (granted kickers and punters are the most poorly paid of any players) even if the player can barely walk or hobble onto the field.

"I feel like I have a free ticket to all the games," says Atlanta's 5-10, 150-pound Bob Etter, nicknamed The Athlete by his coach, Norm Van Brocklin. "I sit there on the sidelines where you can hear all the hitters and pick up knowledge for a future coaching career."

Englishmen and Norwegians, Cypriots and Germans, anyone who has ever kicked a soccer ball will get a look. The Cowboys even tried to make a punter out of Colin Ridgeway, an Australian high jumper.

Denver coach Lou Saban, whose kicker is a tiny Englishman named Bobby Howfield, tells about the time his team came from behind to beat Cincinnati.

"When we scored the winning TD, Bobby was all over me yelling, 'Great chaps! Great chaps!' Then he took off for the end zone and started pounding the players and congratulating them. We had to chase after him all the way down to the end zone and tell him to get in there and kick the extra point."

Sometimes they get delusions of grandeur. After he tied an NFL record with six field goals in a game, the Lions' Garo Yepremian, a 160-pound Cypriot, remarked, "A day will come when I won't miss from 50 yards, but I'm one year away."

When last heard from, Garo was kicking them in the Continental League.

At times their thinking is on a different wavelength from the rest of the team.

"You stand on the sidelines and watch the team drive," said Minnesota's Fred Cox, one of the few field goal kickers who was actually drafted (most come in as free agents or foreign exchange students). "If we make the first down a couple of times with a break or two, you get the feeling that the luck won't hold out. You just have the feeling that the drive is going to stall. Then you start concentrating."

Philadelphia's 40-year-old Sam Baker, a loquacious fellow off the field, says he doesn't talk to other kickers . . . except once, to Charlie Gogolak of the Redskins.

"We were walking off the field one Sunday and the fans were booing us and he said, 'These fans don't know anything. Don't worry about them.' He was just trying to be friendly. My, he's a young-looking fellow."

The pressures can be unbearable. It's one of the hazards of the business.

"A kicker only wears one hat," Turner says. "Hero or goat. You can't say, 'Well, I had a pretty good game.' You either make that winning 40-yarder with 30 seconds to go or you muff it."

"A passer can miss a pass, then come right back on the next play," Baker says. "A guy can miss a block and come back. But if I miss a field goal, I can't say, 'Just watch, I'll kick this one.' "

"I looked down at my holder, Eddie Meador, and I had trouble breathing," the Rams' Bruce Gossett says about a 25-yarder he once kicked to beat Green Bay in the last 55 seconds.

"I said to Eddie, 'I'm scared.' He said the same thing. I figured if I missed it I'd miss it good. It took off like a bullet and must have landed 30 rows up in the stands."

There's even a weird history connected with the longest field goal on record—the Colts' Bert Rechichar's 56-yarder against the Bears in 1953.

"I was down on the field right near the end of the half," says former Baltimore general manager, Don Kellett. "Bert started walking toward the dressing room with me. They had sent Buck McPhail in to try a field goal, but all of a sudden somebody yelled, 'Bert!' and he said, 'What the hell do they want me for?'

" 'Get in there and kick it!' the guy yelled, so Bert did. All he did was set the record. To this day I don't think he'd have made it had he known how far it was. He didn't know and didn't even have time to think about it."

How important is the kicking game? Kansas City coach Hank Stram says it can decide four to six games a season, "and that's factual evidence," he says.

"By that I mean all phases of the kicking game. If a team doesn't have a good punter and kicker, it's in trouble. Look at the teams that have been successful through the years. They've had three things: a quarterback, good defense, and the kicking game. I have seen too many fine teams with excellent offenses and defenses blow a game on a punt return, a blocked field goal, or a weak punt."

The 1969 figures bear him out. Minnesota had the NFL's leading punter and its leading field goal kicker, percentagewise. Kansas City had the AFL's top field goal percentage man, Jan Stenerud, and its third leading punter, two-tenths of a yard behind the leader.

"Stenerud really put the pressure on our defense," the Vikings' Carl Eller said after the 1970 Super Bowl. "He makes you feel you can't give up a thing because he's so dangerous from anywhere inside the 50. I think he was the MVP in the game."

It has always been a mystery to me why the field goal output in the old days of the fatter football wasn't much greater than it is today. A greater kicking surface is always a help to a kicker, and some teams try to sneak practice balls into the game for field goal tries. Balls that have been kicked around a while in practice tend to fatten up.

"The Raiders tried it in one game against us," Turner said, "and the officials spotted it and threw it out. The Raiders said they were just trying to save the cost of a new ball kicked into the stands."

Most kickers preferred the NFL ball, which was slightly rounder than the streamlined AFL ball. But in the last three years that the two leagues used separate footballs, the AFL was ahead on both volume of field goals and percentage.

In 1969 the AFL teams averaged 18.6 field goals for the season, an all-time record, and the combined AFL-NFL average came out to 16.9 per team. They made good on better than 55 percent of them, too. But until 1964, 50 percent was a rarity; in fact it was only accomplished five times by the combined NFL kickers for a season, and never before 1951.

And in the thirties and forties it got downright ridiculous. The All-America Football Conference, with talented booters such as Lou Groza and Ben Agajanian, was known as a kicker's league. Each AAFC team, during the league's four years of existence (1946–49), averaged 5.2 field goals per season. And that's for the whole team. But it was still better than the footless NFL, which in 1943 showed each team averaging two field goals out of eight and a half tries—for the season. There were teams in those days which went 0-for-2 for the whole year, and in 1943 Don Hutson and the Giants' Ward Cuff led the NFL in field goals with three apiece, which was what Stenerud kicked in the first half of the 1970 Super Bowl.

So what was the matter with those old teams and their fat ball which should have been so ideal for kicking? Well, for one thing, field goal kicking wasn't something that a kid would practice in high school and college, knowing that if he got good enough he could make it into the pros on just his leg. The kickers had to be players, too, and a dedicated player just didn't have much time to bother with the boots.

If people wanted to kick, they worked on punting, and the punters of those years averaged about what they do now. Except that people ran those early punts back twice as far. The NFL punt return average in 1941, for example, was 12.7 yards. In 1969 it was 6.4, and it has not been above 10 since 1952. Until then, it was never below 10.

The high averages generally came from quick kicks, which were a great part of the game. It was easier in those days, when the single wing tailback was back there anyway, but today's punters don't go much for yardage. They try to keep the ball high to discourage runbacks. Sam Baugh, who set the pro football punting record back in 1940 (51.3 average), got a lot of help from the roll on his quick kicks. And he only kicked on occasion. The Redskins punted 66 times that year, and 35 of the punts were by Sammy.

The big breakthrough has been in the area of field goal kicking, though, and it has gotten to the point where one club claims it has a full-time scout touring Europe. This gentleman supposedly keeps an eye out for young soccer players who might have the right leg for field goals, and slips them a football now and then for a little practice.

The soccer-style kickers were led into the league by Hungarian-born Pete Gogolak, who kicked for Buffalo in 1964 and '65. In '65 he broke the AFL record for field goals, and soon became a *cause célèbre* when the Giants opened the AFL-NFL player stealing warfare by grabbing him from Buffalo. The merger came a year later, and it might have all been triggered by a kicker, and one who swung his foot sidesaddle at that.

The emergence of the side-footed soccer kickers promoted a whole rash of aerodynamics and time-motion studies about the ideal way of footing a ball. So far the results are inconclusive. The side-footers haven't taken over the game, as was originally feared. They coexist with the traditionals. *Sports Illustrated* once sponsored an overseas contest in which two Americans, Baker and Mike Mercer, took on the cream of the British rugby and soccer crop. Mercer won, but there were too many variables (lack of familiarity with the American ball, weather, etc.) attached to the contest for it to prove anything.

"I don't study myself that closely, and I don't have any set technique," says Norwegian-born Stenerud, a side-footer. "I hit it with my instep instead of my toe, so maybe that gives us a greater surface to hit the ball with. I wear soccer-style short cleats, but they are no good on a muddy day, because my left foot, the one that is planted, will slip.

"Kicking is more natural to Europeans anyway. Give a European boy a ball and his first instinct is to kick it, not to throw it. If a European starts kicking an American football, he'll probably be better than an American who has never done it before. I can't help but think there must be someone, somewhere, maybe in Asia, who can kick the football even better than me, because I never thought about kicking a football until I tried. The first time I kicked one, I kicked it almost as well as I'm doing now."

"I think the soccer style permits you to kick farther," Gogolak says. "For accuracy, straight ahead is just as good. Our way we can put much more power into the ball. Think of the swinging motion of hitting a golf ball. You put your body into it. But the straight-on kicker seems to punch the ball with his foot."

The hunt for kickers goes on. The Chiefs, even after they had drafted Stenerud, held a sort of European kicking junket, probably more for goodwill than anything else. They will never match the Cowboys, though, whose famous Kicking Karavan in April, 1970, covered 10,000 miles and 1,400 candidates, none of whom stuck with the Cowboys.

"They spent $72,000 looking for a kicker and then wound up trading a draft choice for Mike Clark," Baker said. "I'd like to have that $72,000."

Drafting kickers is always a gamble. For instance, the college kicker uses a higher kicking tee, and people wonder how he'll do with the lower one. The tee was given as the reason for the failure of Detroit's Jerry DePoyster, a No. 2 draft. The Lions bailed out, though, with Errol Mann, who had been cut by Denver, Cleveland, and Green Bay, who had had two knee operations, but who caught on with Detroit. Someone once asked him what was different about Detroit.

"No knee operations," he said. "Good holder."

Kickers with sense stay on good terms with their holders—and the centers, too.

"A holder can kill you if he wants to," says Turner, who has probably the best in the business in Babe Parilli. "He can give you the white knuckle—hold the ball down real hard when you get your toe into it—or he can tilt it just half an inch one way or another. Then the whole equation goes kaboom!"

The Cards' Jim Bakken, for instance, says that a change of holders killed his whole 1966 season. He was 15 for 19 through the first nine games, until Charley Johnson, his holder, got hurt, along with center Bob DeMarco. Bakken went eight for his next 21.

"Laces are your worst enemy," says Turner, who buys Parilli and center, John Schmitt, a box of Bering Imperial cigars at the end of the season. "They give you a bad surface. The holder's got to spin the ball before you swing your leg, and he has to bring it down, all in the same movement—within a second. In two years I've seen laces once, and that was on an extra point and it didn't matter."

Studies have hit on 1.2 to 1.5 seconds as the time a kicker safely has to get his boot away without fear of getting it blocked. The optimum distance is between six and seven yards back of the line, based on studies of the angle of the defensive charge, etc.

Most kickers don't kick much in practice or during the off-season. They keep their leg strong through weights or bike riding (Turner has developed his own exercise that involves stepping up and down on a simulated stairway) and figure they'll get their timing in training camp. The good ones check all the game conditions to reduce the margin of error as much as possible.

"We practice at Shea Stadium at the same time as the games, which is a good thing," Turner said. "It gives me an accurate reading on the winds. On Sunday I'm in the game all the time—or at least my head is. I watch every play to see where they're chewing up the field. Joe Namath is very good about that. He asks me every time he comes out where the bad spots are. He's one guy I talk to during the games."

Psychology plays a big part in it, especially with a man as jittery as Turner. Before the 1968 Oakland game, Al Davis, the Raiders' semiowner, semicoach, made the officials examine Turner's shoe, to see if it was legal.

"Sure it shook me up," Turner said. "Then after the game I asked Davis what the hell he did it for. He knew there was nothing wrong with my shoe. He said, 'Why, Jim, you know I didn't do that.' Right to my face. He's amazing."

The NFL's supervisor of officials, Mark Duncan, periodically checks the shoes and throws out the ones with metal in them, or the ones that are double-laced.

"I've looked at some shoes," he says, "that were so heavy I could hardly lift them."

Coaches are always on the lookout for combination kicker-punters. It's Bargain Day when they find one. Don Chandler used to handle both jobs in Green Bay. So did Sam Baker in Philadelphia.

One day Sam was on the practice field, intoning the various kicking credos for a writer. First he gave the place-kicker's standard: "Bend the knee, lock the ankle; bend the knee, lock the ankle." And then the punter's manifesto: "Get the power from the knee and arch the instep." And then he mixed them up: "Lock the knee and arch the instep."

The coffin-corner kick—the punt that goes out of bounds deep in enemy territory—has become a lost art. But the punting game has still become refined and polished, ever since the Browns' Horace Gillom started standing a full 15 yards back (in the late 1940's) rather than the standard 10 to 12 yards.

Watch a coach during punting practice sometime. He'll most likely have a stopwatch with him. He's timing two things, the time it takes between the center's snap and the sound of the kick, and the amount of time the punted ball stays in the air. Either one can be more important than the actual distance of the kick. A quicker delivery means that there will be fewer blocked. It will also mean that the returns will be cut down because the punting team can use smaller, quicker men to cover the kicks, since the defense doesn't have to be held out as long. And the punting team can send more men downfield to cover the punts.

If a punter's boot hangs in the air 4.6 to 5.0 seconds, his job is safe. Few ever stay up much longer than five seconds (Gillom's punts were consistent five-second jobs). Punting into a wind can often be a help, since the wind lifts the nose of the ball and keeps it up longer. A trailing wind can drive it down quicker, often nullifying the advantage in distance.

"The quicker the ball gets to the receiver," Vince Lombardi says, "the quicker it gets back."

A punter will usually do better in a warm climate than a cold one, since his leg feels looser. The ball will carry better in a dry area than a humid one. And Denver, of course, with its thin air, is the punter's Valhalla. Sometimes a punter's average drops between college and pro football, which mystifies some people.

"In college you play in football stadiums where the winds are constant," says Green Bay's Donny Anderson. "In the pros you play in baseball parks with high stands and swirling winds."

Anderson adds a tip to punters—get the right kind of off-season job.

"I had a bad year punting, my junior year in college," he says. "All that summer I had a job for Reed Roller Bit, driving around all day in a car, sometimes 12 hours a day. This was supposed to be the best job they had for a football player at Texas Tech. E. J. Holub had it and Dave Parks had it. But when I started punting in the fall, I felt like I had nothing in my leg at all.

"Next summer I worked for an insurance company in Lubbock [Texas] and I stayed out of cars. I could tell the difference right off."

Stay out of cars, stay out of bars, and if you're a field goal kicker, always buy cigars for your holder. And if you just happen to be passing through Yugoslavia and you see a great big youngster kicking a soccer ball 80 yards, slip him a pigskin and see what happens.

11
Sunday's Madmen: The Suicide Squad

Everyone has some fear. A man without fear belongs in a mental institution—or on special teams, either one.

□ Walt Michaels

Let's put it this way. It helps to know what you're doing, but it don't take no brains.

□ Don Fullmer, describing his job as utility man
in the Kennecott Copper Refinery

It sounds innocent enough. It even has a scientific ring. "Special teams." Run down the field on kickoffs. Help block for the man returning those kicks. Punt and be punted to. Block for the place-kicker, or try to block the other team's kicks. Not bad, right? But when I see those special team specialists earning their $15,000 a year, I start thinking about Henry Schmidt.

Schmidt was a reserve tackle on the 1966 Jets for a few weeks. His eight-year pro career had taken him in and out of four camps, and by the time he hit New York he was just about playing out the string. His salary was $15,000. I used to get a kick out of studying Henry Schmidt. His face was craggy and lined, and when he would get out of the team bus after a 15-minute airport trip, his battered knees cramped and aching, he would hobble like a 60-year-old man.

When the Jets finally cut him, I was surprised to see that he was only 28. He looked like 40. And then I remembered who Henry Schmidt was. Schmidt was the greatest "hot man" I'd ever seen in my life.

The hot man is the wedge-buster on the kickoff teams, also called special teams . . . or specialty teams . . . or "money" teams (to be kind) . . . or simply "teams." The players call it the suicide squad, because the injury rate is so high. And hot man is the most suicidal of suicide squad positions, because the only requirements for the job are speed, size, and an absolute willingness to hurl himself at the four big men that form the wedge in front of the kick returns.

A ballcarrier on the special teams takes his lumps, but he always has the option of downing the ball in the end zone or fair-catching a punt. A hot man has no options. He hits people every time, as hard as he can.

If he's extra good, he might wade through the wedge and somehow pressure the ballcarrier. If he's a superman, he might make a tackle. And those rare tackles are things you frame and nail to the wall, because the hot man is usually going at top speed, completely out of control. When a ballcarrier is hit by the hot man, he sails.

I saw Schmidt in his rookie year with San Francisco in 1959, and if you can picture a guided missile, 6-4, 260 pounds, zeroing in on a target and totally destroying it, that was Henry. He'd split the wedge like kindling, and if he didn't smash into the ballcarrier himself, he'd fly by him at such speed that the poor guy would certainly remember Henry the Hot Man the next time he fielded a kick.

Seven years later I saw what all that wedge-busting had done to Schmidt, and the only miracle was how he had managed to survive as long as he did.

The special teams are the Lafayette Escadrille of pro football. Lift high your glasses, men, for tomorrow we face the Red Baron.

"Lord, don't ever phone me the day after a game," says the Jets' kick and punt returner, Mike Battle, nicknamed Punchy Mike or Joe Don Battle. "I'll either be still getting drunk or lookin' for bail. When you're on a suicide team like I am, you don't wait till next week to start living."

"Momentum. Momentum is what causes the greatest number of injuries in pro football," says the Jets' team physician, Dr. James Nicholas. "Center is a relatively safe position because the contacts come when the momentum is low. The injury rate there is low, and by injury I mean something that disables you for two or more games or requires surgery. The injury rate on special teams is .035, about eight times higher than the next most dangerous position. That means that out of 100 contacts, or plays in which there is contact, you'll get hurt more than three times on special teams. You're going at close to 20 miles an hour, often out of control."

Kansas City's Stone Johnson raced upfield on a kickoff play and threw a block against Houston in a 1963 exhibition game. The impact damaged Johnson's spinal cord and fractured a cervical vertebra in his neck. Eight days later he died.

Special teams claimed the Jets' No. 1 draft choices for 1968 and '69: Lee White, a fullback, and Dave Foley, a tackle. Both injuries occurred in the first game of the season, and Foley's didn't even involve contact. He was running downfield at top speed; he pivoted to make a cut, and his knee collapsed. He was operated on, lost for the season.

"It's especially dangerous for linemen," Dr. Nicholas said. "Backs are used to open-field running and cutting, but linemen aren't."

"Special teams will tell you one thing," Vince Lombardi once said, "who wants to hit and who doesn't. You find out right away."

After the Jets drafted Al Atkinson, a defensive tackle from Villanova, they toyed with the idea of making a linebacker out of him. And while they were experimenting, they gave him the job of hot man on the kickoff team. Midway in Al's rookie season, the Jets beat Denver, 45-10, which meant that the Jets kicked off eight times.

Atkinson made five unassisted tackles on those eight kickoffs, possibly the greatest day a hot man has ever had. Three games later he was the Jets' starting middle linebacker.

"We had to get him off those special teams before he killed himself," Michaels said. "Or killed someone else."

"We were sorry to see him leave us, but glad, too, in a way," said reserve fullback Mark Smolinski, who was the unofficial captain of the special teams.

"I mean it's kind of an incentive type of thing, a contest to see who gets downfield first and into the ball carrier. Al didn't give the rest of us a chance.

"On special teams you've got to hit or be hit. You play with abandon; you turn your body completely loose. It's tough and you can get hurt, but it all boils down to pride. If you do it well, the hitting becomes contagious and carries over to the regular offense and defense."

Coaches spend time thinking up ways to make special teams attractive. They come up with catchy names, or the players do themselves, such as the Rams' Guillory's Gorillas, in honor of former special team captain Tony Guillory. But special teams can also be a special whip in the hands of management.

When the Jets' starting fullback Matt Snell became a salary problem in '68 and threatened not to play any exhibition games until his contract was signed, he got a taste of the kick return unit —second man in from the left on the wedge. He came around.

When the Packers' Jerry Kramer had trouble with his contract a few years before that, he suddenly found himself on the kicking team. He took out his frustrations on the Minnesota Vikings, made his point, and got his raise.

Blanton Collier says he found out about Leroy Kelly, the Browns' perennial All-NFL fullback, through special teams.

"I could see he was a good runner," Collier said shortly after he moved Kelly in for the retired Jimmy Brown. "He was fast, with good balance. But what really struck me was his toughness on kick coverage. He was a vicious tackler. I knew then we had ourselves a good boy."

Starters are occasionally used on punt teams, where the action is more confined and the contact not as sharp—except downfield. They'll pop us as blockers on the return team, since chance of injury is slightly less. But starters on the kickoff unit are a rare sight.

Bud Grant used five of his Viking offensive linemen on his kick return team in the 1970 Super Bowl, but only two starters—both of them defensive backs—on the team that kicked off. And Kansas City's Hank Stram used two linemen and a linebacker to block on the kick returns, but only one starter, cornerback Jimmy Marsalis, on coverage. But when things got tough in the AFL playoff game, Stram threw his 6-7, 275-pound defensive tackle, Buck Buchanan, on his kickoff unit. Buchanan has a history of doing interesting things on special teams.

"Once on a kickoff return a guy from Oakland was coming down my side and the ball was out of bounds or something," Buchanan says. "He got right beside me and I hollered 'Rraagh!' at him as loud as I could. It just scared the drawers off him. He jumped about 10 feet. You've got to shake these guys up to let them know you could have busted them one."

All positions on the kicking and return teams are numbered. On the kicking team they go L1, L2, L3, R1, R2, etc., according to the side of the kicker they are on—left or right—and where they are in relation to the sideline, one is the closest, two the second one in, and so on.

The returning team is generally broken up into four phalanxes. The front rank consists of three linemen, one of whom is assigned to the kicker if he's capable of making a tackle. The other two take the men on either side of the kicker, the wedge-busters.

Behind that front trio comes the wedge, four men tightly packed. They can be either linemen or heavy backs, but they must be good blockers. On either side of the front rank are the wings, generally ends or quick linemen. They have to be good open-field blockers, since they must pick off the wide men, in more open territory. Finally the two kick returners are stationed on the goal line. One fields the kick, the other one makes the call, telling him whether to down it or run it. The advice can be either heeded or ignored, depending on the situation and the personality of the people involved.

All teams have a few plays they can use in their kick returning, and Friday or Saturday is usually kick day, the time they polish those plays. In 1967 the Packers' Travis Williams broke two long kickoff returns for touchdowns against Cleveland. Two weeks later he broke a 69-yarder against Chicago, and two weeks after that, a 104-yarder against Los Angeles. His average of 41.1 per return was the highest in history. Jerry Kramer says it was the crisscross system of blocking by the front three men that sprung Williams. It was a variation on the normal straight-on approach, and the gaps caused by the angle blocks opened the holes for Williams, according to Kramer. The play looks like this (see Fig. 9.)

No special treatment was afforded the kicker, other than the normal straight-ahead wedge, because it was assumed that even if he were left alone, he couldn't handle Williams in an open field. If

Fig. 9

Packers' Cross-Block,
Kick-Return Play

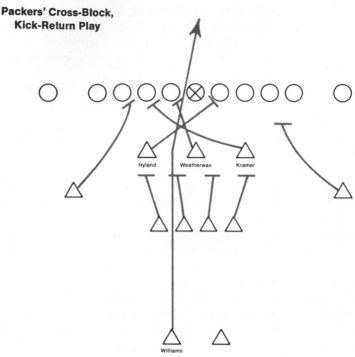

or

a kicker can also play the game, he might be assigned the job of safetyman, in which case he backs up and takes anything that gets through. But a Pete or Charlie Gogolak isn't entrusted with such responsibility, and a permanently assigned safety will back up and keep them company.

Some kickers, such as Detroit linebacker Wayne Walker, head downfield after they kick and play it as any other lineman would. And the Browns' Lou Groza, even when he was fortyish and pot-bellied, considered it a point of honor to get downfield and try to establish himself somewhere in the vicinity of the ball carrier.

The men assigned to cover kicks used to be big and durable, people who were able to take a pounding. But more and more backs are finding their way into the unit, and the little guys who used to man only the L1, L2, R1, R2 positions are now moving as far inside as fourth man. The theory is that shiftiness, open field tackling ability, and ability to avoid blockers are more important than brute strength, although the 250-pound hot man will never be replaced.

It was that reevaluated thinking that brought a Super Bowl and AFL playoff check into the pocket of John Dockery, a 185-pound defensive back who was ending the season with the minor league Bridgeport (Connecticut) Jets when he heard the call from above.

The San Diego Chargers' Speedy Duncan had just broken a 96-yard punt return against the Jets, and Ewbank figured that the best way to shore up his coverage unit would be to bring in somebody sleek and fast. He checked the farm team, decided on Dockery, and activated him for the last three games of the season, just enough playing time to qualify him for the championship game and the Super Bowl.

"I wrote Speedy a letter of thanks," Dockery said. "Next time I see him I'm going to buy him all the beers he can hold."

Every kick- and punt-return man has his own style. It can be the freewheeling mayhem of Mike Battle, or the studious approach of Herb Adderley ("I try to get a visual picture of how they're bearing down. Sometimes I try to draw them in at the wedge in the middle. Then if I can get the end man too close, so he commits himself too soon, I figure with my speed I might be able to turn the corner before he can recover").

Battle made the Jets as a rookie, and his showpiece effort was an 87-yard punt return against the Giants in the big exhibition game in the Yale Bowl. Battle, traveling at top speed, hurdled punter Dave Lewis, and spent the rest of the season trying unsuccessfully to match that one glorious move.

"I've got to get that kid to stop doing that," Ewbank said after

Battle had broken his nose for the second time. "One of these days they'll carry him off in a basket."

"Well, he punished other people, too," someone said.

"Oh yeah?" said Ewbank. "I haven't seen anyone carried off yet."

A good, quick back is often the most valuable man for blocking place kicks. Adderley was a master at this specialized art. He used to go easy the first couple of times, lulling people to sleep, but when the big one came, he'd turn it on and sometimes catch the kicking team napping. "The best side to rush from," Adderley says, "is my own right side. That's the open side. It isn't shielded by the holder's body."

"Adderley made a play that was close to superhuman," Norm Van Brocklin said after Herb had blocked a field goal against his Atlanta Falcons.

"There was nothing particularly wrong with our execution of the field goal. Adderley just willed himself into blocking it."

Usually, though, blocked kicks come from the inside, from the "alley." This free ticket opens up when a defensive lineman either pulls or shoulder-blocks his man out of the way, creating a gap for a teammate to rush through. The players usually decide on this kind of move on their own.

"I remember one time when the other team was kicking an extra point," says the Jets' 180-pound Billy Baird, "and one of our linemen said to me, 'I'll pull the guy out of the way and you run up the alley and try to block the kick. There's nothing to it. It's easy.'

"So I told him OK. Well, he never touched his man, and I took a 10-yard run. The offensive guard was waiting for me, and he straightened up and let me have a forearm right under the chin. I was out for about 20 minutes. That's the last time I ever tried anything foolish like that."

II
How It's Played On and Off the Field

12
Football of the Seventies: Stagg Got There First

In those days, all a football coach needed to get a job was a journeyman's knowledge of the off-tackle play and a yen to kick anyone who happened to be in a crouching position.
□ Jimmy Conzelman, on coaching the Detroit Panthers in 1925

"What would happen if someone came out with a single-wing offense?"
"It would embarrass the hell out of us."
□ question put to Vince Lombardi

If you want a very expert prediction of what football will be like in the seventies, we can offer the opinion that it will be fun to watch and it will make a lot of money from television, and the players will be bigger and faster and stronger, unless there's a sudden famine.

Hank Stram took care of the technical side of the predicting when he said that football of the seventies will be a "variety trend, both offensively and defensively, to get away from the simplistic trend of the sixties." The quarterbacks, he said, will be big, strong, mobile guys like his own Mike Livingston (6-4, 220, 4.7 speed for the 40), who stepped in as a rookie when Len Dawson was hurt in 1969 and won five games for the Chiefs. The offenses will be multiple, Hank maintains, and the quarterback will not be an anchor anymore. He'll move, along with his pocket of protection.

And since Hank and his Kansas City Chiefs are the resident Super Bowl champs, at least for 1970, he is the reigning predictor.

More predictions:

"The great quarterbacks in future years will have to run as well as pass to survive pro lines, which seem to get rougher and faster every season. . . . The pro ends of today are bigger than the guards and tackles were a decade ago. . . . The defense places greater emphasis on rushing the passer. . . . The new development in pro football, therefore, will have to be the running quarterback."

Now this is not a quote from Stram. It comes from an article by coach Paul Brown, "I Watch the Quarterback," which appeared in *Collier's* magazine on October 28, 1955. And Brown, who was at the height of his glory with the Cleveland Browns, predicted that the great quarterbacks of the future would be men like Tobin Rote and Ed Brown and Billy Wade. And the stars, of course, became pure pocket passers like John Unitas and Y. A. Tittle.

Stram is a very nice person to be around, and his coaching strength lies in evaluating personnel and drafting accordingly. Having the full backing of a millionaire owner who could finance the costly drafting procedure during the AFL-NFL war years doesn't hurt either. Stram has fine rapport with his players, and his magnificent handling of the Dawson stories that broke five days before the 1970 Super Bowl game brought the club through its most trying hours.

But Hank, who has been termed an "innovative genius," believes that he invented football, and he will occasionally let the world in on this secret. It makes good copy and it gets written. But when you stop to analyze the Super Bowl, you'll realize that Hank did not beat the Vikings because he switched decades on them and buried football of the sixties with football of the seventies.

He beat them because he had magnificent defensive personnel that could match the brute strength of the Viking attack with its own. It was Louis-Galento all over again, only the Louises this time were men such as Aaron Brown, a defensive end who is a remarkable athlete and something of a legend among scouts ("6-5, 265, and he can run a 4.8 forty"); and Willie Lanier, a 245-pounder who looks like a teddy bear but can cover the run-pass combination as well as any middle linebacker in the game; and Buck

Buchanan, a 6-7, 275-pound defensive tackle who has been all-league for years; the vastly experienced Jerry Mays at the other defensive end across from Brown; and Johnny Robinson and Bobby Bell and Curly Culp . . . the list of super-athletes on Stram's defense is almost as impressive as the Hall of Fame roster Green Bay used to send onto the field in the mid-sixties.

If Stram did use something new it was the odd-man defensive line, with one of the tackles playing directly over the center and the linebackers "stacked," or hidden behind defensive linemen, and even Hank admits that the NFL knew all about this technique of his.

"We used it 10 times against Green Bay in the 1967 Super Bowl" [35-10, Green Bay], he says. "The Packers ran the ball four times against it and gained an average of two yards. They passed against it four times and had one interception, one completion, and two incompletes."

And the idea of a five-man defensive line with a man directly over the center goes back to to the Giants' Steve Owen in the late 30's and probably even farther back. The middle guards who put the centers to the test were either monsters like 350-pound Les Bingaman and 290-pound Ed Neal, who clubbed them to death, or little guys like 205-pound Dale Dodrill and 210-pound Bill Willis, who finessed them. But most coaches are natural copiers, so the odd-front defense and "stack" will probably crop up all over the place pretty soon.

Stram beat the Vikings because he had added strength in Jan Stenerud, the best field goal kicker in football. But even Jan was suspect for a while ("Typical soccer-style low-trajectory kicker," one scouting report read. "Will get a lot blocked").

The KC defense won the game for Hank, and it was only after they established the fact that the Vikings weren't going anywhere, and Stenerud had kicked a few field goals, that Dawson and the offense could operate their high-percentage, low-risk game, which is perfect for sitting on a lead.

So how about those Paul Brown quotes back in '55? Did it show that the maestro who had coached the Cleveland Browns to nine consecutive league or divisional titles was mistaken? Or was it just that Brown, writing for mass consumption, was having his private little joke, a gentle put-on for the 1955 readers who liked things spelled out in the language of clairvoyants and seers—just like the readers of today.

Coaches usually do not like to give away secrets. Some of them systematically turn down invitations to speak at coaching clinics.

"It took me 20 years to learn what I've learned," says the New York Jets' defensive coach, Walt Michaels. "Why should I just give it away? I don't speak at clinics and I don't write books on football."

But they are human. And what's the point of all those 18-hour days and nights of blind staring at a movie screen, if you can't go to a clinic every now and then, puff a little and have some young college coach come over and say, "Gee, I put in that combination defense of yours last fall and my kids really love it. . . ."

The fun of all this predicting, all this "football of the seventies" business, is to look back on it. Usually you'll find that it has all been predicted before.

"Giant Touchdown," a flyer mailed out to the Giants' season ticket holders before the 1953 season, told everyone how coach Owen's new "Swing-T formation" would revolutionize football.

"Owens's latest attacking masterpiece combines all the systems of the basic T. From play to play the Giants will be able to swing from T to single-wing, or double-wing or any variation of these, to select the most dangerous plays. The Swing-T achieves the all-time peak of offense, because it puts the ultimate pressure on the opposition. The Giants no longer may be 'defensed,' in advance of a game. Instead, defenses must realign for the play of the moment, in the few seconds from Giant line-up to snap of the ball."

The key man was supposed to be a 215-pound rookie named Butch Avinger, who was going to man the all-important quarterback-tailback spot. Well, the Giants finished with a 3-9 record in '53 and the offense scored 14.9 points a game, the fewest in the league. And Avinger was gone next year.

Which only proves that no system will work without the personnel to make it work. And Hank Stram's multiple offense which shifts out of an I formation into a T with a moving pocket, and causes the defenses to "realign for the play of the moment," goes because he has those great big horses in the line who make it go.

There is nothing new in football, except maybe TV's instant replay.

Remember the old story about how Notre Dame's famous passing offense of 1913, with Gus Dorais throwing to Knute Rockne, paralyzed the West Point Cadets, who supposedly had never seen such things? A *New York Times* report of the 1912 Army-Carlisle game casually dropped the line: "Both the Cadets and the Indians used the forward pass to great advantage."

Passing supposedly came about when President Teddy Roosevelt loosened up the game in 1906, but don't believe it.

Amos Alonzo Stagg talking about his playing days at Yale in the late 1880's, mentioned that "we used to throw the ball around in practice, but coach Walter Camp wouldn't let us do it in a game because he thought it was too dangerous."

When people tell you that the T with flankers came about fairly recently, drop over to a library and take a look at Stagg's old "ends back formation." He used this when he was coaching at the University of Chicago in the 1890's, and it bears a shocking resemblance to the pro offenses of today.

Stagg, who wrote that he had "50 or more pass patterns in my repertoire" in 1910, also knocks down another hallowed legend, that Rockne's famous "Notre Dame shift," came when Knute watched some chorus girls perform in a burlesque house.

"One of my players at Chicago was Jess Harper, who later became coach of the Dorais-Rockne Notre Dame team," Stagg wrote. And Rockne later said, "I got the shift from Jess Harper, who got it from Stagg, who got it from God."

The multiple offense that Stram tells us will signal the advent of the seventies was known to George Halas and the 1934 Chicago Bears. George used an old-fashioned T formation and spiced it with a single wing that featured Bronko Nagurski blocking for Beattie Feathers, the first 1,000-yard runner in recorded pro history. Five years later Halas had two formations for Sid Luckman, a T and a Notre Dame shift.

And in searching around for ancestors of the modern flanker offense, you might try Carlisle of 1906, featuring Pop Warner's double-wing formation and a trio of great Indian backs, Joe Guyon, Pete Calac, and Jim Thorpe, who could all pass and run.

A few years ago the scouts decided to draft basketball players to put some zip into the passing game, but Dr. Harry March reports in his 1934 book, *Pro Football: Its Ups and Downs,* that in 1906 Eddie Stewart, the coach of the Massillon, Ohio, professional club, went all the way to Cleveland to recruit a well-known basketball star, "Peggy" Parrott, because the pass was becoming so popular.

But let's not be too hard on Stram's multiple offense, with his I that sometimes shifts into a T and sometimes remains an I.

"It's one thing to see it in film, and another to face it in the flesh," said Mike Stromberg, a New York Jet linebacker after he had played against it for the first time. "Somehow the sight of all those guys shifting around gives you a much scarier feeling than you had when you were watching movies of it."

And the Vikings' strong safetyman, Karl Kassulke, said that even though his team had scouted the Kansas City offense thoroughly enough, the different sets "gave us a moment of hesitation. We were not hell-bent like we normally were. We held back a little bit."

Dallas coach Tom Landry is another exponent of multiple offensive sets, or alignments, and the Packers' middle linebacker, Ray Nitschke, allowed that the Landry approach had some value, even though it was at variance with the Packers' more simplistic approach to football.

"Landry has maybe 30 or 35 different offensive sets," Nitschke said, "and you have to be aware of all of them and be sure you're in the right position for them. He doesn't really expect to whip you with the sets themselves. What he wants to do is create a moment of doubt, a moment of confusion in the defense. Once he's done that, then it snowballs. You're out of position on one play, then you worry and think too long on the next, and all at once you're all at sea and you're dead.

"In some ways it's the opposite of our philosophy—beat a club at its strength. We like to say, 'Here's where we're coming and what we're going to do. Try and stop us.' "

If there ever was a true innovator of modern times it was Clark Shaughnessy, who was credited with renovating the Chicago Bears' old T formation to such an extent that the Bears beat the Washington Redskins, 73-0, for the 1940 NFL championship.

Shaughnessy was a compulsive tinkerer who was happiest when he was alone with an 11 × 14 sheet of graph paper, a set of freshly sharpened pencils, and six hours to kill.

"There's a lot of satisfaction in cooking up things and seeing them work, but it's no fun just copying things, or just doing what you're told to do," he said.

"I love to try things. In fact, I always have a tendency to try too much. I usually throw out about three-quarters of everything I work out."

"You're nuts," the Bears' Sid Luckman told Shaughnessy, when Clark tried to convert Sid from a single-wing tailback into a T quarterback. "How can you send a halfback into the line alone, without a back to block for him. You'll get him killed."

"You worry about the signals," Halas told him. "We'll worry about our halfbacks."

And when Shaughnessy was hired by Washington in 1944, for the express purpose of installing the T, the unhappiest man was Sammy Baugh, who had been a tailback for the Redskins for seven years and who was to become one of football's greatest T quarterbacks.

"I hated it at first," Baugh said. "Shaughnessy told me that Luckman actually cried over the thing when they started teaching it to him."

But the football that Shaughnessy tinkered with in the early forties was a different animal from the refined game that Stram and Landry are trying to conquer. Defensive subtlety was almost unknown, and George Halas' nephew, Pete, who was a scout for the Bears in those days, said he was able to get a reading on the type of defensive line the Philadelphia Eagles would come out in by watching the hands of middle linebacker Alex Wojciechowicz. Alex would call the defenses in the huddle, Halas said, by turning his back to the line of scrimmage and spreading fingers across his chest. Elementary mathematics told the scout that a call for a five-man line would need only one hand, but a six would need two.

Halas gave Luckman his scouting report—one hand on the chest for a five-man line, two hands for a six—and Pete takes the credit for the only loss the Eagles suffered in 1949—to the Bears, naturally.

The Bears' modern, revitalized 1940 T formation, with its quick openers and man-in-motion, is treated by historians as the great offensive innovation of recent history. But on November 17, 1940, the Redskins beat the Bears, T formation and all, 7-3, in a regular season game.

Washington, using the standard single wing, had a 7-1 record going into that November 17 game. Chicago's record was 6-2. The Washington offense averaged 27.3 points a game to the Bears' 19.6, and the Redskins' offense was gaining 58 more yards per game than Chicago's.

The legend is that Shaughnessy sent Halas some last-minute instructions for the title game (and it is a mystery how Shaughnessy could take 'time off from his job as the coach of Stanford's Rose Bowl team that year to worry about the Bears). The plan was to send halfback George McAfee in motion one way, and come back to the other side in what is now called a counter play. Hence, the 73-0 whipping, instigated by Bill Osmanski's 68-yard run for the first touchdown—on a counter play.

"Our coaches had spent hundreds of hours studying game movies and charting every facet of the Washington defense," Halas said. "That off-tackle counter play was put in especially to capitalize on Osmanski's power and speed up the middle. But after all that scientific preparation, everything went wrong. Washington had the play jammed up on the inside, so Osmanski veered around end and we salvaged a 68-yard TD."

The answer to that 73-0 mystery is probably a lot more basic than the T formation and the counter plays off the man-in-motion and the hundreds of other playbook explanations that fans have been bored with for years. It comes down to personnel—and emotion.

The Bears of 1940 were a young team, the youngest ever to win a pro football title. They averaged 24.4 years per man, with 11 rookies on the 33-man squad and nine second-year men. They were late in maturing, but by the championship game they had come of age, spurred on by the emotional incentive of their earlier loss to the Redskins and the reported quotes the Washington players had been tossing around.

But the talent on that Chicago team was awe-inspiring. Luckman, Osmanski, halfback George McAfee, end Ken Kavanaugh, tackle Joe Stydahar, guard Danny Fortmann, center Bulldog Turner—all seven were chosen by the Pro Football Hall of Fame as the greatest players of the decade. And there was plenty of talent to back them up. Halas probably could have used Stagg's old ends-back formation and won the championship with that kind of material. The only sheer collection of talent to match it would be Vince Lombardi's mid-1960's Green Bay machine, that had 13 All-Decade selections (more players were picked in the two-platoon era). And history will probably evaluate Lombardi's true genius as a coach by his ability to amass and motivate and evaluate these great players, not by his selection of formations to give them. The material on Stram's current teams may also be so honored someday, and no one has ever questioned his organizational and motivational ability.

The historian's approach to football of the seventies tells us that offensive change is a lot slower to catch on than defensive readjustment, and that Stram's departure from the standard four-man-line defense, with the ends squared up against the offensive tackles, and the tackles facing the offensive guards (actually the odd front with a man directly over the center is a defense that has been popular in the AFL for years), will gain converts quicker than his offensive theories.

Practically all of today's offenses look the same, a 220- to 240-pound tight end set close to the tackle, with a pass receiver flanked wide to the right and another one flanked wide left, and two running backs deployed behind the quarterback.

Shaughnessy introduced this alignment in 1949, when he was head coach of the Los Angeles Rams. The Rams won a Western Division title with it. Elroy Hirsch, whose history of concussions had changed him from a ballcarrier to a pure pass receiver during the 1949 season, was the wingman on one side. Tom Fears, a true end, was wide on the other side. The tight end was 225-pound Bob Shaw.

Stydahar replaced Shaughnessy as coach in 1950. He knew he had to keep the passing attack to accommodate the combined talents of his quarterbacks, Norm Van Brocklin and Bob Waterfield, probably the two finest passers ever to play regularly on one team (Waterfield and Van Brocklin finished first and second, respectively, in NFL passing in 1951). The ball itself had undergone a gradual slimming process since its watermelon days in the 20's, and all the percentages pointed to a heavy passing game.

But Stydahar got out of the two-wide-men-with-a-tight-end approach in 1950 and '51, using a succession of tiny halfbacks— Glenn Davis, Vitamin Smith, Tommy Kalmanir—as either runners or extra flankers, to team with Fears and Hirsch.

It was an explosive and devastating attack that produced total offense and passing and scoring records that still stand. It gave the Rams a divisional championship and an NFL title, but it wasn't the offense of today. It had no tight end. When the defense countered with an overload of defensive backs (San Francisco used six of them in one game in 1951), Stydahar came back with his "Bull Elephant" backfield of Dan Towler, Tank Younger, and Dick Hoerner, three men in the 220- to 230-pound range who destroyed the spacious defenses.

It was only when Fears began slowing down in the midfifties that he moved closer to the line, giving the offense a somewhat modern look, but Fears still didn't carry true tight end's blocking responsibility.

The Chicago Bears effectively used what they called a "slot back" in the late 1950's. This was a modern tight end type of player who lined up in the slot between wide receiver and offensive tackle. He was set slightly behind the line of scrimmage, and Halas' slot backs—Bill McColl, Bob Carey, Jack Hoffman—were all 225-pounders, capable of blocking a linebacker by themselves.

The Bears weren't alone in this alignment, that looked like offenses do now. But right up until the early 1960's, many teams were going with three runners in the backfield, or three pass receivers and no tight end. People were simply afraid to take a chance with something new.

The defense became modern more quickly. The alignments had undergone a succession of changes, from the early Seven Diamond, with seven lineman, one middle linebacker, two halfbacks, and a deep safetyman; to the 6-2-2-1; to the 5-3-2-1. In Philadelphia, Greasy Neale brought in his "Eagle" defense, which got away from the idea of three men in the pass defense area. The Eagle was either a 5-4-2 or a 5-2-4 defense, to fit the occasion.

In 1950, the New York Giants' Steve Owen brought in an "umbrella" defense that was the predecessor of the current 4-3-4.

There were six linemen, one middle linebacker, and four men in the secondary. Occasionally the defensive ends would drop back to cover the short passing zones, and the whole effect was that of the opening of an umbrella.

The Giants alternated their 6-1-4 with a 5-2-4 defense until 1956, when Sam Huff arrived as a man who seemed born to the middle linebacking position, and Landry, the Giants' defensive coach, established the permanent 4-3-4. By 1957 practically everyone was using it, just as they are today.

The year 1956 is officially given as the birthday for the 4-3-4 defense, with earlier Giant alignments occasionally lapsing into the pattern. But I have a program clearly showing that, one year earlier, Washington coach Joe Kuharich substituted linebacker Charley Drazenovich for middle guard Ron Marciniak and put a pure 4-3-4 defense on the field against New York. And I wouldn't be surprised if there exists evidence that Stagg was stopping Michigan cold 60 years ago with a modern 4-3.

There have been fluke formations from time to time. The "Shotgun," which is nothing more than an old Missouri spread formation, or a Pop Warner double wing, enjoyed a brief vogue a few times within the last 10 years. The catchy name (in Detroit it appeared as the "Zephyr") didn't hurt it's publicity. It was quickly defensed back into moth balls.

The only thing that has remained constant is the knowledge that coaches like to copy from each other.

"It's a matter of self-preservation," Shaughnessy once said. "Coaches get fired when they lose, and even when they win sometimes. So they just follow the line of least resistance and go with the pack.

"If a coach dares try something new and it flops, he gets fired because he's a screwball and only a stupid person would attempt such a thing. But if he tries something that's been successful with another team and it fails, he's got a perfect out. He can blame it on his material, and keep his job, particularly if he's a good apple-polisher."

Poor Pop Ivy found out. He came down from Canada in 1958 with his head full of the spread offenses of the wide-open game up north. He used his wide spreads, with four and five pass receivers, at the Chicago and St. Louis Cardinals, and he ended up quitting before the '61 season had ended. His four-year record was 15-31-2. But nowadays, people cheer when the old Ivy spreads come up for a few sequences here and there, or maybe for a full game (Ewbank occasionally uses a double wide receiver pattern on either side, and his ex-assistant, Boston coach Clive Rush, tried to beat Weeb in '69 with an alignment that strung out three wide receivers on the same side).

Coaches, like everyone else, can usually be typed by the experiences of their formative years. Stram picked up the I formation when he was an assistant coach at Purdue 20 years ago, although he modified it slightly. Landry, a defensive specialist as a player and an assistant coach with the Giants, developed Dallas' complicated multiple offense as "the only way to attack the basic 4-3 defense," a defense that he helped create.

And his complicated defensive system at Dallas is designed to stop his complicated offensive system. The complexity never ceases.

Those Giant teams of the midfifties, with Landry in charge of the defense and Lombardi running the offense, has sent disciples to all of pro football's outposts. It was in New York where Lombardi achieved fame with his "Run to Daylight" theory of ball-carrying, which became a major part of his early Green Bay offenses. And Lombardi's Green Bay establishment sent a gang of its own missionaries out into the world.

In 1966, *The New York Times'* William Wallace tallied up 55 Lombardi-Packer emigres in pro football, as either players or coaches. By now the number must be near 100. A man carries his basics with him, but sometimes they can slow him down.

John Rauch spent three years as Oakland's head coach, supervising the application of overall boss Al Davis' "Big-Pass" offense. It produced tremendous success at Oakland, but when Rauch got to Buffalo in 1969, he found an aging and unspectacular passer with a mediocre set of receivers—but a mercurial and explosive runner, O. J. Simpson. He built his offense around Jack Kemp's arm, rather than Simpson's leg, and people wondered whether it might be a holdover from his Davis days.

I find it hard to believe that the basic thinking of football of the seventies will be much different from that of the sixties—or any other era. Organization, motivation, evaluation: the three basics that never seem to change, although formations come and go.

Paul Brown had a genius for organization when he first entered pro football in 1946, and that has not changed. His thinking was remarkably constant with the present—and the concept of the future.

In his first training camp in '46 he dictated the following to the players for inclusion in their playbooks: "First we will write 'A —Form of Running.' Now put numeral 1 under A and write, 'Why?' Then make a dash and write, 'It is the most fundamental factor in winning. You can't lick speed.' "

You can assume that Lombardi will stay basic in Washington. His football in the seventies does not include the multiple offense.

"Every summer we'd put in a lot of that stuff," Lombardi says, "and about the fourth exhibition game we'd say to hell with it and go back to what we had. Formations don't win games."

"Our system at Green Bay is pretty basic," fullback Jim Grabowski once said. "I've talked to the guys on the Bears and I get confused just listening to their terms."

Lombardi's ideas aren't quite as basic as he would have people believe. At Green Bay, for instance, he developed the highly sophisticated passing philosophy of reading defenses as the pattern develops, granting his receivers optional routes against double coverages and zone defenses. The quarterback then has to "read" that option, which follows a predetermined plan, and hit the defense in its cracks, or seams. Lombardi also developed the play action pass, the pass that evolves from a running play, which pins the linebackers down for an instant.

After four days with Lombardi, even an old pro like Redskin quarterback Sonny Jurgensen, a 12-year veteran, was amazed at how much he had learned.

"We had a one-hour meeting last night," fullback Ray McDonald said. "You know how many plays he gave us? Two. Only two plays in one hour. But we saw those plays like we never saw plays before."

Stram and Landry say that football of the seventies will be more complicated. Lombardi says it will stay basic. Sam Baker, the much-traveled field goal kicker, has his own thoughts.

"The extra point is forgotten," he says. "The field goal is forgotten. Might as well let 'em do without goalposts completely. They're a nuisance. People are constantly running into them. And let them replace the grass with a carpet. And stop selling tickets. Just televise the games to be shown at a later date."

13
The Coaches

This is a game for madmen. In football we're all mad. I have been called a tyrant, but I have also been called the coach of the simplest system in football. The perfect name for the perfect coach would be Simple Simon Legree.

□ Vince Lombardi

Some of the players now—I'm not sure whether football is a vocation or an avocation with them. You know what football is to me? It's blood.

□ Sid Gillman

A good coach needs a patient wife, a loyal dog, and a great quarterback, but not necessarily in that order.

□ Bud Grant

Search out the man and you've got the coach. Because the essence of the business is not playbooks and diagrams and the confusing jargon that mystifies even the most dedicated fan. It is emotion and purpose and sincerity; it is channeling 40 collective personalities and egos into the most violent game anyone has managed to think up.

All the coaches know their blackboard stuff, and sometimes superior football intellect will give a man a win he shouldn't have had—or maybe that he should have. But I prefer to look at a team as an extension of a man's will.

Go back to a man's beginnings, and the trip will tell you more about him than a whole pile of magazine articles and "in depth" feature stories and half a dozen pages of quotes.

The newspaper of the Black Panthers puts it another way: "What you are speaks so loud I can hardly hear what you are saying."

I think of Blanton Collier, the shy old man who coaches the Cleveland Browns, and I see a young petty officer at Great Lakes Naval Training Center, leaning over the fence and watching the great Paul Brown work out his superb service team. He's too timid to say anything. He stands there every afternoon and makes notes in a little pad and keeps his mouth shut. And one day Brown gets curious about the curious stranger, so he invites him over for a talk about football. After a few sentences Blanton Collier has joined the Great Lakes coaching staff of Paul Brown and Weeb Ewbank, and a career destined for the high schools of the Kentucky backwoods is suddenly jerked into the big time. Now, when you see Collier running the Browns in his modest way, you think of what Jimmy Brown once said about him, and the pieces come together.

"In a grim and brutal business," Jim said, "he has one quality that makes him stick out—sincerity. Blanton never jives anyone. If he wanted to he wouldn't know how."

"You can accomplish anything you want as long as you don't care who gets the credit for it," Collier had said after he won the 1964 NFL Championship—and lost out as Coach of the Year.

I can't seem to shake the suspicion that this old man with the hearing aid just might be the best of them all, better than Lombardi and Brown and the vastly underrated Ewbank. Collier has no "image" with the public because he doesn't get interviewed very often, and if he does it's not for very long; because he doesn't bother with catchy phrases and he didn't invent anything. And if he doesn't much care for the interview he can bury you with, "How's that again?"

The record speaks for Lombardi: St. Vincent with the booming voice and the lawyer's mind. He likes to come on crude, but he probably knows more about the workings of the human animal than most psychiatrists, and he certainly can motivate and drive and whip a team into success.

But there's something about the picture of Lombardi that doesn't sit right, and you wind up asking yourself, "Is there some other way?" And there are little inconsistencies that won't stay down.

He banned the AP's Ken Hartnett from the Packer dressing room because Hartnett broke the story about Jimmy Taylor playing out his option, and it took Pete Rozelle's pressure to get the writer back into the inner sanctum. And, of course, you rose up at this one, because it hit you where you live, and you come on strong when people start tampering with a reporter doing an honest job.

But there's grudging admiration for a man who wants to keep his family together. And you even have to respect Lombardi a little bit when he gets touchy about Taylor wanting to quit him to be closer to his "business interests" back in Louisiana. And then the Lombardi-to-Washington business breaks. A contract is tampered with, and you think about Lombardi's quote: "I think I'll always be loyal to Green Bay, but I don't have to be there to be loyal."

It. wasn't really a coaching job that Lombardi quit, and it was probably the itch to coach again, rather than to remain in the Green Bay front office, that drove him to Washington. And he couldn't very well step in and tell the Packers' coach, Phil Bengtson, once his own first lieutenant, "Step aside, Phil, I'm ready to come back."

Rating coaches is a fool's game. They have all made their contributions and they all have their strengths and weaknesses, and if you try and do it by the record book you're defeated by the hundreds of little variables that negate any positive judgment.

It's more interesting to look at the man—what he is and where he's been.

Two years after his Block of Granite days at Fordham, Lombardi moved to Englewood, New Jersey, and eight years as coach of St. Cecilia's High School. St. Cecilia—Jersey kids referred to them as "The Saints"—and Lombardi gave them a power attack as basic as those terrible Jock Sutherland, "Sweet Jesus, here they come again," single-wing power plays Lombardi faced at Fordham.

Then there was Lombardi as Earl Blaik's assistant at West Point. He knew all about the brutality of football, but Blaik showed him something else—finesse, and offensive innovation. Lombardi was growing, and in the Gothic world of Grant Hall and The Plain and The Area, he got a greater appreciation of the concept of discipline, total discipline. Maybe he got it from Blaik, maybe from his long talks with General MacArthur, maybe it just seeped in through five years at the Point.

He went to the Giants and molded their offense with his "Run to Daylight" approach, and then he went to Green Bay and cured the sick franchise. The basic simplicity of Lombardi's approach had its hidden subtleties that the player and the enemy could appreciate. His knowledge, his total knowledge, was undeniable. He never would have been able to impose his will on so many men for so long if there existed even a small suspicion that he didn't know what he was talking about. He knew how to evaluate talent and he knew how to draft and trade, but he knew persuasion and motivation best of all. Cut off the lines of communication between coach and players and you might see genuinely talented players become a group of dogs. Let any phoniness show, and the tensions and emotions and hypnotic state that permit men to punish their bodies for five straight months will crack, and the team will split wide open.

A coach can be a whipper like Lombardi or a milder, Weeb Ewbank type. But as long as his sincerity isn't doubted, his players will perform under discipline, even though they might hate the demands that are being made upon them.

The Packers who were part of Lombardi's championship teams at Green Bay sound like they've rehearsed the same script. They speak of the "great love" that existed on the team, and the "family" feeling they all had. They joke about Lombardi and point to his relentlessness, even cruelty, but they speak about him like a father.

Leonard Shecter did a magazine piece on Lombardi a few years ago, and many people considered it a hatchet job. Actually, it was a candid look at the man, the touches of humor and intelligence and bestiality that are now part of the Lombardi image, written by an author with a good knowledge of people but very little knowledge of football. The underside of Lombardi had never been shown before, only the achievements, so many fans (and many writers who called themselves newspapermen but were actually no more than glorified fans) castigated Shecter as an assassin.

The Green Bay players, naturally, rallied to Lombardi's defense. I once asked Jerry Kramer why everyone thought the story was so bad, since it only made public what they knew.

"Well, I'll tell you," Kramer said. "A lot of us laughed about some of the stuff that was in there, like the way Lombardi looks like a pigeon when he comes on the practice field with his chest all puffed out. But it's one thing to say it in the family and another thing to have it out there in the open. It's like someone writing an in-depth look at your father, and a few million people reading it. How would you like that?"

When Lombardi acts crude with his players, he is adopting the most sensible approach to the basic crudeness of the business. There is nothing subtle about slamming into a man. But again, he has that calculating intelligence where people are concerned.

"He'll have a division title in three years," Green Bay cornerback Herb Adderley said when Lombardi went to Washington. "He'll find the players who have been breaking down. They'll change—or be replaced. He'll mold that team. That's Lombardi's great secret. He can sense talent that others miss. And he can realize the personalities in 40 men—who gets the kid gloves and who gets the screaming."

The screaming doesn't work with everyone, and some of Lombardi's former players remember only that aspect of him.

"He coached through fear," said center Bill Curry, a sensitive man who is active in the Fellowship of Christian Athletes. This was after Lombardi had traded him off the club.

"Most of the Packers were afraid of him, of his scoldings and his sarcasm. It's a form of motivation that works for some people. But it didn't work for me."

"Abuse is a lousy teaching method," said San Diego's offensive tackle, Ron Mix, who quit after the 1969 season to devote full time to his law practice.

"Fear—yes, fear of losing money. But you need a certain amount of control. Take money from a player if he doesn't perform. But you can't abuse today's players and keep getting away with it. I wonder what the Packers really thought of Lombardi. Sure, they loved him—as long as they won."

Again, those little inconsistencies in the Lombardi approach, those little doubts. And again the look at Collier and his quiet, low-key style that turned a moody athlete like Jim Brown into a sentimentalist. It controlled everybody, even an offbeat character like his flanker, Gary Collins, who admits . . . "I'm garbage in practice. Games turn me on, not practices." So Collier lets Collins go his way, and so far it has had no disruptive influence on the Browns—as long as Collins performs well every week.

Collier spent 16 years trying to get some algebra into the minds of his Kentucky high-school students, and when people talk of him now they always tell you, "Blanton is a teacher . . . he will get down and show you every little thing you're doing wrong."

I remember the Colts' Lou Michaels once talking about the way Collier coached him when Lou was a freshman tackle at the University of Kentucky, and how Collier actually took a stance next to him and patiently went through the whole thing, step by step . . . let $x = 2y + 7$.

"What do you remember most about him, Lou?" I asked him.

"I remember him staring at me . . . remember, I was just an 18-year-old kid then, and telling me, 'Lou, you're going to be the greatest tackle in college football someday.' "

The old country teacher remains a teacher. The rock jaw of George Halas has appeared in group photos ever since the NFL was just a dream. His idea is total control, although he *did* let Jim Dooley handle the coaching a few years ago. But Halas controls the contracts and the trades, and the tightfistedness that he inherited from the days when people were paid $50 to play a game of football has left its scars.

"Halas would promise something, but he never really gave a damn about you," said the great defensive end, Doug Atkins. There was a contract fight and Atkins found himself shipped off to New Orleans, where he had three great years.

"I don't hold a grudge, but football is tough enough without having to deal with people who are halfway fair. He's unreal. I had to fight and argue for every $1,000 raise."

Old-time coaches want to run the show, and they'll throw extra work onto an already loaded day by holding down two jobs—coach and general manager. General manager means that you can control players' salaries. The five coaches in football who are also GM's are dedicated to the total-control idea . . . or they learned their football from men who were. Paul Brown and Lombardi are coaches and general managers. So is Bengtson at Green Bay. So is Denver's Lou Saban, Brown's defensive captain in the early Cleveland days. And is so is Ewbank, who coached under Brown.

The public is just getting around to evaluating the greatness of Ewbank, who has taken a lot of unfair criticism during his career. He developed two of the game's greatest quarterbacks—John Unitas and Joe Namath—and the people who say that it was just some kind of lucky accident that Weeb happened to be in the same place they were have never seen the coach's quarterback book. Every step, every movement, every detail of execution is carefully diagramed in Weeb's book, which is as fat as a normal playbook. No, Unitas and Namath didn't stumble into their greatness. They were led there by one of the shrewdest quarterback coaches in the business, one of history's cleverest students of the passing game.

Ewbank is a solid judge of talent. He has gotten burned on trades probably less than any other coach in football. And he has an unmistakable genius for organizing his practices, cramming the most into the shortest.

But Weeb grew up in the moonlight era, when he used to sneak away from Miami University of Ohio to pick up $10 or $15 as quarterback of the Hammond, Indiana, semipro team. He had a wife to support. And it has left him with a weakness. He doesn't like to spend a buck.

"You come out of a contract talk with him," says a Jets' defensive veteran, "and you say, 'Never again. Never again will I put out for that man on the field.' Then you're in the game and you look over to the bench and you see him, sorta looking scared and little, and you say, 'What the hell? What's the difference?' and you give it all you've got."

Allie Sherman grew up in Brooklyn and played five years of quarterback with the Philly Eagles, a "smart little guy with a terrific football brain," so the press books said. When he came to the Giants as head coach, he broke up the Sam Huff gang and traded away the heart of the great defense. They were old and cliquish; they represented a threat to Allie's control and Huff had openly insulted him in one particularly ugly incident. His defense deteriorated, although his offense always had some of his ingenuity in it, and Allie tried to salvage the club through trades.

They were credit card trades; "buy now, pay later" trades—high draft choices for marginal vets, who came and went in a depressing parade (only Fran Tarkenton really helped). The Giant organization was a family-store type of operation with a nice guy named Wellington Mara as its owner and a neighborhood way of doing business. And meanwhile, Allie—and Mara—were trading away any hopes for the future.

This isn't a knock on the draft-choice-for-veteran principle. George Allen built a winner at Los Angeles by doing exactly the same thing, but he traded for winners: "I want to look in my locker room and see bald, old men," he said. "Guys who have been through it—winners." So the Rams reversed their pre-Allen youth movement that had brought "great potential" stars into camp, while stocking the rest of the league with proven talent. But Allen is a defensive coach who understands that part of the game. And defense is the place where you want maturity. The marginals that Sherman brought in to play defense never helped him.

Poor Allie, the Brooklyn boy with the corn pone and apple fritters accent ("Why does he talk like that?" one assistant coach once said. "Is it to create an image of toughness? Brooklyn's a tough enough place to be from"), walking around the practice field just before his firing in '69, dictating his thoughts into a tape recorder.

Many people consider the turnover rate of assistant coaches as a gauge of a head coach, and Allie had 16 assistants in his nine years. Ewbank only had eight in his first seven years with the Jets, and Lombardi had only 10 in his nine years at Green Bay.

The beginning, go back to the beginning, go back as far as you can. Al Davis, who runs the Oakland operation (although John Madden and John Rauch before him were the official "coaches"), grew up playing stickball on the streets of Brooklyn, and as he got deeper into football, his New York accent gave way to the dialect of the still and the cypress. His biographies point out that he was a "three-sport athlete"—football, baseball, basketball.

Ah, if only that were so. Then perhaps Al would not be the terror he is today: master spy, master trader, wheeler-dealer, rogue. "He was kind of an eager kid, always trying but never quite making it," says Eddie Miller, a basketball player who roomed with Davis at Syracuse. "He went out for a lot of sports. I was really impressed by how eager he was to make good in sports. He even kept a set of barbells under the bed."

He always had a fine technical mind for the game, and he knew how to evaluate talent and wheedle performance out of people whom others had given up on. And his trading ability is legendary.

But history will remember his chicanery. "I have a spy in every city," is the quote that will stay with him longest, and when he isn't snitching little bits of information here and there, and fibbing to the press (even his fiercely loyal Oakland press), he's employing an almost equally effective technique.

It's an old track and field—or golf—or gin rummy trick called "breaking the other guy's concentration." He'll allot a visiting team a practice site a day or two before a game, and at the last minute switch locations. He will have his groundskeepers unroll their tarps while a team is practicing in the Oakland Coliseum. The suspicion has always existed, although it has never been proved, that Davis turns on the Coliseum sprinklers the night before a game. But the fear of it can sometimes be as effective as the deed itself. And in the 1968 AFL championship game against the Jets in New York, he smuggled some workmen into Shea Stadium the night before the game and had them erect an unauthorized cold-weather heating tent behind the Oakland bench. Milt Woodard, the AFL Commissioner, made him tear it down 30 minutes before game time, but the attempt had served a purpose.

"He broke Weeb's concentration," Jet kicker Jim Turner said. "Before the game, that's all Weeb was talking about—Davis' lousy heater. It got us all thinking about it."

I have overheard AFL players in deep conversation about whether or not Davis really has an electronic wiretap and tape recorder planted in the enemy spotter's booth in his home park.

"I don't think he does," says a former Oakland employee, "because if he did, Johnny Rauch would probably have spread it around the league when he left Oakland to coach in Buffalo. Unless John, himself, didn't know about it when he was coaching for Davis. But I'll tell you one thing. You'd better believe that every room in the Raiders' office building is bugged. At least I think so."

Davis' practices are strictly locked-gate affairs—except to the chosen few of the local press. The status of injured players is kept secret. The league requires all teams to submit an injury report by Tuesday, supposedly to keep injury information in the open and neutralize the gambler with the "inside info," the guy who rushes in for a quick killing right before kickoff time.

Some coaches stick by the rules. The Minnesota Vikings' Bud Grant, for instance, opens his practices to home and visiting press alike, and makes no secret of his injuries. But Davis and Halas and a few others play the injury lists like a Stradivarius, and even Lombardi has occasionally fiddled with the reports.

Full knowledge of a club's injury situation would give the enemy an undeniable edge. So many times Tuesday's "definitely out's" effect miraculous recoveries by game time. And Tuesday's healthy come down with strange ailments before kickoff.

Davis believes in total knowledge, and he has instant recall of the league's complicated waiver regulations. He has also bent the rule that says that a player has to be signed to a contract before he can work out with a team. So has everybody else. Tryoutees and marginals are often smuggled in and out of camp, and sometimes a club will deliberately pick up a player who's been released from a team that's on the schedule in a couple of weeks. The poor guy will be strung along for a while, promised a taxi-squad contract that somehow never materializes. Meanwhile, his brain is picked clean of what kind of automatics his old club is using now, and what players are dragging minor injuries from game to game.

Davis likes to call himself an organization man. He likes to cite the strengths of an organization, rather than the strengths of a particular coach or an individual. But in that area, he'll have to take a back seat to Paul Brown. Brown represents total control.

"Paul Brown," a rival coach once said, "has never gone into anything shorthanded. That's why it's so interesting to me to see how he does at Cincinnati. When he was coaching Massillon High he imported Pennsylvania kids. When he coached Great Lakes he had the greatest collection of talent of any service team, with the possible exception of Fleet City and the El Toro Marines. When he started at Cleveland he raped Ohio State."

He beat the rule that says a man's class had to graduate before he could be drafted. The time in military service took care of that. Lou Groza, Dante Lavelli, Bill Willis, Lindell Houston, Gene Fekete—they all had Ohio State eligibility left when Brown grabbed them for the Cleveland Browns. Special Delivery Jones jumped from the Chicago Bears to the Browns of the brand-new All America Football Conference. Lou Rymkus jumped from Washington. And Brown went across town and denuded the

NFL's Cleveland Rams of Tom Colella, Don Greenwood, and Mo Scarry.

His Browns were one of the youngest teams in the league, and remained so until the league folded four years later. If a player got old, Brown got rid of him, period. The tumblers click. Emotion is a dirty word. Cleveland never lost an AAFC championship, and when people said the Browns were a freak, Paul Brown ran off six straight NFL divisional or league titles.

Total control. The image. The boss. "The thing I remember best about him," says Babe Parilli, who was his quarterback for a year, "is the way the sleeve of his T-shirt used to flap around his arm at practice. He didn't like that. He used to pull it tighter. He didn't like the idea that he had thin arms."

Brown calls the play for his quarterbacks. He probes the egos and emotions of his players with a psychological test all rookies have to take. People laughed at it—then copied it. A sample question:

"If you do not like food or service you get at a restaurant do you protest to the waiter————NEVER————SOMETIMES ————OFFEN————ALWAYS————?"

At Cincinnati he assigns either business manager John Murdoch or PR man Al Heim the job of choosing the movies the team will see the nights before road games. He makes it clear that the movie will be of the upbeat type, ever since one player reported that *Midnight Cowboy* left him "terribly depressed."

Total control, total attention to detail, is nothing new. Lombardi sent his assistant coach, Dave Hanner, down to Florida to pick out a hotel for the Packers to stay in for the 1968 Super Bowl—and this was six and a half months before the season started. "One of the first things Vince did when he got to Washington," says the *Washington Post*'s Dave Brady, "was to establish the schedule for the sportswriters' cocktail hour at training camp. It was 5 to 5:30. And that was that."

"You show me a man who shoots a good game of golf," Ewbank once said when someone asked him how his golf game was coming along, "and I'll bet he neglects his business, or someone else does his work for him. I don't have time for golf."

Paul Brown doesn't play much golf. His only game is the Cincinnati Bengals.

In July of 1969, Brown cut a 30-year-old offensive guard named Pete Perreault, who was picked up by the Jets, where he stayed for the season. The first day Perreault was with the Jets he made a telephone call and came away from it shaking.

"Just talking over the phone, it all came back," he said. He had called the Cincinnati equipment man to find out about some of his gear. "I could feel the tension and the fear. It was like being back in marine boot camp after you'd already gotten out.

"I'll tell you what Paul Brown's training camp was like. Everyone has always talked about the tremendous respect that exists for the man. Actually we were all scared to death. The first day there we all got this big IQ test—you know, 'What has four sides?' and they show you a square and a triangle and an ice-cream cone or something. I don't know how important that test was, but next day five guys were gone. If that doesn't put the fear of God into you, I don't know what does.

"The first time coach Brown met with us he said, 'I run everything here. If something goes wrong, don't bother to complain to your teammates or the assistant coaches or the president of the club. They can't help you. I'm the only one.' No secretary got fired, no one invested five dollars in the club, no one bought a pair of cleats without first clearing it with Brown."

The only problem with a total dictator is that he leaves a terrible void when he goes, as the Packers sadly learned when Phil Bengtson took over for Lombardi in '68. Unless you've got a man like Collier to step into that void.

He took over for Brown in 1963 and gave the Browns a 10-4 record. Next year they were NFL champions. Less than two weeks before the 1966 season began, Jimmy Brown announced his retirement. Collier moved in Leroy Kelly, who had carried the ball only 43 times in two years, and Kelly became an All-NFL fixture. Before the 1968 season a salary dispute (nothing to do with Collier) threatened to tear the team apart, and then the club got rid of regulars Ross Fichtner and John Wooten in a racial flare-up. Two more regulars retired just before the season. After the first three games, Collier replaced starting quarterback Frank Ryan with Bill Nelsen, a Pittsburgh castoff, and Nelsen led the Browns into nine victories in their last 11 games—and into the NFL title game.

There are other men whose greatness will be established before long. Minnesota's flamingly honest Bud Grant, whose steely blue eyes and close-cropped gray hair create the impression of a totally sincere, totally dedicated icicle, tells you that he plays down the emotional aspect of football.

"I can't afford the luxury of emotion," he says. "I don't concern myself with things over which I have no control, like the officiating or the weather or bad breaks that have already happened."

But watch the Vikings on the field—a punishing and basic offense and a total abandon and recklessness on defense—and you think that Grant is turning down the thermostat when he talks about emotion. Something about him must be getting his Vikings to play like Storm Troopers.

Emotion is not a thing that can be sought out and created and fostered. It must come from within. I think of the brilliant and cold Tom Landry and his finely competent Dallas organization, and I think of the quotes that keep coming out of the Dallas camp, year after year—about how the "new" Cowboys are going to be killers, not artisans, about how "we're going to start giving that final, killing lick" (middle linebacker Lee Roy Jordan), or how "from now on I'm going to make the guy playing opposite me worry about just surviving the game" (defensive tackle Bob Lilly).

Landry's Cowboys were last-minute victims to Lombardi's Packers in successive NFL championship games. And you remember what Wellington Mara said about the days when both of them were assistants on the Giants.

"Lombardi went from warm to red hot. You could hear him laughing or shouting for five blocks. You couldn't hear Tom from the next chair. Landry was a theoretician and Lombardi was a teacher. It was as though Landry lectured to the upper 40 percent of the class and Lombardi lectured to the lower 40 percent."

Perhaps it's the Dallas system, the theory of operation, that discourages killers. On defense, his "containing and reacting" philosophy might tend to discourage the punishing, murderous impulses that are kept alive in Minnesota and Los Angeles, with their all-out pass rushes. And Landry's big-play offense, with tremendous team speed and quick touchdowns, might not encourage the slogging brutality of the Minnesota or Kansas City attacks.

Lombardi's emotional symphonies, with their crashing crescendos and heavy percussion, were replaced by the chamber music of

Phil Bengtson. And although the Packers tried to motivate themselves, they couldn't do it without a dictator in command. Bengtson is a nice guy, cool and remote. I remember him as the line coach at Stanford in 1950, carefully correcting, carefully explaining.

The Stanford players respected Phil, but the guy they loved was Finney Cox, a fiery redhead who could get down on all fours and throw a blocking dummy over his shoulder with his neck. And when head coach Marchie Schwartz was replaced by freshman coach Chuck Taylor in 1951, Bengtson left and Taylor brought in his own line coach.

Jim Dooley took over for Halas at Chicago. He brought a pile of 25,000 silver dollars out on the field one day, just to show his players what championship and Super Bowl money really looked like. It didn't work.

"When Dooley tells you to kill, you just have to laugh," one Bear player said. "He just wasn't that kind of ballplayer himself."

People like to smile at Kansas City's Hank Stram when he gets tricky in his strategic concepts. He is a phrasemaker ("Mike Garrett knows how to bleed yardage; Our defense was aged in disaster; Camouflage Slot; Moving Pocket," etc.), and his message board in the locker room is spiced with catchy items, such as his advice to overweight players:

UGLY FAT . . .

You Can't be Fat . . .

. . . And Fast, too.

FAT IS HARD TO SEE, FAT IS HARD TO
DETECT, IT HIDES UNDER THICK SKIN,
IT ENSLAVES AND SLOWS THE WHOLE
BODY, AN UNTRAINED EYE CANNOT FIND
FAT.

LIFT · RUN · DIET · WORK

The legacy of poor Joe Kuharich might be a parade of his famous non sequiturs: "The charge of that blocked kick came either from the inside or from the outside. Every coach must view a player with three different eyes; trading for a good quarterback is quite rare but not unusual; we were three points behind but that's not the same as being even; I'm not vacillating you. I can only answer a question about a conclusive."

I think of George Allen, who coaches the Rams, and I remember what someone once said when he read a story about Allen's 18-hour working day: "No business should be like this." He drinks papaya juice to calm his queasy stomach, and eats a lot of ice cream, "so he doesn't have to spend time chewing," his wife says. "It would take his mind off football."

Sometimes he expends his normal 18-hour day and watches films until after midnight. Then he goes to a motel for three hours' sleep, and comes back to the office for more work. His wife buys his shoes and clothes for him ("They're on approval," Allen says. "If they don't fit, they go back"), and when he needs a haircut, she makes the appointment for him at the airport barbershop, and he comes in on the day of a game trip.

Mel Durslag, the Los Angeles columnist, tells the story about the time Allen showed up for a football writers' luncheon in the tasteful wardrobe his wife had laid out for him—new sport jacket and slacks, button-down shirt with a stylishly striped tie. And white sneakers.

"I forgot to take my shoes this morning," he apologized.

And while all this was going on, Allen's boss, Don Reeves, who had fired eight coaches in 20 years before he hired Allen (average life-span—2.5 years), was brooding because he was being "left out of things."

So he reverted to form and canned the coach who had brought the Rams success. This was at 8 o'clock on the morning after Christmas of 1968, and it prompted Allen's famous understatement: "This was probably the biggest Christmas shock of my life."

It took a rebellion by Allen's fiercely loyal players to get him his job back.

The nature of the business leaves many imponderables. Some questions seem to come up all the time. For instance:

Q: Why can't Dallas win the big ones?

A: This is unfair. The Super Bowl situation, in which 26 teams are boiled down into only one winner, has left a string of teams that "can't win the big ones," i.e., Dallas, Minnesota, Baltimore, Los Angeles, Cleveland. It's going to get worse.

Q: If those coaches are so smart, why do they trade away so many great players? Just look at the quarterbacks who gave their new team championships—like Unitas from Pittsburgh to Baltimore, and Van Brocklin from L.A. to Philly, and Lamonica from Buffalo to Oakland, and Tittle from Frisco to New York, and Ryan from L.A. to Cleveland, and Nelsen from Pittsburgh to Cleveland, and Morrall from New York to Baltimore, and Dawson from the NFL to Kansas City.

A: Again, unfair. Lots of these trades looked good at the time and no one questioned them. Hindsight is always 20-20. Remember that Morrall was laughed out of New York by the same writers who deified him a year later. Every coach has traded someone who came back to hurt him. Repeat, every coach. Lombardi let Timmy Brown go and he became a star at Philadelphia. Ewbank traded Fuzzy Thurston from Baltimore to Philly. Brown sent Bill Quinlan and Willie Davis and Henry Jordan to Green Bay, and even Al Davis got burned when he traded Richie Jackson to Denver for very little. Remember that at the time these men are traded they aren't always the players they are two or three years later. And sometimes there are things we never hear about—like contract troubles or the other players' attitude about a guy.

Q: How important is all this strategy business, really? All this game-plan stuff?

A: Well, they all have to know it, but emotional motivation is probably more important. I remember a Columbia University football writers luncheon before Columbia played Dartmouth, and John Toner, the backfield coach, was working out a kind of formula on the blackboard. He was showing how many different sets Dartmouth's Bob Blackman used, and how many adjustments you have to make to meet every variation . . . and the variation of every variation. The geometric progression got near the four-figure mark and a writer asked him, "How much real value is all of this?" John's an honest guy, so he told him, "Practically none. But it's something you just have to do."

Q: Do great players make great coaches? How about great quarterbacks? They're so smart, and all.

A: Otto Graham and Frankie Albert never made it as coaches with Washington and San Francisco. Neither did Bob Waterfield at L.A. Roman Gabriel said he never taught him a thing. One doesn't follow the other.

Q: Why did Lombardi quit coaching to become a general manager when he loved coaching so much?

A: He said, "When I first came, our total income was $600,-000. Last year it was nearly $5½ million. More and more decisions become necessary."

Q: What do they say at half-time. How important is it, really?

A: Usually the teams break down into groups, offense with the offensive coach, defense with the defensive man. They talk strategy and adjustments (although it's too late to really change anything). Most of the good coaches feel that it's just a matter of doing well what they know how to do best. But don't think that they still don't give old-fashioned pep talks. A stadium guard outside the Washington dressing room between halves of the 1969 Redskin-Eagles game once said Lombardi spent the whole time screaming at just one guy, tackle Jim Snowden, who let his man tackle Sonny Jurgensen for a safety. He said that Lombardi screamed at the guy that he was yellow, among other things. Lombardi obviously didn't think that he had a yellow ballplayer on his hands, or he would have cut the uniform off him. The coach probably figured that a good half-time scream session would get everyone's adrenalin flowing quicker than 15 minutes at the blackboard.

Q: Can coaches tell when their team is "up" for a game?

A: This is one thing everyone agrees on. It's impossible to tell. Every coach has his story about how his team took the field with blood in its eye and then played like dogs, and vice-versa. Some say that, once the game starts, the special teams—the kickoff and punt teams—will give the clue. If they're really hitting, then the team is up. Landry says he can't tell until the Cowboys get a touchdown scored against them. If they come right back, he says, they're ready to play.

Q: Remember that 30-minute TV special on Kuharich, how crazy he got on the bench? Do they all get like that?

A: The best of them come unhinged either on the bench or in the few minutes before a game starts. Jerry Kramer tells about the time Lombardi walked over to cornerback Bob Jeter before the 1967 College All-Star game and said, "You ready to go, Herbie?"

So Kramer turned to safetyman Willie Wood and said, "Well, Bart, let's have a great night." And you remember Joe Namath's book, where he tells about Ewbank sending the Jets out with, "OK, you Colts, let's go out and win this baseball game." Well, before the Miami game in '69, the last official AFL premerger game the Jets were going to play, Weeb tried to impress everyone with the historical significance, but he got all balled up. He told them: "Let's go out and win this All-America game." Paul Rochester, the defensive tackle, said the players figured that the seniors were going to be introduced before kickoff.

Q: Is the pay good for coaches?

A: Lombardi's first Green Bay contract called for $45,000 a year, and Jerry Kramer figured out that during the season, by the hour, the Green Bay coaches earned less than Green Bay garbage men. Lombardi's contract was renegotiated five times, and he was making $100,000 a year when he left Green Bay. His 5-percent stock deal at Washington means that he makes more there. But the money isn't what makes a man want to coach a professional team.

Q: What is it then?

A: Prestige, for one thing. Lombardi had a street named after him in Green Bay. A drink, too. And before he moved to Washington, the Alexandria, Virginia, city council voted unanimously to ask him to "consider living in our beautiful, old and historic city." And it's a disease that infects them, too. Paul Brown had it made in the five years he was out of football, still getting paid off on his Cleveland salary. He spent five years on the beach at La Jolla, California, but when Ewbank visited him, he told Weeb, "Don't ever leave it. Don't let them do it to you." He also said that losing is rotten, but it's better than no football at all. And when Lombardi was GM at Green Bay, he said he was pretty unhappy in the press box, "where I can't even root."

Lots of players can't figure out why a man would want to coach. The Rams' defensive tackle, Merlin Olsen, says, "A coach just isn't treated that well. The respect is lacking, unless they do fantastically well, and only a small percentage of them really do. Some of the finest coaches in the country go through their whole careers unnoticed and unrecognized, just because they happen to be in the wrong place. A few of them even get hanged in effigy."

When Miami first started interviewing coaching applicants back in 1966, the organization got a series of letters that began with one from a hotel clerk who felt he was the right guy because he had "a gift for organization." An itinerant evangelist wrote that "I could never lose. I am pure of heart." And another applicant was a Pittsburgh trash collector who thought he was exactly the man for the job . . . maybe because he could clear out the dead wood.

There's an intern's report on file at the Scripps Clinic in La Jolla, where L.A. coach Joe Stydahar collapsed after his Rams won the '51 NFL title. "This patient," the medic wrote, "is laboring under marked mental tension."

That's got to be one of history's great understatements.

14
Game Plans...
And Other Deep Thoughts

When Weeb first came to New York, he gave us a playbook; we'd been without one for three years. It's a sensible sort of thing for a professional football player to have.

□ Larry Grantham

No, I didn't say the team's strongest point is the game plan. That sounds like something a sportswriter might say.

□ Norm Van Brocklin at a press conference
after Cleveland beat Atlanta, 30-7

"Why we have a playbook."

"The proper execution of a push-up."

"Dealing with newspapermen: learn who you can trust."

It's all part of a playbook, that mysterious thing that can cost a player $500 if it's lost—or swiped. The basic offense and defense and diagrams are only part of the whole picture. Club rules, even rules of life (depending on the moral nature of the head coach), timely hints for behavior—they're all there. It's the philosophy of a professional football club; it's like a newspaperman's Style Guide; or the Ten General Orders for a soldier on guard duty.

"The plays and diagrams and things like that, they all write down themselves in the book," Jets' coach Weeb Ewbank says. "We lecture and they write. They learn it better that way. We used to have them write down the other stuff, too, the club rules, but it just took too much time."

The offense gets one playbook, the defense gets another. The books usually run upward of 100 pages. An economical one can

go 100. But this isn't as tiresome as it sounds. Diagrams are deliberately large, to facilitate comprehension, and a few of them can
eat up a whole page.

The book usually starts with the Club Rules, subtitle Basic Information: fines, player rating systems, a hint at salary trends,
dealing with the press, basic stances, how to use the machines,
how to wear your equipment, how to run, how to exercise, and
mental attitude all carefully spelled out. This is included in all
books, and through the years the section has become more basic
as the college background of the new talent becomes more diverse.
And by now the coaches probably realize that many of the rookies
come to camp with very little in their heads—except, possibly, the
knowledge of how to ask for money.

The offensive book will then have a basic information section:
quarterback calls; the huddle; the terminology; the play numbering
system; the numbering of the backs; formations, both offensive
and defensive (the offensive players must learn to recognize defenses); the two-minute drill; the "automatic" or checkoff system at
the line; where to sit on the bench; the pregame warm-up; the
means of calling signals.

Signals, surprisingly, can be called in hundreds of different
ways. The quarterback can say "hut, hut, hut," without breaking
his rhythm. He can say, "hut-hut, hut-hut"; or "hut-one, hut-two";
or he can get tricky with broken rhythm calls such as "hut, hut-
hut, hut-hut-hut," which are supposed to throw the defense off,
but can foul up a rookie on his own team, too. It's generally expected that when the snap number is, say two, the player is supposed to be off on the "hut" and into his man by the time two
comes around.

The book then settles into diagrams, broken up by frequency
charts for formations (on first and 10 we were in a flank-right 61
times last season; on second and seven, 43 times, 28 times in a
slot-left, etc.) and then actual plays from those formations.

The more "basic" coaches such as Lombardi might have 60 to
75 running plays in their books and the same number of passes.
People like Halas, who claims that his men have to learn 500
plays, don't really use 500 different plays. They are just switching
terminology and calling each variation of a play a new play. It

adds to the mystique. Actually there are only so many different plays that are possible, and the number is a lot less than 500.

A defensive playbook usually contains an early section on "Defensive Philosophy," which starts with the No. 1 philosophic imperative—Prevent Scoring. Then come things like Theory of Pass Defense, which concerns zone or man-to-man preference; Theory of Blitzing ("We blitz to create confusion and sow destruction," etc.); and standards of achievement.

Both the offense and the defense have standards, i.e., hold the other team to 250 total yards in a game, hit enemy passer for loss four times; complete 55 percent of your own passes. There are generally between 15 and 20, and they'll be repeated on a giant board, if the locker room is spacious enough. And from game to game the actually achieved figures will be entered next to the ideal, so the players can see if they were good boys or bad boys.

After the players have attended all their lectures and diagramed all the plays on the little blank charts provided in the playbook, they are expected to study; read and study. Some do and some don't. The bright students learn everyone else's assignments as well as their own. If they're certain of making the club, they do it so they'll be able to perform with greater intelligence. If they're worried, they do it in case they're asked to change positions. The more things you can do, the better your chances. Some people are instinctive athletes who know the requirements of their own position (when they throw a pass to my man, don't let him catch it; when the guy tries to block me, knock him on his ass and go after the passer, etc.), but they haven't the foggiest idea of what everyone else is trying to execute.

"It's amazing," says the Jets' free safetyman, Billy Baird. "I've seen guys who couldn't even tell you how the numbering system goes. They know their own position and their own assignment on each play, and that's about it."

"It took me 40 years to collect this playbook of mine," Ewbank says, "but it doesn't mean a damn thing if you don't have the people to put it to use."

Assume that everyone has worked hard in camp and everyone knows his playbook. Now it's September and the season is about to start. The scouting reports on the first game or two are brief.

They're based on the tendency charts and frequency patterns and film reports from exhibition games and last year's action. As the season goes on, the reports become complete. And the coaches' life takes on another aspect—the movie projector.

The first two days after a game are a race against time. The coaches get their own team's movies and look at them (the actual grading of players is done in the off-season). They get enemy films and perform the tedious, nonthinking, mechanical task of "breaking them down." It is during this period that coaches go buggy, or get "square eyeballs," as Jet line coach Joe Spencer likes to say.

"I haven't gone to a movie in five years," Cleveland's Blanton Collier once said. "My eyeballs couldn't take it."

The Jets were once playing a game in San Diego, and Weeb Ewbank and Sonny Werblin and a couple of writers spent an evening in Tijuana, right across the border. They were taking a stroll down the main drag when a little guy holding something that looked like two cans of film approached the group.

"Movies?" he said. "Feelthy movies?"

"Christ, no," Ewbank said without breaking stride. "I've been looking at movies all week."

The endurance contest begins when the processor sends the films of the most recent game that next Sunday's opponent has played. Monday evening is preferred, and then the staff will work long into the night on the film. Tuesday morning is the deadline, since it gives the coaches only a few hours to break down a film before the players arrive around noon. A favorite trick of George Halas was to tamper with the film he was sending out, and every time the Bears had a long gainer, the film would become strangely blurred or smudged. The league now requires play-by-play sheets to be sent along with the film, so people will know what's coming and report any shenanigans to the league office.

Two offensive assistants get the other team's defensive film and two defensive men get the offense. They set up their projectors in two rooms, and one coach calls out formations while the other one writes. The writer can go through a whole session without ever seeing the movie.

"Once we tried a computer," says Boston head coach Clive Rush. "But it was faster just to write everything down on a big, yellow, legal-size pad. You have to feed stuff into the computer, and by the time we set up the feeding system, we could break down one whole quarter."

Breaking down merely means sectioning off the paper according to period of the game, score, down, and distance to go, and position on the field, i.e., left hash mark. Then as an alignment is read off, in the viewing team's own terminology, it gets recorded in the proper space, so that by the end of the session, a frequency, or tendency is determined. The actual plays get broken down later.

"Some people get tricky," says Jet defensive coach, Walt Michaels. "Like Paul Brown. He scouts his own team and deliberately goes away from his own tendencies. But I think that maybe these people are just fooling themselves. When the going gets tough, people usually revert to their traditional patterns. It's a psychological principle: you do best what you do most, and vice-versa."

Coaches try to stay a game or so ahead of the race. When a film of, say Baltimore vs. Los Angeles comes in (and especially in an important game such as this one . . . a lopsided game gets less weight on the charts), Baltimore gets the immediate study, if that's the enemy on the coming Sunday. But L.A., which might be on the schedule in three weeks, will get broken down and charted, too. Then you're a few weeks ahead of the game.

"It's a reflex," Michaels says. "Anytime I can latch onto a film, I'll grab it and break it down."

The first breakdown is only for alignments. It takes only one viewing of the film to get them. For instance, the offensive coach may read off, "first and 10, they're in a 5-1 under; second and five, 4-3 with one-free." He's merely giving the defensive formation, although the execution of the defense—which requires a more careful film study, sometimes up to 10 or 15 repetitions—comes later.

The conversation of the defensive coaches may sound like this: "First and 10, flank right; second and two, slot-right, backs divide."

A team gets the films of the last two games the enemy has played. The two-week-old game comes in on a Thursday night, nine days before the opponent is to be faced. So while the Giants are preparing for Cleveland on Sunday, the coaches are spending the Thursday and Friday pregame nights breaking down films of the Steelers, whom they will meet a week from Sunday.

The films are studied, broken down, and shipped off. And with careful horse trading among friends in the profession ("You help me with some films, old buddy, and I'll help you"), a team can have half a dozen film reports of an enemy by October—plus in-the-flesh scouting reports.

By the time the players report on Tuesday, the game plan is ready. There isn't enough time to include the chart of the latest Sunday game, but it's no tragedy.

"Teams don't change that much in one game anyway," Ewbank says. "And if they did, we could always have the players write some adjustments into their game plan.

"Some coaches give the players the game plan on Wednesday. We like them to have it on Tuesday, even though it's a light work-out day. They seem to work better when they have that thing in their locker."

On Tuesday, the players look at films of their own last game, unless it was so dreadful or so easy that the teaching value is negated. They'll get a quick look at the enemy—with further study coming later in the week. Most quarterbacks sit down with the offensive coach for private study, and the ones who really care have a projector at home. They borrow films. Occasionally a lineman will do the same thing.

When Los Angeles' rookie Mike Lahood replaced Joe Scibelli at offensive guard in 1969, he got a projector in a hurry. The first opponent he studied was the 49ers defensive tackle, Charlie Krueger.

"I figured I had 11 years of Charlie Krueger films to study." Lahood said, "and he had none of me."

And then there's the game plan, the mystical game plan that's treasured like the original Book of Kells. In form, there is nothing unusual about it. The defensive game plan is generally longer, running 45 pages or so, since the enemy offensive plays must be diagramed. The offensive plan, diagraming mainly the enemy defenses, is shorter. The size varies with the complexity of the enemy's operation. A game plan against the Kansas City offense might set a record for length. Another one—against Green Bay, for instance, would be briefer.

What it amounts to is a statistical analysis of what the enemy is *likely* to do, and what is the most logical thing for you to do to prevent him from doing it, or to defeat him when he tries it.

"Basic psychology," says Michaels. "You project yourself into the other coach's brain and determine what you would do if you were him. Then you try and counteract it."

The game plan is divided into three sections. First comes a scouting report, which is a preview of things to come later in the book. It puts in statistical terms the enemy operation, which is later spelled out in diagrams and frequency charts.

Next in the offensive game plan is the ready list, or short list, culling the playbook for the choicest morsels to throw at the particular opponent. The extra-special favorites, maybe six or seven running plays, and the same number of passes, might get starred. Of course, each play is really two plays, because it's understood that it can go to either side. And there is an infinite number of basic formations each play can originate from.

Then come the enemy defenses. The formations are diagramed, probably six to a page, with the sheet split down the middle. The same formation will be shown lined up in two different ways—left and right. This would all go under the heading of "Primaries," or basic alignments. And next to each formation is neatly written the frequency of use—on first and 10 this was used 62 percent of the time, etc.

Then a few pages of blitzes, each one identified according to the formation of origin. The names of these blitzes are a kind of anagram game, i.e., a WHAM blitz gets its name from the letter W, which identifies the weak-side linebacker as the blitzer. A SLAM blitz might indicate that the strong-side linebacker is coming. And then, of course, there are combinations. All variations are carefully spelled out.

Pass coverages come next, the infinite varieties of zones and combinations and half-zones, all broken down into situations in which they occur. Finally there are "Key" defenses, complicated maneuvers in which certain players follow certain tip-offs and gear their actions, or rotate their zone accordingly. The Key defense represents the height of sophistication, and requires an extremely mature group of players to make it work. The Jets held

Baltimore to seven points in the 1969 Super Bowl with a Key defense. The club dropped it in '69 when less experienced people filled in.

The defensive playbook is an exact reversal of the offensive one. After the scouting report come the team's own defenses, with the choice ones listed. Then the enemy offensive sets and plays, pages and pages of diagrams. And at the end of all game plans is usually a little area marked, "Special Notes," and another for the player to fill in, as dictated.

"I like to keep my own notes, sort of as a supplement to the game plan," Baird says. "Most of the time they deal with personnel—any changes a guy may show from year to year. If you've been around long enough, you get a pretty good collection of these things."

There are things the movie camera doesn't tell, though, so assistants are sent out on personal scouting missions.

"You get a different feel of the game, a different view when you're there in the flesh," says Baltimore scout Ed Rutledge. "You want to see things like what's going on on the bench, and how hard people are really hitting, and how they go through their pregame drills, and the injury situation the camera can't pick up."

But sometimes the scouting books come up short. Green Bay, with its violent blocking and great execution and rugged tackling, used to give scouts a boring day.

"Nothing fancy," said the Colts' Dick Bielski after watching the Lombardi Packers work. "How do you scout blocking and tackling by experts?"

Lombardi adds another twist to the normal scouting operation. After every game his players sit down and grade the men they have faced head on. They rate them on four categories—ability to diagnose plays, lateral movement, toughness, and quickness. A two- or three-year stack of these ratings gives Lombardi a pretty good line on a man—plus solid trade information.

The actual relay of information during a game involves two telephones. An offensive and a defensive coach sit in the spotters' booth next to the main press box. The offensive coach talks to a reserve quarterback while his offense is in the game, and to his No. 1 QB when the defense is in. The assistant coach does the same thing—relaying the information his binoculars have picked up to either a reserve linebacker or defensive back, or to his defensive signal caller, depending on who's in the game.

The head coach stands on the sideline and makes substitutions and decisions ("Touch my hat means we accept the penalty; leave it alone and we decline it"). A nearsighted field captain who can't see his coach is in trouble. It is the coach's job to keep his sanity, and scream at the officials, if they need it.

The world of the game plan and the scouting report is not a be-all, end-all. And the older a coach gets, the more he realizes it. But it's the kind of blind chess that tickles the intellect. And sometimes, like the man who cracked the Japanese Code in World War II, a scout sees that certain little something and seizes it and watches his message reap a huge reward. It will keep him smiling through the whole off-season.

NFL coaches sat in the stands and watched the thoroughness with which Joe Namath cracked Baltimore's zone defense in the '69 Super Bowl. They were like the European generals who came to America to stand at observers' posts and watch our Civil War, with a detached, clinical interest. And before the fourth quarter of that 1969 Super Bowl was over, the coaches and scouts were fidgeting in their seats, anxious to get to their frequency charts and diagram sheets at home.

The decline of the Colts from '68 to '69 was the decline of a great defense. Retirement of some of the old hands could have been one reason, and the spotty pass rush, which left the zone defense vulnerable to passes with time to set up and read, was probably the biggest reason. But, underneath it all is the typical scout's suspicion that the Jets had shown the NFL something about how to beat Baltimore, and people spent the better part of their off-season analyzing this showpiece game. The Kansas City-Minnesota Super Bowl will get the same scrutiny.

"I talked to the Rams' Diron Talbert," Baird said. "He told me that they watched our Super Bowl films more than we did. He said their game plan was 108 pages long for the Baltimore game next year."

Breaking down film and setting up tendency charts and drawing up game plans are all tiring, but not really that difficult. The whole thing can become a crutch to lean on. Emotional motivation is a much trickier game.

"You make all sorts of plans, but sooner or later in any close game the unexpected always happens," Paul Brown once said. "You fool somebody, or they fool you, and that's the ball game. Football would be awful dull if things turned out any other way."

15
Training Camp Days

It would be great if you could remove your head and just send your body to training camp.

□ Larry Bowie, ex-Minnesota Vikings' offensive guard

There are many eyes that see a training camp. The coaches see it through eyes that are filled with hours and minutes and unreasonably tight schedules: "By Sept. 1 your roster must be down to 49 players; by Sept. 8, 44," etc. They think in terms of cramming the most learning into the least time and force-feeding their playbooks into the brains of the rookies.

Camp is a giant warehouse of talent, and the coaches must evaluate, decide, and make quick judgments. And at night they spend many hours scanning the waiver list to see if they can latch onto some bargains that were cut from other clubs.

For the writers covering the club, camp is a picnic. The reporters who want them can have their own rooms on the campsite, and if there isn't a refrigerator stocked with cold beer in their own room, there's one down the hall. It's a time for getting to know the coaches and their assistants in the informal chitchat of the dining hall or the tavern. It's a breeze because there is usually very little "hard copy" that comes out of camp. The season hasn't started, so the reporters don't have to crank out stories that start: "What's wrong with the Colts?" Or the Rams or the Dolphins.

They write features and mood pieces and close-ups of rookies, relaxed in the knowledge that this kind of story usually reads just as well as the exposés, and are infinitely more fun to write.

The veterans who are secure in their jobs see camp through eyes that have seen it all before. They run and sweat and curse the heat, but it's still low-key for them because the pressure hasn't really started yet. The ones with a thirst try to figure out a way of beating the curfew, and this is fun, too, because they know that most coaches accept the late-hour sneak-outs and the fines as part of the game. After all, the season hasn't started yet, and thirsty veterans often make the best players anyway.

Sometimes a different kind of problem comes up on clubs that have a closely knit veterans group: the problem of saving a buddy his job when a rookie threatens to take it away from him. It can be brutal on the rookie, especially if he comes to camp with a big reputation and an even bigger bonus. And many a sensitive youngster never makes it because the veterans ride him off the team—in subtle ways, such as a steady hammering on the field, even in dummy scrimmages, and the silent treatment when practice is over. For the veterans, though, it's a matter of relative morality. What's more important, saving your best friend's job or worrying about a rich rookie's tender sensibilities?

For the borderline veteran, camp is a horror, and he views every wind sprint, every set of calisthenics, as an excuse for the coach to unload him if he doesn't perform well enough. The man who has a working knowledge of his body knows that, once he gets to a certain age, sprinting and excercising in 90-degree heat will take that much more away from the energy he is desperately trying to hoard for the contact scrimmages, which he knows are the real tests of who stays and who goes.

The high-draft rookie knows that he's almost assured of a spot on the roster, since 1) he probably has a no-cut contract, and even if the club trims him from the roster it must still pay him his full salary, which will usually swing the economy-minded coaches over to his side, and 2) cutting a high-draft choice right away lays the coach's original judgment wide open to assaults from the press and the owners. The rookie should be responsible enough to want to absorb the system as quickly and as thoroughly as he can. And the high-priced youngster must be careful that he doesn't rub any of the veterans the wrong way, since they can make his life intolerable on the field. He knows he can expect little help from the coaches in this area. Their primary interest is seeing how well he takes the pressure. "Intestinal fortitude" is their name for it.

"Sometimes I wonder, when I read some rookie quoted in the paper about how confident he is about making the team and how he doesn't expect pro football to be that tough," says the Rams' defensive tackle, Merlin Olsen.

"It's the worst thing a rookie can say and it shows that he's either very confident or very stupid. No one who has played the game for a while thinks it's very easy at all, and the longer you play the tougher you realize it is. A rookie who says stuff like that is just digging his own grave, because the veterans will read it and remind him about it every day."

"Rookies are like children," says the Jets' defensive back, Jimmy Richards. "They should be seen but not heard.

"I remember how a couple of them ran their mouths the first year I was in camp, how they didn't think a couple of the veterans were so good and how they were going to beat them out. But a few days later they were gone. The veterans don't talk to you for two reasons. One, you're a threat to their job, and two, they don't want to bother getting friendly with somebody who might be gone in a few days anyway.

"I kept to myself and I kept quiet. I figured if nobody noticed me, maybe they'd keep me around."

"I used to practice by myself that first year in camp," says Ram quarterback Roman Gabriel, who was a first-round draft choice in 1962. "I'd throw the ball, and then run and pick it up, and throw it back. That was my practice."

Camp is usually a nightmare for the low-draft rookie, but the pressure he faces isn't as severe as that of a marginal vet. The low-draft or free agent knows his status pretty well before he even gets to camp. Unless he's very naïve, he realizes that he won't get as long a look as the rookie who represents a sizable investment by the club, and he knows that, statistically, the chances of his making the squad are slim. Sometimes that can be an even greater incentive.

"This is what's exciting. This is the thrilling part of training camp," said the Jets' defensive back, John Dockery, a Harvard graduate who had been sent down to the minor leagues and re-called.

"It's the wondering that makes it exciting—wondering if you'll be around next week. Sometimes I feel sorry for guys like Joe Na-math, never knowing what this is like."

Long after I have forgotten about individual touchdown passes and great goal line stands, I will remember some of those rookies' faces in the Jets' training camps I covered.

I remember the first time I interviewed Lee Jacobsen, a pale, slender linebacker from Nebraska. He said his father owned a popcorn farm.

"That's right, popcorn. It's a different kind of corn. Let me tell you, there's good money in it."

The Jets brought in a free agent one year named Bill Connor, a 6-7, 270-pound defensive tackle, the terror of the Atlantic Coast League. I saw him the day he left, sitting in Weeb Ewbank's office with a face as long as a field goal.

"I just don't like to hit people anymore," he told the coach.

The same year, the Jets drafted Tom Myslinski, a square-jawed offensive guard from Maryland. His cut personally pained Ew-bank, who got more sensitive about the job of cutting as he got older.

"You'll never see a better attitude on a kid," Ewbank said that night at dinner.

"The tears were streaming down his face when I told him he was cut. 'It's my pass blocking, isn't it?' he said. I told him it was.

" 'I know it,' he said. 'I just can't keep those guys out of there.' "

Some rookies try to make it through sheer mayhem, such as the Jets' punt returner, Mike Battle, who waged a frantic war with everyone on the field. To the veterans he was known as "Joe Don Battle," or "Crazy Mike," but that first day in camp he opened up with some of the stuff that lay below the surface.

"I quit school my senior year at Southern Cal and got a job as a garbage collector, just to strengthen my legs," he said. "I didn't get paid for it. I don't know what I'll do if I get cut from here. I don't know how I'll ever go home. I'll probably have to sleep in a garbage can."

"I had a job in a bakery, taking metal cake tins out of the

stove," said Bob Taylor, a halfback who was cut after the exhibition season started.

"They paid me five dollars a week and I thought it was big money."

The year Joe Namath announced his retirement—and then came back—the Jets brought an extra quarterback to camp, Harold Olson, a free agent from Illinois State. The day Namath reported, Olson was cut. The two quarterbacks took part in one practice session together.

"At least I had that," Olson said. "I can say I met him. That's all the people back home will ask me about—Joe Namath. I wonder if he'll remember my name."

The Giants' defensive backfield coach, Emlen Tunnell, has a special place in his heart for low-draft rookies, especially the ones from the poorer homes. Not all assistants are so concerned.

"Do me a favor, will you?" he once asked a writer. "Go over to some of these guys with your notebook and pencil and pretend you're interviewing them, even though you don't really intend to write anything. It'll mean a lot to them. It'll give them something to remember."

The actual cutting is handled by the coach, but the most feared man in camp is the assistant equipment man or assistant PR director, the one who has the unenviable job of knocking on the player's door and delivering his dreadful message—"Coach wants to see you." He is called The Turk, a reference to the traditional vision of a scimitar-wielding Turk. The big cut night (which usually precedes the day in which rosters have to be trimmed to conform to league standards) is called The Night of the Turk.

"I had that job for two years," said a college kid who used to work in the Giants' camp in the summer. "Then this year they told me I was going to be Turking again and I told them to go to hell. I'd go back to summer school first.

"So they left me alone for a day and then they said, 'OK, if you won't Turk then go over to the gym and help the trainer. You can sort out the used jocks and socks and put them in the laundry bin.'

"I was happy. It was nice, honest work."

Sometimes the job is handled by phone, which is just as bad.

"You just sit up in your room and concentrate on making the

phone not ring," Dallas rookie Charlie Collins told sportswriter Steve Perkins.

"One morning the phone rang at 9 o'clock. My roommate said, 'It's for you.' It was the girl on the switchboard. My head was buzzing so bad I could hardly make out what she said—'Coach Meyers wants to see you.'

"I bounced from wall to wall going down the hall. The one thing that kept going through my mind was, 'But I'm not ready to stop playing football.' I asked the girl where coach Myers' room was and she said, 'Not coach Myers—Curt Mosher is the one who wants to see you.' I could have kissed her. Mosher had a Dallas radio station on the line that wanted to interview me."

The thing the veterans remember most about training camp is the conditioning, the sheer physical drudgery. Camp starting dates are set by the club and they vary from team to team, but they're all within a week apart, in the first part of July. The rookies report a week earlier than the veterans. But some vets with a particular problem, such as overweight, might be invited back early, with the rookies. When a coach is putting in a new offensive system, he might invite his quarterbacks back early, too.

The first few weeks of practice involve two workouts a day, one in the morning, one in the afternoon. There is usually a squad meeting for an hour before each session, and on every other evening there is another meeting, in which the players break down into smaller groups, by position. The assistant coach in charge of the position conducts those meetings. Each squad varies the schedule, alloting more or less meeting and practice time, according to the experience and physical condition of his squad.

Two-a-day workouts last until the week before the first exhibition game, usually the first week in August. Most team physicians feel that the majority of injuries occur during those double practice sessions, since the physical stamina and resistance to injury are lowered.

"You need the two-a-day workouts to do all your conditioning work," says Dallas coach Tom Landry. "That's when you get them in shape for the season. Once the games start, you can't spend time on it. But before a game, whether it's a regular-season game or an exhibition, they need a few days to get their legs back, so you have to knock off the two-a-days."

The degree of severity of the workouts varies with the different philosophies of the coaches. Vince Lombardi runs a punishing camp. Weeb Ewbank's is generally milder. Sometimes a coach will change his style, easing up one year, cracking down the next. Norm Van Brocklin ran an easy camp his first year with the Minnesota Vikings. The club was an expansion team, stocked with veterans from other clubs, and Van Brocklin didn't want to punish people.

Next year, with an influx of rookies, he cracked the whip.

"I never saw anything like it," said the great halfback, Hugh McElhenny. "We scrimmaged during the week, even in the regular season. In 10 years of football I'd never seen that."

Landry used to have everyone run a mile in camp, and he made his players do it until they ran it within a specified time—six minutes for backs and ends, seven minutes for tackles, etc. He did it until his tight end, Pettis Norman, collapsed one day during the fourth lap and needed emergency treatment from a heart specialist. Landry's current program calls for four laps, with one minute's rest in between.

Players who report to camp overweight receive special treatment. Ewbank used to fine his jumbos, like 330-pound Sherman Plunkett and 300-pound Jim Harris, a dollar a day for every pound they were overweight. But some coaches merely resign themselves to the fact that a player who "plays fat" stays fat in camp. And as long as he does well in the scrimmages, the coach will look the other way while he waddles through the conditioning work.

Detroit's Buddy Parker resigned himself to the fact that his All-League defensive middle guard, Les Bingaman, carried 300 to 360 pounds during his career. One day at camp he discussed Bingo's weight with line coach Buster Ramsey.

"That boy's put on a few pounds," Parker said. "He must weigh 400."

"Bingo doesn't go much over 330," Ramsey said.

So they made a steak bet, Parker maintaining that Bingaman's weight was closer to 400 than 330. The only scale they could find was in a feed and grain store in Ypsilanti, Michigan, and when Bingaman stepped on it, the needle stopped at 349½.

"See that," Ramsey said. "I told you he wasn't overweight."

After the Rams lost to Minnesota in the 1969 Western Division championship game, the quotes that came out of the Los Angeles dressing room led back to the same thing—all the work that had gone into bringing the team so far, especially the camp work.

"A whole season, all that work, the two-a-day workouts—all of it down the drain in one game," said Deacon Jones, echoing the sentiments of his teammates.

But the professional football player is still not as finely conditioned as the college athlete. The reason is twofold. For one thing, professional players need extra bulk to stand the week-to-week pounding. If they got too finely tuned in August, they would be worn down in December, 20 games later. And college football has 10 more minutes of playing time than the professional game—almost a full quarter more.

The reason is the time-out rule. In college football the clock stops each time there is a first down, and doesn't start until the sticks are moved into place. The rule was put in to create more plays for the TV fan. And in college football, a team must put the ball in play within 25 seconds. In professional ball the limit is 30, which amounts to another five seconds per play. In 1968, for instance, the top six college teams averaged 80.9 plays per game. In the pros, the top six averaged 63.1.

"There are about two players in this camp who could make it through one of Bear Bryant's practices," said Jet rookie Mike Hall, fresh off the Alabama campus.

"All my life I was told to keep my weight down, keep my weight down," says Boston's defensive end, Karl Henke. "I knew I had to get it higher for pro ball, but every time I'd gain it would go right to my belly and I couldn't stand the sight of myself, so I'd lose it again.

"Then I showed up in camp and there were all those big fat linemen with their big fat butts, shoving me around. I felt sick."

Every coach has his idea of what the training camp setting should be like, and most of them agree on one thing—it shouldn't be near the temptations of a big city. So most clubs take their players to college campuses that are remote.

Two years ago the Jets switched to the campus of Hofstra University in Hempstead, Long Island, about 30 miles from Manhattan. The first thing the players noticed were coeds, lovely ones in all shapes and sizes. Hofstra's summer school was in full session.

"Weeb—the players—they're all going up to the girls' rooms," an assistant gasped one night.

"Well, that's one good thing about this place," Ewbank said. "If they want it, it's right here on campus. They don't have to go driving into New York at all hours for it. And you know the ones that are going to get it are going to get it somehow."

The Jets' old camp was at Peekskill Military Academy. The bedsprings were ancient and they would collapse under too much stress. The field was uneven. The food was terrible. But even Peekskill was better than the Titans' old training base—East Stroudsburg, Pennsylvania.

"Not once during that hot, dry summer of 1962 had anyone watered the field," said Alex Kroll, an offensive tackle on the '62 Titans. "Don Maynard's legs took six weeks to loosen up after sprinting on the concrete-hard surface."

The Dallas Cowboys switched their camp to Thousand Oaks, California, after spending their initial season of 1960 in St. John's Academy in Wisconsin.

"The place was like a medieval castle," recalled Jerry Tubbs, a linebacker on the early Cowboy teams. "All it needed was a moat."

The buildings were old and dark, and the players dressed in a basement that was so murky that they named it The Dungeon.

"It was so damp in that basement," said Jack Eskridge, the equipment manager, "that a player could leave his shoes overnight and find them covered with mold in the morning."

The players roomed two to a cubicle, with a bare light bulb in the center of the room. Every night, when the lights went out, the dorm would be filled with hooting and groaning, and somewhere a player would invariably yell, "Quiet down there! This is the warden." At breakfast one morning one player asked another: "Was that you rattling your cup against the bars last night?" The camp's biggest hero that year was defensive tackle Ed Hussman, who killed a bat on the second floor of the players' dorm one evening.

The club moved to St. Olaf College in Northfield, Minnesota, next year, and the players used to dress in a converted cow barn. Next year the site was Northern Michigan College in Marquette, near the Canadian border. The pipes used to freeze at night, the temperature rarely got above 50 degrees and the trainer reported a record number of knee injuries. "They just can't get loose," he said. "It's not warm enough." Thousand Oaks, though, with its hot days and breezy nights, proved to be the answer.

"I'll never forget my first camp, Atlanta in '66," said the Giants' linebacker, Ralph Heck. "Black Mountain, North Carolina. A little YMCA retreat 25 miles from Asheville. They just hacked a practice field out of the woods, where no air could get in. They held their first practice at 10 A.M. The first rookie passed out at 10:16."

Sometimes a club's choice of practice venue is dictated by finances—or lack of them. The Miami Dolphins' first camp was in St. Petersburg, Florida. There had been an offer from Suncoast Sports, Inc., to underwrite the camp cost of $70,000, but when the club arrived, it found no Suncoast Sports, Inc., only John Burroughs, whose son was a linebacker candidate. The field was a thin layer of sod over seashells, which Burroughs, Sr., used to go over with a roller every day. When the son was cut, the father, and roller, vanished, and the team practiced on just seashells.

Players dressed in their hotel rooms, which were decorated by socks and jocks and pads hung up to dry, which gave an interesting smell to their living quarters. The hotel dining room served so much Chinese food that middle linebacker Wahoo McDaniel once remarked, "From now on they'll have to carry me to practice in a ricksha."

Coaches are not always the best judges of the training camp attitude of their squad. Two days before the 1957 season, Buddy Parker quit as Detroit coach.

"This is the worst team I've ever seen in training camp," he said. "They have no life, no go; they're just a completely dead team. I know the situation. I don't want to get into the middle of another losing seaon."

So Buddy went to Pittsburgh, where he had a 6-6 record, and George Wilson took over at Detroit. Three months later, after Detroit beat Cleveland, 59-14, to win the NFL championship, Wilson said, "These are the fightingest damn bunch of guys I've ever seen."

The strangest week of training camp I've ever seen came in 1969, when Namath was weighing his decision to sell Bachelors

III and come out of retirement. He paid one or two secret night visits to camp to talk to the players. Johnny Sample, the defensive back, was his liaison man with the press.

And I'll never forget John, standing in the middle of the press room, feeding us Namath quotes.

"What was he wearing tonight?" someone asked one time.

"Uh, let's see. Blue bell-bottoms. And a sort of a T-shirt, and a gray, make that a blue golf jacket over that."

16
Football and the Medics

Houston, October 9, 1960: About four minutes after the kickoff we were huddled on about our 35-yard line. God it was hot. It was hard to get air and the gritty grime of sweat caused my pads to slip across my skin. Next to me in the left guard spot, Howard Glenn's voice seeped out the words, "I don't think I can make it." I looked over to him, slapped him on the butt in a gesture of encouragement and Al Dorow called the play. It was a pass which was completed to Don Maynard.

Back in the huddle again, we leaned forward with hands on knees wait-- ing for the strategy from our quarterback. Hot stinging water ran into my eyes, causing them to burn with salt. To my right, Art Powell, the end, said, "Damn it's hot," and to my left, Glenn repeated, "I don't think I can make it."

When the play was over and we started to move back to huddle again, Glenn was moving slow as if cramped. "Howard, you OK?" I asked. "I . . . I'm sick," he said. "I gotta go out." Then another voice said, "Naw, stick in here, Glenn. Suck it up." There were flecks of foam in the cor- ners of his mouth and I caught the faint smell of a horrible odor.

"I . . . I can . . . I can make it," he said, gasping. "C'mon, call the play!" someone shouted. Again I slapped Glenn on the butt. The odor he expelled was getting worse and the heat made it cling about us. We didn't make the first down and we punted and Glenn stayed out of the game.

After the game we found Howard sitting nude in a metal chair and holding a towel to his chest. We backed away, looking at his body twitch. He was straining to breathe and that odor was still with him. He still clutched the towel to his chest. "Why in hell don't you get a doctor to him!" Powell shouted at the trainer.

I was just pulling my shoulder pads away from my body when I turned to see Glenn's body fall—like a drunk's—to the floor. He was sprawled flat on his back, staring toward the ceiling. I didn't think he could see. Quickly, I went to his side. All around him, the other players had gath- ered, water from the shower dripping from their bodies.

A fit of uncontrollable coughing seized him. "It's . . . it's coming out," he said in a weak voice.

"Turn 'im over!" Powell shouted.

Then the smelly, yellow-green mucus bubbled from his mouth. Several hands seemed to reach in and wipe it away. He struggled with his tongue, and his eyes bore no pupil. Soon an ambulance came to take him to a Houston hospital.

On the plane back, Ed Bell reached across the seat and touched me on the shoulder. "Don't take this as final fellows," Ed said to Art Powell and me, "but Steve Sebo *[general manager]* boarded a few minutes ago and said that Howard died at the hospital." . . . All I could see in my mind was Glenn's body lying in the water on the cement floor. He died a lonely death.

It took time and reasoning for me to get over Howard Glenn's death. Even today, it enters my mind often. I wonder if he really died from what was reported, a broken neck suffered in the game with Dallas the week before.

□ Ernie Barnes, N.Y. Titan tackle, 1960

The tragic death of Howard Glenn was not wasted because it brought a new breed of doctor into the game: Men such as Dr. James Nicholas, orthopedic specialists, top men in their field, doctors who attacked the problem of football injuries with dedication.

"I had been in private practice up until then," said Dr. Nicholas, who is known for the repair work he did on Joe Namath's knees, and for the back operation he performed on President John F. Kennedy.

"I was doing research on bones—what made them hard and soft, why bone injuries were so severe in older people. Harry Wismer, the Titans' owner, was one of my private patients. He kept asking me to come over to the Titans. The money he offered was negligible—something like $2,000 for the season. But after Howard Glenn died, I went. I've been with the Titans, and Jets, ever since."

The world that Dr. Nicholas entered was just emerging from the orthopedic dark ages. Only the most advanced of the team physicians believed in immediate knee surgery. Players hobbled around on torn ligaments that had been packed in ice and thrown in a cast.

"One thing they didn't have in my day," Bronko Nagurski said not too long ago, "was all this knee surgery. When you got hurt, you went ahead and played."

"We weren't at all sure about knee operations back when I

played," said Sammy Baugh, the coach of the Titans in 1960. "We were kind of leery about them. We'd crip around and try to play anyway."

"I remember one season we played 29 games with only 16 men," the Chicago Cards' old fullback, Ernie Nevers, says. "You couldn't afford to get hurt. We had one guy with a trick knee and he'd tell us, 'Listen, if you see me down and unable to get up, for God's sakes, jerk my knee back in place so I can go on playing.' "

Many clubs back in 1960 had team doctors who were kind of lovable old oddballs, friends of the owner, or just super-fans. There was the Giants' Doc Sweeney, for instance, who hated everybody who played for the other team. The famous Doc Sweeney story concerns the Chicago Bear who suffered a gashed cheek against the Giants in the Polo Grounds. The Bears had no doctor along on the trip, so Doc Sweeney was drafted into service for an emergency stitch job. When the job was finished, it was discovered that he had stitched the player's tongue to the inside of his cheek.

"He talked too much anyway," Doc Sweeney said.

"One time we were up at training camp and a priest passed out from heat prostration while he was watching the practice," the Giants' publicist, Don Smith, remembers. "It was late in the afternoon and Doc Sweeney was taking a little snooze, so they woke him up and rushed him out to the field.

"By now our two trainers, Johnny Johnson and John Dziegel, were working on him. Doc Sweeney rushed in and started to take his pulse.

" 'Why, this man's pulse is perfectly normal,' the doc said.

" 'For Christ sake!' Johnson yelled. 'That's my arm you've got there.' "

The first thing Dr. Nicholas learned when he entered this strange world of medical science was that he was dealing with a different kind of patient than he had ever seen, than most doctors ever see.

"I had to reevaluate my thinking, change my standards," he says. "A doctor who sees normal patients in his regular practice doesn't understand what professional football players are able to live with. When you first come in, you think of them in terms of the patients you were used to treating, and I was overly cautious at first. I shuddered at the callousness of the people in the game.

But there are certain injuries, injuries that would keep normal people out of action for a couple of weeks, that a man can play football with. They're painful, but they won't lead to further damage. You have to learn to draw the line between those kinds of injuries and the ones that might get much worse if you let the man play."

Very few team physicians are in football today to make money. They are in it because the violent, dangerous life the players lead is medically challenging. A team doctor might get paid a $5,000 to $10,000 retainer for the season, and a few might get more, but it's only a small fraction of what they could make if they devoted the same time to private practice. The game has attracted some of the country's top orthopedic specialists, and the closer they get the more they realize that research—careful, scientific research that exists in other areas—has been dreadfully lacking.

And they realize another thing: the deeper they go into research and the more facts they uncover, analyze, and present to the professional football establishment, the farther they get from that establishment. And the tougher their job becomes.

"We are outlanders in the eyes of the establishment," said one team physician who wished to remain anonymous. "There are two reasons for this. First of all, the more information we uncover about injuries, the worse it is for the pro football image. People in the Commissioner's office don't like to read about injuries. It gives the game a bad name, as far as they're concerned. And a lot of the newspaper stories are distorted for dramatic effect, with very little actual knowledge behind them.

"Then there's the question of the Players' Association and insurance payments and the compensation laws. The more we uncover, the more it stirs up these people, and the owners don't especially care for that.

"In 1969, Dr. Nicholas headed a group called the Team Physicians' Committee. It still exists, and the top men in the business are on it, men like the Buffalo Bills' Joe Godfrey, and vice president of the American Academy of Orthopedic Surgeons; and the Cards' Fred Reynolds, who's head of orthopedics at Washington University of St. Louis and a past president of the academy; and the Denver Broncos' Mack Clayton, who is head of the University of Colorado's orthopedics department. They had the backing and help of three of the country's leading medical groups.

"They wanted to do independent research into the nature of injuries in pro football, an area that had hardly been touched. Sure, you read gimmick stories every so often about some new cleat that's going to cut down injuries or about how AstroTurf is going to be a cure-all for all knee injuries. But no one had scientifically researched the whole injury question. They asked the Commissioner's office for help. Do you know how much they got— $10,000 in 1969, and then nothing in 1970. I'd like to see figures comparing that $10,000 with the money spent researching something like television, which is the biggest money-maker in the game.

"The only other medical area where pro football spends money, that I know of, is the University of Michigan computer study in frequency of injury by position, the one started by the Eagles' Dr. James Nixon. I think they get something like $20,000 a year from the club owners."

Pro football has often shown unique intelligence in some aspects of the game—i.e., television—but has a history of a penny-wise, pound-foolish approach to the whole problem of injuries. There are clubs that will delay surgery on a player, hopeful of squeezing an extra game or two out of him, even though it might cost him a full year—or a career.

The Oakland Raiders have perhaps the saddest record in this respect. The team's managing general partner, Al Davis, has the overall say on all club matters, including medical ones, and three of his best recent players—defensive back Kent McCloughan (knee), defensive tackle Dan Birdwell (knee) and defensive tackle Tom Keating (achilles tendon)—were delayed surgery cases. Keating missed the entire 1968 season, Birdwell the entire season of 1969, and McCloughan dressed for the 1969 games but was virtually useless.

In high-school and college ball, where medical treatment is on a more primitive level, the situation is even worse.

Joe Namath suffered extensive ligament damage in his right knee in his senior year at Alabama, but he was packed in ice and sent on the field in a few weeks, and he has had to live with a set of 70-year-old knees ever since. Terry Hanratty suffered knee ligament damage in his senior year at Notre Dame, but the university held off on surgery. And it was only after Hanratty, who now quarterbacks the Steelers, went home and privately contacted the Buffalo Bills' Dr. Godfrey that his knee was repaired.

Injuries are getting to be the most important factors in determining a team's chances for success or failure. The 1969 Super Bowl champions, the New York Jets, went through the season without any significant injuries to veterans. The 1970 champions, the Kansas City Chiefs, sent their same defensive team on the field every week of the season—and in all three postseason games. The Chiefs' big injury was to quarterback Len Dawson, a chancy type of thing that had people keeping their fingers crossed, right up until the Super Bowl was wrapped up.

Dawson suffered knee ligament and cartilage injuries early in the season. An operation would take him out for the year. No operation meant that he would eventually come back with a wobbly knee that could go at any time. The choices were put squarely to him, and he took the gamble. He was 34 years old. He had a chance to cash in big. He knew the same chance might never come again. The knee was put in a cast for five weeks. It emerged wobbly, but it held up for the rest of the year. It will probably wobble a little for the remainder of his career.

Other quarterbacks haven't had it so easy. The Year of the Quarterback—1968—put 18 of pro football's 26 starters out of action for two games or more. Buffalo had five quarterbacks laid up at one time or another. In 1969 a rash of sore arms hit six of the game's finest quarterbacks. The newspapers ask, "What can be done to protect pro football's stars?" There are editorials about the brutality of pro football. And there are cure-all diagnoses—such as the Monsanto Corporation's steady drumbeat about its synthetic grass product, AstroTurf: "Buy AstroTurf and watch knee injuries disappear"; "Statistics show that AstroTurf cuts serious injuries by 60 percent." Or 40 percent, or 50, depending on which ad you read.

The medical fraternity winces at these ads, which are usually the result of the barest of scientific study.

"You need at least five years' study of artificial surfaces before you can make any meaningful conclusions," Dr. Jack C. Hughston said in the March 5, 1970, *Medical Journal.* Dr. Hughston is chairman of the American Academy of Orthopedic Surgeons' committee on sports medicine. "On the basis of three years of football statistics collected in Seattle, there is no appreciable difference in the rate of serious injuries on artificial and real turf." Seattle was one of the early AstroTurf pioneers.

There are doctors who maintain that artificial turf may cause more serious shoulder injuries, because the players travel at higher speeds. And Dr. Nicholas says that the ripple-sole shoes or soccer shoes that players wear on pseudo-turf cause foot injuries similar to those suffered by ballet dancers.

"Some of those injuries may take eight to 10 weeks to heal fully, as long as some knee injuries," he says. "Dallas halfback Calvin Hill suffered his foot injury on synthetic turf, and it never did come around all season. And look at the Houston Oilers. Ode Burrell broke his leg on AstroTurf, and Pete Beathard, their quarterback, broke his foot on the same surface."

Artificial turf may indeed be the answer to knee injuries someday, but no competent researcher likes the way the pseudoscientific data is dropped on the public. Monsanto, for instance, takes out regular ads in the *Sporting News,* ads that are designed to look like actual newspaper stories.

The members of the blue-chip study group, the Team Physicians' Committee, keep pushing on with their research—on their own.

"The big problem," Dr. Nicholas says, "is the lack of historical data. Full medical records weren't always kept. And if they were, a lot of them were thrown out. Most club doctors now realize that the best way to attack the problem is to try and find out what causes injuries, and once you've isolated the causes you can start working on them."

Some clubs ask all rookies to fill out medical questionnaires that can run up to five pages long. These documents try to isolate the player's entire history of injuries, and tell the doctor something about the person himself. Some questions:

". . . Did your injury require, a) hospitalization b) aspiration (draining) c) injection d) bracing e) cast f) operation g) crutches h) special studies (EEG, spinal tap) i) one month or more of rehabilitation j) re-operation?

". . . Were you treated by a) an orthopedic surgeon b) general practitioner c) trainer?

". . . Do you think your injury was a) avoidable b) unavoidable?

". . . Do you think that you received a) excellent b) fair c) poor care?

". . . Do you take pep pills before a game?

". . . If you answered yes, do you have any idea what the strength of the pill is?

". . . Do you gain, lose more than 10 pounds in the off-season?

". . . Which functional part of the body seems hardest to train a) arms b) legs c) wind d) endurance?

An injury during the professional season isn't just an injury. It's a vital statistic that's fed into the Team Physicians' Committee's computerized study that matches anything IBM could think up. Every conceivable circumstance surrounding the injury is covered. For example:

FIELD AND CONDITIONS: Temperature——Humidity—— Playing surface (dry——hard——wet——mud——frozen—— holes——uneven——)

ACTIVITY: Calisthenics——Drills——Sprints——Passing ——Running——Punting——Kickoff——Field Goal/PAT—— Fumble——Interception——Other——

CONTACT: Nail——Clip——Blind side (or believed)—— Crackback——Blocked——Tackled——Rule Infraction——

And, of course, every article of equipment is accounted for.

The results of these surveys can tell a prospective pro some interesting things about his injury prospects. If, for instance, he is a loose-jointed person, if he can touch his toes no matter what kind of shape he's in, he'll get a ligament injury sooner than he will break a bone or pull a muscle.

If you're a five-year veteran, your chance of serious injury is less than that of a rookie. The law of natural selection works here, and the injury-prone people have been weeded out in high school and college and the first few years in pro ball.

You're more likely to get hurt in the exhibition season than during the regular season, thanks to the heat and the two-a-day workouts. The odds are 2-1. You're more likely to get hurt on the road than at home, thanks to the unfamiliar conditions. Again, 2-1 odds.

The chances that you'll undergo an operation sometime during your professional career are about one in four. And if you do nothing but play on special teams—punt, kickoff, etc.—the chances of your getting hurt are three times greater than those of an offensive or defensive regular (offense is slightly safer than defense, because the offensive player knows when a contact is coming).

The University of Michigan study tells us that the safest position in football is offensive center. The area is the most congested, and the momentum is less. The centers might have to live with headaches for a day or so, but their legs usually won't get torn up by the violent open-field contacts.

Special teams, naturally, are the unsafest positions. Then come running backs (again, the momentum factor). Defensive end and linebacker are trouble positions; offensive line and defensive tackle, relatively safe. Wide receivers and cornerbacks vary. Some years are worse than others. Until lately, quarterback was a safe position.

"The biggest factor in predicting injuries is momentum," Dr. Nicholas says. "That's why we don't have drills like the Nutcracker in our training camp. It's brutal."

The Nutcracker is a showpiece type of thing in which one lineman works against another one, within the confines of two dummies. The offensive man blocks the defensive man, and a back runs through the hole, keeping within the area marked off by the dummies. Sometimes the drill is expanded to include a second offensive lineman and a linebacker.

"It separates the men from the boys; it tells us who our hitters are," is the way Nutcracker coaches put it, but it's costly, too. The Giants' fullback Tucker Frederickson, began his whole parade of knee and leg injuries in a Nutcracker drill one day in camp, and the same club lost another runner, Allen Jacobs, in a 1969 Nutcracker exercise.

The world of the coach and that of the team physician are often miles apart.

"It must be murder to be a doctor under Vince Lombardi," a

sympathetic physician once said. "It must be a constant battle with yourself."

The Redskin coach practices what *New York Post* columnist Larry Merchant once called, "The pick-up-your-bed-and-walk school of medicine—or the Church of Lombardi Scientist." His approach to injuries is mental: ignore them and they'll go away. His Packers won three championships by shrugging off aches and pains, sometimes even more serious hurts. But most veterans seem to learn to play with pain.

"Bruises, cuts, pulls, twists, sprains, and so forth we call 'hangnails,'" says the Rams' defensive tackle, Merlin Olsen. "The only 'injuries' are broken bones or things which destroy your movement. Injuries drive you to the bench.

"I was only benched four times in my first six seasons. The last time, I had my ankle torn up and it was agony to try to stand on it. But it was also agony to sit and watch someone not as good as me botch up plays. So I conditioned myself to play with pain.

"In San Francisco once, I was kicked in the groin early in the game and again before halftime. It hurt terribly, but I kept telling myself I was a coward looking for an easy way out. I brainwashed myself into carrying on. I finished the game. In the locker room afterward I couldn't untie my shoes. I was in the hospital four days.

"Our wives say we keep complaining, and it's hard to put up with our moans and groans. We do take it out on them. You can only ignore pain so long. When the game is over and you're home, you give in to your misery. Some mornings after games I've gotten out of bed and collapsed. My legs just wouldn't support me. There have been Mondays when I couldn't raise my arm."

In a 1968 exhibition game, Ram quarterback Roman Gabriel had his hand stepped on. The hand was X-rayed and the picture showed two older breaks that had healed. He had played with them and said nothing. But the highest pain threshold in pro football probably belonged to 6-8, 270-pound defensive end Doug Atkins.

"In one game," said New Orleans defensive coach Jack Faulkner, "Doug came over to the sideline and said, 'My leg feels funny.' He was still walking around on it that night. All he had was a broken tibia."

"You get caught up in a game and you do strange things," Dr. Nicholas said. "One time one of our safetymen, Mike D'Amato, got hit on the head. On the sidelines I asked him where he was and what quarter it was. He answered perfectly. Then I asked him to count backward from 100—by sevens—and he did that, too. Then I asked him his wife's name and he said, 'Barbara,' so I let him go back into the game.

"About two minutes later I said, 'Hey, wait a minute. His wife's name is Rita.' So I got him out of there."

All doctors have their favorite stories about coaches. The Raiders' Dr. Kendall Small remembers the time linebacker Archie Matsos banged his head against Denver fullback Cookie Gilchrist's knee in an exhibition game.

"He was in convulsions as he came down to the ground," Dr. Small says. "He was out for 20 minutes and I feared for his life. As I was examining him, a coach came up.

" 'Will Arch be ready by next Sunday?' he asked."

At one practice session, Oakland quarterback Tom Flores took a blow on his bicep. "I took him into the trainer's room and applied ice," Dr. Small says. "Just then a coach came up. 'Is that the coldest ice you can find?' he said."

Lombardi once said that "fatigue makes cowards of us all." His rigid training sessions leave a trail of fatigued bodies, but his athletes generally have better luck avoiding those fourth-quarter injuries that don't usually happen earlier in the game.

Players always look for an easy answer to fatigue. The amphetamine family of pep pills, such as Benzedrine ("bennies") and dexedrine pop up in many dressing rooms. Some players figure vitamin B_{12} shots are the answer, although medical science hasn't yet proved it. And there are milder forms of pick-me-ups, such as energy-producing dextrose pills, honey . . . even candy bars. The bennies actually provide a quick jolt, but they also present a medical problem—hyperactivity, or a nervous system that can run haywire.

"Some players just can't operate without them," Dr. Small says. "They've come to depend on them as much as their helmets. I've seen players take drugs that would make you and me climb the walls.

"Most team physicians disapprove of strong drugs. But the

coaches want them—for some athletes won't play without them. So what's a doctor to do? Well, he just turns his back. The trainer sets the pills out where the athletes who need them can see them, and he goes on with his taping."

Worst of all, say many doctors, the pep pills can jag up a player to the extent that he performs at a much more violent tempo than he normally would, causing more injuries to himself and others.

The area usually affected by these violent collisions is the unsuspecting knee. When God designed the human knee, he wasn't thinking about Gale Sayers or Leroy Kelly. If he were, he would have made it like the shoulder, a joint that can swivel around in all directions. The knee can only go front and back, like a hinge, and when it's forced to go sideways—either through a blow or the wrong kind of cut—it gives.

If the athlete is lucky, he suffers only damage to the cartilage, or menisci, which cushion the bones that lead into the knee. Removal of dislodged cartilage is a relatively minor operation. If he's especially lucky, he'll suffer only a "sprain," which is actually a partial tear of one of the four ligaments that hold the knee together. This can mend by itself. But if he's unlucky, one or more of the ligaments will tear, which can cause a snapping sound like the breaking of a bone.

In 1968 Sayers suffered what is known in medical slang as "The Terrible Triad of O'Donoghue, named after the University of Oklahoma's Dr. Don H. O'Donoghue, a pioneer in knee surgery. Three of the four ligaments (medial and lateral collateral, anterior and posterior cruciate) were torn, and the whole knee had to be rebuilt, using muscle tissue in place of the torn ligaments. (Actually there is a worse injury, a Terrible Quartet type of thing in which all four ligaments go. The Giants' center, Greg Larson, suffered this, but came back through surgery and intensive weight lifting.)

Dr. Theodore Fox, the Bears' orthopedist, diagnosed Sayers' injury immediately. He performed an operation that night. Three months later Sayers was lifting weights and jogging, and next season he was as good as new.

"Factor X—drive and motivation," Dr. Fox said. "Factor X elevates a player one plateau. It makes a star out of an average player and a superstar out of a star. My operation will contribute

60 percent to Sayers' recovery. Gale's strong desire—Factor X—will add the other 40 percent."

Dr. Fox was being modest. Instant diagnosis is often difficult to perform during a game.

"You have to be heartless," Dr. Nicholas says. "You have to test the mobility of the knee right away—before it fills up with blood and fluid. If you wait until it swells, it's too late. And to test it, you have to move it from side to side. It hurts. Sometimes the player lets out a yell, and the people watching look at you like you're a sadist. You're not damaging anything any further, but you can't be squeamish in something as important as this."

"You've got to operate right away," Dr. Fox says. "Wait 24 hours and the injury is like a bag of mush. It really would be like trying to stitch together two bags of cornmeal mush."

The great stars like Sayers and Namath make the headlines. The doctors do, too, but only in time of tragedy. A club pays them the same money that it tosses away on a bonus for a sixth-round draft choice. Pete Rozelle hasn't yet seen fit to bless the research these men perform. The owners wince when the subject of injuries come up at all. The cure-all corporations such as Monsanto don't like football's medics because they won't endorse the quick-cure schemes, like AstroTurf. And all the coaches want to know from the doctor is "When are you going to have our guy ready for us?"

But these men could well control the future of the game. Someday pro football may catch on.

17
All-Americans Unmasked: The Art of Scouting

I wish I could stick a needle in a boy's arm and measure desire.
□ Gil Brandt, Director of Player Personnel, Dallas Cowboys

I didn't know what free agent meant, until I saw my first paycheck.
□ Pete Gent

They're there every year, the free agents and low-draft choices who have made it big, a constant embarrassment and reminder that the computers and their science can only take you so far.

Willie Wood wasn't drafted. He got a look from the Packers when he jumped up and touched a goalpost. Minnesota grabbed Lonnie Warwick off an Arizona railroad gang. Thirteen rounds of picks went by before the Rams' gave Deacon Jones a call, and this was when the AFL-NFL talent war was raging.

The New Orleans Saints were starved for talent in 1967, but they waited until the very last round, the 420th player selection, until they picked Dan Abramowicz, who was trying to tell people he had broken every pass catching record at Xavier U.

He was an end without speed or size, but the New Orleans coach, Tom Fears, was once a slow end himself, and he saw just enough. Two years later Abramowicz led the NFL pass catchers and made one All-League team.

"If I was a scout, I wouldn't have grabbed Danny Abramowicz very high, either," Abramowicz says. "He didn't have much speed or size. You've got to be careful in the draft. You can't afford too many mistakes. But the low pick hurt my pride. It put a burning sensation in me to prove myself."

"Sure, guys like that come up every once in a while—sleepers," says Gil Brandt, who heads the Dallas Cowboys' scouting operation, the most sophisticated and high-priced operation in football.

"But you go broke trying to find the Ray Berrys and Tommy McDonalds. For every guy like that, a guy who defies the odds, there are hundreds of low drafts who wash out, people you never hear about. Pull one inside straight and you spend the rest of the night losing all your money trying to do it again."

People remember the rags-to-riches stories, the free agents and low drafts who buck the system and beat the odds. But the proven way to success is a steady stream of intelligent selections in the first few rounds of the college drafts.

The Kansas City Chiefs built the most powerful team in football because millionaire owner Lamar Hunt had the cash to sign the draft choices. The Chiefs didn't lose too many bidding wars to the NFL in the days of the troubles, and 16 of their starting 1970 Super Bowlers were drafted in the fifth round or higher. Eight of those 16 were first-round picks.

First rounders always make the squad, because their price tag is so high that it would be financially unsound to cut them, to say nothing of the way the press would handle such a move. In 1969, 18 first-round choices became starters, for all or part of the season, and a 1969 survey showed that 24 second-round choices made the squad; 21 third-round men; 16 fourth rounders; 10 fifth rounders, and nine sixth rounders. After that, it gets chancy because of the volume of teams drafting.

A team that is low in the standings will generally trade high draft choices for proven veterans. Sometimes it works, sometimes it doesn't, depending on how shrewd the team is and how good a spy network it has. A veteran goes on the trading block. If your informants tell you, "Don't touch him; he's all banged up," you lay off. But if you get the word that the problem is money, or there's a personality clash involved, you might take a chance. George Allen bailed out Los Angeles that way, and when the Rams finally arrived, he began to stockpile draft choices through trades. He had three first-round picks in '69.

Vince Lombardi built such a talent storehouse at Green Bay that, when he left the organization, there were still 10 No. 1 drafts on the club. And he had built up so many extra first-round picks, through trades, that the no-redshirt rule (no drafting for future years) had been put into effect.

The draft system is not infallible, though. In 1965, Tucker Frederickson and Donny Anderson were the blue chippers among the college running backs. Gale Sayers was just a speed burner with questionable size and a questionable future.

"Anderson is the finest back I've seen in 15 years," Green Bay scout Jerry Burns said—just before the Packers donated $600,000 toward the enrichment of Anderson. "The only college back I'd compare him with would be Hugh McElhenny when he was playing for the University of Washington. If Anderson isn't a star in the NFL, then everybody will miss their guess."

They're still waiting for Anderson to get there, and Sayers has been called one of the great runners of all time.

"We'd made our mind up about Butkus, our other No. 1 pick [from Pittsburgh], but I wasn't so sure about Sayers," George Halas said. "I'd drafted Ronnie Bull away from Lamar Hunt in '62, and I didn't want to get in a bidding war with Hunt over Sayers, especially since Gale would have been a big draw in Kansas City. I'd run the risk of losing him, and besides, there were plenty of other backs around.

"Then the night before the draft I saw some movies of the All-America team. I saw three of Sayers' runs that I had seen before. Then I saw a fourth one—from his sophomore year in 1962—a 96-yard TD run. It was a revelation. Gale showed me one move, a right-angle cut at full speed, that was simply incredible. Right then and there I realized I was watching somebody who could be the greatest runner of all time."

That same year—1964—Alabama quarterback Joe Namath finished 11th in the Heisman Award balloting. Four quarterbacks were ahead of him—Notre Dame's John Huarte (No. 1), Tulsa's Jerry Rhome (No. 2), Michigan's Bob Timberlake (No. 4) and California's Craig Morton (No. 7). Jet coach Weeb Ewbank was interested in Rhome. But the club's owner, Sonny Werblin, had a show business outlook on the game. He was looking for more than a quarterback. He wanted a man he could build into a personality.

"I met Rhome and all I saw was a crew-cut, introverted little guy with a squint," Werblin said. "I said to myself, 'This is not the man we'll build a franchise around.' "

So the Jets traded their rights to Rhome to Houston ("He said he wanted to play in Texas anyway," Ewbank said) and got the Oilers' No. 1 draft rights. And the quarterback turned out to be Namath. Werblin took care of the publicity angle with the $427,-000 package, and a star was born.

Then there's the other side of the coin. George Sauer, Sr., the Jets' chief scout, was old-fashioned enough to believe in scouting his talent himself, in the flesh.

"One year I drove down to Delaware with my wife to scout the Delaware-Buffalo game," Sauer said. "I was interested in John Stofa, the Buffalo quarterback, and a Delaware back—I think his name was Brown. It was a cold, miserable, rainy day, and, as usual, I was roaming up and down the sidelines without a coat.

"Well, Stofa didn't look like he had a strong enough arm, and the other kid didn't show me much, but every time Delaware had the ball and they ran it near one Buffalo kid, there would be this tremendous crash of bodies. I checked the program and the boy's name was Gerry Philbin, a defensive tackle. I wrote that name down.

"When I got back to the car, my wife was already inside, warming up the motor. I sat there shivering for half an hour before I could drive.

" 'No player is worth this,' she said.

" 'This one is,' I told her."

Philbin has been an All-AFL defensive end for two years.

The gambles pay off. The Colts awarded a twelfth-round draft choice to Preston Pearson, a 6-1 basketball player at Illinois. He hadn't gone to school on scholarship. And the whole football situation had been rocked by a slush fund scandal. Baltimore owner Carroll Rosenbloom got the tip on him from a friend of a friend who had seen him play halfback at Freeport, Illinois, High School, so the Colts gambled, and in his rookie year Pearson led the NFL in kickoff returns.

It's an inexact science, but so is medicine. The cure for cancer is just over the horizon, but the common cold still taunts us. And the free agents, the lowliest chattel of all, are always around to prove the value of humility.

Ewbank built the Jets from a garbage franchise into a Super Bowl champion through his choice of free agents. He had made friends in his NFL days, and people didn't mind passing along tips to Weeb. The Jets' whole Super Bowl defensive backfield consisted of free agents; also middle linebacker Al Atkinson, who had been cut by Buffalo; offensive tackle Winston Hill, an old Baltimore castoff; center John Schmitt and the record-breaking field goal man, Jim Turner, who couldn't make it with Washington.

The errors aren't only limited to the drafting table. The College All-Star game in Chicago, which runs its operation like a peanut stand, is a famous talent waster. Otto Graham didn't play Sayers in the '65 game. He didn't like his "attitude." Graham let John Sample and Ray Nitschke sit side by side on the bench for his All-Stars in the '58 game. He used Greg Cook only as a last-resort third-string quarterback in the '69 game, and Cook almost pulled the thing out for him. And Calvin Hill, the Cowboys' No. 1 draft in '69 and the only rookie to make All-NFL, wasn't even chosen for the '69 game. He finally came along because of the dropouts, but Graham didn't see fit to use him.

"Every time I think of Herb Adderley, it scares me to think about how I almost mishandled him," Vince Lombardi once said of the great Green Bay cornerback. It was only an injury that moved him over to defense.

"I will definitely be an offensive slotback with Green Bay," Adderley said just before he reported to the Packer camp. "I'll occasionally run a sweep or reverse. Lenny Moore's job with the Colts is a carbon copy of my job. I just hope I can be nearly as good."

Drafting has progressed from the old days, though, when people used to show up at the meetings with copies of Street & Smith's *Football Yearbook* in their pockets.

"In 1936, the first year they had the draft," Halas says, "all the names were put on a blackboard. If a man's name wasn't on that blackboard, you couldn't pick him. So there was always a big scramble for free agents. We came into that session with about 14 names, and when we got down to our last selection, there were two names left on the board. One of them was Danny Fortmann, a guard from Colgate.

"I said to myself, 'Fortmann, that sounds like a nice name, and Colgate is certainly a fine school. I'll take him.' He became one of the great guards in pro football."

The Giants' legendary story is about how Wellington Mara was trying to figure out whom to pick in the last round in '53, and he happened to glance at a copy of the *Pittsburgh Courier* that was lying open on a table. The paper had picked its Negro College All-America team, and the face of Morgan State's Roosevelt Brown was staring up at him. Mara liked the expression on Brown's face, so he picked him, and Brown became an All-NFL offensive tackle for years.

The only thing wrong with the story is that the Giants had three more rounds of drafting left, and on the twenty-eighth round they took Joe Ramona, a defensive guard, who made it with the club, and on the 29th and 30th they picked Bob Griffin, a back, and Stavros Kanakas, a linebacker, who didn't.

During the AFL's battle for survival, draft sessions were a grim business. The AFL would hold its secret drafts a couple of weeks before the rest of the world, and as a club picked a player, it would dispatch a "baby-sitter" to track him down and try to sign him.

"Around the fourth round," the Jets' PR man, Frank Ramos, recalls, "the room would be just about empty. Everybody was out looking for the guys they had drafted. So they'd have to adjourn the meeting and hold it over until the next day."

James Bond could have gotten a steady job during those war years. The AFL's Lamar Hunt once placed a long-distance call to first-round draft choice Roman Gabriel. The Rams' Elroy Hirsch, who was camped in Gabriel's room as a baby-sitter, got the call instead, imitated Gabriel's voice, heard the whole AFL pitch, and finally signed off with, "Yes, Mr. Hunt, I'll certainly consider your offer."

Oakland superspy Lee Grosscup once rerouted an NFL sleuth by imitating the voice of the guy's general manager.

"I told him to get his ass over to Seattle in a hurry because the AFL was stealing his player," Grosscup said. "There was a blizzard out there, and he got locked in. It took him out of commission for three days."

One year Don Klosterman, the Dallas Texans' general manager, tried to keep first-round pick Buck Buchanan, a 6-7, 287-pounder hidden in the Klosterman household.

"How do you propose keeping this one a secret?" his wife

asked him one day. "I've just given him 80 pancakes, 12 eggs, and a loaf of bread I had to borrow from a neighbor whose husband is sports editor of a Dallas paper."

"Maybe we can stick some acorns in his hair," Don said.

Sometimes the talent hunt got extreme. Most AFL clubs held open tryout sessions in the spring. The hopeful and the hopeless; they'd show up in Army fatigues, khakis, sneakers, sandals, and swimsuits. One year the Old Blue and the Manhattan Rugby Clubs were having a match in New York's Van Cortlandt Park. A few of the ruggers looked past the sidelines and the sparse foliage was full of naked men. The game stopped and the invasion was investigated.

"Don't mind us," Weeb Ewbank said. "We're having our Jets' tryouts, and we're changing clothes in the bushes. We couldn't use the lockers because they're holding a high-school track meet here today."

The names of the draft choices are supposed to be a secret, but there is cooperation between friends. It's always existed, ever since George Halas bribed Pittsburgh's Art Rooney to draft Sid Luckman on the first round and then trade him to Chicago. The bribe was Eggs Manske, an end. And in 1970, Cleveland owner Art Modell called Green Bay general manager and coach Phil Bengtson to make sure that the Packers still had confidence in their quarterback, Don Horn.

The Packers drafted second. Miami drafted third, but Cleveland was in the process of trading Paul Warfield to the Dolphins for their pick, which Cleveland was going to devote to Mike Phipps, a quarterback. Before he could complete the deal, Modell had to be sure Green Bay wasn't looking for a quarterback.

"We still had an 'out' clause in our deal with Miami," Modell said. "Just in case Horn got hit by a bus in the meantime. It was an option to call off the Warfield deal in case of an Act of God."

The drafting is based on scouting, and scouting is often a matter of inches and pounds. A college player who has the foresight to keep the tape on his ankles on the day that a scout measures his height might pick up an extra $10,000 or so. Tape can hide pieces of wood or metal against the bottom of the foot, and these little elevators can add as much as an inch in height. And hunks of metal stashed away somewhere on the body can give a player 10 more pounds, which look a lot healthier on the scout's report.

"I used to come into camp at about 230," said Dallas' former offensive guard Mike Connelly, "but I'd weigh out at 240. I'd put two five-pound weights in the waistband of my jock and wear a T-shirt over it. Jim Myers, our line coach, always used to say, 'You don't look that heavy. I guess you just got a real solid build.' "

Every coach has his own rigid set of standards for each position. Dallas coach Tom Landry usually won't give a second thought to a linebacker who's shorter than 6-2, an offensive lineman who's under 6-3, or a defensive lineman who's shorter than 6-4. And Brandt takes no one's word for anything. He likes his own scouts to do their own measuring and weighing.

"We've had 260-pound tackles who came into camp at 225," Brandt says, "and one quarterback who was listed at 6-2 measured 5-11½."

"Beware of the half inch," says the Jets' Joe Spencer. "It usually means they're trying to hide something. A man who says he's 6-3½ might measure out to 6-2."

"Eight different scouts weighed me at the East-West game," said Oklahoma halfback Steve Owens. "They just won't take each other's word for it. So you step on the same scale you've just stepped down from two seconds before, and the new scout looks over your shoulder and says, 'hmmm,' like it's all big news."

"Gravity pulls a guy tighter," says Charley Mackey, the West Coast scout for the BLESTO-V syndicate. "A guy lies in bed all night long and everything relaxes—ligaments, tendons, muscles, the whole structure relaxes and lengthens. I've measured height changes during the day that have gone down one inch."

"I'm 6-3," Gabriel says, "but for some reason I've always been listed as 6-4. One day I said to our PR man, 'Why don't you list me at 6-3, my true height?' He told me, 'You can't begin shrinking now.' "

Even more rigid are the speed standards—no slower than 4.7 for wide receivers and cornerbacks; maybe a tenth of a second or so slower for safetyman, 4.9 for running backs, and 5.0 to 5.4 for linebackers and linemen. These vary more than the heights. A man's speed can depend on whether he's wearing light padding or just shorts—or whether he's nursing a slight injury he doesn't feel like admitting—or simply on how he feels that particular day.

"The thing you've got to remember," Brandt says, "is that a man slows down the more he gets hit. No one ever gets faster in pro football. You pick up a back who runs a 4.8 and maybe in a few years he'll be 4.9 and a few years later he'll be 5.0 and too slow to play."

It's tough to keep height and weight figures secret, but a slow time is seldom released to the press. You only hear about the speedsters. It's embarrassing for the slow ones, who might have been clocked while they were injured. And it's not the smartest policy if the club is thinking about a trade. Speed is best left in vague terms.

There's an old maxim: "You can't find a substitute for speed," so the World's Fastest Humans have always been a target for the pro scouts. If the scouts look hard enough they can generally find some football in every sprinter's background, but a lot of money has been donated to flyers who washed out. Bob Hayes, the Olympic sprint champion, made it big with Dallas, but Hayes was a football player at Florida A & M before he was a sprinter. And for every Hayes there are a dozen failures, i.e., Ray Norton, Frank Budd, Henry Carr, Tommie Smith, the Ohio State Glenn Davis, etc. The jury is still out on Miami's Olympic champ, Jimmy Hines.

There are three scouting syndicates; BLESTO-V (Bears, Lions, Eagles, Steelers, Vikings—with the TO standing for Talent Organization); CEPO, or Central Eastern Personnel Organization (Cards, Giants, Packers, Redskins, Falcons, Browns, Colts); and Troika (Rams, Cowboys, 49ers). New Orleans bought its way into Troika by giving Los Angeles a second-round draft choice, but a year later the Saints dropped out of the syndicate, preferring to go independent. The clubs in the old AFL worked independently, although there is some horse trading among old buddies.

A syndicate such as Troika has eight area scouts, each one taking one of the eight areas of the country. They work roughly six months out of the year, hitting the college camps during spring training and the fall season, covering the big games in their area as they come up. They get paid as much as an average college coach, and the job offers far better security. There are also part-time scouts who will do special assignments, on request, such as taking a second or third look at a particular player.

The syndicate reports come into the parent clubs all year long, so that by the time the draft meetings come up each member comes into the meetings with a fairly fat book of syndicate data on perhaps 1,500 college seniors. Every team has this same computerized set of reports. In addition to the basics—height, weight, speed at 40 yards—there is a capsule comment on each man, plus a number indicating how many reports there are on him. O. J. Simpson got 26 CEPO reports in 1968.

"The more reports," says St. Louis' Dan McCarthy, a member of the CEPO group, "the more reliable the information. If you get 10 or more reports, you've got a pretty good reading. We use this as a cross-check of our own private club scouting reports, but if it comes down to a borderline thing, a good, solid CEPO rating could swing it."

A report will carry a precise evaluation, i.e., "14th of 152 tackles graded," plus a rating, which follows a system that is just about the same everywhere: the lower the number, the better the player. In BLESTO-V's terminology, an 0.0 to 0.6 rating means superstar. (Simpson holds the syndicate record at 0.4); 0.7 to 1.2 means almost certain to be a starter . . . right on down to 3.1 and more, which means forget it. Other systems simplify things by dividing the ratings into four groups—the 1's, 2's, 3's, and 4's. Scouts live with these numbers so much that they shorthand their conversations. So a girl with a Raquel Welch build might be an 0.6, but her face might be 3.4.

Member teams have a moral obligation to turn all names of prospective draftees over to the syndicate—but that's all they have to do, simply report the names. There's nothing to say that a club's scout can't devote extra hours to a sleeper, and keep the extra information private, once he's dropped the name.

You'd wonder why a club such as Dallas, which takes such pride in its own scouting network (Brandt plus four main scouts work the year round and draw a much higher salary than syndicate scouts), would want to hook up with a group. The reason is that the club can use the syndicate personnel to perform the menial tasks of checking out the hundreds of rumors that come in each year.

"Say we hear of a 6-5, 250-pound tackle from Whitworth College in Washington," Brandt says. "We get a hold of the Troika people, and they check him out and report he's 5-11, 215. So we haven't tied up one of our own people for a day on a wasted trip. Syndicate scouting eliminates a lot of wasted hours for your own men."

Brandt's job is a constant, year-round grading, evaluating, and rating process as reports keep coming in from Troika and Dallas scouts. He'll stay with a player throughout the boy's college career, and all files find their way into a giant office called the Book Room. The current year will get one whole area, with a set of blue portfolios indicating prospects, white ones indicating nonprospect seniors, or "maybes," and different colored binders designating sophomores or varsity-eligible frosh. The room contains a five-year working file, with black folders signifying rejects for that year. After five years the names go into the storeroom. The cost of the heavy portfolios alone runs well into four figures—1,000 or so at $6 apiece.

The Cowboys' heavy rating work is handled by an IBM computer. Brandt feeds the monster a diet of carefully programmed information from four separate personnel sheets. He alerts it to the prime considerations in the Dallas scheme of things, and the machine rates the players for him.

"The categories usually stay the same," Brandt says, "but every year you change the evaluation of them. If you're concerned about speed, you might mark off 'speed' as a 14-percent consideration for tight ends, up 3 percent from the previous year. Or maybe you decide that size is becoming more important in centers than quickness—so the two categories get a reevaluation at that position. The same thing for intelligence, toughness, desire—any category in which a prospect is rated."

A vice on one rating might be a virtue on another. In 1968 the Jets drafted a 6-6, 270-pound offensive tackle named Sam Walton. There was some basketball playing in his history.

"Agile ex-basketball player," the Jets' rating said.

"Fat, lazy, basketball," read the CEPO report.

The area of intelligence testing was considered a joke when

Paul Brown started it in the 1940's, but people are beginning to fall in line now. The notion that a player can be dumb off the field but a genius once he puts on the pads and cleats has been discredited in 99 out of 100 cases.

"You can't use intelligence testing as an absolute," Brandt says. "There are a lot of variables. We give a short-form IQ test that measures alertness as well as basic intelligence, since it has a few trick questions, but a kid with a solid education—say prep school and Ivy League—will grade out higher than a boy from a small local college. It doesn't mean the Ivy Leaguer is basically smarter.

"And you have to keep in mind when you gave the boy the test. He'll do best before he eats anything, early in the morning. He'll do the worst after practice."

The IQ test devotees believe that brains can explain a lot of inexplicables, for instance why a top draft choice with all the physical tools doesn't move in as a starter until he's been around for three or four years.

"Check the punt returner who catches the ball on the one-yard line when he should have let it go into the end zone, or the guy who jumps off side in a key situation," one scout says. "Ten more points on the IQ and he probably wouldn't have made the mistake."

Sam Baker, the veteran field goal man, tells about the first time his 142 IQ was put to the test.

"The team psychologist gave me a battery of tests," he says. "Personality, IQ, capability, dexterity, you name it. All of us on the club took them and then, later on, the psychologist had little private talks with us to explain how we did.

"The first thing he said to me when I walked in was, 'You know, you're not a genius. You know it, don't you? You know it, you know it!' I figured he was sore because I had a higher IQ than he did."

Testing the IQ's of college players can be a tricky business. Most coaches have an instinctive distrust of pro scouts (fostered and encouraged by the NCAA, which is always attuned to potential loss of revenue from pro competition). If they hear IQ tests, they might throw the scout off the campus.

"A lot of times," one scout says, "we have to con 'em a little and tell them we're giving the kid a personality evaluation test."

And a college coach might look at the whole nature of a football player differently. A 5-11, 210-pound guard might be a killer for him, even though the boy's pro chances are nil. And when a scout tells him the kid doesn't have a chance, but points, instead to a lumbering 6-5, 250-pounder who's busy finishing off an ice-cream cone, the coach might get furious. ("You'll always take a chance on a great big guy," Brandt says. "Most really big kids mature a lot later").

"Don't forget," says the Jets' Walt Michaels, "a coach's first obligation is to his own college kids—not to you or to professional football. A lot of times you'll ask him for prospects and he'll mention a marginal player who's just been a good, solid citizen for him for four years. He figures he might be able to get the kid a little bonus money. Who can blame him? You just have to understand that."

Brandt has always taken care to stay in good graces with the collegians. He'll extend any courtesy the Dallas organization is capable of, and Cowboy and Troika scouts will be repaid by seats in the press box during games. This is an invaluable aid to scouting. The stands don't offer the same view of the action, and even if they did, the jostling might not allow much writing.

The Dallas scouting organization is built on a very solid foundation—the Texas millions of owner Clint Murchison, Jr. Murchison owns the Cowboys' office building. He allows free use of funds in scouting procedures, and the organization's president, Tex Schramm, will spend it on whatever he and Brandt see fit. Pennies are not pinched in the Cowboys' office.

"Take a look at our office building itself," Brandt said one day. "Where everything should be cement, it's done in terrazzo here. And where everything is usually terrazzo, ours is in solid marble."

The reward for a hard year of scouting is usually a trip to the All-Star games . . . Blue-Gray, North-South, East-West, Hula Bowl, Senior Bowl, etc. The hard-core investigating has already been done. There are no sleepers in these games, only blue chippers. But what the scout can pick up from this kind of action is how talent performs when it meets talent head on. This gives him a better line on the small-school player.

But after the computers have coughed up their last load of IBM cards; after the CEPO and Troika and BLESTO-V books, all

Fig. 10A   **NEW YORK JETS**   Date _____

Name _____

(Last)   (First)

School _____

Hometown _____ Transfer _____

Competition
Remaining _____ Position _____

Hgt. _____ Wgt. _____ Age _____

Time _____ Dist. _____ Gear_____

         Quickness   5 – 4 – 3 – 2 – 1
         Agility   5 – 4 – 3 – 2 – 1
         Strength   5 – 4 – 3 – 2 – 1
         Toughness   5 – 4 – 3 – 2 – 1
         Desire   5 – 4 – 3 – 2 – 1
         Size Potential   5 – 4 – 3 – 2 – 1
         Speed for Position 5 – 4 – 3 – 2 – 1
         Character   5 – 4 – 3 – 2 – 1
         Aggressiveness   5 – 4 – 3 – 2 – 1
         Pride   5 – 4 – 3 – 2 – 1

Squad Workout _____ No _____

Movies Seen: vs _____ vs _____ vs _____

Comments:

Pro Rating Guide
5. Will be a STAR in professional football.
4. Will make a professional FIRST TEAM.
3. Will make a professional SQUAD.
2. Has an OUTSIDE CHANCE to make a pro squad.
1. REJECT – Not enough ability.

Fig. 10B

DALLAS COWBOYS FOOTBALL CLUB				INITIAL YE
DATE MONTH YEAR	SCHOOL	NAME LAST	FIRST	INITIAL REGISTER

9	8	7	6	5	4	3	2	1
EXACTLY LIKE HIM FITS HIM TO A "T"	A LOT LIKE HIM		MODERATELY LIKE THE MAN		A LITTLE LIKE HIM		NOT AT ALL LIKE HIM DOESN'T FIT HIM AT ALL	

HE DOESN'T ALWAYS COOPERATE
::9:: ::8:: ::7:: ::6:: ::5:: ::4:: ::3:: ::2:: ::1::
HE IS QUICK AS A CAT
::9:: ::8:: ::7:: ::6:: ::5:: ::4:: ::3:: ::2:: ::1::
HE WANTS TO WIN AT ALL COSTS
::9:: ::8:: ::7:: ::6:: ::5:: ::4:: ::3:: ::2:: ::1::
HE FINALLY CATCHES ON AFTER MUCH REPETITION
::9:: ::8:: ::7:: ::6:: ::5:: ::4:: ::3:: ::2:: ::1::
HE IS AS STRONG AS A BULL
::9:: ::8:: ::7:: ::6:: ::5:: ::4:: ::3:: ::2:: ::1::
HE RARELY THINKS OF ANYONE BUT HIMSELF
::9:: ::8:: ::7:: ::6:: ::5:: ::4:: ::3:: ::2:: ::1::
HIS MOVEMENT IS AWKWARD IN WAVE DRILL
::9:: ::8:: ::7:: ::6:: ::5:: ::4:: ::3:: ::2:: ::1::
HE WILL BREAK HIS NECK TO CARRY OUT HIS ASSIGNMENT
::9:: ::8:: ::7:: ::6:: ::5:: ::4:: ::3:: ::2:: ::1::

HE CAN RETAIN WHAT HE HAS LEARNED AND DOESN'T
REQUIRE REPEATED CORRECTION
::9:: ::8:: ::7:: ::6:: ::5:: ::4:: ::3:: ::2::
HE CAN OVERPOWER A MAN OF EQUAL SIZE BY BRUTE FOR
::9:: ::8:: ::7:: ::6:: ::5:: ::4:: ::3:: ::2::
HE WOULD JUST AS SOON MISS PRACTICE
::9:: ::8:: ::7:: ::6:: ::5:: ::4:: ::3:: ::2::
HE DOESN'T REGAIN HIS BALANCE ONCE HE HAS LOST IT
::9:: ::8:: ::7:: ::6:: ::5:: ::4:: ::3:: ::2::
HE DOESN'T STOP UNTIL THE WHISTLE BLOWS
::9:: ::8:: ::7:: ::6:: ::5:: ::4:: ::3:: ::2::
HE IS VERY QUICK TO LEARN ASSIGNMENTS
::9:: ::8:: ::7:: ::6:: ::5:: ::4:: ::3:: ::2::
HE DIGS IN AND YOU CAN'T MOVE HIM
::9:: ::8:: ::7:: ::6:: ::5:: ::4:: ::3:: ::2::

9	8	7	6	5	4	3	2	1
EXCEPTIONAL RARE ABILITY	REAL GOOD		ABOVE AVERAGE		AVERAGE COLLEGE ABILITY		POOR	

OFFENSIVE ENDS & FLANKERS

RECEIVING SHORT
::9:: ::8:: ::7:: ::6:: ::5:: ::4:: ::3:: ::2:: ::1::
RECEIVING LONG
::9:: ::8:: ::7:: ::6:: ::5:: ::4:: ::3:: ::2:: ::1::
AVOID BEING HELD UP
::9:: ::8:: ::7:: ::6:: ::5:: ::4:: ::3:: ::2:: ::1::
FAKING AND CUTTING ABILITY
::9:: ::8:: ::7:: ::6:: ::5:: ::4:: ::3:: ::2:: ::1::
RUNNING ABILITY AFTER CATCH
::9:: ::8:: ::7:: ::6:: ::5:: ::4:: ::3:: ::2:: ::1::
ABILITY AS A BLOCKER
::9:: ::8:: ::7:: ::6:: ::5:: ::4:: ::3:: ::2:: ::1::
CATCHING IN A CROWD
::9:: ::8:: ::7:: ::6:: ::5:: ::4:: ::3:: ::2:: ::1::
HANDS
::9:: ::8:: ::7:: ::6:: ::5:: ::4:: ::3:: ::2:: ::1::

DEFENSIVE LINEMEN

ABILITY AGAINST THE RUN
::9:: ::8:: ::7:: ::6:: ::5:: ::4:: ::3:: ::2:: ::1::
ABILITY TO KEY AND DIAGNOSE
::9:: ::8:: ::7:: ::6:: ::5:: ::4:: ::3:: ::2:: ::1::
PASS RUSH — CUP OR AGGRESSIVE
::9:: ::8:: ::7:: ::6:: ::5:: ::4:: ::3:: ::2:: ::1::
LATERAL MOVEMENT
::9:: ::8:: ::7:: ::6:: ::5:: ::4:: ::3:: ::2:: ::1::
TACKLING
::9:: ::8:: ::7:: ::6:: ::5:: ::4:: ::3:: ::2:: ::1::

OFFENSIVE LINEMEN

PASS PROTECTION — CUP OR AGGRESSIVE
::9:: ::8:: ::7:: ::6:: ::5:: ::4:: ::3:: ::2:: ::1::
BLOCKING FOR THE RUN
::9:: ::8:: ::7:: ::6:: ::5:: ::4:: ::3:: ::2:: ::1::
QUICKNESS OF INITIAL MOVE
::9:: ::8:: ::7:: ::6:: ::5:: ::4:: ::3:: ::2:: ::1::
PULLING ABILITY
::9:: ::8:: ::7:: ::6:: ::5:: ::4:: ::3:: ::2:: ::1::
DOWNFIELD BLOCKING
::9:: ::8:: ::7:: ::6:: ::5:: ::4:: ::3:: ::2:: ::1::

LINEBACKERS

EFFECTIVENESS AGAINST INSIDE RUNS
::9:: ::8:: ::7:: ::6:: ::5:: ::4:: ::3:: ::2:: ::1::
ABILITY TO WARD OFF BLOCKERS
::9:: ::8:: ::7:: ::6:: ::5:: ::4:: ::3:: ::2:: ::1::
ABILITY TO KEY AND DIAGNOSE
::9:: ::8:: ::7:: ::6:: ::5:: ::4:: ::3:: ::2:: ::1::
PASS COVERAGE ABILITY
::9:: ::8:: ::7:: ::6:: ::5:: ::4:: ::3:: ::2:: ::1::
LATERAL MOVEMENT
::9:: ::8:: ::7:: ::6:: ::5:: ::4:: ::3:: ::2:: ::1::

OFFENSIVE BACKS

POWER RUNNER
::9:: ::8:: ::7:: ::6:: ::5:: ::4:: ::3:: ::2::
OUTSIDE RUNNING ABILITY
::9:: ::8:: ::7:: ::6:: ::5:: ::4:: ::3:: ::2::
ABILITY TO BREAK TACKLE
::9:: ::8:: ::7:: ::6:: ::5:: ::4:: ::3:: ::2::
ELUSIVE RUNNER
::9:: ::8:: ::7:: ::6:: ::5:: ::4:: ::3:: ::2::
OVERALL RECEIVING ABILITY
::9:: ::8:: ::7:: ::6:: ::5:: ::4:: ::3:: ::2::
BLOCKING — PASS AND RUN
::9:: ::8:: ::7:: ::6:: ::5:: ::4:: ::3:: ::2::
HANDS
::9:: ::8:: ::7:: ::6:: ::5:: ::4:: ::3:: ::2::

DEFENSIVE BACKS

OVERALL ABILITY AGAINST THE RUN
::9:: ::8:: ::7:: ::6:: ::5:: ::4:: ::3:: ::2::
ABILITY AGAINST PASS
::9:: ::8:: ::7:: ::6:: ::5:: ::4:: ::3:: ::2::
ABILITY TO KEY AND DIAGNOSE
::9:: ::8:: ::7:: ::6:: ::5:: ::4:: ::3:: ::2::
PURSUIT
::9:: ::8:: ::7:: ::6:: ::5:: ::4:: ::3:: ::2::
TACKLING
::9:: ::8:: ::7:: ::6:: ::5:: ::4:: ::3:: ::2::
HANDS
::9:: ::8:: ::7:: ::6:: ::5:: ::4:: ::3:: ::2::

QUARTERBACKS

ABILITY TO THROW SHORT
::9:: ::8:: ::7:: ::6:: ::5:: ::4:: ::3:: ::2::
ABILITY TO THROW LONG
::9:: ::8:: ::7:: ::6:: ::5:: ::4:: ::3:: ::2::
ABILITY TO TIME PASS
::9:: ::8:: ::7:: ::6:: ::5:: ::4:: ::3:: ::2::
DELIVERY
::9:: ::8:: ::7:: ::6:: ::5:: ::4:: ::3:: ::2::
ABILITY TO SCRAMBLE
::9:: ::8:: ::7:: ::6:: ::5:: ::4:: ::3:: ::2::
COURAGE
::9:: ::8:: ::7:: ::6:: ::5:: ::4:: ::3:: ::2::
QUICKNESS TO SET UP
::9:: ::8:: ::7:: ::6:: ::5:: ::4:: ::3:: ::2::
DETERMINATION TO STAY IN CUP
::9:: ::8:: ::7:: ::6:: ::5:: ::4:: ::3:: ::2::
RUNNING ABILITY
::9:: ::8:: ::7:: ::6:: ::5:: ::4:: ::3:: ::2::
POISE
::9:: ::8:: ::7:: ::6:: ::5:: ::4:: ::3:: ::2::
QUICKNESS OF DELIVERY
::9:: ::8:: ::7:: ::6:: ::5:: ::4:: ::3:: ::2::

PROSPECTS OF PLAYING IN THE NATIONAL FOOTBALL LEAGUE

CINCH	REAL GOOD	GOOD	SLIM
::9:: ::8::	::7:: ::6::	::5:: ::4::	::3:: ::2::

DO NOT WRITE BELOW THIS LINE

::1:: ::2:: ::3:: ::4:: ::5:: ::6:: ::7:: ::8:: ::9:: ::0:: ::1:: ::2:: ::3:: ::4:: ::5:: ::6:: ::7:: ::8:: ::9::
::1:: ::2:: ::3:: ::4:: ::5:: ::6:: ::7:: ::8:: ::9:: ::0:: ::1:: ::2:: ::3:: ::4:: ::5:: ::6:: ::7:: ::8:: ::9::
::1:: ::2:: ::3:: ::4:: ::5:: ::6:: ::7:: ::8:: ::9:: ::0:: ::1:: ::2:: ::3:: ::4:: ::5:: ::6:: ::7:: ::9::
::1:: ::2:: ::3:: ::4:: ::5:: ::6:: ::7:: ::8:: ::9:: ::0:: ::1:: ::2:: ::3:: ::1:: ::2:: ::1:: ::2:: ::3:: ::4::

IBM H91641

DALLAS COWBOYS FOOTBALL CLUB

SCOUT:_____DATE:_____   PLAYERS NAME:_____

HOME ADDRESS:,_____   SCHOOL:_____

HOME TELEPHONE:_____   SCHOOL ADDRESS:_____

TELEPHONE: _____

DESCRIBE
PHYSICAL
BUILD

TIMED: 40 yards in Shorts

Football shoes_____   Height:_____ By:_____

Tennis shoes_____   Weight:_____ By:_____

Barefooted_____   Personnel Test: Yes____ No____

Did Player run with someone: Yes___ No___   Score:_____

General Physical Impression:

General Personal Impression:

Fig. 10D

					NAME				
Scout		Date		School			Last		First

9	8	7	6	5	4	3	2	1
Exceptional, Rare Ability		Real Good		Above Average		Average College Ability		Poor

CHARACTER
9 8 7 6   5 4 3 2 1

QUICKNESS, AGILITY, BALANCE
9 8 7 6   5 4 3 2 1

COMPETITIVENESS, AGGRESSIVENESS
9 8 7 6   5 4 3 2 1

MENTAL ALERTNESS
9 8 7 6   5 4 3 2

STRENGTH and EXPLOSION
9 8 7 6   5 4 3 2

OFFENSIVE ENDS-RECEIVING
Receiving Short
9 8 7 6   5 4 3 2 1
Receiving Long
9 8 7 6   5 4 3 2 1
Avoid being held up
9 8 7 6   5 4 3 2 1
Faking and Cutting Ability
9 8 7 6   5 4 3 2 1
Running ability after catch
9 8 7 6   5 4 3 2 1
Ability as a blocker
9 8 7 6   5 4 3 2 1
Catching in a crowd
9 8 7 6   5 4 3 2 1
Hands
9 8 7 6   5 4 3 2 1

DEFENSIVE LINEMEN
Ability against the run
9 8 7 6   5 4 3 2 1
Ability to key and diagnose
9 8 7 6   5 4 3 2 1
Pass rush — cup or aggressive
9 8 7 6   5 4 3 2 1
Lateral movement
9 8 7 6   5 4 3 2 1
Tackling
9 8 7 6   5 4 3 2 1

OFFENSIVE LINEMEN
Pass protection — cup or aggressive
9 8 7 6   5 4 3 2 1
Blocking for the run
9 8 7 6   5 4 3 2 1
Quickness of initial move
9 8 7 6   5 4 3 2 1
Pulling ability
9 8 7 6   5 4 3 2 1
Downfield blocking
9 8 7 6   5 4 3 2 1

LINEBACKERS
Effectiveness against inside runs
9 8 7 6   5 4 3 2 1
Ability to ward off blockers
9 8 7 6   5 4 3 2 1
Ability to key and diagnose
9 8 7 6   5 4 3 2 1
Pass coverage ability
9 8 7 6   5 4 3 2 1
Lateral movement
9 8 7 6   5 4 3 2 1

OFFENSIVE BACKS
Power runner
9 8 7 6   5 4 3 2
Outside running ability
9 8 7 6   5 4 3 2
Ability to break tackle
9 8 7 6   5 4 3 2
Elusive runner
9 8 7 6   5 4 3 2
Over-all receiving ability
9 8 7 6   5 4 3 2
Blocking — pass & run
9 8 7 6   5 4 3 2
Hands
9 8 7 6   5 4 3 2

DEFENSIVE BACKS
Over-all ability against the run
9 8 7 6   5 4 3 2
Ability against pass
9 8 7 6   5 4 3 2
Ability to key and diagnose
9 8 7 6   5 4 3 2
Pursuit
9 8 7 6   5 4 3 2
Tackling
9 8 7 6   5 4 3 2
Hands
9 8 7 6   5 4 3 2

QUARTERBACKS
Ability to throw short
9 8 7 6   5 4 3 2
Ability to throw long
9 8 7 6   5 4 3 2
Ability to time pass
9 8 7 6   5 4 3 2
Delivery
9 8 7 6   5 4 3 2
Ability to scramble
9 8 7 6   5 4 3 2
Courage
9 8 7 6   5 4 3 2
Quickness to set up
9 8 7 6   5 4 3 2
Determination to stay in cup
9 8 7 6   5 4 3 2
Running ability
9 8 7 6   5 4 3 2
Poise
9 8 7 6   5 4 3 2
Quickness of delivery
9 8 7 6   5 4 3 2

PROSPECTS OF PLAYING IN THE NATIONAL FOOTBALL LEAGUE

9	8	7	6	5	4	3	2	1
Cinch		Real Good		Good		Slim		None

neatly printed and packaged, are delicately carried down to the draft meetings; the coaches sit in the office by the phones and play hunches—right up through the very drafting.

"You go back to our office after a draft session," says the Giants' publicist, Don Smith, "and you'll see all these ratings on the blackboard. Maybe 20 players carefully rated at each position. As the guys are picked their names are crossed off, but after that first day you might see numbers 15 through 20 crossed off the list, but four through eight still left on it. People play hunches."

Paul Robinson, a track star at Arizona, played only one year of football, but every time he was put through a computer the card came out reading "Can't miss—star." But almost three full rounds went by—81 players—before Robinson was claimed by the Cincinnati Bengals. He became the AFL's Rookie of the Year and its ground-gaining leader with 1,023 yards.

"The scouts," said Dan Rooney of the Steelers, "didn't have the courage of their own convictions."

18

The Armament Factory

I played football before they had headgear, and that's how I lost my mind.

□ Casey Stengel

There exist great love affairs in football—a man and his helmet, or maybe his shoes, or maybe a pair of worn-out old shoulder pads that he filched from a high-school locker, but he knows fit just right.

A player will sit by, stony-faced, while his best friend is cut from the team, but let them put his headgear on waivers and he'll break down and cry.

"We once had this terrible free-for-all on the field when I was playing for the Browns," says Walt Michaels. "Fists flying everywhere. I was on the bench at the time, so I tore my helmet off and ran out on the field to get in it. Whack! whack! I got two off the head right away and down I went. Whack! and I was down again.

"They finally broke it up, and when we got back in the locker one of our guys said, 'Hey, Walt, what did you ever take your helmet off for? That was the dumbest thing I've ever seen on a football field.'

"I'm still trying to figure out why I did it. Reflex, I guess. Anyway, I coach the guys now to keep their helmets on at all times. And make sure the chin strap's buckled. A helmet is a boy's best friend."

"I kept adding features to mine," said defensive end Bob Dee, an original Boston Patriot who finally retired in 1967.

"I started out with a double face bar, then added a third bar because I was getting cut on the chin. I also added a horseshoe bar at the top of the helmet to protect myself from getting a forearm in the eye or the nose.

"I also had it repaired every year until my last season. I didn't let 'em paint it that last year because it was getting worn and I was afraid they might take it away from me. I didn't want to lose it.

"I cracked it near one of the ear holes in practice. I don't know how. It was just a plain old dummy scrimmage. Just hit it right, I guess. Anyway, the crack got worse. The helmet was pretty well battered out of shape, too. The edge of the top kept digging into my skin, and I'd come out of every game with a bloody forehead. But I wouldn't let 'em get rid of that old baby of mine."

Pads were smaller and less ferocious in the old days. The Packers' famous pass catcher, Don Hutson, probably set the record for stinginess.

"I remember the first time I saw Hutson," said ex-tackle Bruiser Kinard. "He had on a little bitty ole pair of shoulder pads he bought in Woolworth's or maybe his wife made them."

"I'll tell you why," Hutson said. "We had to buy our own."

They love those old pads and helmets, but there's one set of equipage that has drawn evil looks ever since the dawn of football, and that's the family of dummies. Blocking dummies, tackling dummies, sleds, reaction testers—the business has come a long way since the days when Illinois coach Bob Zuppke said, "I keep dummies on the field to make the alumni happy."

The early dummies fell into two classes. There was the single dummy that one player would hold and another one would block, and old Giants talk about the way coach Steve Owen's craggy Oklahoma face would light up as he'd yell, "Git it! Go git it!" to his linemen. Then there was the two-man sled that's still in use; two dummies mounted on metal runners and attached to a base, upon which a coach stands and yells, "Drive! Drive it now!" until the blockers' legs start quivering.

The Edison of the dummy business was a Connecticut squire named Marty Gilman. His first breakthrough in the field was the

Springback, which would bounce off the grass by itself, ready to be knocked down again.

"I got the idea," Gilman said, "when Lone Star Dietz of the Carlisle Indians said he'd like a dummy that picks itself up like a spittoon in a saloon."

Then came the Fightback, the Tackleback, the Chargeback, the Runback, the Breakthrough and the Big John, a huge inflated parody of a defensive lineman, with arms upraised. Big John's role was to give quarterbacks the idea of passing under pressure.

The Giants under Allie Sherman were very big on Gilman dummies, which came in all colors. A visitor to the Giants' Fairfield, Connecticut, camp took a look at the rainbow collection on the field and dubbed the place, "The Lollipop Farm."

Vintage Giants remember the two weeks that Joe Don Looney was in camp as a rookie in '64. Looney, king of modern flakes, took an instant dislike to one of Gilman's monsters whose forte was striking back at tacklers after they hit it.

"Joe Don sidled up to it and gave it a lick, and the thing knocked him on his ass," a veteran Giant recalls. "So Joe Don went berserk and attacked the dummy and punched it with his fists and kicked it and screamed at it.

"I don't want to say who won that fight, but the dummy is still here, and who knows where Joe Don is right now."

Gilman's masterpiece, though, was a special contraption called the Ramback. The Giants tried it out in 1966, and Vince Lombardi also gave it a look, but the world wasn't really ready for it. The Ramback worked this way:

A great foam rubber dummy swiveled back and forth, capable of striking out with 1,200 pounds of thrust. Stationed at either end were transparent helmets with red spotlights inside them. A coach would mount an elevated platform and sit in front of a control panel. A lineman would take a stance in front of the dummy. The coach chose a button from rows of red, yellow, and blue knobs. He pushed it and a helmet lit up. That was the "get ready" signal. Then he pushed another button, the other helmet lit up, and bam! the dummy shot out at the lineman, who was expected to meet the machine's thrust with that of his own. A gauge measured the player's reaction time, another his thrust power. The team physician stood by, just in case.

None of the Giants volunteered to test out the Ramback, so Allie Sherman grabbed Willie Young, a 270-pound rookie tackle. Willie stopped the Ramback's charge, teetered a little, and then, dazed, staggered off to rejoin the rest of the linemen. "He's amazing," said Shaeffer Smith, the electrician who had installed the machine. He pointed to Young, who was still walking in circles. "He actually stopped the machine's thrust. And his reaction time was 30-hundredths of a second. Amazing."

The Ramback claimed no victims for a couple of days, and then one afternoon Sherman happened to be walking by. He looked around to make sure no one was watching. Then he decided to see if it was as tough as its reputation.

"I was all set to give it one of my patented shoulder blocks," the coach said, "when it struck out at me. I just escaped. It must have been around feeding time."

Another day after practice, a few rookie linemen were standing a safe distance away, eyeing the Ramback suspiciously. Veteran safetyman Jimmy Patton passed by, stopped, and put his arm around a youngster's shoulder.

"Son," Patton said in a low voice, "tonight when you're safe asleep in your room, that thing is going to light up and come walking across the grass and come into the dorm and up the stairs —and get you."

"Heh, heh," said the rookie, shuffling his feet.

The machine cost $5,000 and Gilman first unveiled it at a coaches' convention in Washington the preceding winter. "He kept one in the living room of his hotel suite," said Bob Brooks, a sporting goods salesman who was at the convention.

"One night he was throwing a party and a drunk wandered in and saw the machine. 'It ain't so tough,' he said. 'Gimme a crack at it.' Marty didn't say a word. He just put down his drink and got behind the controls. Everyone got set and Marty pushed the button and the thing fired out—and knocked the drunk into the bathroom, 10 feet away."

The Giants finally decided the Ramback was too tough for human consumption and they got rid of it late in the training season.

"They hitched it up to a truck—with chains—and dragged it off the field," said Don Smith, the Giants' publicist. "It reminded me of the bullfights, when they hitch the bull up to a team of horses and drag him out after he's been killed."

The Jet's killer-dummy is called Big Bertha. It's simpler in design, but scary enough in its own way. It consists of one huge blocking, or tackling dummy, attached to a lever by a set of coiled springs. The tension—and the force of the dummy's power—can be increased by adding more springs. One spring is for backs, two for linemen. And then there's a third spring. The Jets chose Steve Chomyszak, a 6-6, 280-pound defensive tackle, to try out Big Bertha at three springs.

Chomyszak can press 400 pounds; he's been called the strongest man in football. He got down in a stance and waited. "Hey, Steve," someone called. He turned his head for an instant, the Big Bertha fired out, and Chomyszak was stretched on the ground, unconscious. The Jets found out all they wanted to know about the third spring. They have never used it since.

The world of the personal equipment isn't so ferocious now, but in the old days, players would tape pieces of fiberboard and plaster—even sheet metal—to their arms to increase the power of the blow. When officials began to scrutinize the armaments more closely before each game, the illegal weaponry decreased. The old padding was of the heavy leather and fiberboard variety, and a full set of equipment could weigh up to 30 pounds, even more on a wet and muddy day.

Lightweight plastic and foam rubber have replaced the cumbersome old gear, but a big man can still carry a heavy load.

"One day when we were at Utah State," said the Jets' kicker, Jim Turner, a college teammate of the Rams' 270-pound Merlin Olsen, "we were messing around with some of Merlin's equipment, sort of trying it on. The weight of it almost brought me to the ground. That helmet—my God, it weighed about as much as all my equipment combined."

Players take special care of their helmets and shoes, but anything in between can be haphazardly regarded, even discarded (except shoulder pads). Players were always fiddling around with the old buckle-and-strap hip pads, trimming them down to the bare minimum, streamlining them for added speed, and then throwing them away entirely. In the mid-1950's, about the same time that face bars on helmets became mandatory, girdle pads put in an appearance. The pads fit neatly into pockets of a special type of shorts, giving a girdle-like effect, but even those are discarded by many players.

"The only people who seem to wear them all the time," said Dallas equipment man Jack Eskridge, "are offensive linemen and quarterbacks."

"I wore them until about four years ago," the Cowboys' All-NFL linebacker, Chuck Howley, said in 1969. "I don't like that extra weight, which isn't all that much, but you get a feeling of restriction."

"I threw away my rib pads in college," the Packers' offensive guard Jerry Kramer once said. "Then my hip pads went in my first few years at Green Bay. Then I got smaller knee and thigh pads. I kept cutting down the size of my shoulder pads, too. You hit with your head, not your shoulder. I finally found a nice pair of little ones, high-school discards or something, but the equipment man finally threw them away. He was ashamed of them."

"The only pads I wear are shoulder pads," the Jets' former cornerback, John Sample, once said. "Maybe it goes back to my college days at Maryland State. There weren't enough pads to go around, so only the seniors got a full set, and only about six of those sets were any good. I just got in the habit of playing without much padding, and I couldn't stand the extra weight. The only risk I run is if someone hits me across the thighs on a block, since I don't have any thigh pads. But defensive backs are supposed to be able to avoid downfield blocks anyway."

Most players don't wear any pads when they come out for their pregame warmups. "They're just too lazy," said Ray Berry when he was an assistant coach at Dallas. "It's easier to wait until the last minute. I always wore them at all times. Helmet, too. I wanted to get used to looking for the ball over the face bar."

Berry's words turned prophetic when the Cowboys' flanker, Bob Hayes, dove for a ball in a warm-up before the Jets' exhibition game in 1969 and separated his shoulder. It cost him part of the regular season.

"See that," said the Jets' George Sauer, who always wears his pads. "If he would have had shoulder pads on, he wouldn't have gotten hurt." Next week most of the Cowboys wore their pads to warm-ups.

The helmets have always been subject to the most careful scrutiny. Just as man once searched for a way to fly, doctors have always felt that the helmet which absolutely eliminates brain concussions is right around the corner, just waiting to be discovered. So far no one has.

In February, 1969, Miami's 245-pound fullback, Larry Csonka, told the National Commission on Product Safety that the regular helmet was unsafe. During his rookie season of 1968, he had missed three games because of concussions and dizziness. He said the problem was finally solved when he was outfitted with a new, experimental helmet that hadn't been released because "it sells for a few more dollars." But in 1969 his concussions came back, new helmet and all.

St. Louis trainer Jack Rockwell said the answer was The Headliner, a Rawlings product that offered an extra-wide leather headband and extra padding and suspension that could be adjusted to give the head a snug fit. Philadelphia equipment man Johnny Robel swore by a Riddell product called the Air Helmet, designed to cushion the shock with 12 inflatable pads (air was pumped in with a perfume atomizer contraption) and plastic containers filled with methyl alcohol. It turned the player's head into a walking drugstore.

"It feels," said the Eagles' flanker, Gary Ballman, "like I've grown an orange skin on my head."

The medical journals occasionally report cure-all helmets, such as the one designed by Dr. E. Dale Mattmiller, director of Ohio University's health services. The August 7, 1969, issue of the *Medical Tribune* carried his report. Dr. Mattmiller said that his plastic-foam helmet, which looked like a mushroom, had cut down on head injuries during the four years he experimented with it. The only trouble was that his guinea pigs were intramural football players at Ohio University, and he had no way of comparing their size or hitting power with that of professional football players.

"We've never had a serious head injury since I've been with the club," said the Jets' veteran equipment manager, Bill Hampton, "and we don't do anything special. Maybe it's just luck. Maybe the guys just know how to wear their hats right."

Joe Namath *did* request an additional face bar on his helmet after the 1967 Oakland game in which Ben Davidson broke his cheekbone.

"I once asked for it before," he said, "and they talked me out of it. They said it would cut down on my vision. Vision, hell. This beak of mine is too big a target for some of those guys."

Bobby Layne held out against face bars of any kind until he retired in 1962, long after face bars became mandatory. He was football's Ted Williams, who always refused to wear a plastic batting helmet. And the last of the original barless hard noses was Boston defensive tackle Jess Richardson, who played naked-faced until his retirement in 1964.

Football shoes have become a personal trademark with some of the game's stars. Lenny Moore taped the outside of his shoes and called them "Spats." Namath's white leather shoes are famous. So were Alvin Haymond's green ones when he was with Philadelphia. San Diego's punter-kicker, Dennis Partee, has 14 different pairs of shoes. New Orleans' kicker Tom Dempsey wears a special leather-reinforced shoe that costs between $100 and $200 a pair (and Dempsey had to sweat out the league office's great shoe purge of 1969, when metal reinforcements were outlawed). And the NFL's pass-catching leader in 1969, Danny Abramowicz, says he has gone through as many as 17 pairs in a season.

"I haven't had toenails on my big toes in two years," he says. "They turn black in preseason practice and then I lose them, and then I have nothing until the season's over. They grow back just about the time we're ready to go to camp next year.

"I blame it on the shoe manufacturers. There are special shoes for backs and linemen and kickers, but nothing for pass receivers. Yet nobody cuts as often or as hard as a receiver. I paid $25 a pair for those 17 shoes I went through, but it's not the price that bothers me. I'd pay double or triple that, if only the shoes would work. I wore a special lightweight pair in one game, and by the third quarter the things were worn out. I had to send to the locker room for a new pair."

The special shoe that kicker Ben Agajanian wore to fit his toeless right foot drew a lot of interest when Ben was helping conduct the Cowboys famous Kicking Karavan in 1967. One high-school youngster asked him how he could get a pair like that.

"Well," Agajanian said, "first you get yourself a hatchet . . ."

Soccer-style shoes are becoming fashionable for receivers, and many players prefer to use their own rubber-cleated shoes when they play on Houston's AstroTurf, rather than indulge in a selection from the Houston storehouse of 250 assorted ripple soles.

And when George Allen took his Rams to play in Minnesota for the 1969 NFL Western Division championship, he took along four different kinds of shoes—regular cleats, the longer mud cleats, ripple soles for a frozen field, and Canadian Broomball shoes for a field covered with ice.

"Yes, we have them, too," Viking coach Bud Grant said. "I brought them down from Canada three years ago. The shoes have 19 suction cups on the bottom. They're for running on ice. Broomball is a game like hockey. You play it with a broom handle and a soccer ball. Except that you don't wear skates; you wear broomball shoes."

Fig. 11

Explanation of equipment:

A Shoulder pads . . . $30
B Rib pads . . . $9
C Girdle hip pads and supporter . . . $10
D Lineman's hand pads . . . $3.50 a pair
E Forearm pads . . . $4.50 a pair
F Elbow pads . . . $2.25 a pair
G Arm pads . . . $2 a pair
H T-shirt . . . $.75
I Thigh pads . . . $5.65 a pair
J Knee pads . . . $2.65 a pair

K Shin guards . . . $4 a pair
L Sweat socks . . . $.75 a pair
M Helmet . . . $20
N Face mask, cage type . . . $4.25
O Chin strap . . . $1.25
P Jersey . . . $44 ($22 each for road and home)
Q Pants . . . $34
R Leather belt . . . $1.50
S Long hose . . . $3.50
T Football shoes . . . $25

PLUS: Sideline cape ($39); sideline jacket ($25); practice jersey ($2.50); practice pants ($8); thermal winter gloves ($9).
TOTAL: $292.05
Most clubhouses have their own washing machines for practice gear, but game uniforms must be sent out to be laundered, at a cost of about $120 per game. Unless you play extra-dirty football.

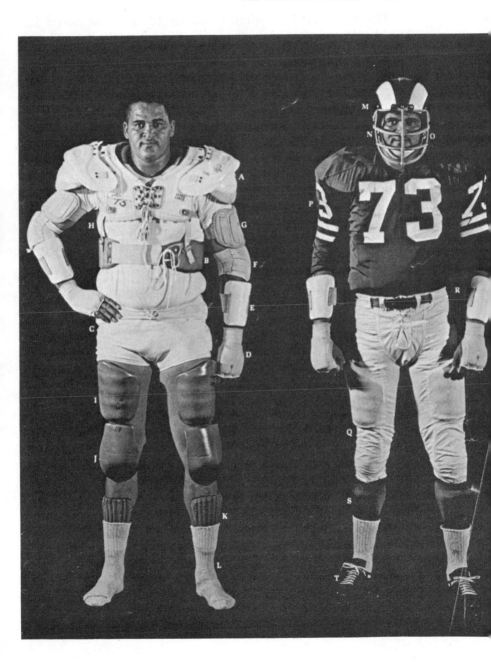

The home team is required to furnish 12 new footballs (at $25 each) for each game. A high-scoring game costs the team money, unless it has a couple of equipment men in the end zone, shagging footballs. When the Bears beat the Redskins, 73-0, in the 1940 Championship game, George Halas became alarmed at the amount of balls all the scoring was costing him.

"We started running out of footballs," says Bulldog Turner, the Bear center that day. "After one of our last touchdowns, Bob Snyder—he was the holder for the extra point—told me, 'Coach said to make a bad pass from center. He said we were losing too many footballs.'

"I told him, 'I'm going to put the ball right back in your hands, and if you don't want it, drop it. I'm not making any bad passes.' So I centered it back there, and he just turned it loose and let it lay on the ground. And the guy who was kicking—damn if he didn't kick it up through there and lose another ball."

Until the NFL-AFL merger, the NFL used a ball called The Duke, and the AFL used the slightly slimmer J5V. The AFL ball was supposed to be better for passing, but a group of quarterbacks, among them math Ph.D. Frank Ryan, were given a blindfold test, and they couldn't tell the balls apart. In the 1920's the ball was 23 inches around the middle, and most of the passers threw it in a sort of shot-put motion. Half an inch was taken off the ball in 1931, another inch in '34. It can go as little as 21¼ inches in circumference now.

The cost of outfitting a player is close to $300 wholesale (add about 30 percent for retail prices for individual items). See Fig. 11 for a breakdown of these items.

19
Keepers of the Faith: The Officials

We are under a Constitution, but the Constitution is what the judges say it is.

□ Charles Evans Hughes, 1907

First there were three officials, then four. Then in 1947 there were five, and in 1965—six (plus two rodmen, a boxman, and an alternate on the sidelines). Someday they may decide to platoon the officials like football players, or bring them in by the busload.

But some things never change. Officials will always catch hell from the players and coaches and sportswriters and fans. Maybe even from their wives.

"I once got this letter," said the retired Ronnie Gibbs, who refereed in the NFL for years. "It went like this:

Dear Mr. Gibbs. I just want you to know that I certainly appreciate the job you fellows do, because I know that no one has a harder time of it nor gets less appreciation. And even if people might criticize you, I understand your problems and think you do a fine job. P.S.—Please forgive the fact that this letter is written in crayon, but they don't allow us any sharp objects where I am.

Off the field, the officials might look like anyone else, except for a few tired lines around the eyes. On the field they line up like this (see Fig. 12).

Fig. 12

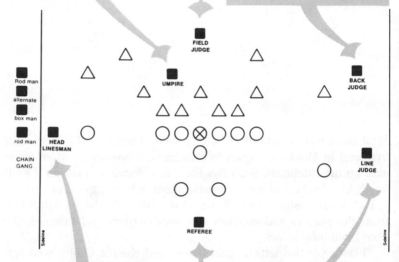

(Cover deep punts, fair catches and deep passes—watch for pass interference and illegal "picks"—time the 30-second count for putting ball in play—time the halftime and time-outs—rule with back judge on field goals)

(Check equipment—watch for linemen downfield—wipe wet ball—watch the holding—keep the linemen calm)

(Watch illegal "picks" on deep passes—count numbers of defensive players—work with field judge on signaling field goals—watch for clips on long runs—mark deep out-of-bounds)

FIELD JUDGE

UMPIRE

Rod man
alternate
box man
rod man
CHAIN GANG

HEAD LINESMAN

BACK JUDGE

LINE JUDGE

Sideline

Sideline

REFEREE

(Watch for offsides—watch for out-of-bounds—supervise chain gang—supervise subs on your side—watch pass interference—work with line judge and signal TD's on goal line plays—watch the side clips)

(Official timer—mark out-of-bounds—help linesman on goal line plays—shoot the gun at end of game—watch offsides—make sure scrambling quarterbacks don't cross the line before they throw forward pass—watch backward laterals)

(Run the game—put ball in play—start the clock—notify teams about time-outs—announce penalties—bring in chain gang—watch for backward passes—watch for cheap shots on passer—watch for roughing the kicker)

Officials hunt in packs, or teams. A team stays together for the season, and there are 13 of them—one for every Sunday game—plus a couple of alternate teams. Pay is figured according to length of service, not official duties, so a back judge can earn as much as a referee, if he's been around as long.

The scale is $250 a game for the first three years of service; $300 for the next two; $350 for six to 10-year vets, and $400 a game for officials with 11 years or more in the game. A divisional playoff game is worth $750; a conference championship, $1,100 and a Super Bowl as much as $2,000. The league provides expense accounts on the road, plus air travel cards.

The crew is expected to check into the hotel in the city it's working 24 hours before game time. On Saturday night the referee opens up the film of last week's game, spreads out the rating sheets by the two coaches involved (if they have bothered to fill them out), reads the report and comment from the league office, hands out play-by-play sheets. Then the group watches itself on film.

On Sunday morning there's a quick rule check, and the trip to the stadium. The officials are expected to get there no later than an hour and a half before kickoff time. They check with the TV people, the chain crew, and the home team, to make sure the required 12 new footballs are on hand—plus a hand pump on the sideline.

"Everything they do is closely scrutinized," says Mark Duncan, pro football's supervisor of officials. "We like to remind them that we have 800 to 900 applicants for the few jobs that open up every year, counting the screwball applications we have to throw out.

"We'll scout college officials, too, just like the clubs scout players. We'll even send a man to look at a good high-school official, if he's really exceptional. Some guys are turned down right away. A fat man, for instance, doesn't stand a chance. Officials have to do a lot of running out there. Besides, there's the image to think about.

"Back in the New York office we start looking at films as soon as they come in, usually late Monday afternoon. The No. 1 thing we watch for is whether or not an official was in the right position to make a call. We don't question his judgment.

"It's tough to figure out the temper of a game from watching films. That's why we send observers out to watch the games in the flesh. They rate officials' conduct and their control of the action. One thing we always want to do is discourage all that talking on the field, by officials as well as players.

"Talking is a woman's prerogative. Our officials should be above that."

There's paper work involved in all of this. The observers on the scene fill out a sheet. So does the league. And so do the coaches. The grading system on all of this is 0 to 5. Three is the cop out number, the "satisfactory" grade that coaches automatically put in when they're tired and don't want to think about it too much.

"If a guy wants to remain an official," Duncan says meaningfully, "his average better not drop below three."

The rating sheets are shown in Figs. 13A, 13B, and 13C.

Coaches who scream about the officials on Sunday generally calm down when they get around to filling out the grading sheets later in the week. Some coaches are easy markers . . . live and let live . . . some are tough. The reports are weighed according to the care the coach takes in filling his out. Dallas' coach Tom Landry, for instance, has a reputation as a meticulous and careful grader.

"About 60 percent of the coaches' reports are excellent—really great," Duncan says. "They're not just bitching. They're genuinely trying to improve the caliber of officiating. They'll point out things they feel are constructive, even if it means criticizing a call that helped them in the game.

"Of course there are some you file in the wastebasket. They're just ridiculous. And you never hear a word from some coaches. They never bother to send their reports in. Good, bad, indifferent . . . who knows? The reports start coming in toward the end of the week, and it's understandable. The coaches are so damn busy at the beginning of the week.

"But it's amazing how the attitudes of some these coaches change after they've had a chance to look at the films. One thing is universal. They don't show any sense of humor on these reports. Everything is deadly serious."

The league is very sensitive about coaches criticizing the officials when newspapermen are around. It fines people. The Jets

Fig. 13A

NATIONAL FOOTBALL LEAGUE
Officials Evaluation Report

_____( ) _____ ( ) Date _____

THER: Fair _____ Cloudy _____ Rain _____ Snow _____ Observer _____

DITION OF FIELD: Dry_____ Wet _____ Muddy_____ Temp. _____

ng Scale

Excellent — 5   Good — 4

Satisfactory — 3   Poor — 2   Unsatisfactory — 0

PERSONAL OBSERVATIONS	Ref.	Ump.	HL	LJ	BJ	FJ
a. Appearance (Dress — Physical)						
b. Manner in which Pre-Game duties conducted						
c. Composure (Pre-Game)						

OFFICIATING COMPETENCE ON FIELD

	Ref.	Ump.	HL	LJ	BJ	FJ
a. Basic position (Before snap)						
b. Mechanics (After snap)						
c. Judgement						
d. Reaction under pressure						
e. Application of Rules						
f. Decisiveness						
g. Temperament (after disputed calls)						
h. Reaction to pressure from bench						
i. Cooperation with crew						
j. Game control						
Total						
Ave.						

ments: (Use back side if necessary)

Fig. 13B

NATIONAL FOOTBALL LEAGUE
Film Report

GAME NO._____   _____ (   )
                                                            Home Team

DATE_____   _____ (   )
                                                            Visitors

TYPE OF GAME   QUALITY OF FILM

Routine ( ) Excellent ( )						
Difficult ( ) Good ( )						
_____ ( ) Poor ( )						
_____ ( ) _____ ( )	R	U	L	LJ	BJ	FJ
Position and Coverage						
Judgement						
Reaction Under Pressure						
Decisiveness						
Game Control						
FILM RATING						
OBSERVER						
COACH						

Fig. 13C

COACHES REPORT

DATE _____   GAME _____   ( ) _____   ( ) _____   ( ) _____
                                    HOME TEAM   VISITING TEAM

POSITION	REFEREE	UMPIRE	LINESMAN	LINE JUDGE	BACK JUDGE	FIELD JUDGE
NAME						
JUDGEMENT						
GAME CONTROL						
POSITION AND COVERAGE						
REACTION UNDER PRESSURE						
DECISIVENESS						

RATING SCALE: 5 (Excellent) 4 (Good) 3 (Satisfactory) 2 (Poor) 1 (Unsatisfactory)

COMMENTS:

_____
Signature

drew two stiff ones in succeeding years in Oakland, the first one in 1967 after Ben Davidson broke Joe Namath's cheekbone with a late shot, and the next one, a $2,000 whopper after the 1968 game. An assistant coach stormed outside the officials' dressing room after the game. That cost. The team doctor joined him. More money. And although Jet coach Weeb Ewbank refused to comment about the officials, he was held responsible for some newspapermen getting their hands on closeup game films and ripping the officials in print after a couple of viewings.

The game movies can be costly to players, too. The officials missed the sight of the Jets' cornerback, Randy Beverly, clotheslining Buffalo flanker Haven Moses in a 1968 game. But the league office caught it in the movies and stepped off their own penalty on Beverly—$100.

"I just bumped him," Beverly said.

"Bumped him?" a league official said. "You might as well have hit him with an ax. He was out a minute."

"That's what we call bumping."

The difference between the officiating of today and the earlier-vintage law enforcement is like the difference between J. Edgar Hoover and Wyatt Earp. In the early book, *Pro Football, Its Ups and Downs,* Dr. Harry March describes a one-ref game of 1906 —the Canton Bulldogs vs. the Massillon Tigers.

"Big Bill Edwards was brought in all the way from New York to run this contest, and he did just that, RUN it. Canton coach Blondy Wallace sent in a 215-pound substitute with a water bucket, to carry some instructions. Big Bill caught him in his subtle task and grabbed him by the neck and threw him 10 yards across the sidelines, water bucket, dipper and all."

The AFL's supervisor of officials, Mel Hein, says that the man responsible for an extra official being added to the crew could have been Chief Johnson, the old center.

"Chief was my sub on the Giants," Mel said. "He was an Oklahoma Indian and he knew how to walk softly. There weren't enough officials to go round in those days, and Chief's favorite trick when he was on defense was to sneak up to the ball while the other team was in the huddle, and nudge it about two feet with his foot. The crowd would start yelling, so the officials knew something was up, but Chief was too sneaky ever to get caught at it."

Pro football still makes its spectacular boo-boos, though. The Green Bay Packers beat the Baltimore Colts in a special Western Division playoff in 1965 when field judge Jim Tunney ruled that Don Chandler's field goal was good. The movies showed that he blew it, and they also show Chandler kicking the turf in disgust after he missed the kick. The NFL is still red-faced about that one, and now there are two officials (one on each goalpost) to call the kicks.

Then there was the famous three-downs case in the 1968 Bears-Rams game, a game that cost L.A. a shot at the Western Division title. Norm Schachter, one of football's most highly respected referees and a noted educator and scholar, blew that one. So did his whole crew. So did the assistant coaches in the press box, and the writers, and Ram quarterback Roman Gabriel—and even Pete Rozelle, watching the game on TV. It was a case of mass hypnosis. A holding penalty wiped out one of the Rams' four downs toward the end of the game when time was running out, but they never got the extra down back. They settled for three, and Schachter's crew was suspended for the rest of the season for its arithmetic lapse.

"It was one of the most amazing things I've ever seen," Duncan said. "It's pretty rare when a whole crew can lose track of a down like that. And how about the Ram coaches in the spotters' booth? How come they didn't phone the bench and start screaming about it. No, they missed it, too. And how about Gabriel?"

"I saw where one of the men on the chains was quoted as saying that he noticed it and mentioned it and was told to mind his own business, but I don't believe that he really caught it. If he did, he wouldn't have shut up about it. I know him. He'd have raised hell."

Someone asked Bear coach Jim Dooley if he knew what was going on.

"We don't count plays," Dooley deadpanned, "until we get the ball."

Ask a defensive lineman what he thinks about officials, and it's a 5-1 out-bet that he'd tell you, "Why don't they do something about the damn holding?"

Holding is like jay-walking. It's illegal, but it won't get called unless it's blatant. (See Fig. 14.)

Fig. 14

Boston Patriot guard Len St. Jean grabs a handful of the Jets' John Elliott's jersey. Mike Taliaferro gets ready to pass, and the referee watches but sees not. Where was the umpire?

For years, the Dallas Cowboys have been forwarding their game films to the league office, accompanied by a play-by-play sheet with "holding plays on Bob Lilly," carefully circled. The Cowboys might have given up by now. And the great defensive tackle has learned to live with it.

"I guess they figure if you don't let people hold Lilly," said the Cowboys' defensive line coach, Ernie Stautner, "it would be unfair to the game."

"The official is right behind me," Lilly said, "and when I charge one way or the other, my body shields off one of the offensive lineman's arms. And that's the one they use to give me the business with.

"OK, so the ref can't see it, and I cope with it the best I can. But then you get a play right in the open and they blow that one, too. That gets you mad."

The officials work on a part-time basis. During the week they are lawyers and schoolteachers and businessmen. Someone once asked Duncan if he ever thought of having his officials work on a full-time basis during the season.

"It couldn't happen," he said. "What would they do during the week? Look at movies all the time? What good would that do? You get experience by game conditions, and where would they get it during the week? You couldn't have them traveling around looking for scrimmages to officiate. Baseball and basketball have full-time officials because their sport is on a daily basis. Football isn't.

"I know one thing. Coaches wouldn't want officials hanging around their training camp the whole time. They'd get too close to a team."

Most officials say that they welcome the newest TV innovation —the instant replay—which allows the fans another look at their closer decisions.

"It's one of the greatest things that ever happened," says Tommy Bell, a referee with close to 10 years of service behind him.

"The people at league headquarters are going to see the films and grade us anyway. It's better to let the fans look at the play right after it happens. Nine out of 10 times we're right. I think it gives the general public confidence in us when they can check for themselves."

Officials pass out from heat prostration when they work the summer exhibition games, and they freeze in the winter. Schachter worked the 1967 NFL championship game in Green Bay when the wind-chill factor was 37 below. He wore eight layers of clothing, but his nose and feet froze, and he was laid up eight days after the game. Worst of all—his whistle froze.

There are other occupational hazards—like George Halas.

"I once criticized him for storming up and down the sidelines in a game in San Francisco," Gibbs once said.

" 'But the fans love it,' he told me.

" 'In Chicago, yes,' I said. 'But not in San Francisco.' "

They learn to put up with sharpshooters like Johnny Unitas, who will occasionally try to flimflam the world when he comes out to call the coin toss.

"We'll receive down at that end," he might say if he wins, whereupon the other guy will say, "We'll kick up here then." It's up to the referee to explain, "No, son, you've got the choice of the goal you want to defend. We've already established that you'll kick."

Bell says he once got even and even managed to shake up Namath, who seldom gets shook.

"I worked the '69 Super Bowl and Namath came up to me late in the game and told me, 'You know, you're doing a pretty good job in this game, even if you are an NFL official.' I thanked him and said, 'That's nice, Joe, but you know my team is still losing.'

"He didn't know how to handle that."

20
TV: The Hand That Feeds Us All

When talking, be as brief as if you were making your will; the fewer the words the less litigation.

□ Baltasar Gracián, The Art of Worldly Wisdom

Somewhere in this world there must exist tapes of some of those early 1948 and '49 pro football telecasts, and how I would love to spend a day going through them again. Every time I get a little annoyed at NBC's Al DeRogatis and his complexities or CBS' Frank Gifford and his easy expertise I snap out of it by thinking of those vintage telecasts, the golden throated, empty-brained pronouncements that passed for knowledge:

"Blocking and tackling is the name of the game . . .

"Defense is the name of the game . . .

"The last two minutes is (are?) the name of the game . . ."

They couldn't even get the names right in those days, and I'm sure Cleveland end Mac Speedie used to chuckle about that phantom pass catcher, "McSpeedie," who impersonated him on TV every week.

When people cry endlessly about the TV time-outs today and the little man in the red hat who tells the ref when to blow the whistle, I remind them of Jimmy Powers and his garbled version of the Friday Night Fights or Bob Edge, endlessly droning, "In again out again Finnegan," during the basketball games.

Of course, the obvious conclusion about TV is that if it weren't for those little men in the hats, the New York Jets wouldn't be around today, and neither would the Players' Pension Fund and the Super Bowl.

TV has bankrolled professional football, lifted it into a multi-million-dollar industry, into the nation's No. 1 spectator sport. It has turned us all into financial voyeurs (was the new pact $150 million or $184.4?). And it has kept us indoors on Sunday; that day that used to be devoted to church and lemonade on the porch and long walks in the woods or the park—it's now Mad Sunday with it's Violent World and Fearsome Foursome and Doomsday Defense and Eleven Angry Men.

Yes, TV did all that; the guy who tells you to buy a car, sip a beer, think of your future, buy some insurance, take a loan . . . wait a minute, don't go out to the kitchen for the commercial. They're paying $75,000 for that minute.

But TV is not judged by its nine-figure contract that people are suddenly very hush-hush about. It's measured by the guy who tells you: "That was a square-out to the split end, but the linebacker dropped over in the zone coverage and broke it up." The announcers, the color men, the audio part of the video, they're the image of TV as far as the world is concerned.

"Announcing is our weakest link," says ABC Sports president Roone Arledge, whose network will televise 13 Monday night games during each season from 1970 to '73. And a CBS executive was quoted in *Sports Illustrated* as saying: "Compared to the technological advancements we've made, our announcing is like having an old iron gargoyle stuck on the front of a new skyscraper."

The gentleman is being a little too hard on his announcers. Comparing them to "blocking and tackling is the name of the game," you would have to say they've come as far from those early days as the technology—14 cameras, "creepy-peepy" portables, stop motion, disc recorders, instant replay—has come from the two-camera setup of the late forties.

A sportscaster makes around $50,000 a year now, and some of the top names—Chris Schenkel, Curt Gowdy—can take home as much as $350,000, figuring all the extra work. The modern play-by-play man has learned to keep his mouth shut (sometimes), and follow the monitor next to him instead of the action on the field, just so he won't announce something that the guy in his living room can't see. And he must keep his sanity and composure while a steady stream of messages—mention the astronauts in the crowd, mention the governor, plug the Monday night movie—pour in.

The background, or color man is caught between two worlds. He must keep it simple so he won't frustrate the missus, and he has to explain what's going on with more than a passing knowledge, so people won't forget that he played the game for 10 years or so.

The early announcers were hired for their voice, not their brain. The ensuing set of color men were ex-pros whose knowledge was above question but whose delivery was often garbled or wooden (I still remember Red Grange "analyzing" a 50-yard pass play by drawing a straight line on a blackboard to indicate the receiver's route). Then came the modifications. The ex-player idea was retained as basically sound, but the men started to take diction lessons and acting lessons, and how-to-avoid-being-complex lessons.

"I'll never forget my audition," the late Paul Christman once said. "It consisted of putting me in a studio and having me simulate a football game . . . 'Here we are in the Polo Grounds, fans.' I stumbled around for a while and afterward, Bill MacPhail [CBS sports boss] said it was the worst thing he'd ever heard."

Christman survived, though, and eventually made it to the top of the field, because he had one admirable quality—a sense of humor. He refused to take himself seriously.

"I remember one game when a team was on its own five," Christman said, "and I was going through this long shpiel about how they had to dig it out and how tough it was, and while I was talking, boom, they threw a 35-yard pass and got right up to the 40. So what could I do? I made a joke of it."

The head-to-head confrontation, the *mano a mano* came in the first Super Bowl. NBC, with its top gun, Christman, was jointly televising the game with CBS, whose No. 1 boy was Frank Gifford. It was a clash of styles, the careful, somewhat wooden Gifford against the loose and easygoing Christman. The Cards' old QB, Pitchin' Paul, against ex-Giant Gifford, who had been nicknamed "Slick" back at USC.

"If people want to make a competition out of it," Gifford said, "well I can't help that. I'm sorry they're doing it. Christman is a fine announcer, but he doesn't have any more knowledge of the game than I do. He isn't better equipped, I can tell you that. I'll just try to work my tail off and do the best job I can.

"I know I've worked my tail off getting ready for this game. I've looked at Kansas City films [NBC's Kansas City was playing CBS' Green Bay], running them back over and over again so much that you could take the numbers off the players and I'd still know every one of them. I've gotten all the statistics—everything."

"I've never liked to clutter my mind with a whole bunch of facts," Christman said. "I rarely prepare for a game in a formal way. My job is to interpret the action and that's it. I remember we were doing a Buffalo game, and Charley Warner ran back his thirty-third kickoff of the season, a club record. There was nothing else doing, so I mentioned it.

"Then I started thinking, Now what the hell does a guy watching the game care about a club kickoff return record? So I followed up with something like, 'Now that statistic ought to keep you up all night.' I was never able to do this stuff with a straight face."

No one ever did decide how the Christman-Gifford battle came out. The Nielsen ratings gave CBS a 22.6 (12,410,000 homes) and NBC an 18.5 (10,160,000), which seemed to indicate a CBS victory. But NBC had been running much farther behind CBS during the regular season ratings, and the important thing was that the two networks had polled a combined 41.4 rating, which meant that 79 percent of all the televiewers in the United States were watching the game.

Christman remained at the top of his field up until his death in early 1970, but there were signs that his off-the-cuff delivery was starting to flatten out a little. Some players laughed at a few of his favorite pronouncements, such as, "Quarterbacks often like to get hit early in the game. It loosens them up."

"I've never liked to get hit *any* time in the game," Joe Namath said. "I'm loose enough without getting my head knocked off."

And Gifford has shown an improvement over his early days, when he lived in fear that too incisive an analysis of mistakes would offend the men he used to play alongside.

"Occasionally I'll see a guy goofing off, a guy who obviously didn't come out to play ball that day, but I won't mention it," he once said. "My job is to discuss overall strategy. I owe that much to the players.

"But I remember one time a guy I knew pretty well got beaten badly on a pass play. He gambled on the interception and lost, and I mentioned it. The next time I met him we sort of halfway kidded about it, but I knew we'd never have the same social relationship. Our wives wouldn't either."

There's something looking over these announcers' shoulders these days—the instant replay, the greatest second-guessers of all time. The referees say the gimmick is wonderful. The color men say it adds to the pressure. It means that every time they say, "The hole opened up when the guard and tackle cross-blocked," the producer in the control booth says, "Well, let's see," and he replays it, and the fans sit there second-guessing.

The whole thing amounts to a deeper and better analysis. And if at times DeRogatis, probably the best in the business, gets over-analytical, at least the viewer can feel he is being approached on an intellectual level, not the idiot level of those early telecasters.

The image of the ex-ballplayer rooting for his hometown buddies bothered CBS, though, and before the 1968 season the network instituted its Great Purge, trimming its 16 announcing teams (one for each team) down to eight. The octet works on a rotating basis, thereby keeping a fresh approach and eliminating hometown bias. The idea has remained, along with the ex-pro as color man.

"I honestly believe that the TV viewer prefers to listen to an ex-player, quite content to let him talk conversationally, even if he does split his infinitives and leave his participles dangling," says ex-Ram linebacker Don Paul, who was purged in '68. "There are polished announcers who don't know a sideline pattern from a stolen base."

With the increased technological and financial advances, though, has come secrecy. The TV contract used to be announced with such pride ("Photographers rushed in," *Sports Illustrated*'s Bill Johnson wrote of the historic CBS and NFL contract in 1964, "reporters shouted. Bill MacPhail, deafened by questions and blinded by flashing bulbs . . . said later . . . 'That was my greatest moment in sport' "). But the terms of the latest package have never been released, leaving the various reporters to take educated guesses and quote "reliable sources," and each other.

"The reason for the secrecy isn't hard to figure out," says a reliable source who mentioned that if he doesn't remain unnamed he will no longer be a source, or even a TV employee.

"It's gotten too big. There's too much money floating around. Once you get into money like that, there's all sorts of tax things that people start worrying about and the fear of antitrust investigations by some Congressman who wants to make a name for himself.

"No, everyone feels that it's better left unpriced, but it isn't too hard to figure out, if you use logic."

Ah, but who can understand figures that run into hundreds of millions. The best leak so far came from a CBS executive who said, cagily, that "CBS is paying no more than it did before, and NBC is paying a lot more than it used to, and CBS is paying about $3 million more per year than NBC." Another executive said the combined yearly package for the two networks is "around $33 million." So this is the way the package breaks down:

CBS: $18 million per year for 4 years · · · · · · · · · · · $72 million
NBC: $15 million per year for 4 years · · · · · · · · · · $60 million
ABC: $8.6 million per year for 4 years · · · · · · · · · $34.4 million
4 Super Bowls at $2.5 million each
　(NBC and CBS alternate) 　· · · · · · · · · · · $10 million
4 All-Star games at $1 million each · · · · · · · · · 　$4 million
　　TOTAL FOUR-YEAR TV PACKAGE · · · $180.4 million

A collection of newspaper clips from those two weeks after the deal was announced make for lively reading. The *New York Post*'s early-afternoon edition on the day of the announcement set the four-year combined figure at $95 million, which, if true, would have meant that pro football would be suffering a 40-percent reduction from its old package. The next edition corrected the figure to $100 million, which would have meant only a 36-percent decrease. And the late edition that same day corrected the figure again, setting the new price at $176 million, which was more logical. The *Sporting News'* TV columnist, Jack Craig, rushed into print with a $150 million figure, correcting it, in a later issue, to $184 million. And so on.

The president of CBS-TV, Robert Wood, was alternately quoted as saying, "The $70,000-per-minute price that advertisers have to pay will not be affected," and, "The $75,000-per-minute price that advertisers have to pay will not be affected." What's $5,000 a minute?

CBS acknowledged that some one-minute ads for the 1970 Super Bowl went for as much as $125,000 a minute, but then a CBS executive bragged at a party, "We got $200,000 from Hartford Insurance Co. for a one-minute ad in the 1970 game."

This financial "Can You Top This?" can go on forever, and it all makes you wonder about the significance of this great mass of figures that the newspapers and magazines drop on the fan. Does it make him enjoy the game anymore? Does it make Sonny Jurgensen's passing look any sharper, or Buck Buchanan's hitting look any harder? Does it make the announcing any clearer or the commentary any more revealing? And more significant: will it keep him in his seat during that one-minute commercial, or will he still duck out to the kitchen to make that chicken sandwich?

The significant thing about the new package is it makes you believe that the market has just about topped out. The increase in revenue that each pro football team will get (each club will get $1.6 million a year under the share-alike plan. Last year the NFL teams got $1.2 million apiece and the AFL teams, $950,000) comes mainly from the money that ABC is pouring in. CBS and NBC are upping the payments a little bit, but nothing like the increases that used to greet every new package in the past.

In 1948, for example, the old AAFC Baltimore Colts' owner, Bob Rodenberg, said that the club got $50 to televise a game into Washington and $100 to televise it in Baltimore. "Radio still dominated the scene," he said, "but all we could get from them for the season was $7,000."

The TV market grew, and NFL Commissioner Bert Bell had the foresight to black out the local area in those early years. In 1953 a District Court ruling upheld the practice, which prevented TV from swallowing up football the way it had devoured boxing and baseball. The clubs negotiated their own TV contracts, and in 1956 and '57 CBS held contracts with 11 of the 12 NFL teams.

All 12 were covered in 1958, 11 of 12 in '59, 10 of 13 in '60, and 11 of 14 in '61. In 1959 Green Bay was collecting only $30,000 a season for its telecasts, and the Giants probably represented the top of the market when they pulled in $200,000 in '61.

The AFL had gotten a deal from NBC, though, which called for $1,785,000 a year, with increases that would bring the five-year package close to $11 million. In '62 the NFL got a two-year contract from CBS that called for $13 million, and the race was on. In '64 the NFL got CBS to up its payoff to $14.1 million for each of the next two years, and the AFL was assured of financial security when NBC came through with a contract that eventually became $42 million for five years. CBS' next contract with the NFL—for the '66 and '67 seasons and an option on '68—called for $18.8 million a year, and in 1969 MacPhail said that the network was paying the NFL $22 million, including a $2.5 million payoff for the Super Bowl.

The huge jumps of the past seem to have calmed down, and the new package represents only a slight increase when you combine the NBC and CBS revenues. CBS pays more now because the cities under its scope include the top five market areas in the country —New York, Chicago, Los Angeles, Philadelphia, and Detroit. NBC's top draws are New York, Boston (No. 6), and Oakland (No.7), and even the three teams that swung over in the merger— Pittsburgh (No. 9), Cleveland (No. 11), and Baltimore (No. 12) —don't help NBC's overall picture that much.

The networks have been crying for the last two years about over-exposure, that they can't sell their advertising time, etc., and someone must believe them, if only slightly. But they'll probably all come close to selling out during the 1970 season. Advertisers realize that pro football gives them a great big audience that the prime time shows never reach—the young, wage-earning males. It's a lot easier to try to sell a car to a roomful of men on Sunday than it is to the ladies who watch "Bewitched" or "The Ghost and Mrs. Muir" on weekday nights. And the 1970 packages (CBS' "Red, White and Blue" for $75,000, $50,000, and $35,000 per minute; NBC's "Green and Red," each averaging out to about $45,000 a minute; and ABC's $65,000 a minute) are not significantly higher than those of '69. And even if the networks just barely manage to break even on football, as they claim, the prestige of being associated with pro football should be enough to keep them going—and paying.

During the 1970 season, though, all eyes are on ABC and its intrusion into evening prime time. The feelings are mixed. Does an NBC or CBS man root for ABC to make it, thereby showing the superiority of football—never mind the day or hour—over Family Entertainment? Or is he a team ballplayer who sticks with his own network against the invader, even though it means rooting against pro football and its image, which his own network is trying to promote. And everyone likes the idea that the addition of ABC means that for four years people don't have to worry about the shadowy network of Howard Hughes, the man no one knows but everyone fears.

The ABC telecasts will start at the exact same hour that NBC's blockbuster, "Laugh-In," ends. "They'd be crazy," an NBC man says, "to try and buck 'Laugh-In' head on." "That never figured into our plans, one way or another," an ABC man says. "Everyone in the business knows that 'Laugh-In' is on the way out anyway."

And then there's the business about pro football sharing ABC with its sworn enemy, the NCAA, which dreads all intrusion of the pro game. "The Monday night games on ABC will promote the NCAA telecasts for the following Saturday," says an ABC man, "but the NCAA Saturday games won't say a word about the pro game that Monday. We spoke to Pete Rozelle about it and he understands."

Will pro football really become overexposed? There's an awful lot of football around.

"Too much, much too much," says the Rams' defensive tackle, Merlin Olsen. "Six preseason games, just for TV. That's too much. And now Monday night football. That means that during the season there will be high-school football on Friday night and Saturday; college football on Saturday; pro football on Sunday and again on Monday night. Four of the week's seven days will have football.

"If a man likes chocolate pudding he will eat all you give him until one day he'll stop eating it and probably never eat it again."

Almost lost in this whole maze of high finance is that original concession to TV—the TV time out. This slight bending of the rules to accommodate the hand that feeds us all, a practice which Vince Lombardi once said hit at the very moral fiber of the game (he now accepts it . . . "They're paying all that money"), is just about unnoticed now. It did get a little raw, though, when they ran a kickoff over in the 1967 Super Bowl because TV wasn't ready.

"TV hardly interrupts a game at all," says veteran referee Harry Brubaker. "Usually the 12 normal time-outs the two teams can take, plus the touchdowns and kickoffs and two-minute warnings and changes of period, provide all the time we need. But if play has run continuously at the start of any period, I can expect the TV man on the sideline to put his arm on his shoulder, indicating I'm to call a time-out."

"We never break up a drive," says referee Norm Schachter. "I remember calling a TV time-out in that Dallas-Green Bay sub-zero game in '67 and Bob Skoronski asked me why I was calling a time-out in that freezing cold. I said, 'This one's for the players' pension fund.' That ended the conversation."

And even the biggest TV blunder of modern times, when *Heidi* popped up to chop the last minute off the Jets-Oakland game in '68, can be put to good use. Three weeks later newspapers carried an NBC ad for *Pinocchio,* following the Kansas City-San Diego game. It's guaranteed to turn a good mood sour within a minute.

PINOCCHIO SAYS—I'D RATHER CUT OFF MY NOSE THAN HAVE THEM CUT OFF ANY OF TODAY'S AFL ACTION. SPORTS FANS CAN RELAX. SEE ALL THE ACTION ** AND PINOCCHIO, TOO (7 PM) ON NBC!

NBC reported a marked improvement in ratings for *Pinocchio. Heidi,* too.

III
Characters and Contemplations

21

A Gallery of Ruffians, Flakes, and Oddballs

Joe Don Looney; never was a man more aptly named.

□ George Sauer, Jr.

I think of E. J. Holub, the multi-knee operationed center of the Kansas City Chiefs, and I think of a night in Rice University Stadium after an exhibition game in 1967. The Chiefs had just beaten the Houston Oilers in a Texas football classic that was notable for a 10-minute brawl on the field, and the P.A. announcer kept reminding the fans, "Stick around after the game, folks, for the grandest fireworks display in the State of Texas."

So 20 minutes after the game, there was E. J., sitting on the stone ramp leading to the dressing rooms, his soaking uniform clinging to his back, his false teeth in his right hand, watching the rockets flashing across the Texas sky.

"Not yet, man," he said to the assistant coach who told him to get his ass inside and take his shower. "I simply *love* fireworks."

I think of Larry Eisenhauer, the defensive end for the Boston Patriots, and I wonder whether old Dutch still makes the trips. Dutch is Larry's father, a crew-cut 6-3, 275-pounder who used to raise hell for the Long Island Aggies in Farmingdale.

"Want to see one of Dutch's scouting reports?" Larry once said before a Jets-Patriots game. He pulled out a single sheet of lined

305

yellow paper. "To beat the New York Jets," the report read, "you must get Joe Namath and double-team Emerson Boozer."

"Of course he lets us work out the details for ourselves," Eisenhauer said.

When the Patriots played San Diego, they would stay at a place called the Stardust Motel. The big feature of the Stardust was the Mermaid Bar. The drinkers would drink and look at four young water ballerinas performing in front of them in a glass pool. One hot night Larry's dad felt like a swim.

"Where's the pool, Larry," old Dutch said, and of course Larry steered him over to the Mermaid.

"It almost made me swear off booze for life," a writer said. "There I was having a nice quiet drink, and all of a sudden this goddamn whale in a blue woolen bathing suit was swimming right at me."

"How was your swim, Dad?" Eisenhauer wanted to know after Dutch got through with his show.

"OK, Larry, but I got the damnedest feeling that there were a whole lot of eyes on me."

One afternoon a Charger PR man stopped by and handed the Boston players a bunch of Charley Charger coloring books. The Patriots took them over to poolside, and the rumor that night was that Eisenhauer had spent the rest of his day dutifully coloring his Charley Charger book.

"It's a goddamned lie," Eisenhauer said later. "I wasn't coloring the thing. I was just reading it."

Life would be indeed dull if America's football players rolled off the assembly line saying "Yessir," and "Nosir," and "Gee, I think all the credit belongs to my teammates, sir." It's people like Eisenhauer and Sam Baker and Alex Hawkins ("I went to high school in Charlestown, West Virginia, and I'd get myself ready for the big game by playing solitaire, having a chew of tobacco, and listening to Webb Pierce sing, 'I'm in the jailhouse now.' ") who make things interesting. Yes, even the Joe Don Looneys, who bring you into another dimension.

Looney's dossier reads like an old Henry Aldrich script. By the time he got to the University of Oklahoma he had logged time at Texas, TCU, and Cameron JC in Lawton, Oklahoma. He was canned at Oklahoma for slugging a student assistant coach, and then came the pinball trip through the pros—New York to Baltimore to Detroit to Washington to the Army to New Orleans, all within six years.

Before his senior year at Oklahoma, he had spent a summer in a Baton Rouge, Louisiana, health studio. He was 6-1, 224, when he left. He could run the hundred in 9.8, lift 290 pounds in a military press, 450 in a squat. He drank a gallon of milk a day and swallowed 20 different kinds of protein pills.

"Have you considered his attitude?" someone asked Wellington Mara after the Giants drafted him No. 1 in December, 1963. "I have considered those shoulders, those legs, and those 224 pounds," Mara said.

He lasted with the Giants for 28 days. People remember him punching and flailing at Allie Sherman's recoil-blocking dummies. Trainer Sid Morett remembers that Looney wouldn't throw his used socks and jock into a bin so marked, because, "No damn sign is going to tell me what to do." He wouldn't talk to reporters because, "They just get things fouled up," and when publicist Don Smith pushed a note under his door, Looney pushed it back out. "And don't you bother me either," he said.

Practices bored him and he preferred playing catch with a nine-year-old boy on the sidelines. In scrimmages he ran the seven-hole when he was supposed to run the five-hole. "Anyone can run where the holes are," he said. "A good football player makes his own holes."

He wouldn't have his ankles taped ($50 fine); he was late to meetings ($50); he missed bed check ($50). "Finally," Smith said, "he owed us so much in fines that he couldn't afford to play for us."

"It's not fair," he said, when he missed the 11 P.M. bed check by 10 minutes. "The night before, I was in bed at 10. They still owe me 50 minutes."

In August he was traded to Baltimore, and after a few workouts the Colt coaches said his attitude was 100-percent improved. He scored a touchdown on a 58-yard run against the Bears and came off the field in tears. Joe Don was ready to blossom.

Then in November he broke down a door and slugged the male

member of one of two young married couples cowering in the hallway. It was all a big mix-up, he said at the trial. He and his buddy were looking for the apartment of some nurses, and besides that, he was pretty upset because Barry Goldwater had gotten beaten so badly in the Presidential election.

And when Looney's lawyer, William D. MacMillan, suggested probation before the verdict, he gave the world a definitive appraisal of his man: "This verdict would keep the two couples from having a feeling that Looney might develop a 'persecution complex,' over the matter, and the two other couples would not have a future fear of Looney retaliating against them."

A week later Looney jumped into the ring during a tag team wrestling bout involving Red Berry and Bruno Sammartino in the Civic Center and helped quell what he figured was a riot. Promoter Phil Zacko thanked Joe Don for protecting his wrestlers. "He should be commended," the promoter said.

Baltimore coach Don Shula couldn't see it that way, and before the next camp opened, Looney was gone—traded to Detroit for Dennis Gaubatz. And while the Lions' coach Harry Gilmer was explaining, "I believe that with his rookie year behind him, things will straighten out. I don't believe he will be a problem," the Colts were relating a few Looney stories they had held back until then.

There was, for instance, the time he cut out of a party carrying a blanket. "Where are you going?" someone asked him. "I'm going to sleep in the cemetery," he said. "It's nice and peaceful there."

Next morning a teammate asked him how it was. "I had a good talk with a guy about death down there," Joe Don said.

There were the stories that John Unitas told—about the time Joe Don asked someone to "watch my cheeseburger for me," while a team meeting was going on; about the time the team was gathered in the locker room for the pregame prayer, and someone heard a noise in the equipment room, and there was Looney, listening to the radio and doing the Mashed Potato all by himself; about the time in practice when Joe Don got off a 60-yard skyscraper of a punt and stood there watching it, hands on hips, and finally asked, "How'd you like that one, God?"

Gilmer rubbed his hands and said that the Lions' running attack could center around Looney. The Detroit publicity department predicted that Joe Don could be the first 1,000-yard runner in the team's history. But Looney's first real headlines in Detroit involved a fight in the parking lot of the Golden Griddle Pancake House in Royal Oak. There was something about a tab for $3.28 and a misunderstanding over who should pay it, and the scene finally ended with Looney trying to smash a beer bottle and use the jagged end, just like people did in the movies, only the bottle wouldn't break.

Then there were problems with his back, and finally, in one September game in 1966, Gilmer told Looney to carry a message in to quarterback Milt Plum. "If you want a messenger," Joe Don told the coach, "call Western Union." That ended his career in Detroit. Next stop, the Redskins.

"We're walking down Washington Boulevard in Detroit the day after Joe Don got traded by the Lions," says Bob Tate, a Detroit bartender and a friend of Looney, "and Joe looks up and says, 'You know, Tate, I sure am glad I'm not a building.'

" 'Yeah, Joe,' I said, 'it would be awful hard on you moving from town to town.' "

In Washington he achieved instant stature. He scored a touchdown in his first game ("It was a twin-two-sweep-trap . . . that means as much to me as it does to you"), Coach Otto Graham said he was finally shaping up, the headlines involved the "New" Looney, and the honeymoon lasted right up until he announced he was playing out his option because of a salary squabble.

He wound up in the Army for a year, and finally New Orleans picked him up as a free agent. He packed up his mastiff hound, the one he had loaded down with barbells ("to build up the dog's leg muscles") and almost converted into a health food addict with a sunflower seed and wheat germ oil diet, and headed south. The last report on the dog was that he had made a raid on a nearby hen house.

"I might have known," sighed Doug Atkins, the Saints' giant defensive end. "The minute the kid straightens out, the dog goes bad."

There were gamblers and drinkers and bummers in the old

days. There were a few eccentric geniuses like Johnny Blood, Green Bay's itinerant poet and world traveler, roaming over the landscape, immortalizing places like the old Astor Hotel in Green Bay ("the only hotel in the world," Blood once said, "where you can call collect at 2 A.M. and get money"). But these were mostly poor men, and if not for football they'd be loading trucks and hauling freight and plowing rocky little patches in no-name towns.

"Jug Earp, Mike Michalske, Cal Hubbard," the Green Bay druggist, John Holzer, once said, reciting the names of the old Packers like a roll call of famous World War I infantry divisions.

"They played their hearts out for $35 or $50 a game. They had a fierce desire, an almost animal desire for contact."

"I remember one time when Bronko Nagurski was horsing around in a second-floor hotel room with a teammate," said retired referee Ronnie Gibbs, master of the apocryphal, "and Bronk fell out the window. A crowd gathered and a policeman came up and asked, 'What happened?'

" 'I don't know,' said Nagurski. 'I just got here myself.' "

George Halas tells about a 1933 Bear game in which Nagurski knocked out Philly linebacker John Bull Lipski.

"Bull had great recuperative powers, and he came back in the game and tried to tackle Bronko again, and he was rendered unconscious again. Two of the Philadelphia substitutes came off the bench and started to drag Bull off the field. Bull came to near the sidelines and started muttering something about getting back in there.

"But play had already resumed, and the Bears were headed in his direction on a sweep with Nagurski leading the interference. Bronko overtook Lipski and the two subs about five yards from the sidelines, and WHAM, he threw a block that sent all three of them flying into the Eagles' bench.

"Poor Lipski was knocked out for the third time, a record that should stand until another Nagurski comes along, if one ever does."

When some of these old-timers become coaches, they evaluate their talent in an elemental way. They set their linemen on each other, one-on-one. The guy who survives is the first stringer. The Giants' old coach, Steve Owen, was saved from the Oklahoma dust bowl by football and he never forgot it. He lived by two mottos: "Football is a game played down in the dirt and always will be" . . . and, "Football was invented by a mean son of a bitch, and that's the way the game's supposed to be played."

In 1924 Steve tried out for the Kansas City Cowboys in old Blues Park, along with a character named Milt Rhenquist of Bethany, Kansas.

"The Swede was dressed in overalls and work shoes," Owen wrote in *My Kind of Football*. "He weighed about 240 and had heavily calloused hands. The Swede in scrimmage battered one half of our regular line. He wasn't scientific, just effective."

They used to say that the Steelers' Ernie Stautner, who played defensive tackle at 230 pounds, could have been transported 40 years back into time, pound by pound, and he would have fit right in with the leather-helmet boys. Ernie knew one move, the straight all-out shot, dead on his man, with every sinew and nerve dedicated to that one killing charge.

Once in camp a rookie lineman challenged him to a fight, so Ernie, a trifle mystified, but no less vicious, beat hell out of the youngster.

"Some damn fool college coach told that kid," Ernie said, "that the best way to make a pro team was to lick the toughest veteran they had."

The year after he retired, Stautner coached the Steeler linemen. The first time Ernie's rookie protégé, Ben McGee, faced the Giants' great tackle, Rosey Brown, both men were thrown out for fighting.

"That guy was working my head over with his forearm," said the usually mild Brown. "I took that stuff from Stautner for 10 years, but I'll be damned if I'm going to take it from a rookie."

The ruffians of football come in all packages, from the wildly flamboyant Eisenhauer to the cold, tight-lipped Dan Birdwell, the defensive tackle of the Oakland Raiders.

"I've got bruises all over my body from bumping into Dan around the kitchen," says his wife, Diane. "Or taking a gouge from him while he's asleep. He won't even play with our three children for fear of injuring them."

"I kept listening to Birdie all game long, bitching about the holding," said his teammate Tom Keating. This was after one of the Jets-Raiders bloodbaths on the Coast. "We all knew something was going to happen. Then there was this pileup, and Dave Herman's [Jet offensive guard] hand was sort of sticking out of it, on the ground. Birdie ran over and stomped on it with his cleat. He looked like he broke every one of his fingers."

Eisenhauer's No. 1 enemy is the dressing-room wall. "I've calmed down a little," he said a couple of years ago. "I really used to get psyched before a game. I'd try to tear anything apart— walls, doors, lockers, my teammates sometimes. They stay away from me now."

The biggest challenge is the Buffalo dressing room. "It's kind of small," Eisenhauer says. "Not much room to get up a head of steam. But I got that little partition one time. I got it with my helmet."

There's a slightly puckish twist to his nature, and the Patriots publicity department once tried to cash in on it . . . until they learned not to fool around with the unknown.

Boston used to have a daytime kiddie show called "Boom Town"—Rex Trailer and his sidekick Pablo. Someone sold them on the idea of filming a show at Fenway Park, and the action would center around the Patriots' football team. Pablo would grab the ball and run for a TD with all the Patriots chasing him. Eisenhauer, an extrovert, was picked to be one of the chasers.

Once the action started, though, a hidden bell clanged and all the 6-5, 250-pounder saw was an enemy player running for a touchdown, a guy who had to be stopped. So he stopped him.

"I'm kind of ashamed of it now," he said later. "Pablo was only about 5-3, and he was slow, so it wasn't any trick catching him. I didn't really hurt him. I just sort of jumped on his back. But what the hell? Why give a guy a free touchdown?"

For a while there was a whole thing about Baltimore linebacker Mike Curtis. Mike, the Animal, mean Mike, who liked to run his bicycle into walls when he was a kid, etc. He said, no, it was all a misunderstanding and he gave out the phony quotes just to ease the tension, and you know, underneath it all is the soul of a Rachmaninoff. But there is a very nasty story his parents once told about an exquisite torture that the preadolescent Curtis dreamed up for baby chicks. We won't go into it now, but if it's true, it shows that under many a rough exterior beats the heart of a true sadist.

Everyone has his favorite candidate for meanest player ever. A straw vote among recent veterans—players and coaches—would probably elect Hardy Brown. Physically, Hardy wasn't very impressive. He stood a shade over 6-0 and weighed 196; he had light sandy hair and a bland face. His speed wasn't much, and he didn't have any great talent for pass coverage.

What Hardy had, though, was a right forearm, sometimes a shoulder, that he turned loose with killing force and velocity.

"When he hit a guy," said his old teammate on the 49ers, Ed Henke, "it sounded like a rifle going off in the stadium. He missed a lot of tackles, but he just killed 'em when he hit 'em. There were no face guards in those days, and he had a shoulder block that could numb a gorilla. It was a skill nobody could duplicate."

Brown began in the old All America Conference, with Brooklyn and Chicago. Later on he played for the 49ers, Colts, Redskins, and Cards in the NFL.

"I won't say he was the toughest player who ever lived," said St. Louis assistant coach Chuck Drulis, who has been in the NFL since 1941, "but he was the meanest. He enjoyed hurting people. He broke more noses and caved in more faces than anyone else. I once saw him knock two players out on the same play. Good backs like Frank Gifford, Kyle Rote, and even big guys like Dan Towler feared him. They hated to run fakes into the line because Hardy hit them so hard."

There was no explaining Hardy and his magic forearm. He was like that psychiatric phenomenon, the Idiot Savant . . . a man with the IQ of a 4-year-old, but with one super-developed talent, such as absolute recall of any note of music he ever heard. The outer world is blocked off, the psychiatrists say, and the Savant's entire being is channeled into that one great talent. So it was with Hardy Brown. Every ounce of his 196 pounds, every instinct on the football field, was directed to that one lethal, numbling blow of his right forearm—or shoulder.

Y. A. Tittle, who played against him in the AAFC and then with him at San Francisco, used to enjoy Hardy, which was sort of like having a pet Gila monster around the house. In his autobiography, Y. A. wrote: "Hardy once threw a shoulder block into Joe Geri of the Steelers so hard that he popped Joe's eyeball clean out of the socket."

And Y. A. also likes to indulge in legend . . . this from the days when he played against him.

"We ran a play at Hardy one game, and one of our guys was lying on the ground," Tittle once said. "Then we ran a play the other way and Hardy stretched another guy. So I called the Bootsie play—everybody get Hardy Brown. When it was over, there were two of our guys lying on the ground. There was a lot of grumbling in our next huddle.

" 'The hell with this,' one guy said. 'Let's go back to the old way. At least he was only picking us off one at a time then.' "

In 1951 Brown was credited with racking up 22 NFL backs. Don Paul of the Rams said they got up a kitty of $500 to go to the player who took Hardy out of action. No one collected it. One particularly vivid memory is the shot that Hardy delivered to Mr. Outside, L.A. and West Point halfback Glenn Davis, on an end sweep.

They met at the corner, and there was one of those Daffy Duck sequences in which the body keeps running but the head stays in place. They carried poor Davis off the field and I still have visions of that deathly white face, and his head bobbing lifelessly from side to side.

The game attracts them all, the killers and cuckoos, and plain stand-up comics like Detroit's 250-pound defensive tackle, Alex Karras, whose world, off the field, is a never-ending series of incredibilities.

"I see myself as a man on horseback, in an attractive policeman's uniform," Alex says, "singing and playing the guitar to the girl I love. The problem is finding the right girl, one beautiful enough to match my own sheer brilliance and personality. It may never happen."

Alex likes people to know that he has lived other lives—in the company of Adolf Hitler and George Washington, for instance. ("Hitler was no ordinary Joe. He had this obsession to hold his breath for more than three minutes.")

And if you're ever in Athens, try to find someone who watched the 1957 Balkan Games. Alex threw the shot put in that competition.

"It was open to anyone of Greek or Slavic ancestry, so I signed up and got a free trip out of it," Karras said. "I told them I threw the shot and discus, even though I never tried it in my life. On the boat going over, our coach told me there was no place to throw, but I could practice my form.

"He watched me and then he said, 'Your style is pretty unorthodox. What kind do you use?' I told him, 'step-over.' I finished last in the shot put with a 32-footer, and it was actually the best throw of my life."

In Dallas, they were saddened when Danny Villanueva, the Mexican-American kicker left after the 1967 season. When he first came to the Cowboys in 1965, he took the regular team psychological exam, and the psychologist reported to club officials that he shouldn't be called "Taco," the nickname the Rams had given him. "It saps his confidence," the psychologist explained.

"How about calling him 'Toro'?" said a sportswriter.

"Great," said the psychologist.

Then Villanueva walked over to meet the press.

"Call me Taco," he said.

In 1966 he ran a fake punt 23 yards against the Cards, which started people speculating that perhaps he had been a halfback in college.

"What were you in college?" a writer asked him afterward.

"I was a Mexican then, too," said Danny.

Sometimes the coach sets the tone. The old Colts were an incongruous bunch, but as long as they kept winning, Weeb Ewbank let them go their own way. The country boys used to like to play tricks on their Irish tackle from the Bronx, Artie Donovan. One night at training camp some of them buried a dead groundhog under his bed sheets.

"You hillbillies ought to have your mind on football," Artie said when he found it. "Just look at that poor dead fish."

And there was the time the late Gene, Big Daddy, Lipscomb, the Colts' other All-Pro tackle, made his off-season wrestling debut. He scored a pin with his secret hold, a "hammer slam."

What, his teammates wanted to know later, was a hammer slam?

"Just squeezin', I guess," said Big Daddy.

Ewbank's Jets left some unforgettable vignettes, before they started getting good. There was the midnight dive that Don Maynard took, fully clothed, from the high board at the swimming pool in Oakland's Edgewater Motel. Don collected $50 for his stunt.

"You going to fine him?" someone asked Ewbank the next day, which happened to be the day of the ball game.

"Hell, no," the coach said. "If I fine anyone it'll be those other guys—for dumbness. Maynard's so crazy he'd have done it for nothing."

And there was the time that Weeb figured that a trip to the hot mineral baths in Sonoma would be just the thing to remove the kinks after an Oakland game. So he detailed his traveling secretary, John Free, a nervous little guy, to shepherd the team bus up to Sonoma.

"We passed by a winery," Free recalls. "The sign said Free Samples, Tasting Room. Everyone started banging the floor of the bus. They made me stop the bus, and we toured the winery. They all got half stoned, and the ones that didn't, smuggled bottles of wine under their shirts and drank them on the bus on the way back to camp.

"That night at supper Weeb looked at the guys slumping over their plates and he said to me, 'See that, John? Those baths did help. I've never seen the players so relaxed.' "

The true personalities have their character molded before they ever hit the pros. When Texas Tech's Donny Anderson was being alternately wined and dined by Houston and Green Bay before he signed his $600,000 contract, he'd make sure to remind the gentleman in charge of the particular evening's entertainment: "No college broads."

"How's your speed?" a writer asked him just before he reported to the Packers' camp.

"All I've got to be, stud," said Donny, "is one step faster than Hornung."

Michigan State coach Duffy Daugherty has his own testimonial —to one of his boys who never even reached the pros.

"His name was Mad Pat," Duffy said. "He got so worked up he went around the tunnels banging his head against the wall. Then he was hammering at the door of the dressing room, roaring and shouting. He put his hand clean through the door once. Out on the field before the Purdue game, he started hitting all their defensive backs before the game even started. I had to break it up, and I'd tell him, 'You stupid son of a bitch, why do you want to make these guys madder than they already are?'

"A hell of a competitor."

22

We Never Lose a Game in the Press Box

A sportswriter looks up in the sky and then asks you: "Is the sun shining?"

□ Sonny Liston

It took a newspaper strike, a long one, to convince me that I really liked my job as a sportswriter.

The first clue came during one of those depressing interviews that might land me a job until the strike was settled.

"Well, you report in at nine and you leave at five," the guy said, and I got my hat. Nine to five? I'd forgotten that kind of world existed. My time schedule is measured by the pro football schedule—kickoff is 1 P.M. Sunday, press luncheon is 12 noon on Monday and 11:30 A.M. on Wednesday. In between, I'm on the phone; I make the practices in the afternoon; I talk to people; I hustle up stories. The sheer volume of work is greater than the average 40-hour week, but no one tells me that my day starts when I come into the office at nine and ends when I leave at five.

I used to laugh at the guys who said, "What a racket you sportswriters have. All you do is get paid to watch games." I laughed because it was the thing to do, and what did they know about all the slammed doors and "no comment" statements and people who yelled that you misquoted them, to save their own necks?

But I had been jolted by that nine to fiver. I really do like being a sportswriter. In fact I like it better than almost anything I could think of, except maybe a movie star or a food taster for the Michelin Guide.

There are some things I don't much care for. The thing I hate most is the schizophrenic existence right after a game. For three hours you've been tucked away in a warm press box, watching something you sincerely enjoy. There are coffee and sandwiches, a meal before the game and snacks while the action is going on (I'll never forget the brownies in the Cotton Bowl press box).

People hand you statistics and play-by-play sheets—even quotes—and, if you're so inclined, you can just about let that mass of mimeography write your story for you. But when you leave this protective world for the dressing room downstairs, you're thrown into a completely different setting, a dingy corridor where 50 or 100 people crowd together like transports on a slave ship. There's always a wait for the doors to open, and for some reason the special cops outside those doors seem to have an instinctive dislike for newspapermen. You can't stop to give these guys much back talk, either, because, if you indulge in that luxury, you'll lose precious time getting into the dressing room, and you might lose valuable field position, which, as most experienced dressing room jockeys will tell you, is everything.

The very mechanics of transmitting your story are an anachronism. You type it, and hand it to a Western Union telegrapher, who has to type it all over again. This comes into your office, where it's edited and sent out to the composing room, where it's typed all over again, this time by a linotype operator who may or may not be hitting all the right keys, depending on the kind of celebrating he had done that weekend (Sunday nights are dreaded by most reporters).

Two sets of fingers have typed your story after you did, and you check the first edition on Monday, and "played very well," comes out "played like hell"; and "88 yards rushing" comes out "388," and a day later the players say, "How the hell could you write that?"

I remember I once spent an hour and a half after a game doing an intricate study of the passes thrown into each area and how a team's zone defense had been scientifically picked apart. And, of course, Monday's paper had all the numbers garbled, which is the type of error that doesn't get picked up by the editors on the desk. I stopped leaning on statistics so much after that one.

The coaches and players you talk to often have a very foggy notion of the way a writer works. This is especially true of the athlete who's been severely burned by an unfair story. He knows all he wants to know, and 50 complimentary feature stories sometimes never undo the damage that once was done.

"The stories I like to read, in fact the ones most ballplayers like to read," San Diego's offensive tackle, Ron Mix, once said, "are the ones about contract problems, and holdouts, and guys who are playing out their options. Why don't you guys write those kind of stories more?"

"OK, Ron," I said. "How much are the Chargers paying you this year?"

"Well, I think that's kind of a personal matter, don't you?"

And that's why people don't read more contract stories, or, if they do, they read about prices that are often guesses. Not all, though. Every writer who has been around for a while has his pipelines, his tipsters, who keep him informed about some of the things that go on. Management doesn't want you to know what the players are making, because the knowledge will only work against them. The players who are underpaid will demand more money, but the high-priced guys will never say, "Gee, I think you ought to trim my salary a little to make it conform to the other guys at my position."

The players are naturally secretive about their paycheck. For one thing, they're told never to disclose it. Some of the lower-paid ones might be ashamed if people knew how little they were working for. And some of the top money players feel that it's best if their price doesn't get out . . . sort of killing the goose that lays the golden egg.

A club will leak the information about a huge package, like Joe Namath's $400,000, for publicity purposes, keeping the price vague and never spelling out the exact amount, but letting you know that this is a helluva thing for football and mankind.

Big-money signing sessions are often hilarious.

"Is he making $75,000?" you ask a club "spokesman."

"Oh, no, not that high."

"How about $60,000?"

"Well, I think he's worth more than that."

"How about $70,000."

"Well, ha-ha, now you're trying to pin me down."

So the writers get together and decide to go with $70,000, and next day's banner headline reads: "Joe Doakes Signs for $70,-000."

I've always found that the toughest stories to write were the ones about the business deals that might be taking place, the things from the Commissioner's office, prospective mergers, franchise shifts, etc. And I've often wondered just how much people like to read them.

I've had people come up to me and say, "Gee, so-and-so wrote a wonderful story on the merger talks," when all he had done was taken a pass, stayed for maybe half an hour, looked around and "Written the Scene," as it's called. . . . "Twenty gaunt and haggard men huddled in the decaying elegance of the Hotel Boris Karloff and plotted the destiny of America's greatest sport," etc. etc. And the poor guy who has worked all night, and picked up some good information from his tipsters, and done a thoroughly researched job of reporting, gets the quick read.

Writing the Scene is the biggest copout in our business; also the easiest kind of story to do. You walk into a dressing room after a big game. The star quarterback's locker is crowded to bursting. There's no chance of getting near him. The coach is mobbed. Half a dozen players each have a knot of reporters around them. So you stand back and take a look and write, "The smell of sweat and liniment rose from the dressing room like great clouds of smoke from an angry steam engine; in a corner of the dressing room, with its inch of blue carpeting and psychedelic light patterns bounding off the ceiling, a young man slowly cut the tape off his battered ankles . . . ," *ad infinitum*.

Most writers can crank out this kind of nonsense forever. The tough part is getting that inside position on the star quarterback, taking that elbow in the ribs or kick in the shins, writing the hard quotes, and making some sense out of them. Then you can Write the Scene if you want to. Most good interview stories are personalized . . . if a guy look tired, or is bleeding, or took a sip from a bottle of Lithuanian beer while he was talking to you, it should be part of the story.

There's another part of our business that gives most writers nightmares—the scoops. The scoop, in newspaper work, is not dead, as some people would have you believe. It is very much alive, even more so now that there's a big competing medium— television. The traditional newspaper reporter's fear is that he'll be somewhere while something important is happening someplace else. But it happens. Win one, lose one; try and have a winning record and don't jump out the window when you blow one.

"Competing against him isn't so touch," a writer once said about a demon reporter who worked for a rival daily, "except for those two or three mornings a year when you open his paper and say, 'Oh, God.' "

But you are often measured by your superiors on how many scoops you got, how many stories you broke, even though the story proves to be without foundation. And if you can get other papers to respond to the story by "knocking it down," or writing a piece that contradicts your story—even if the knock-down piece is entirely accurate—the score is 1-0 in your favor.

There's the story about the two Philadelphia writers who were covering a 76ers basketball game. They decided to have a little fun, so they planted a bogus story about Philadelphia general manager Jack Ramsay rumored to be in line for the Commissioner's job. A couple of New York papers bit for this one, although the other Philly writers weren't fooled.

Next day one of the two Philadelphia reporters was in his office, chuckling about the prank, when his sports editor pointed to the New York story about Ramsay taking his new job and yelled, "How the hell could you get the beat on this? Write a story knocking it down."

So the poor guy had to pretend to make a phone call, and then type a by-line piece that began, "Jack Ramsay today denied rumors that he was going to the Commissioner's office . . ."

When the Len Dawson story broke on Tuesday before the Super Bowl, one of the first reporters to interview him was Ken Denlinger of the *Washington Post*. He wrote down Dawson's quotes . . . "I have absolutely not been served with a subpoena . . . I am absolutely innocent of any wrongdoing . . ." and drove back to the main press room to call his story in to the desk. The *Post*'s columnist, Shirley Povich, overheard the conversation, but he got the quotes slightly balled up. He thought Dawson had dropped the word "absurd," into his denial. He mentioned it to someone, and his conversation was overheard by a New York columnist in the next seat. This gentleman took a deep pull on his pipe, tilted his chair back, and called his desk to dictate his Wednesday column:

" 'It's absurd,' Len Dawson told this writer in confidence last night . . ."

I've found that one of sportswriting's most cherished axioms: "Never forget that the ballplayers need you a lot more than you need them," doesn't always hold up. I would like to believe that it's true, but unfortunately it's not. Many players have cashed in on their publicity, but I honestly feel that most of them would just like to be left alone. Without publicity, attendance would suffer, consequently finances, consequently salaries. But without football to cover, our autumns would be deadly dull, unless we could work up some enthusiasm about covering cross-country or the Ukrainian Soccer League. And if there ever really was a doubt about who needs whom, it was dispelled the first few times I saw reporter-player squabbles. Four times out of five it's the writer who makes the first peace overture, not the player (although the reverse is usually true with coaches).

In the old days, the writers were right down on field level. They couldn't watch the plays open up, but they could hear the curses and the hitting, which is actually the best way to see a game— except that we've all become a bit too stodgy to be able to handle that kind of a workday now. When the Giants played the first game in the Polo Grounds, on October 11, 1925, the morning paper writers got seats in the baseball press box, in the lower deck behind home plate, or deep in the end zone. The afternoon paper reporters got seats in the stands—lower deck between home and first base. But when the Chicago Bears brought the barnstorming Red Grange in at the end of the season, a press box was set up on the upper deck, at midfield, and that became the standard for future press boxes.

Some teams allow you in the locker room before a game—up until an hour before kickoff. Then strategy might be discussed, and such things are not for writers' ears. Unless it's a big game, I usually don't go into the locker room ahead of time. Most of the players don't like a bunch of people hanging around asking them, "How do you feel?" every five minutes, although a few of them welcome the break in the tension. The writers who follow the Jets got a bonus before the 1969 Super Bowl. They got off the team bus with the players, and walked into the dressing room with them, the usual procedure for any game. They were treated to some memories that will always remain—Johnny Sample's strange, lonely ritual in the empty shower room as he "psyched" himself for the game; George Sauer lying on his back with his feet in the air, pretending he was a "frog upside down"; Don Maynard desperately trying to work the soreness out of his leg, right up until he had to go out onto the field.

We all thought it had been an oversight on the part of the club, letting us in like that, but Weeb Ewbank was one step ahead of the game.

"I didn't want the players to feel too much tension," he said afterward. "So I tried to make everything seem like just another road game, all the conditions. And that included having the writers around, as usual."

Every reporter has his own method of watching a game, and scoring it. Most of them use a longhand system that duplicates the mimeographed play-by-play sheets that are handed out after every quarter. Some of them use a chart book filled with sheets that represent the field and the yard markers. You use different-colored pencils for the two teams, and detail their progress up and down the field, using symbols for different types of plays—i.e., straight line for run, wiggly line for pass, dotted line for kick, snapped pencil and perhaps a drop of blood for a play you miss, etc.

By the second half, the morning paper writers with early deadlines are usually deep in their typewriters, sending "running" accounts of the game, or play-by-play. A lot of them can only glance up to catch a play here and there, and every long pass or dramatic run is followed by a chorus of "what happened?" in the press box.

With about five or six minutes to go, whether the game is a runaway or a cliff-hanger, there's usually an exodus from the press box, as the writers start heading for the dressing room. This is a part of the job I hate, because I like to watch the game until the very end. It's not always possible. In a stadium with a direct elevator from the press box to the locker room, you can wait until the final whistle and then race out like a madman, knock over a few fans, hop the elevator, and arrive at the locker before the door is opened. But in a place like the Sugar Bowl (1970 Super Bowl), with a system so archaic that a guide had to lead the press to the dressing rooms, you had to leave early or you were dead.

Late arrival outside the Kansas City dressing room, even though its door stayed locked for 15 minutes after the game, meant that you would lose your chance for a ringside seat for the No. 1 postgame story—Len Dawson. You wouldn't be anywhere near his phone conversation with President Nixon; you wouldn't be able to fit in the trainer's room while Dawson answered questions for a dozen or so writers—while 60 or so milled around outside. Through judicious trading of quotes after the game, you might come up with the same basic quotes as anyone else, but you would have that left-out feeling, which unhinges so many of us.

The worst part of a post game dressing room is the en masse questioning of a losing quarterback or a losing coach or the cornerback who has allowed the winning touchdown. If there's anything in the world these people don't want to do it is talk to a gang of reporters, and sometimes the brusqueness and insensitivity of some of the writers is surprising. I would dearly love it if someone would think up a better way of handling these situations, but so far no one has.

I used to enjoy talking to Chicago White Sox manager Eddie Stanky and getting a reading from him about the press. There was always a free give-and-take of ideas with Eddie, and he never kept his feelings hidden.

"The thing I can't understand," he once said, "is how you guys can go over to a pitcher who's just lost a tough game, and start popping those questions right away: 'What was that last pitch you threw? How do you feel about losing?' Stuff like that.

"Maybe I'm getting old, but once upon a time there were older writers covering a club, and the first thing they'd do would be to go over to the guy and put their arm around his shoulder and say, 'You lost a helluva tough game out there, but you pitched great.' Then they'd gradually work into their questions, and they'd usually get better answers."

It's a good idea, but it has to come from the heart. It has to be genuine, or it will be spotted right away and the reporter will be written off as a phony.

I'm often amazed that some people connected with our business can show so little understanding of it. Or maybe it's pretense. Joe McGinniss wrote a *Saturday Evening Post* piece on Washington quarterback Sonny Jurgensen, who likes to duck out on reporters after a game, win or lose. McGinniss describes a 1968 game in which the Redskins beat Philadelphia, 17-14, and Jurgensen met him afterward, apologizing for his lateness because a couple of writers nailed him in the hall while he was sneaking out.

"Sonny Jurgensen does not like to talk about a game right after it has been played," wrote McGinniss, an ex-newspaperman. "He prefers to wait a day or so and sort things out in his mind. It is a sensible approach, and undoubtedly leads to more intelligent conversation, but sportswriters want quotes for their stories, and want them right away."

Yes, we do. But when a quarterback throws a winning pass in the last two minutes, how do you explain to your readers, "Sorry, dear reader, but Mr. Jurgensen will not comment on that pass. He's busy sorting things out in his mind."

A basic antagonism exists between the press and the TV people, even though we don't like to admit it. We bristle while we stand outside a dressing room, squashed together like grapes, knowing full well that inside, the lights and the mikes of CBS or NBC or ABC are in full operation, recording the comments forever. It's like the guy in the VW who sees the chauffered Rolls drive by. It pains us deeply and always sends up a ripple of reflex grumbling—"Damn TV guys, why should they be in there?" etc. —but it's a fact of life. They paid big dough for the rights to the game so they travel first-class. Newspapermen will always be around.

Actually, the TV man is not the newspaperman's real enemy. It's the magazine writer. A magazine staffer or a free-lancer can cover a club or an individual on the club and do a hatchet job and leave, never to return. But what he has left is a group of very angry ballplayers, or perhaps just one, who vows: "Never again will I trust those newspaper bastards." So the regular beat men are left to clean up the wreckage and try to smooth things over. The magazine writers are the guerrilla fighters—they hit and run—but the regular writers are the foot soldiers, the infantry.

The Sunday work is only part of the regular assignment. There are advances to write, feature stories, postgame follow-ups on Tuesday, prospective trade stories, etc. Once the season is humming along smoothly, I can organize my work week as follows:

Sunday: Cover the game.

Monday: Follow up on game, or look ahead if someone is injured, or next week's opponent has injury.

Tuesday: Day off, except if you're on the road. Then you do a feature story.

Wednesday: Press luncheon. Talk to coach. Talk to opposing team coach (phone). Talk to players. Watch practice.

Thursday: Generally a feature story on opposing team player, by phone. Watch practice and write about any injury report, etc.

Friday: Do pregame Saturday advance. (That's the big advance for our paper because we don't come out on Sunday.) Also do advance on college football game I'll be covering.

Saturday: Cover a college game. If pro team is going on the road, it will generally leave Saturday morning, so if you're covering a college game, you might have to make your own travel arrangements.

Of course any of this can be broken up by special situations; any big stories that are breaking in the league itself (especially if you have a good pipeline on that club), or anything unusual concerning one particular individual. Then you'll write about him for the better part of the week.

Every coach has his own feelings about writers at practice. Ewbank opens his Jet practices to visiting and New York press, but if he's putting in a triple-whammy offense for Sunday's game, he will remind the reporters: "I don't mind you writing that I'm working on new stuff, but please don't include a diagram," which is a perfectly reasonable request. Bud Grant likewise opens his Minnesota practices.

"I once had an office in Canada overlooking the visiting team's practice field," he said. "I could sit there and watch their practice, but it never helped me one bit."

"How about your injuries?" someone asked.

"Maybe the gamblers would be interested," he said. "We report our injuries to the league office, like we're supposed to do."

At the other end of the scale is Al Davis, who runs the Oakland Raider workouts, their locker room and the team offices, and everything else connected with football in the area, with a heavy fist.

A few of us went out to Oakland five days early to cover the Raiders-Chiefs playoff for the 1968 Western Division title. It was my greatest week for kickouts. In fact three of them came in one day.

On Wednesday morning I dropped over to the Raider offices and was told that I was in the way. Would I please leave. At noon I stopped by at the locker room. Ben Davidson's new bar, Big Ben's in Hayward, was opening up that night and I wanted to get directions on how to get there.

"It's kind of complicated so you better check this map on the wall," Ben said, but I never got a chance. A white tornado had arrived: Johnny Rauch, the coach, in a flurry of arms and legs, and I found myself being hustled out of the locker room.

"The board—look at the map on the board!" Davidson yelled, but I was traveling too fast to focus on the bulletin board.

"No writers in our locker room!" Rauch yelled, and as I passed two Oakland writers, they flattened themselves against the wall to permit smooth egress.

Now it was a challenge. I simply had to get to the practice. I scouted around, and a 13-year-old equipment boy told me that on Wednesdays they held practice at Cal State at Hayward, in a sunken bowl-like stadium that was high on a hill. I got there about half an hour after practice started. The Forbidden City. Shangri-La.

Except that I was too high up to see anything. I sat there for a while, watching the workout, and nothing much happened, so I got bolder and moved closer. My fatal error. A frozen tableau. Everyone staring, and piercing the chilly December afternoon was the voice of Davis—"He's from New York! Get him out of here!"

Up the stairs, like a dutiful cocker spaniel, trotted a fat little guy called Bugsy Engelberg, the kicking coach. I made it tough on

Bugsy. I moved to the very top step, so he had to trot all the way up, to puff out his message that I had to leave.

And the last sight I saw of Cal State at Hayward, through the rearview mirror of my car, was little Bugsy standing in the middle of the street, a towel flapping around his neck, as he watched the car to make sure it left. That night I mentioned to a writer that I might have come close to the one-day record for getting thrown out of places.

"I think the record is four," he said. "But getting kicked out by a kicking coach adds a touch of class."

Newspapermen have been suspect, or at least avoided, ever since the game started making money. Red Grange might have set the tone in 1925 when he hopped a train to the Chicago Bears after his last college game—Ohio State—and booked a stateroom under an alias, to escape reporters. Sometimes an interview can be an exercise in blank verse.

Some reporters will not take an "off the record" statement, since they feel it compromises their integrity. I don't have such mental discipline. I'll take one, and then try to talk the guy out of it, if it's to his advantage anyway—at least I'll try to get it in under "an informed source." Pete Rozelle and other experienced interviewees set the ground rules beforehand—"This is for direct quotation; this is for attribution but not quotation; this is for neither attribution nor quotation . . ."

I have always shunned the tape-recorder approach. Mechanical gadgetry usually kills any spontaneity in an interview, but it is excellent for say, a book, when the narrator wants all his thoughts in print anyway.

"I hate those things," Ewbank says. "I like a writer to interview me with a pad and pencil, so I can see what he's doing. Those tape recorders pick up every damn word you say."

The literal transcription of a conversation is often upsetting. Profanity, when taken out of context, can assume a totally different flavor.

"There may be some profanity when 40 hard-charging men and six demanding coaches are mixing it up on the field," the Packers' Phil Bengtson said after one practice session. "But, frankly, you don't expect to see it in print anymore than you expect a photographer to take a picture of us in the locker room with our clothes off."

One fellow who annoys newspapermen, coaches, and athletes alike is the extra-aggressive man with the microphone, the guy who's always shoving it under someone's nose in the middle of an interview. After one 1969 Redskins' game, a man shoved his microphone between Vince Lombardi and Jurgensen during a conversation.

"You would stick that thing in a coffin," Lombardi told him.

"I have my own way of dealing with those guys," says Jimmy Cannon, the columnist. "When I see a microphone, I just string together every four-letter word I can think of until the guy goes away."

It's a sort of unfortunate maxim that the stupidest questions often produced the best and liveliest answers. An interview may be progressing along on perfectly logical grounds until some guy pops up with: "What was the turning point of the game?" (a favorite question among idiot-interviewers), which might draw a response like . . . "How the hell can you ask for a turning point in a 47-0 game?" . . . and then blam, blam, blam, four or five snappy quotes that might never have come out.

A reporter once interviewed Art Aragon, the fighter, after he had been beaten unmercifully in a bout.

"What would you do next time?" the guy asked.

"Next time," Aragon said, opening a puffy eye, "I'd throw you the hell out of here."

And don't forget that it was only after needling and prodding that Lombardi issued his famous 1967 post-Super Bowl quote that at least a few NFL teams were better than Kansas City, a statement that was to stay with the Chiefs right up until their Super Bowl victory three years later. And Lombardi's full quote ended with: "That's what you wanted me to say and I've said it for you."

It's a tricky business, taking down somebody's remarks and translating them into copy and headlines. Often an innocent statement will explode. And there exists a group of people in every town, whose single function in life seems to be to call up quoted athletes and coaches to tell them, "Gee, did you see what so-and-so wrote about you?"

And of course next day you hear about it, and the first thing you ask is, "Did you read the story?" and the answer, "No, but I didn't have to. I was told about it." So you tell him: "How would you like it if I missed the game, but wrote a story about how lousy you were?" But it doesn't usually make any impression. And sometimes, if it bugs you enough, you'll go and produce the story and show them that what was written and what they were told about were completely different animals.

You have to be careful about the meaning in which a statement was given. Players like to put the press on. Coaches love to. There are writers who take everything literally, and don't stop to try to figure out what really happened. It's part of the business.

"I don't know how Paul Brown did it, but he sure managed to control the press in Cleveland," Ewbank once mused. "I wish I could have that in New York, but it's impossible. The guys here are too interested in sensational stories."

"How would you like to be an editor and have a 'controlled' writer covering the club for the paper?" someone asked him. "Don't you think the readers deserve a better shake than that?"

"It's just that in places like Cleveland, the newspapermen were more community minded," the coach said. "They didn't want to do anything to hurt the club."

Every team has its "house men," reporters who take the easiest way out and make sure to stay in good graces with the people they have to talk to every day. For every ripper, and there are some reporters who deliberately like to stir up controversy, there are a dozen house men. But the rip is remembered and the house story taken for granted. Until a few years ago, George Halas had a captive press in Chicago. Then it became open warfare on the Bears' boss, and he retaliated with some very pointed phone calls to his friends who edited newspapers, and there was some shuffling of assignments. Al Davis enjoys almost complete immunity from any embarrassing questions in Oakland. And he pays his locals back by laughing at them.

"We'll make a decision on McCloughlan later on this week," Rauch told a Bay Area press luncheon four days before the Raiders played Kansas City in the '68 playoff.

"They're so dumb I've got to laugh," Davis said later that day.

"Kent McCloughlan was operated on for torn knee ligaments this morning."

Coaches cherish some of the old-time writers, especially if they're a little bit foggy about the game. The coaches realize that these people will seldom hurt them. Occasionally the coach will drop some little tidbit to one of his regulars, some minor scoop, just to make sure that their jobs are secure. Sometimes a guy will call the coach and say, "I quoted you today, but don't worry, I didn't say anything important." And the coach will feign annoyance, attaching a naughty-naughty tag to the idea of quoting him on something he didn't say. But he really loves it. It gives him a kind of minor hammer, and it solidifies the relationship.

I firmly believe that most coaches mistrust the reporters who show signs of learning too much about the game. They don't like to read something that says, "The Eagles scored their winning touchdown because Joe Doakes blew a zone coverage." They'd much prefer a writer to come up and say, "What happened on that last TD?" so they can tell him, "How the hell can I tell until I look at the films." And of course, by the time the films are studied, it's generally a dead issue.

In the old days it was simple. A club simply bought off the writers with food or booze or just flat-out cash. This might still work in some places, and it's tough to turn down a good feed every now and then—as long as the club is paying for it and writing it off on their taxes. But the blatant bribe is passé in most big cities (although it still exists). For one thing, the newspaper business is more competitive now. There are more young writers coming along, and a quick twenty under the table might set off a rash of exposés, or at least create enough scuttlebut to make it very uncomfortable for the club.

Coaches will fib a lot, and occasionally deal you a great big lie. There *is* a difference. I can't really criticize a man for some slight fibbies to the press, if it means maintaining the morale of his squad or protecting a player he's worried about. I don't dig the falsehoods that are dropped out of pure self-preservation, though, the ones that generally involve contract disputes and irritate the players as much as the newspapermen.

The worlds of the coach and the newspaperman are often in conflict. A coach who is sincere is worrying about his team and his players ahead of everything else, including buttering up the press. A writer, unless he's an out-and-out house man, is trying to do an accurate job of reporting the team, the good and the bad. Sometimes he feels he has to write something, even though it might annoy the coach or a player. I can compromise my conscience, though, and withhold something that will deeply injure a player or a coach, provided it isn't essential to my coverage of the team. But there are reporters who never get off the white stallion, who feel that every bit of barracks gossip is fair game for their readers. These guys might get a reputation as flamingly honest reporters, but after a while not too many people will talk to them.

Sometimes a coach will let you step in and help him get his team ready for a game. This comes under the heading of using newspaper stories to psych the boys. It gets a lot of mileage when enemy players are quoted at any length. Any statement can be taken out of context and used as a whip.

"I think we have a helluva chance this Sunday," says Joe Smith, the enemy's defensive left end. So next day the clipping is pasted on the locker of your offensive right tackle, who will be playing against poor Joe.

"See what that dummy, Smith, said?" some assistant coach will remind your man. "A helluva chance. He's your man, and he said that, a stumblebum like him."

"We don't let any off-season bravado slip by unnoticed," Bengtson says. "I have a drawer in my desk for clippings from out-of-town papers that will be of use next year."

The thing that probably bugs the players most about writers, though, is this: "How can a man know how to write about what we're doing on the field when he has never done it himself?" And occasionally, when a writer pops up who has played a little football: "Yeah, he played in the Ivy League, where they put doilies under their helmets."

All this generally comes out when the writer treads on the very tricky ground of expertise. We all indulge in it, and often we are dead wrong. I find it almost impossible to analyze a game and tell, for instance, whether a team is in a man-to-man pass defense, or whether it is using a masked or hidden zone defense. Sometimes the players and coaches can't tell themselves until they see the films. But I keep trying for this deep analysis anyway, and often

I'm dead wrong. It's fun. It's human, this desire to analyze. But it can lead to error . . . and we all do it.

Some of the notables of the various news media make a habit of it. Many times they're badly burned, but the theory is that the public has a short memory. Howard Cosell, the TV man whose hard-interview technique I admire, gets ridiculous when he turns to the area of football expertise, but Howard loves to do this.

Misinformation is spread around the country wherever you look. The biggest ads for the movie *Paper Lion* showed a picture of John Gordy rushing the camera, and the pseudo-scouting report read: "John Gordy, Detroit Lions, Guard, 6-4, 240 pounds, Quick Moves and Likes to Hit . . . A Vicious Blocker . . . See How He Creams the Paper Lion . . ." Now anyone with any sense knows that Gordy played offense and the paper lion, George Plimpton, played quarterback—also offense—so there was no way one offensive player was going to cream the other. But someone sat in an office and thought it up, and it was catchy, so it connected.

Sometimes we newspapermen are just as guilty. We love to sit around the office in the off-season and dream up trade stories. Sometimes we'll drop one into a column, purely speculative but with just a hint of credence, so the poor reader will think he might be on to something. We'll set it off by a tricky lead-in, i.e., "How's this for a trade . . . ?" I look back at some of the prospective trades I've set up and shudder with horror. If I were a coach, I'd save some of those floopers and show them around a couple of years later. Oh, yes, I don't make off-season trades anymore.

Sometimes a slight kindness stays with you for years. I'll never think about the town of Green Bay without remembering the time I went up there on a rainy Thursday to do some interviews before a Bear game. I had a couple of hours to kill, so I asked one of the women behind the Packer ticket counter where I could find a good place for lunch.

"There's a good restaurant about half a mile away," she said, "but it's raining. Here," she said, tossing me her car keys. "Better drive over."

Occasionally, newspapermen are scouted like players. In 1966, Atlanta's sports publicity director Jan Van Duser, published a little guide for his fellow NFL PR men on the Atlanta media representatives:

"Al Thomy—He's a digger and will devote time to you. A bachelor. Has swizzle stick, will travel.

"Furman Bisher—Whatever your own assessment, this controversial man is widely admired, widely cursed, and . . . most important to him . . . widely read.

"Jesse Outlar—Night owl, so don't call before 11 A.M.

"In the broadcasting field we have some enthusiastic fellows. Only time will tell which of the disc jockeys calling themselves sports men really can differentiate between the Fearsome Foursome and the Beatles."

And sometimes we blush when we are parodied. Miami owner Joe Robbie did a whimsical piece for a Dolphin game program in which he pretended to be a journalist writing an in-depth piece on newspapers. His first call was supposedly to Ed Pope, sports editor of the *Miami Herald*.

"First thing, can you tell me please your total budget, your salary, and the salary of every writer on your staff?"

"I'm sorry."

"Also, the salary of your rim men and copyboys?"

"We consider that confidential."

"But it's of great interest to the public. I'm checking out rumors that Miami sportswriters' pay is the lowest in the league, next to Denver."

"We don't give out that information."

"But," I argued, "pay has a direct bearing on the product. Can you at least tell me how much expense money you give your photographers when they cover Dolphin games out of town?"

"We don't send photographers on Dolphin road trips."

"Oh," I said. "Cheapskates," I wrote in my notebook.

Maybe 30 years ago, when reporters were two-fisted drinking men who came into the office at 3 A.M., pushed their fedora back and took a story "off the wall" because their fingers couldn't find the holes on the telephone dial, maybe, just possibly, it was a happier time all around. Certainly a less complicated period. I read some of those wonderfully whimsical pieces written in those days . . . even the poetry (yes, newspaperman wrote actual poetry) . . . and wonder that maybe we're missing something with all our in-depth studies today. One poem, written by the *New York Herald-Tribune*'s Don Skene in 1930, stays with me. It's a parody of Tinker-to-Evers-to-Chance, substituting some of the jaw-breaking names of the Fordham players:

> These are the horns of the Fordham Ram,
> Elcewicz, Wisniewski and Pieculewicz.
> Butting the foe with a scoring slam,
> Elcewicz, Wisniewski and Pieculewicz.
> Savagely singing a touchdown tune,
> Making telegraphers fumble and swoon,
> Ready to die for the Old Maroon,
> Elcewicz, Wisniewski and Pieculewicz.

23
The Lost World: Football's Minor Leagues

God, I don't want to go back down there again. They tear your shoes off
down there.

　　　　　　　□ Jimmy (The King) Corcoran, July 30, 1968, two days before
　　　　　　　he was cut by the New York Jets

Beneath the magic and glamour and hard-rock solvency of professional football lies a hidden world, a kaleidoscopic network of
shifting franchises and unfulfilled promises that the ordinary fan
knows nothing about. If you live in a big city with an NFL or
AFL franchise, you may be dimly aware of the existence of this
substratum that is loosly termed the minor leagues of football. If
you come from a smaller community, you might have a more intimate picture.

At the top of this world there is the Atlantic Coast Football
League and the barely alive Continental Football League. And at
the top of these organizations are the clubs with definite AFL or
NFL tie-ins. These are the fat cats of minor league football.
Working your way down, you pass through the semipro leagues
whose more attractive members are usually snapped up by the top
two minor league federations.

And working your way down from there you come to the fly-
by-nights, the lost and the hopeless, with an ever-shifting cast of
players and owners and general managers and coaches. It is this
world that I know more intimately.

There is a drawer in my desk marked, "Important Documents,"

and somewhere in the middle of the confusion are two pieces of paper that I prize above all others. One is a letter that bears the heading, "Greater Morristown Sports Association, Inc; Also Known as MORRISTOWN COLONIALS." And the other is a check for $2.50, made out to me and signed by the Paterson Pioneers, Inc.

The letter is signed by Charles W. Frost, secretary of the Morristown Colonials, and it goes like this:

> We have finally concluded arrangements with the Equitable Life Assurance Society in which it has been determined that only a very small percent of our players were covered for loss of income during the last season. With this no coverage decision, we, the Association, are entitled to rebates of those premiums unused.
>
> For some reason the company made a check out to your order. Rather than request them to reissure the drafts we thought the endorsement of the check to the Association would be the quicker approach.
>
> Please sign the enclosed draft on the back where provided and return to us. We naturally are planning on these funds to help liquidate some of the Association obligations.
>
> Your cooperation would be appreciated.
>
> > Very truly yours

I keep it as a sort of microcosm of minor league football's lower depths. We were supposed to cover all our players by insurance, Mr. Frost was telling me, but we didn't. But the insurance company sent you some money by mistake ($25), since you weren't covered, and could you please let us have that money back, so we can bail out quicker?

I wonder what Pete Rozelle's lawyers would say about that one.

The Colonials represented my last fling at semipro football. (No minor league ever uses that term. From biggest to littlest, they call themselves "professional football.") I played a few games for the Colonials, just for kicks, about three years ago. Like most teams in this kind of world, the club began with high hopes and lofty aspirations that "the Colonials will create better business opportunities for all of you throughout the Morris County and Northern New Jersey area."

And of course the club went broke after one season, and there were the usual round of frantic phone calls in December . . . "Could you please get the equipment back to us as soon as possible? We're trying to get what we can for it." Until I felt an ominous twinge in my right knee on one kickoff play, and clearly read the message that I was too old for this kind of nonsense, playing for the Colonials was a lot of fun.

The check for $2.50 from the Paterson Pioneers represented the sum total of payment for my services at offensive guard for the Paterson, New Jersey, representative in the Eastern Football Conference in 1960.

The Pioneers were the brainchild of a couple of local dreamers who persuaded a young Leonia, New Jersey, realtor to sink his money into the venture. Bob DeMarco, a Northern New Jersey hero who was on his way up to the St. Louis Cardinals, was a regular figure at those early practices, which were supervised by Russ Carroccio, the old middle guard for the Giants. The whole operation was notarized; we signed legally acceptable player contracts, and everyone felt sure he was on his way to the NFL (there were vague hints about a mysterious tie-in with an "unnamed NFL club").

The fans turned out to see us in our league opener in Paterson's Hinchcliffe Stadium. We lost, 8-6, to the Union County All-Stars in a dull, miserable game, and the fans of Paterson had seen enough. They didn't come out anymore.

We had some fair ballplayers and some poor ones and some local hotshots such as Bob (Tootie) Harrell and Ralph Vigorito. Ralph and Tootie, our halfbacks, were supposed to draw the fans into the stadium every Saturday night. We had one or two men like Dick Dalatri, our 240-pound center and defensive tackle, who were clearly better than the competition. Dick was one of the few players who actually did move up—four years as a starter with the Montreal Alouettes in the Canadian Football League.

After our third game no one had seen a dime in wages and half the team was ready to pack it in. The owners made an impassioned plea one night after practice . . . "Stick with us a little while longer." We had a team meeting and Dalatri, our captain and player rep, stood up on a bench and said, "What do you say? Let's give these guys a break."

That was enough. No one quit, although I did have a private session with the paymaster and asked him at least to reimburse me for the toll money I was spending crossing the George Washington Bridge from New York for practice two nights a week (my contract called for $25 a game). He wrote out a check for $2.50 on the spot, and even signed it.

We lost a couple more games, and by now it was obvious that only a miracle would get us any of our money. But we had a good little drinking group and no one wanted to break it up. There was Red Mosca, the 235-pound quarterback, and Big Artie Ackerman, who worked as a skip chaser for a loan company in Newark, and Dalatri, and 260-pound George Parozzo, the horse player who had once been named AP Lineman of the Week for William & Mary, and a 270-pound colored tackle named Doug Hinton who had been the county half-mile champ but had eaten his way out of a track suit and into a football uniform. Doug used to show up at practice in a little kid's beanie hat.

After the workouts we'd get our beers in Benny's Bar in Paterson, a little place overlooking a softball diamond. Someone would always pick up the tab for us. In Paterson we were big men.

"So what if we go broke," Dalatri used to say. "We're having a helluva time, aren't we?"

One night one of us staggered over to the phone and called up our fullback, Reggie Powe. "This is Paul Pioneer, the owner of the Pioneers," he was told. "Just wanted to tell you that you're cut from the team." Reggie stayed away from practice for two nights until the coach personally drove by his house to find out what was wrong.

We played a game in Swedesboro, New Jersey, and four of us nearly missed it because we had fallen asleep at the beach that afternoon in Atlantic City, about 60 miles down the Black Horse Pike. We spent the first half sobering up, and even Sam Stellatella, our left linebacker (who had once kicked the extra point that won the Liberty Bowl game for Penn State over Alabama), was too groggy to play his usual game on the bench—checking the stands for the girl friends of the offensive players. When the offensive guy was in the game and Sam was out, he would make his play for the girl.

After our sixth loss, the owners got the clever idea of saving money by cutting the high-salary boys, the $50-a-game players, even though no one was getting paid anyway. Ackerman got the ax and so did Parozzo and Hinton.

"Aw, hell," Doug said that night down at Benny's. "There's lots of stuff I can do. I had a good job on a garbage truck back in the city. I can get that again."

He sat there and talked and the tears were rolling down his face. And it was a hell of a sight, the tears and the big moon face and the little beanie.

"I'll be all right," he said.

The team officially folded after our eighth loss, 33-6, to a Jersey City team called the Alvicks on a cold, damp night, with the fog rolling in and obscuring the lights. There were 200 people in the stands. Nineteen of our players showed up. An old Army buddy of mine came down with me to see the game, and Dalatri grabbed him outside the locker room.

"You ever play offensive tackle?" Dick asked. The guy shot me a wild look and moved up to the stands in a hurry.

Officially, the Pioneers were kaput, but Dalatri managed to wangle an exhibition game in his hometown, Spring Valley, New York. The Fire Department sponsored it, and Dalatri got the powerful Franklin Miners, led by the legendary Gunderman brothers, to play us. Somehow, somewhere, he managed to round up 35 assorted Pioneers, including a lantern-jawed, punchy little quarterback we'd never seen before. The guy brought an old leather helmet with a crack down the middle, and we nicknamed him "Cannonball" on the spot.

We lost to the Miners, 35-0, but our game plan was to steal the Miners' guarantee money of $300 and use it for one final, grand farewell party. Unfortunately Sol Rosen, the Miners' owner, got there first.

Sol, who until 1968 was the Commissioner of the Continental League, had been over the route before. He had one of the trainers stuff the money in the equipment bag and take off with it as soon as the game was over. We came away blank.

While we were showering, Frankie Fero, our general manager,

grabbed all the uniforms out of our lockers and hustled them out to a truck. But someone caught him and made him give them back to us.

"It's funny, seeing Sol commissioner of our league," said Dalatri in 1966, the year he played for the Continental League's Brooklyn Dodgers.

"He still laughs about that night in Spring Valley. I played for him at Franklin the next year, before I went up to Canada. We beat the hell out of somebody one Saturday and drank all night. Next morning, about 8 o'clock, Sol called us up and said that the Marines had canceled out of a game with Fort Dix and there would be $50 apiece for us if we'd drive down to Dix and fill in.

"Somehow we managed to get down there. The guys who were sober started the game, but then Fort Dix drove down to our four-yard line, so all the drunks went in. We stopped them and won the game, 32-14, and the soldier across the line from me said, 'Would you please breathe in some other direction? I'm getting drunk.' "

Next year I played for Mount Vernon, and the star of the team was Johnny Counts, who went up to the Giants a year later and finished second in the NFL in kickoff returns. The coach was Bill Elder, the old Notre Damer, who told us he scouted the enemy by "reading every newspaper clipping about them I can get my hands on."

Two years later I gave it another try—the Westchester Crusaders in the ACFL, and the highlight of our season was when our 260-pound right tackle, Fred Hovasapian, got thrown out of the league for assaulting a referee in a game against the Mohawk Valley Falcons in Utica, New York.

The Atlantic Coast League is now the solid entry in minor league football, with the Continental League on the verge of collapse and the Texas League barely surviving by servicing the football-starved masses of the Southwest.

The reason why the ACFL has made it while the CFL has starved is one of approach. The Atlantic Coast League modestly confined itself to the Eastern Seaboard. The Continental League spread its boundaries from ocean to ocean, from Florida to the state of Washington, deluding itself that this national approach to scheduling would draw the fans into the parks and help cover the enormous travel costs.

"Let's face it; this is essentially a bus league," says the ACFL's vice-president, Barney Kremenko. "Sure, you take a plane trip when you have to, but if you think you can operate that way for a whole season you're just kidding yourself."

The ACFL has another very solid asset, a guaranteed hookup with most of the Eastern NFL and AFL teams. It has a guaranteed labor force of taxi squadders from its parent teams. The NFL team pays the boys their taxi squad salaries, thereby cutting down a sizable chunk of payroll expense for its minor league affiliate. And until legislation from Pete Rozelle's office ended the practice, an NFL team could equip its farm team with an entire coaching staff, the men to be paid from the treasury of the big club.

The Continental League claimed looser tie-ins with the big leagues. Geography killed any practical application, though. The ACFL team was often based an hour or two away from its parent club (i.e. Bridgeport Jets and New York Jets; Long Island Bulls and New York Giants; Pennsylvania Firebirds and Philadelphia Eagles), so a player could hop in his car and make both teams' practice sessions. Hundreds of miles often separated the Continental League team from the NFL club it claimed as its affiliate, and the only time the minor league club would see its lend-lease taxi men was on the game night.

The disintegration of the Continental League started after the 1969 season, which had begun with a tentative membership of 23 teams, representing such far outposts as Honolulu and Monterrey, Mexico. By the time Commissioner Jim Dunn had grouped the 7,000-mile monster into four divisions and worked out a 138-game schedule and figured out piggy-back trips (two teams sharing one charter flight), the Honolulu franchise had moved to Portland, Oregon, and the teams from Monterrey and El Paso had folded.

After the season, in which only three teams claimed they could show a profit, four of the CFL's showpiece entries jumped to the ACFL—league champ Indianapolis; Orlando and Norfolk, which had drawn the CFL's record crowd (20,334) in 1967; and Rosen's Jersey Jays from Jersey City. In desperation the CFL turned to its most sensible segment—the Texas League—for help.

"I attended the CFL's reorganization meeting in Sacramento in the winter of 1970," said the Texas League's George Schepps, "just to see if they were going to get out of the jam. I was sitting there minding my own business and I heard the speaker say, 'We would now like to introduce our new commissioner, George Schepps.' It was news to me."

When last heard from, the CFL was still trying to hold itself together—somehow—while the ACFL was firmly divided into a Northern and Southern Division as follows:

Northern Division	*Southern Division*
Long Island Bulls (Giants)	Penn. Firebirds, Pottstown, Pa. (Eagles)
Bridgeport Jets (Jets)	Roanoke Buckskins (Redskins)
Hartford Knights (Bills)	Richmond Saints (Saints)
Jersey Jays, Jersey City (Browns)	Indianapolis Capitals
Jersey Tigers, Elizabeth (Colts)	Orlando Panthers
	Norfolk Neptunes

Stadiums in both leagues are in the 7,000 to 30,000 seat range. The record ACFL crowd was around 30,000 for a Roanoke-Hartford game in 1969. Tickets are scaled to a maximum of $4.50 to the Long Island Bulls play on Hofstra University's AstroTurf or $5 to see Orlando's legendary quarterback, Don Jonas. All clubs push general admission tickets in the $1.50 to $2 range, as well as dollar student tickets, supermarket giveaways, and any other scheme that will bring people into the park.

The weekly payroll is not allowed to go higher than $5,000 for any team in either league. The roster limit for ACFL teams is 36, which means that each player averages $140 a game. The CFL teams can carry as many as 35 men or as few as 30, depending on the finances, so the players probably get a little more money.

The real financial incentives are the "Personal Services" contracts. "Play football for my club," an owner might tell a quarterback, "and you'll get $15,000 a year to do PR work for my lumber business."

Orlando's Don Jonas, the CFL's Most Valuable Player for three years, turned down a contract with Denver to stay in Orlando, where he makes $30,000 a year as a full-time public-relations man for the club. He also has his own TV and radio show. He told the Broncos he might consider coming for a long-term, no-cut contract, and they told him to stay in Orlando, which he was only too happy to do.

Pottstown's Jimmy (The King) Corcoran, a freewheeling quarterback whose flaky antics got him dismissed by, in turn, the Jets, Patriots, and Eagles, pulls down a six-figure package as the ACFL's top drawing card.

"Get this picture," says Jimmy, who is known as the King of Pottstown.

"The stadium lights go dim. It's time for the intros. Now's the big moment, the moment they've all been waiting for. They introduce The King. The King comes running out between the goalposts. The fans go wild.

"I give 'em a wave. The flags go up. The cannons go off. It's the highlight of the night. Ten thousand fans go out of their minds.

"Pottstown—an out-of-sight place. Thirty thousand people in the place, and 33 percent of the population's in the stadium every Saturday night to see The King play.

"We play this game the other night. A national magazine is there to take pictures of The King. My fans don't let the photographer down. I'm walking off the field at half time and I'm mobbed by 15 broads. I'm the Joe Willie of Pottstown.

"It's like wrestling. When we go out of town I'm the villain. That's all the papers write about for a week. Pictures, quotes; half the stuff I don't even say, but who cares? It makes the fans crazy. They're all out there yelling for me to get killed.

"We play in Roanoke and 15,000 people show up. I've just signed a franchise deal for some hot dog and hamburger stands, so the first time I get out there, they're all yelling, 'Hey, King, pass the mustard! Hey, King, make mine rare!' I mean it's loud. You can't hear a thing. So I give 'em the act, the hands in the air bit for silence. They eat it up. It drives 'em wild. Then I throw a touchdown pass and I bow to the crowd—three times."

But Pottstown was still Pottstown, a town you can't say with a straight face. Jimmy was lukewarm to the club, until its owner, E. L. Gruber, explained the facts of life to him.

"He owns BVD," Jimmy said. "He's the majority stockholder in CBS. He's got oil wells in Canada, and he's caught more swordfish than any man in the world. I went out and saw his house in Pottstown. It goes for a million and a quarter. Three hundred acres of manicured land. Gold faucets. His own police force to guard it. Then I started to get the picture on Pottstown. You wouldn't believe the place. They've got about 50 millionaires living here."

Mr. Gruber gave Corcoran a noninterest loan of $90,000. He got the fast-food franchises and his own real-estate office ("It hasn't even opened yet, and every day there's 30 or 40 people banging on the door to get in and give me their money").

"I'm not in Joe Willie's class yet," Jimmy says. "But I'm eating, man. I'm eating."

It's a long way from Miller Stadium and the Paterson Pioneers and the Morristown Colonials.

24

Statistics Are for Losers
—and Sportswriters

I can prove anything by statistics except the truth.

□ George Canning, 1826

There are three kinds of lies; lies, damned lies and statistics.

□ Benjamin Disraeli

Every time I hear a ballplayer tell me, "Statistics are for losers," or the other maxim: "The only statistic that matters is win or lose," I wonder why everyone crowds around the bulletin board when the league stats are posted. The punt-return men look and see if they've gone up a couple of spots or slipped a few. So do the kickoff returners.

The stars, like Joe Namath or Lance Alworth, pretend they don't care, but they'll sneak looks when they think nobody's watching. And after a game, the stat sheets are the first things grabbed up, especially if "tackles" and "assists" and "pass defense plays" are noted. Then the defense suddenly becomes statistic minded.

Everyone tells you that statistics don't matter, but those stats have a strange way of making an appearance during contract talks —on both sides of the table.

The basic things you have to remember about the statistics you read in the paper every week are 1) they're not accurate . . . almost but not quite, and 2) they are not as meaningful as they could be.

Statistics are not accurate because there is a human element involved. During a game the yardage is entered on a master sheet, or a work sheet, by the two men the home club hires to handle its stats. At the end of the game, it's tallied up and phoned in to Seymour Siwoff and the Elias Sports Bureau, Inc., in New York, a baseball statistics bureau that Pete Rozelle hired in 1960 to make some order out of the statistical chaos.

Seymour and his 16-man staff then have 15 hours to get everything added up and prepared for release, so the papers and the clubs can get it for the Tuesday editions. But often those two men in the press box are in a hurry to go to dinner that Sunday night, so they don't recheck their stats with the official play-by-play sheets, and an error in addition remains an error—forever, or until the Elias Bureau has enough breathing time to spot it and fix it. It doesn't always happen.

Plays are often forgotten in the excitement of the game. The most common error involves two running backs or two receivers with similar-looking numbers, i.e. 35, and 36, or 87 and 89. Number 35 might get No. 36's 10-yard gain, and 87 might get credit for the pass that poor No. 89 caught. These errors are never apprehended, and they happen in *every* game, including the big ones at the end of the season. The Kansas City Chiefs, for instance, got robbed of a rightfully acquired first down in the 1970 Super Bowl. Leroy Kelly never got credit for one hard-earned five-yard gain in the 1969 NFL Championship game. It happens everywhere. Players seldom notice the mistakes, and even if they do, they rarely do anything about it. But there are exceptions.

Late in the 1966 season, the Jets' George Sauer was battling San Diego's Lance Alworth for the AFL pass-catching lead. In one game the Jets' statisticians credited Sauer with a catch that tight end Pete Lammons had made. Sauer brought the play-by-play sheets to the team's PR man and showed him the error—which was corrected. Sauer finished second to Alworth that year—but by more than one catch.

Exhibition game statistics are scanned, noted, and then thrown away. They are completely unreliable. The statisticians are often hometown collegians, and many times they don't even know the professional scoring rules. So they'll credit a quarterback's dumps to "yards lost rushing," as it's done in the colleges.

"Meaningful statistics" are anything that can give you an insight into a player's contribution in the game, or his worth at his position. For instance, if you read that Leroy Kelly gained 82 yards on 23 carries for a 3.6 average, you know nothing. Ten other backs in the league might have done the same thing that Sunday. But if you are told that he carried the ball eight times on third-down, short-yardage situations and got the first down on seven of those eight tries, you've learned something about the kind of a day Kelly had.

Two punters might have the same average—say 40 yards per kick—but one might have had his punts returned for two yards all day, and the other for 150 yards, and you'll never know it by checking the punter's record in the papers. A passer's stats don't tell you what he did in the last two minutes of each half, or what the score was when he got the bulk of his yardage. And a 50-yard passing play is still 50 yards on the books, whether the quarterback laid a perfect 50-yarder into someone's hands, or whether he threw a little safety valve pass and the receiver shook off three tacklers and gained the 50 on his own.

The Xerox Company began to recognize the need for more incisive statistics toward the end of the 1969 season, so they handed out little analysis sheets in the press boxes, showing a runner's performance on each of the four downs, a passer's breakdown according to downs, his performance in the last two minutes, etc. They never got much notice in the papers because everyone was too busy with other things to try and dissect a bunch of new, albeit meaningful, statistics. The only stories I saw that mentioned them at all were offbeat features about how nutty Xerox was, how they'd dream up anything for a little publicity.

I have developed my own set of statistical rules in an attempt to separate general statistics ·from "meaningful statistics." I try to keep track of the passing game with a chart of my own that I found out is called a "field chart" (Boston coach Clive Rush once explained to me what I was trying to do).

The purpose of this intricate bit of mumbo jumbo is to show not only passes and completions, but to give a history of each receiver and each pass defender. Every pass thrown to a man, whether it results in a completion, an incomplete or an interference penalty, is noted in the offense section (for the receiver) and the defense section (for the pass defender). I try to use symbols for such things as the type of pattern, whether or not the defender made a good play, or if the pass was poorly thrown (on an incomplete)—also, what kind of a misfire it was: overthrow, wide, etc., or whether it was just a deliberate throwaway. (See Fig. 15.)

The tally I can get at the end of the day tells me 1) how many times each receiver was thrown to, 2) whether the offense was picking on a certain defender, and 3) if the passer was having a bad day, what particular type of misfortune was he having.

On running plays I try to note the blocks by the lineman, if the play picks up anything worthwhile . . . usually four yards or more, depending on the situation. I write the number of the players making those blocks under the gain itself (which I have recorded in my chart book). If the defense comes up with a good play . . . holds the runner to three yards or less, or keeps him from a first down on a short yardage situation, worries the passer into a bad throw, covers the receiver well, etc. . . . I put the number of the defensive man (in different-colored pencil) underneath the play.

All this tells me how a blocker did during the day (blocking stats are never given out). It also tells me how many "meaningful" defensive plays a man made. A mere record of tackles will tell you something, but there is a difference between a lineman making a tackle after he's been driven eight yards downfield, and a defensive man tackling a runner for a loss. And when a man rushes the passer and chases him into the arms of someone else, only the tackler will get mentioned on the official sheet, but actually it was the rusher who did the work. So I give them both a call.

A meaningful punting statistic to me is the one that tells you about the runbacks. Never mind the average yardage of the punts themselves, unless it's something phenomenal. At the end of the season most punters end up within a few yards of each other anyway. They pay off on runbacks—and on how many punts are returned and how many are fair-caught.

All this dedication requires a very busy pencil during the game, and there are limits to how much you can write down in the break between plays. Just as an experiment, I pushed myself to the limit during the 1970 Super Bowl. I tried to get the lineup of players on kicking and punting teams, and I tried to diagram the defenses both teams used, but I had stepped over the line. It was too much. I started missing plays, and finally I snapped and regressed completely, sitting there stunned for a whole series while someone else filled in my chart book for me.

It taught me one thing, though; how far I could go with this stuff.

Statistics are like love; you're either hooked or you're not. I happen to be a statistics nut, and I wouldn't wish it on other people, and I try to keep my game stories relatively uncluttered with numbers, although if I come up with some *particularly* meaningful stats, I'll try to drop them in . . . quietly.

Most successful statisticians are in love with their work. A statistic isn't just a cold number, it's a little story. And a good statistician can usually smell out something that doesn't sound right.

"When I redid all the old books," says Siwoff, the most dedicated statistician of them all, "I had to throw out a lot of old stuff and just start in all over again. A stalwart . . . like Jimmy Brown and Joe Namath . . . will get personalized treatment. I'll go through every game of their career and make sure their lifetime totals are correct. Don't forget, the AFL didn't hire our service until 1967, and the stats before that were a mess.

"For instance, nowhere in the AFL prior to 1966 is there a record of just who played in which game. When I asked them about it they said, 'What do you need that stuff for?' And six years before that, when I first started with the NFL stats, I found some weird things. For one thing, there was no record of trades. Merle Hapes and Frank Filchock, the two Giant players who got in trouble for failing to report a bribe, had been wiped out of the books. But I went and researched them. You don't pass moral judgments with statistics."

Siwoff pointed to a jumbled pile of papers in a corner.

"See that pile," he said. "The league records were worse. I had to rummage through all of them to try and get lifetime records. I lost a couple of years on Bronko Nagurski. It was frustrating as hell. Don't forget that statistics never even got into the papers until Bert Bell begged them in in the 1940's. And they were only publicity gimmicks in those days.

Fig. 15

OFFENSE

SE 25 PITTS	FL 89 TAYLOR	TE 84 ARBANAS	RB 21 GARRETT	FB 45 HOLMES
+20 pop l Sh msd +20 sl in l KR zone INT PL 26 SHAR - tn-in l	+9 curl RT MB +8 out RT MB X go nt ez MB ✓ N nt post KR w/MB O HUNG +10 out RT MB +3 out RT MB ✓		+16 DN L SH - BLTZ COV X dn l HILG deft at line <u>6 McVeA</u> X 0 over fly l WWR	

SE 84 WASHINGTON	FL 80 HENDERSON	TE 87 KRAMER	RB 41 OSBORN	FB 30 BROWN

TRANSLATION

PITTS

Caught a 20-yard pass vs. Sharockman on a pop pass on left side—Sharockman missed the tackle.
Caught a 20-yard pass vs. Krause on a left slant-in . . . zone coverage.
26-yard interference penalty on Sharockman on a left turn-in pattern.

TAYLOR

Caught a nine-yard curl pass on right side vs. Mackbee.
Caught an eight-yard square-out right, vs. Mackbee.
X (incomplete) on a go, or fly pattern, right, vs. Mackbee, who made a good play (✓) in the end zone.

DEFENSE

3 40 ?SALIS	TS 46 KEARNEY	FS 42 ROBINSON	RCB 18 THOMAS	LLB 78 BELL	MLB 63 LANIER	RLB 51 LYNCH

CB 46 ACKBEE	FS 22 KRAUSE	TS 29 KASSULKE	RCB 45 SHAROCKMAN	LLB 60 WINSTON	MLB 59 WARWICK	RLB 58 HILGENB'G
√ TLR CURL RT. TLR OUT RT u: ge RT EZ √ TLR OUT RT TLR OUT RT√ ↙ /KR	+20 PTS sl in l ZONE N TLR RT. POST O HUNG w/MB		+20 PTS pup l MSD INT PL 26 PTS +n in l +16 6RT dn l BLTZ COV		Xo OVER McV Fly l	X CRT dn l defl at line

N (intercepted) by Krause w/MB (double coverage with Mackbee) on a right post pattern...o hung (o indicates bad pass that hung)
Caught a 10-yard square-out right, vs. Mackbee.
Caught a three-yard square-out right, vs. Mackbee, who made a good play (✓)

GARRETT

Caught a 16-yard pass, straight down the field, left, vs. Sharockman, who had the coverage because the linebacker on that side blitzed.
X (incomplete) on a straight-down pattern, left, vs. Hilgenberg...ball was deflected at the line.

McVEA

X (incomplete) on a fly pattern, left, with Warwick covering...o over (indicates bad pass, overthrow)

"I can look through the books and smell a phony statistic. Beattie Feathers, the old Bear halfback, gained, 1,004 yards rushing in 1934. No one had ever gone over 1,000 before, and no one did it again for 13 years. You see a statistic like that and it shakes you. It's like a bolt of lightning. I'm not saying anything, but I have a feeling some punt and kickoff returns were added into that rushing total."

Siwoff admits that things are far from perfect. Some modifications and amendments will have to be made. He would like a passer's totals to show the yardage of the pass and the yardage gained after the catch, so people can get a true reading on the actual passing efficiency, but that would put greater strain on the stat men in the press boxes. He's still looking for the perfect formula to rate the passing leaders at the end of the season.

The other categories are pretty well standardized. Runners are ranked by total yardage, receivers by total catches, punters, punt returners and kick returners by highest average. But no one has ever been quite sure how to rate the passers.

From 1931 to 1945 the leaders were ranked according to completion percentage, although you find mysterious inconsistencies when you look through those old books. From 1946 to '49 they were ranked according to how they rated in the league in six separate categories—completions, percentage, yards gained, touchdowns, fewest interceptions, and lowest interception percentage. By 1949 the category of interceptions was dropped. The system was junked in 1950, and for the next 10 years passers were rated by only one criterion, average yards gained for each pass they threw.

In 1960 the six-category grading system was restored, only this time average-yards-per-pass became one of the six categories. The NFL dropped two categories in 1962 (total yards gained and total completions) and installed the rating system that is used today. The AFL did the same thing five years later when Siwoff took over.

The system works like this: Say a passer finishes first in the league in pass-completion percentage. He'll get a grade of "one" in that category. If he's second in TD passes, he'll get a two; first in lowest interception percentage (total passes attempted divided into interceptions) and he gets a one; and, say, fourth in average yards per attempt, he'll get a four. The grades are added, and his total comes out to eight. Another man, say with grades of three, four, four, and one, will end up with a total 12, so he'll be behind the passer with eight. It goes down the list, with any passer who has thrown 140 passes or more (10 a game) eligible to be graded. Lowest grade wins.

"One category still bugs me," Siwoff says. "Touchdown passes. It's an absolute total. Every other category is on a percentage basis. I'm trying to figure out a way of making touchdown-passing efficiency become a percentage category, too."

People are always willing to help. The best system I've seen was suggested by an ex-Columbia tackle named Alfred L. Ginepra from Santa Monica, California. His idea is to grade touchdown passing by dividing the TD passes into the total completions, and you come up with a figure representing touchdown efficiency. If you apply the system to the 1969 passing totals, Daryle Lamonica would move from the No. 3 spot in the AFL to No. 2, replacing Joe Namath. And Len Dawson would break out of his sixth place tie with Steve Tensi and shoot up to the fourth spot. In the NFL Craig Morton would move up a notch, and Roman Gabriel would suffer a slight dip. Cleveland's Bill Nelsen would stay the same, and Joe Kapp would shoot all the way up from No. 10 in the league to No. 6. The system seems to reward winning quarterbacks.

Some statistics that are mindlessly repeated as gospel don't make any sense. People will tell you that a quarterback's record of how many third downs he cashes into first downs is the real tip-off on his ability. They say that 50 percent is the desired figure. Right, and $100,000 a year is the desired income, too, but few of us reach it. No quarterback has a 50-percent, third-down record for a season. Some passers kill you on first and second down, and they could run up a 28-0 count without cashing a single third down. Third-down efficiency is a nice little statistic to play around with, but it's not the whole answer.

During the year the Jets won the Super Bowl, for instance, Joe Namath had a 29-percent efficiency rating on third-down- and fourth-down-short-yardage (when the team went for it) situations.

But the Jet defense allowed rivals only 27 percent. Next season, Namath was up to 33 percent, but so was the Jet defense, so the team slipped.

Namath is an avowed scoffer at statistics. Sauer likes to look at them, but he has reservations.

"Going into the last game in 1968 I was leading the league in pass catching," Sauer says, "but our last game was an easy win over Miami, and I came out early and I only caught two passes that day. Alworth caught me for the title. But suppose I'd have caught a lot of passes and taken some unnecessary chances and gotten hurt? I'm out of the championship game. The thought of it would have haunted me for the rest of my life."

Jimmy Brown used to say that every time he broke another record he turned into more and more of a statistic, instead of a person. But sometimes the have-nots show an uncommon interest in numbers. Philadelphia fullback Tom Woodeshick, for instance, has a lifelong goal of reaching 1,000 yards rushing for a season.

"The men who get 1,000 yards are the elite," he said toward the end of the 1968 season, when he was within smelling distance of the magic number. "Very few have done it. I want to be one of them. I want the prominence and standing that go with it. And if I don't get it because of those three quarters I missed in one game, or the 60-yard run I got called back against the Bears, if I fall a few yards short, I'm going to be very disturbed. Right now I'd have to say my chances are getting slimmer—just like me." (He never made it.)

The *Dallas Times-Herald*'s Steve Perkins tells about the time he helped Bob Hayes win a championship—the 1968 punt return title. The Cowboys were beating Pittsburgh pretty easily in the next to last game of the season. Hayes had just returned a punt 90 yards for a touchdown, and he was well in front of the rest of the NFL's punt returners. But he was still one return short of the minimum 14 needed to qualify. Perkins told him about that on the sidelines during the Pittsburgh game.

"Suppose they don't kick to you in New York next week, or you have to fair-catch them all?"

"OK," Hayes said, and he handed Perkins his cape, ran a punt back three yards, and ran out again. "Does that do it?"

Against the Giants the following week, Hayes returned a punt 63 yards for a touchdown. "I have just figured it up," Perkins wrote, "and if I hadn't talked Hayes into running back that three-yard punt against Pittsburgh, which dragged his average down, he would have broken Jack Christiansen's NFL punt return record by a full yard."

And that's why they build a press box for writers—and statistics nuts—and keep them off the field.

25

Strictly Personal:
The Greatest Player

Paul Brown once had been asked, "How'd you like to have that Doc Blanchard?" And he replied: "The man I've got in mind is called Marion Motley and he's better than Blanchard."
□ *Sport* Magazine, November, 1952, History of the Cleveland Browns.

He was the greatest all-around football player I ever saw. The man was a great, great linebacker. Believe me, he could do everything. He had no equal as a blocker; yes, he could do it all.
□ Blanton Collier

Nothing devastates a football team like a selfish player. It's a cancer. The greatest back I ever had was Marion Motley. You know why? The only statistic he ever knew was whether we won or lost. The man was completely unselfish.
□ Paul Brown

I first became acquainted with Marion Motley when I bought a copy of *Pro Football Illustrated,* 1947 edition. It cost a quarter, but it was one of those giant-sized magazines that used to be put out in those days and it was loaded with pictures, so I figured it was worth it.

I was thumbing through it on the subway home from school, and there was this picture that stopped me dead. It was a full-page shot of Motley, running right at the camera, with his face sort of sqwunched together and his lower lip sucked in, and what looked like a scar running down one side of his cheek. I thought he was the toughest-looking man I'd ever seen in my life.

A couple of weeks later, when I saw Motley's Browns play the Yankees in the Stadium, that first impression was confirmed. He was the toughest football player I'd seen. I didn't keep stats in those days, but I seem to remember that Motley averaged about 10 yards a carry, which is fancy stepping for a 238-pound fullback, and I know for an absolute fact that he scored three of the Browns' four touchdowns.

He backed up the line on defense, and I can still see him on one play, reaching out with one hand and grabbing the Yankees' little Buddy Young by the seat of his pants and holding him up in the air for the crowd to see.

A few weeks later I went to the Stadium again, this time for the Browns against the Yankees for the All-America Football Conference championship. I was sitting in the upper deck, above home plate. My binoculars caught Motley coming right at me, 51 yards on a direct hand-off over the middle, the last 10 or so with the Yanks' Harmon Rowe riding his back and slugging him in the face.

The papers next day had a quote from Motley, answering a photographer who asked him to smile.

"I can't," he said. "My teeth were knocked out."

The record books show that he gained 109 yards in 13 carries that day, which was a typical kind of day for Motley—a lot of yards, not many carries—the kind of day that left you wondering what kind of stats he could have run up if Paul Brown had decided to build his attack around him in those days, instead of around Otto Graham's passes.

I watched Motley right up until his last, hopeless days when he tried a comeback with the Pittsburgh Steelers in 1955, and if there is a better football who ever snapped on a helmet, I would like to know his name. There's a statistical table at the end of this chapter, detailing the numbers that made up Motley's professional career, but it's a kind of meaningless way of evaluating this remarkable player. It would be like trying to describe a waterfall in terms of gallons per second, or a sunset in terms of light units.

There has never been a set of statistics to measure the force and intensity of a man's hitting power, or his effectiveness as a pass blocker, unless you use a seismograph, and that would probably run into too much money. And until they start playing football with adding machines, I have to believe that the force of the blow is still what the game is all about.

Giving a quick look at the table, though, you'll note that Motley averaged 5.7 yards a carry during his pro career, which is half a yard better than the lifetime average of Jimmy Brown, probably the greatest running back who ever lived.

Brown was the best runner I've ever seen, but Motley was the greatest all-around player, the complete player. He ran, of course, and he caught flare passes and turned them into big gainers, and he backed up the line in an era in which the rest of the world was switching to two platoons, and he pass-blocked like no other back who ever played the game.

"That young fella, Jimmy Brown, has been getting a lot of heat because he didn't block," Motley said a year ago. "Let me tell you something about that boy. When he first came up to the Browns, he asked me to show him a few things about pass blocking. We were pretty good friends, used to play golf together.

"Well, I showed him, and he seemed eager to learn, but the system just didn't call for it. That was Paul Brown's way. He had you helping him where you could help him most, and he didn't want to hear anything else."

I talked to people who were connected with Motley in the old days, and tested their reactions when I told them that I thought he was the greatest player I'd ever seen.

"The people who talk about Motley are talking about the Motley who played in the NFL—on two bad knees," said Denver coach Lou Saban, who was the defensive captain of the Browns during their AAFC years.

"The Motley they saw was just a shadow of the old Motley, even when he made All-Pro in '50 and led the league in running. Don't forget, he was 26 years old in his rookie year—in 1946."

"I think you've made a very wise choice," said the Jets' coach, Weeb Ewbank, who was on the Paul Brown-Blanton Collier staff that had Motley as its fullback at Great Lakes Naval Training Center and then Cleveland.

"You know, you think about those old days of pro football, and you wonder about some of the great stars then and how they could stand up nowadays. Take Bill Willis, for instance. One of the great middle guards in the game, but where would he play today—at 210 pounds?

"But Motley would be the same now. He weighed 238 and he could keep up with any back except maybe Buddy Young. He just might be the greatest player at that."

"We had a scrimmage between Great Lakes and the College

All-Stars," Collier recalled. "We finally went into a seven-man line, with Marion as the linebacker, in an effort to hold them. Pretty soon it developed into a struggle between Marion and the All-Star offense—and you can believe me when I say it was a standoff."

"Marion lived right near me," said Jets' line coach Joe Spencer, who was a young tackle on the '49 Cleveland team. "One day after practice I was counting my pennies and trying to figure out the cheapest way to get home. Marion didn't say a word—except 'Get in,' when he pulled up his car.

"So every day we used to drive to practice together and drive home, one of the greatest stars in the game and a guy just fighting to stay on the club. But that's the way he was. If you were his teammate, he would do anything for you."

During 1969 I decided to hunt up some old movie film on the Browns' early games and see for myself whether the recollections of a 14-year-old high-school kid would stand up. It's generally a bad play to make, messing around with the cherished memories.

I remember Cus D'Amato telling the story about how he forced Jimmy Jacobs, the fight film collector, into showing him old movies of George Dixon, the featherweight champ.

"When I was a kid," Cus said, "all my father would talk about was George Dixon, the greatest fighter that ever lived. It was George Dixon this and George Dixon that. Before every meal, he'd lift a glass of wine to George Dixon.

"So I asked Jimmy if he had any old films of Dixon and he said he did, but that I wouldn't want to see them. I said show them to me anyway. I watched one, and I said, 'That's not George Dixon,' and he said, 'I'm afraid it is.' The guy fought like a zombie.

"I got this terrible pain in my stomach, watching that film. It really hurt. I said, 'Jimmy, for Christ sake, shut off that projector.' "

The films of Motley didn't break my heart. They just showed me that my vision had been remarkably clear in those days, probably better than now. He was dynamic and terrifying, and it was his pass-blocking that really lifted him into a different dimension.

"Why is the Cleveland passing attack so good," a radio interviewer once asked Gail Bruce, San Francisco's fine pass-rushing end of 20 years ago.

"Well, you rush Graham, and put on a move and beat your man, and there's Motley waiting for you," he said. "Next play, you beat your man with a different move, and there's Motley waiting again. Pretty soon you say, 'The hell with it. I'd rather stay on the line and battle the first guy.' "

Motley's style was a numbing, paralyzing head-and-shoulders shot that would lift defensive ends and tackles and dump them on their fannies.

I finally hunted Motley down the day before the Jets-Colts Super Bowl in Miami. He was down there to help with a fund-raising campaign for a group called the NFL Alumni Committee. The idea was to try to get some kind of pension installed for some of the old players, the ones who were broke and could use a little help.

I told him I'd like to do a chapter of a book on him, and he gave me a kind of uh-huh look.

"I've talked to guys who said they were going to do stories," he said, "and somehow I don't get to see those stories. They say they'll send them, but they never do."

We were in his room in the hotel, and aside from a slight bulge around the midsection that a green golf sweater didn't quite hide, he looked formidable, still the Motley from *Pro Football Illustrated,* 1947.

He had been burned by Paul Brown, who discarded him after his value was exhausted. He had been burned by Otto Graham, his old teammate, who turned him down when he had asked him for some kind of a scouting job in the Washington organization. This was when Graham was the coach of the Redskins. He had owned a bar in Cleveland and lost it, and he had gone along with a weird idea about coaching a girls' football team in the Cleveland area, a scheme that also went down the drain.

"I was in the Yankee Stadium," I told him, "the day you knocked Tom Casey out of football."

Casey had been a 175-pound defensive back for the Yankees. He was probably the only man I ever saw stop Motley head on when Motley was going full tilt. Casey woke up in Bronx Veterans' Hospital, and he never played any more football.

"I see him every now and then," Motley said. "He's Dr. Thomas Casey now and he lives in Shaker Heights, right outside of Cleveland. We kid each other about that play and he'll say, 'You S.O.B., you ended my career.' And I'll tell him, 'I couldn't help it if you got in front of me.' "

I told Motley that I was in Kezar Stadium in San Francisco the day Norm Standlee tackled him near the 49er bench, and I remembered Motley crawling all the way across the field and out-of-bounds so that the Browns wouldn't have to take time out. I mentioned this, too.

"Young man," he said, squinting at me, "you've got a good memory. I pulled a muscle in my leg on that play. I would have scored if not for that. I liked old Norm, though. Always did. He was another guy who played linebacker and fullback at the same time."

Motley's legs were the saddest story of all. If not for a couple of crippled knees, he probably could have had five more great years.

"The first time I hurt my knee was in college," he said, "at the University of Nevada. I had started at South Carolina State in Orangeburg, and transferred to Nevada in 1940. I spent three seasons there, hurt my knee, and went back home to Canton, Ohio.

"My knee was pretty bad, but I got a job with Republic Steel. I was a pieceworker. I burned scrap iron out of the steel with a torch, and it'd get awful hot up there on top of the steel where I worked. I honestly think that all that heat mended my knee. The muscles around the knee had been torn. When I hurt it, I played the next week, but it would get stiff and swell up on me. But that heat fixed it up."

On Christmas Day, 1944, Motley entered boot camp at Great Lakes. The coaching staff had Ewbank and Collier and Paul Brown, who had coached Massillon High when Motley was the rival fullback for Canton McKinley.

"I was about 210 or 215 at Great Lakes, but I was fast," Motley said. "Just how fast, I couldn't say. I'd been timed in 10-flat for the 100 in college, but it was only an intramural meet, and I don't know how good the timers were. In high school I once raced the best 220 man in the school. He gave me 20 yards, and when the race was over I still had that 20 yards he gave me.

"Paul Brown was a little different at Great Lakes. In the beginning he didn't call all the plays. I think he was a little leery of it.

"Anyway, I wrote to him when I got out of the service and he was coaching the Browns. He wrote back that he had enough backs at that particular time and he couldn't use me. But then they got Bill Willis in camp, and in about a week they decided they were going to keep him. He was the only Negro in the league. The AAFC sort of had this unwritten rule about keeping the league all white, but rules like that didn't mean anything to Brown.

"About a week later I got a phone call from Bob Voigts of the Browns. I was all set to go back to college and get my degree, but he asked me, 'How would you like to try out for the Browns?' I said I'd like it fine. Later I found out that the only reason they called me was that they needed a roommate for Bill Willis for the road trips.

"Gene Fekete was the fullback and I worked at linebacker. One day we had this scrimmage and I was making a few tackles and shaking a few people up and someone asked Willis, 'What's the matter with Motley today? He trying to kill somebody?'

" 'No,' Bill said. 'He's just trying to make this football team.' "

Fekete hurt his knee in the league opener against the Miami Seahawks, and Motley became the Browns' fullback, as well as their linebacker.

"People knew the players pretty well then," Motley said. "Most of the ballplayers came from Ohio State, and Brown had gotten a few off the Cleveland Rams, which had become the Los Angeles Rams. But they couldn't place me. They didn't know I was colored and they'd ask each other, 'What's that, a French name, or what?' They figured out the story, though, the first time they saw my picture in the paper.

"You know, colored kids in those days just never thought about professional football. It was just too farfetched. But I remember I used to read the stories about the old pros in *Liberty* magazine. I remember there was once a story that the old star, Dutch Clark, wrote himself about being approached by gamblers who wanted him to throw the game. He turned them down and they threatened him. And then he went out and played his best, and he wound up in the hospital with broken ribs. But he scored the winning touchdown, right through the goalposts.

"He was fighting and squirming, but he made it through those posts. That was my impression of professional football, fighting your way through the goalposts."

Motley's first contract was for $4,500 ("I signed the first thing they put in front of me"). His last one for Brown—for the 1953 season—came to $11,500. In between he had spent a few years averaging 55 minutes a game; he had lost a few teeth when he misjudged a tackle on Frankie Albert; and he lost a few more in that championship game in 1947, not to Harmon Rowe's fists, but to an elbow.

"It was on an extra-point play," he said. "I was setting to block, and someone caught me with an elbow. It drove my teeth right back up into the roof of my mouth. I didn't even catch his number.

"We had four plays for me and that was all; an end run, a buck up the middle, a trap, and a screen pass. I'd only carry the ball eight or nine times a game, and inwardly I'd have the feeling that I should have carried more. But Paul Brown was a winner, and he didn't need any advice from me."

Brown was once accused of running a pass-and-trap offense, which was kind of a silly rap to hang on a coach who won the league title every year it was in existence, but Brown answered his accuser normally.

"All right, so I'm a trap-and-pass coach. But any coach having Graham and Motley would do what we do. He'd be crazy not to."

The beginning of the end came in 1951 when Motley collided with linebacker Tony Adamle in a scrimmage. Once again, the damage was to his knee.

"He hit me with a reverse body block with a leg whip," Motley said. "I'd never teach that kind of block to anybody."

He dragged through the 1951 season, but by 1952 he'd run into something new. The Giants' Steve Owen had devised a defense that assigned one man, linebacker John Cannady, to Motley, on a permanent basis.

"One time I ran over to the sidelines, and there was John, right alongside me," Motley said. "I said, 'John, what the hell are you doing over here?'

"He told me, 'Coach Owen said that if Motley goes home, you go with him. If he goes in the stands, you go along with him. So here I am.'

"Anyway, what that accomplished was that it took away my trap play."

By 1953 Brown had a new fullback, a chunky blond-haired kid from Indiana named Chick Jagade who yelled and screamed when he ran. "The most reckless football player I've ever seen," Coach Brown said of Chick.

"I had some kind of a bonus clause in my contract in '53," Motley said, "Something about $1,000 extra if my yardage was up with the leaders. I was doing OK in the beginning of the season, and then I could feel myself getting eased out. I finally got the picture in Chicago, when Brown said to me, 'Well, Motley, this is Chick's hometown, so we're going to let him play today.'

"I said to myself, 'You son of a bitch,' but there was nothing I could do about it. I just let it roll. Next season in early camp I was running downfield on a kick team and I felt something tear in my knee. I came back from the injury, but I knew I was finished in Cleveland. They had all those backs like Curley Morrison and Maurice Bassett and Dub Jones and Chet, the Jet, Hanulak. They didn't need old Marion anymore.

"When he traded me to Pittsburgh in '55, I still thought I could play some good football. I felt my speed coming back when I ran the sprints. Then I hurt my knee again, and that was it. I told them I was through."

You have to wonder what kind of records Motley would have set if he had carried the ball 20 to 30 times a game, like Jimmy Brown did half a decade later. Or what he would have been like if he would have come into the league with a heavy bonus and a no-cut contract.

"I think it takes something away from these kids now," he says. "They just don't have the same desire to make the club. It's like a job to them, an easy job, and they don't seem to be putting out the way we were."

He was standing up now, buttoning his sweater.

"I've got a meeting to go to, with that NFL Alumni Committee. Do me a favor. If you're writing an article, mention somewhere that it would be a good thing if Rozelle could find a way to lay aside a little pension money for some of the old-timers who are needy now, guys like Jack Manders. He had the cartilage taken out of his knee this year, and he's on crutches. How much do these kids have in their pension kitty now? Ten or 15 million? Maybe they can turn some of it loose for us old guys."

MARION MOTLEY: CAREER RECORD

Year	RUSHING					PASS RECEIVING				TOTAL POINTS		KICKOFF RETURNS		
	Games	Attempts	Yds.	Avg.	TD	No.	Yds.	Avg.	TD	TD	Pts.	No.	Yds.	Avg.
1946	13	73	601	8.2	5	10	188	18.8	1	6	36	3	53	17.7
1947	14	146	889	6.0	8	7	73	10.4	1	10†	60	13	322	24.8
1948	14	157	964 *	6.1	5	13	192	14.8	2	7	42	14	337	24.1
1949	12	113	570	5.0	8	15	191	12.7	0	8	48	12	262	21.8
1950	12	140	810 *	5.8	3	11	151	13.7	1	4	24	—	—	—
1951	11	61	273	4.5	1	10	52	5.2	0	1	6	—	—	—
1952	12	104	444	4.3	1	13	213	16.4	2	3	18	3	88	29.3
1953	12	32	161	5.0	0	6	47	7.8	0	0	0	3	60	20.0
1954	Did not play.													
1955	7	2	8	4.0	0	0	0	0.0	0	0	0	—	—	—
Totals	107	828	4720	5.7	31	85	1107	13.0	7	39	234	48	1122	23.4

* Indicates league leader.
† returned one intercepted pass for touchdown

26
The Image-Makers:
A Look at the All-Alls

Me, you mean they actually picked me, with Namath and all those guys to choose from?
□ New York Jets' offensive guard Randy Rasmussen, when told that the New York writers had picked him as the team's offensive MVP for 1969

The All-All explosion has finally arrived. Chronology seems to inspire this outbreak of All-All picking. An end of a decade will do it (the AFL, after 10 years of existence, picked it's All-Time team in 1969), and a positive milestone, like the NFL's 50-year anniversary, simply drives the pickers wild.

Remember the furor with which the Associated Press greeted the end of the first half of the twentieth century? The wire service picked its "Greatest Athlete of the First Half of the 20th Century" in all sports, finally rolling all the greatests into one greatest, Jim Thorpe, who happened to be destitute at the time. The AP picked its Greatest Upset, Greatest Sports Thrill, Greatest Game . . . I can't remember the full list of Greatests, although I've got them all written down somewhere.

So the Pro Football Hall of Fame has commemorated the NFL's 50 years of existence by picking its All-Stars of each decade, and then boiling them down into one All-Star team, which is perfectly all right with me, because I happen to enjoy all this All-All picking, and most other people do, too, even though it's fashionable to scoff at it.

Oh, there are inconsistencies. Four members of the Cleveland

Browns made the All-Star squad of the 1940's, even though the Browns were strictly an All-America Football Conference team and not part of the NFL during that period. The reasoning was that the AAFC was incorporated into the NFL in 1950, so its history had a right to come along with it. Which is fine, except that the AFL, which became part of the NFL in 1970, got totally neglected on the All-Star team of the 60's. But that's the way it goes with All-Star picking. You make a dozen friends and 100 enemies.

The yearly All-Pro picking is left to the wire services and the players and the coaches. The Hall of Fame picked a combined AFL-NFL team in 1968 and '69, and so did the Professional Football Writers Association. Only the coaches' picks got tangible rewards, because from those choices came the 35-man NFL Pro Bowl and 33-man AFL All-Star game squads. The winners of these two games got $1,500 apiece, the losers, $1,000.

Coaches and players sneer at newspapermen's efforts to pick all-anything. But in 1969, *Sports Illustrated* tried polling the assistant coaches of each team, since these men look at more miles of film than anyone in the game, and the results were hilarious.

The coaches couldn't vote for their own players, which was supposed to encourage objectivity, but somehow two Dallas offensive centers, Dave Manders and Mal Walker, wound up with one vote apiece. Minnesota cornerback, Bobby Bryant, received one vote as a safetyman; San Diego's Ron Mix got two votes, placing him among the top six offensive tackles in the AFL, even though he had been out for the whole season with a pulled leg muscle.

Sam Walton, an offensive tackle for the Jets, received a vote, even though he had been cut from the squad in midseason, so *Sports Illustrated* frantically called the coach who had voted for him, and the answer was, "No, I meant the other guy on the Jets." Fourteen different NFL guards got votes; and on one NFL team, four different assistant coaches picked five different cornerbacks. Maybe Atlanta's head coach, Norm Van Brocklin, had the right idea. He forbade his assistants to pick anybody.

The NFL used to pick its official All-Star team from 1931 through 1942, at which time the wire services (AP, UPI, and the now defunct INS) took over. In 1955 NEA (Newspaper Enterprise Association) joined the group, and although this was proba-

bly the most highly respected team, since the players did the se-
lecting, it took six years for the NFL to recognize the picks in its
annual *Record Manual*. The *Sporting News'* All-AFL team was a
players' poll team, and its All-NFL divisional teams were picked
by its own staff.

Both AP and UPI follow the same technique. Two or three
writers who regularly cover a team are designated as official pickers from that city. When there's a scarcity of regular reporters, the
wire service uses one of its own men who covers the club. The
ballots are tabulated and the choices are made accordingly. Negli-
gent writers, or people whose picks are erratic, are replaced.
("One Dallas guy had 10 Cowboys on his 1969 team," reports a
UPI official).

The only drawback to this system, unless you figure that writers
are not qualified to judge talent, is that a man may not get to see
all the teams in the league. He has an intimate knowledge of the
club he travels with, but he only gets one or two looks—
sometimes none at all—at the players on other clubs. But it's expected that the reporters will go heavy on the men of their own
team, and when all the ballots are in, the whole thing is supposed
to balance out.

The NEA, or NFL players' team (coaches picked the NEA's
All-AFL teams), has its weaknesses, too. Murray Olderman, the
NEA's executive editor and formerly its sports editor, originated
the idea and handles the whole thing, and he reports that only 60
percent of the players send in ballots, despite repeated prodding.

But this is probably the best team of all, and history bears it
out. Men like Merlin Olsen, the Rams' defensive tackle, Green
Bay safetyman, Willie Wood, and Green Bay and Philadelphia
center, Jim Ringo, were all picked by NEA one year before the
rest of the world discovered their greatness.

"Ringo told me that he was flying home from Green Bay after
the 1956 season," Olderman said, "and he stopped off at O'Hare
Airport in Chicago. Our picks had just come out, and Ringo was
the center even though the Packers had finished 4-8 that year. He
had never been picked before, and no one else picked him that
year.

"I remember I led off the story with something about how the
players weren't impressed with a big reputation or a team's rec-

ord. They selected according to pure talent. Ringo said that he looked over the shoulder of a man reading a newspaper in the airport, and he saw the story and tears came to his eyes."

The coaches' ballots, which many a general manager will use around contract time, showed Olderman one thing. Coaches are lousy spellers. "There's no predicting how they'll spell even a name like Smith," he says.

"But the players aren't much better. We have an award called the Third Down Trophy that we give out every year. A team votes for its own MVP, and one year the Boston Patriots picked Gino Cappelletti, the flankerback and kicker. We counted it up, and Gino's name was spelled 17 different ways."

One other danger of having the players make the selection is the horse trading—"You pick me, I'll pick you"—and the habit players have of voting for their buddies. But things probably cancel themselves out, with 600 ballots coming in.

The Pro Bowl and AFL All-Star game selections were unfair because the coaches' primary aim was to put a team on the field, not to pick a collection of All-Stars. The selections had to be made strictly by position, i.e., they *must* pick a man who regularly plays left defensive end and one who plays right defensive end, left offensive tackle and right offensive tackle, etc. So if there were, for instance, four outstanding left defensive ends in the division and no decent right defensive ends, only one of the outstanding left group will get picked, to be joined by the best of the mediocre right group.

The players aren't officially told about this, though, and sometimes they are deeply hurt by the obvious injustices. It hurts financially, too.

The rest of the squads are supposedly filled in by the runners-up in the balloting, but a lot of horse trading goes on here, too. And if a player comes up injured before the game—or if he's merely worn out from the overlong season—the coach of the particular All-Star squad can fill in as he sees fit, usually with men from the team he coaches during the regular season. Hence, seven members of Van Brocklin's 6-8 Atlanta Falcons showed up on the West's 1970 Pro Bowl squad, also coached by Van Brocklin.

Players look at these games with mixed emotions. The AFL All-Star game was such a bush-league operation that the players weren't even covered by any insurance, until Oakland defensive tackle Tom Keating tore an Achilles' tendon in the 1968 game, causing the whole situation to explode. Players enjoy the week in the sun and the fraternization with the stars of other teams. The game can be low key or high key, depending on the individual.

"I remember we were playing in the Pro Bowl one year," says Walt Michaels, who was a linebacker on a few of the Eastern Division teams. "Jim Parker was the West's offensive guard, and Ernie Stautner was our defensive tackle playing over him. Jim just wanted to take it easy, but Ernie was playing like a madman.

" 'Pro Bowl, Ernie—Pro Bowl,' Jim said.

" 'You're getting paid ain'tcha?' Ernie told him. 'Shut up and play.' "

The selection to the squad usually means more than the actual game itself. Herb Adderley, the Green Bay cornerback, was furious when he found out that the Packers' coaching staff hadn't voted for him for the 1970 Pro Bowl game. He demanded to be traded all winter.

But Dallas offensive tackle Ralph Neely came away from the 1967 Pro Bowl shocked by the inefficiency of the whole thing.

"Only one thing about the whole deal amazed me," he told Dallas reporter Steve Perkins. "The downright disorganization and downright stupidity of the Washington coaches who had our team. I heard Otto Graham ran things pretty loose, and I know you can't do much coaching with an All-Star team in one week. But this was ridiculous."

One final note on All-All picking. The most neglected position seems to be strong safetyman. The AP and UPI All-NFL teams always choose two free safeties. The last strong safety they picked was Richie Petitbon in 1963. The All-AFL pickers have considered Kansas City's Johnny Robinson a strong safetyman on their team for two years, even though the Chiefs' coach, Hank Stram, had switched Johnny to the free safety spot.

But nobody's perfect.

Oh yes, there is also a second-place bowl game in Miami for the runners-up. Vince Lombardi had a way of describing it:

"A hinky-dinky football game, held in a hinky-dinky town, played by hinky-dinky football players. That's all second place is, hinky-dinky."

Index

373